LifePrints 1

ESL FOR ADULTS

TEACHER'S EDITION

Janet Podnecky
Robert Ventre Associates, Inc.

with

Allene Guss Grognet
Center for Applied Linguistics

and

JoAnn (Jodi) Crandall
University of Maryland - Baltimore County

New Readers Press

ISBN 0-88336-044-6

Copyright © 1993
New Readers Press
Publishing Division of Laubach Literacy International
Box 131, Syracuse, New York 13210-0131

All rights reserved. No part of this book may be reproduced or transmitted in any form or by any means, electronic or mechanical, including photocopying, recording, or by any information storage and retrieval system, without permission in writing from the publisher.

Printed in the United States of America

9 8 7 6 5 4 3 2 1

Table of Contents

Introduction: Using *LifePrints* 4
    Student Performance Levels 22
    Scope and Sequence 24

Preliminary Lessons 26

Unit 1   **Neighborhoods** 32
Unit 2   **Families** 46
Unit 3   **Keeping in Touch** 60
Unit 4   **Getting from Here to There** 74
Unit 5   **Feelings** 88
Unit 6   **Discovering Patterns** 102
Unit 7   **What Did You Do Before?** 108
Unit 8   **The Cost of Things** 122
Unit 9   **Getting Well** 136
Unit 10 **Asking for Help** 150
Unit 11 **The Spice of Life** 163
Unit 12 **Discovering Patterns** 177

Tapescripts 183

Index of Functions 191
Index of Structures 192

Introduction: Using *LifePrints*

Welcome to *LifePrints*. This introduction to the Teacher's Edition will help you understand the rationale behind the program and the relationship among its various components. It will also explain the methodology inherent in the units of this Teacher's Edition (TE) and give you a step-by-step guide to conducting the suggested exercises and activities.

There are eight major sections in this introduction:

- I Philosophy/Principles of the Program
- II Principles of Second Language Acquisition
- III Creating a Learner-Centered Environment
- IV The *LifePrints* Program
- V Developing Literacy and Reading Skills at Level 1
- VI Features of Student Book 1 Lessons
- VII Testing and Assessment
- VIII Classroom Management

The core of the introduction is section VI, which describes the activities and exercise types for developing oral/aural language and reading and writing at this level.

I

Philosophy/Principles of the Program

LifePrints begins with the premise that adult language learners bring diverse life experiences that are rich sources of sharing in the ESL class. These experiences, together with the learners' current needs and desires, form the basis for learning the new language. By tapping into familiar roles and experiences, *LifePrints* allows such learners to see their past experiences as valuable in their new environment and helps them sustain their dignity during a time of transition.

LifePrints also assumes that adults enter the ESL classroom with a life-centered or task-centered orientation to learning. Adults perform many different roles in their daily lives. They are worker, spouse, parent, friend, citizen, and more. These roles often become sources of their self-identity. The role of student may be a new and frightening one to many adult ESL learners. They do not necessarily want to learn *about* the English language; they want to learn to *use* English in performing their various adult roles. For them, English is not an end in itself; it is a tool with which to do something else. Adult ESL students are fully functional, at least orally, in their native language. *LifePrints* gives them the ability to start transferring to a new language and a new culture what they have done and can do as adults.

The organizing principle of *LifePrints* is not language; it is context. Language learning is contextualized in the everyday life experiences of immigrants, their neighbors, their coworkers. The lives of the characters in the book are entry points into the lives of the individual adult learners, and the lessons immerse the learners in situations where they can hear and see and practice language that is relevant to contexts in their own lives. The linguistic and cultural skills presented in the pages of *LifePrints* are transferable to real contexts in the lives of adult ESL students.

Another principle of this series is authenticity. What would a native speaker hear or say or read or write in a given context? What communicative role do English-language speakers play in a given situation? Are they primarily listeners, as when a doctor is giving them medical advice? Or are they speakers, as when giving someone directions to the library? Are they readers, as when looking up a telephone number? Or are they writers, as when completing a work log at the end of their shift? Or do they combine skills, like listening and writing when taking a telephone message, or reading and writing when completing a form? Learners are asked to practice only those linguistic skills that are authentic to the contexts or roles in which they will find themselves using English.

II

Principles of Second Language Acquisition

The acquisition of a second language is a complex process, representing a delicate balance between the learner and the learning situation. There is no single way in which all learners acquire another language. Many factors pertaining to each learner come into play, including age, preferred learning style, previous education, first language and its similarity to English, and motivation. The teacher has little control over these factors. What the teacher can do, however, is shape and reshape the language learning environment so that all learners have the greatest opportunity to acquire the English language skills they need to function as adults.

Throughout this introduction, we use the terms *acquisition* and *learning* interchangeably, irrespective of the cognitive processes involved. Some researchers and teachers contrast these two terms, assuming that they represent two different psychological processes. They apply *acquisition* to "picking up a language through exposure, using subconscious processes" and *learning* to the "conscious study of a second language." Other researchers and teachers argue that a sharp distinction between *acquisition* and *learning* is theoretical, not real. In both the acquisition and learning modes, basic principles underlie curriculum development.

These are some of the principles that guided the development of *LifePrints*:

- **The goal of language learning is communication in both oral and written form.**
  Learners should emerge from the language-learning classroom better able to understand and make themselves understood, as well as having greater facility in reading and writing English, than when they entered the classroom. Without being fluent in English, they can communicate on various levels, as described in the Student Performance Level document (pages 22–23).

- **Communication is a process, not a sequence of memorized patterns or drill and practice exercises.**
  Function is more important than form. That is, what the learner *does* with language is more important than what he or she *knows about* language. Errors are therefore a necessary step in language acquisition. What is being communicated should be the focus, not the accuracy of what is said or correctness in the form of language. This is not to say that form—grammar, punctuation, and pronunciation, for example—is of no concern. Teachers need to focus on form, but at the right time in the learning process and in terms of furthering meaning. Too much attention to form too early will inhibit rather than encourage communication.

- **Language is most effectively learned in authentic contexts.**
  Contexts should reflect the world in which learners are expected to communicate in English and, as much as possible, they should come from the learners themselves. A corollary to this principle is that language is best presented not as isolated sentences or words but as meaningful discourse. The learning of grammar should also emerge from authentic contexts and should comprise a process by which learners discover patterns in language they already know and use.

- **Comprehension precedes production.**
  Learners need time to listen to language and to absorb what is happening in a variety of

communicative situations. They need many and varied opportunities in which to be exposed to spoken and written English, using visual clues such as pictures, film, and video, and realia (things from the real world that learners can see and touch).

- **Production of language, both oral and written, will most likely emerge in stages.**
  Beginning language learners will respond first nonverbally, then with single words, then with two- or three-word combinations, later with phrases and sentences, and finally by linking sentences together to form discourse. Although students should be encouraged to progress in their language learning, they should not be forced to produce language beyond their ability.

- **Key to student participation is a low anxiety level in the classroom.**
  For adults, language learning is by its nature an anxiety-laden pursuit. The more the teacher and the textbook focus on "doing something with language"—for example, solving a problem, finding new information, describing a thing or situation, or buying a product—rather than on "learning language," the more likely students will be to engage in the process of "acquiring" language. *LifePrints* will help the teacher establish a learning environment in the classroom where students can actually function in English through task-oriented activities.

- **Linguistic skills should be as integrated as possible.**
  Adults interact with others and with their environment by using all their senses. By integrating listening, speaking, reading, and writing in meaningful, interesting, and interactive activities, *LifePrints* simulates the processes in which adults interact with their environment. The term *whole language* has been used to describe this integration of skills. In the following pages we present some particularly effective listening, speaking, reading, and writing strategies. We suggest that these strategies be used together whenever it is feasible and authentic to do so.

III

Creating a Learner-Centered Environment

If language learning is to be successful, the learners' needs, not the grammar or functions of language, must form the core of the curriculum. Before discussing the creation of a learner-centered environment, we ought to look at who our learners are. Adult ESL students are a diverse group, ethnically, linguistically, and culturally. Some are immigrants, some are refugees, and some were even born in the United States. Some are newcomers, while others have lived and worked in this country for a long time. Some had strong academic preparation in their native countries but have weak oral skills; some have strong oral skills but weak or nonexistent literacy skills; and some have problems both with oral interaction and with reading and writing in English. Often these students are grouped in the same classroom, so teachers will have to focus on the language needs of each type.

- Learners who have had academic preparation in their native countries must develop the practical oral language skills necessary to function in everyday life in their new cities or towns, to express their ideas in English, and to work in an English-speaking environment. These adults, who are likely to be newcomers to the United States, may even be comfortable with some reading and writing in English. Literacy in their native language is a part of their life-style, and they can use that literacy as a tool in learning a second language.

- Learners who have lived and worked in this country for a number of years have some oral English interaction skills, and they may have developed cultural coping strategies for living and working here. They may have limited formal education in their native countries or in the United States. Their literacy skills in any language may be low or nonexistent, and their academic and study skills may be lacking. Many of these learners come to the ESL classroom looking for programs that upgrade their oral English skills, as well as for literacy skills that prepare them to benefit from academic, vocational, or job-training opportunities.

- Learners who are new to the United States, and who lack both oral and literacy skills needed to access information, express ideas, and solve communication problems in English, are also likely to lack cultural coping strategies. They need strong developmental programs that help them acquire the language, literacy, and cultural skills necessary for learning and working in this country.

In addition to background, each adult comes with his or her preferred learning style. In general, *learning style* refers to one's preferred patterns of mental functioning. At least twenty different dimensions of learning style have been identified, far too many to detail here. Some people prefer to learn by watching, listening, and reflecting on their observations. Others are more comfortable learning by using abstract conceptualization, analyzing, and then acting on an intellectual understanding of the situation. Others learn best by doing and by active experimentation, while still others learn from feelings and specific interpersonal experiences. What this means for teachers is that a variety of strategies must be built into lessons so that all learners can draw on their preferred learning styles.

Teachers can use *LifePrints* to help learners with varying learning styles to observe, question, infer, and brainstorm—all activities that imaginative learners find useful. Full-page illustrations with prompt questions ("What's happening here? What do you think will happen next?") and semantic webbing are examples of activities that are effective with visual learners. Analytic learners can find patterns, organize, identify parts, and classify by means of activities such as using English to create charts and graphs. Commonsense learners can problem-solve, predict, experiment, and tinker with language. Dynamic learners can integrate, evaluate, explain, and reorganize the learning. In short, teachers using *LifePrints* can choose from a variety of activities that are consistent with students' learning styles and with their own. Research has shown that teachers tend to teach from and to their own learning style, so they should be aware not only of learners' needs but also of their own preferences and behaviors.

Creating a *learner-centered* environment is at the core of *LifePrints*. "Learner-centered" means that learners are in control of their own learning and direct what happens in the classroom. It also means that the curriculum is communicative-based rather than grammar-based and that language lessons center on relevant aspects of learners' lives. Finally, a learner-centered classroom calls for a collaborative effort between teacher and learners, with learners always playing an active role in the learning process. It is perhaps easier to describe than to define the learner-centered principles that guided the development of *LifePrints*.

- In an adult learner-centered class, learners and teacher become partners in a cooperative venture. The teacher creates the supportive environment in which learners can take initiative in choosing what they want to learn and how they want to learn it. This does not mean that the teacher has given up control of the classroom. The teacher must structure and order the learning process, guiding and giving feedback to learners in such a way that learners have the right amount of freedom. Too little freedom, as in a traditional teacher-centered curriculum, will stifle learners; too much freedom will make learners feel that the teacher has abandoned them.

- What happens in the language classroom should be a negotiated process between learners and teacher. The content and sequence of *LifePrints* lessons do not preclude the use of the program in a learner-centered curriculum. Indeed, the program is a starting point for classroom interaction and for student generation of adult learning materials. The language presented and practiced in *LifePrints* is based on issues, situations, and contexts that language-minority adults have expressed as crucial in their lives. Many of these same issues and situations will also be important in the lives of the learners in your class. The participatory process means that teachers must know their students and ask them what they think and what they want to learn and do.

- Problem solving occupies a good portion of any adult's life, so it is not surprising that problem-solving activities are a necessary part of learner-centered curricula. Problem-solving exercises are prominent in *LifePrints*. In beginning units, learners are asked what they would say or do in a particular situation, or about their own experiences in similar circumstances. Later on, they are asked to present the pros and cons of a situation, to negotiate, or to persuade. Learners are also asked to generate problem-solving and simulation activities from their own lives. By presenting and solving problems in the classroom, learners become confident of their ability to use language to solve problems and to take action in the larger social sphere.

- The traditional roles of the teacher as planner of content, sole deliverer of instruction, controller of the classroom, and evaluator of achievement change dramatically in a learner-centered curriculum. When the atmosphere in the classroom is a collaborative one, the teacher becomes facilitator, moderator, group leader, coach, manager of processes and procedures, giver of feedback, and partner in learning. *LifePrints* lends itself to these roles, giving suggestions to the teacher for whole-class, small-group, paired, and one-to-one activities.

- In managing communicative situations in a learner-centered environment, teachers set the stage for learners to experiment with language, to negotiate meaning and make mistakes, and to monitor and evaluate their own language-learning progress. Language is essentially a social function acquired through interaction with others in one-to-one and group situations. Learners process meaningful discourse from others, and they produce language in response to other human beings. The teacher is responsible for establishing the supportive environment in which this can happen. This does not mean that the teacher never corrects errors; it means that the teacher knows when and how to deal with error correction and can help learners understand when errors will interfere with effective, comprehensible communication. *LifePrints* introduces and then recycles vocabulary, grammar, and functions. This helps both learners and the teacher in the monitoring and correcting process.

IV

The *LifePrints* Program

The *LifePrints* Program is composed of four separate but linked components for each level:
(1) the Student Book (SB)
(2) Audiotapes ( )
(3) the Teacher's Edition (TE), and
(4) the Teacher's Resource File (TRF).

The Basic English Skills Test (BEST) is an optional feature of the *LifePrints* Program, providing a means for assessing placement and progress of adult ESL learners.

Encompassing three levels, *LifePrints* is designed to enable adult learners who have little or no oral and/or written competence in English to handle most everyday survival, social, and job-related situations independently, using oral and written English. Student Book 1 is designed for adults at Student Performance Levels (SPLs) 0–1; Student Book 2 for those at SPLs 2–4; and Student Book 3 for those at SPLs 5–6. A description of the SPLs appears on pages 22–23 of the Teacher's Edition.

Student Book

There are 12 units in each Student Book. Ten (Units 1–5 and 7–11) focus on content, for example, housing, health, shopping, cultural adjustment, and employment. The other two (Units 6 and 12) focus on the grammar (structures) that learners have used in the preceding five units. A full Scope and Sequence for each Student Book, covering functions, structures, culture, and life tasks, is included in the Teacher's Edition for that book.

These are some of the features of all three student books:

- Authentic language use at all levels.
- Adult contexts relevant to the lives of learners, their families, and friends.
- Visual stimuli for language learning, where appropriate, and a progression from visual to text-oriented material. While effective for all language learners, this progression taps into the natural learning strategies of low-literate individuals who often use visual clues in place of literacy skills.
- An emphasis on paired and group work, because learners acquire language through interaction with others on meaningful tasks in meaningful contexts.
- A whole language orientation, integrating listening, speaking, reading, and writing, to reflect natural language use.
- Activities that help students transfer what they learn in the classroom to the world they live in.
- Grammar learning as a discovery process, with a focus on understanding the rules for language that students have already used and internalized. The discovery of rules is contextualized and at the discourse level whenever possible.
- An integration of new cultural skills along with new linguistic skills. *LifePrints* recognizes that adults need to understand and acquire a layer of cultural behaviors along with language. The situations presented help learners explore cross-cultural beliefs, attitudes, and values, and to compare and contrast expected behaviors in their native countries with expected behaviors in the United States.

Audiotapes

Because *LifePrints* learners are asked to engage in active listening, not to read conversations, there are no written dialogues in the student books. Instead, the audiotapes, an integral partner with the student books, offer real listening opportunities by providing all conversations on tape. In keeping with authentic language, they offer authentic listening practice, exposing learners to different voices and relevant listening situations in which learners will find themselves. Learners are given the opportunity to listen to a conversation several times, to ask questions about it, and to develop strategies for understanding what they hear. Most important, learners are not forced to produce language they are not yet ready to produce.

Teacher's Edition

The layout of the *LifePrints* Teacher's Edition allows for a full view of each student page, along with the purpose of the lesson, materials needed, warm-up, presentation, and expansion activities. For each unit, the *learning objectives* are listed and categorized by linguistic functions, life tasks, structures, and culture. Key and related vocabulary are also provided for easy reference. Following is a description of the learning objectives sections in the TE, with suggestions on how to use them.

1. **Functions.** Functions focus on what people want to do with language or what they want to accomplish through oral communication. Functions can be categorized in different ways. The functions in *LifePrints* relate to *personal matters,* such as identifying oneself and one's family, and expressing needs or emotions; *interpersonal matters,* such as expressing greetings and farewells, expressing likes/dislikes and approval/disapproval, persuading, and interrupting; and *giving and seeking information* by, for example, reporting, explaining, describing, asking, clarifying, and directing. An index of functions for this level of *LifePrints* appears on page 191.

2. **Life Tasks**. Life tasks refer to coping skills required to deal with aspects of daily life in U.S. society, such as shelter, employment, food, clothing, transportation, and health care. The life tasks included in *LifePrints* are listed in the Scope and Sequence. It should be noted that when put into the statement "The learner will be able to . . .," these life tasks become functional life skills or competencies, correlating with adult competency-based curricula such as the California Adult Student Assessment System (CASAS).

3. **Key and Related Vocabulary.** For every subject or topic, some vocabulary is key, or content-obligatory; that is, without those words, one cannot discuss the subject. Other vocabulary is related, or content-compatible; these are words that modify, describe, or complement the key vocabulary. For each *LifePrints* lesson, the most important key and related vocabulary is listed. At a minimum, learners should be able to *understand* these words in context. The subject matter and the proficiency level of the class usually determine whether the teacher should expect learners to *use* this vocabulary actively in conversation.

4. **Structures.** Although grammar is not isolated for practice in each lesson, certain structures are primary and appear frequently in the lesson. Many of these structures are brought together in Units 6 and 12, where learners are asked to discover patterns of grammar and then to practice the structures in new contexts. To help teachers give explanations where necessary, notes in the Teacher's Edition focus on the important features of a particular structure. The Scope and Sequence lists the primary structures for each lesson, indicating whether they are introduced for the first time or are being recycled.

5. **Culture.** Items inherent in the subject matter of the unit that are cross-cultural (for example, family, shopping, medical care, gender roles, and child-rearing) are noted in the Teacher's Edition. There is often a crossover between cultural points and life tasks. We suggest that, whenever possible, learners discuss cultural similarities and differences so they can reflect on ways of doing things in their native culture and of performing the same tasks in U.S. society, without making value judgments in either case.

Besides outlining the objectives for each lesson, the Teacher's Edition gives detailed suggestions for the teaching of each Student Book page. We use the word *suggestions* because the steps presented are meant as guidelines, not as absolutes. After considering the needs and learning styles of the students in your class, as well as your own teaching style, you might blend them with the suggested steps for teaching the lesson. To feel comfortable with each student page, make your own lesson plan; include, along with the approximate timing, a "grab bag" of possible whole-class, small-group, paired, and one-to-one activities. Gather any needed materials well beforehand and, if you have time, practice-teach the page (without learners) to get a feel for the flow of the lesson, for monitoring your own speech, and for noting what you think might be difficult points for the learners. Suggested teaching steps include the following:

1. **Teacher Preparation and Materials.**

Gathering materials is an important step, so the TE suggests the materials and any special preparation needed for the lesson. Most lessons require a cassette player for the listening activities, but other equipment and supplies may be needed as well. A language course that is contextualized in survival situations must rely on pictures and real objects to convey meaning. Building a *picture file* for the first time will take some work; however, after you have gone through the book with a class once or twice, the file will need only periodic updating. Highly visual magazines, mail-order and other catalogs, and newspaper advertisements and Sunday supplements are good sources of illustrations for survival situations. Pictures of houses; the inside of clinics/hospitals and various workplaces; items in grocery stores, supermarkets, and department stores; and people interacting in both everyday and problem situations are examples of visuals for your file. Include pictures that can be used for sequencing and strip stories. In some cases you will want to cut and mount the picture before class; in others you will want to have learners look through a magazine or catalog to find items as part of the class lesson. From time to time, the TE also suggests asking learners to provide pictures as out-of-class work.

For some units you will also need realia. An empty milk carton, an aspirin bottle, a soiled piece of clothing, a bus schedule, or a hammer and screwdriver can make the difference between learners really understanding and internalizing language and having only a vague idea of what a word or concept means. Particularly at the beginning and intermediate levels of language learning, the gathering of materials is a crucial step in the teaching process.

2. **Warm-up.**

The Teacher's Edition gives suggestions for getting started on a lesson and for eliciting concerns, information, and questions from the learners. Casual conversation with the whole group or a few learners, or small talk on a given topic, can be an icebreaker. Movement, chants, dances, and songs can both stimulate and relax learners so they are ready to attend to class business. The most important part of warm-ups for adult learners is tapping into their prior knowledge and experience, and using their backgrounds to prepare for the lesson topic. Brainstorming activities that involve both learners and teacher in generating vocabulary, multiple associations, and illustrations on a specific topic can set the tone for the entire lesson. Warm-ups help learners organize information about a subject, while lowering their anxiety level and getting them to use the English they have already acquired.

3. **Presentation.**

This section is the heart of the Teacher's Edition in that it gives step-by-step suggestions for each page. It includes:

- Suggested language for asking questions and eliciting information. "Teacher talk" often gets in the way of the learners' understanding what they are supposed to do. In giving instructions, teachers sometimes use more complex grammatical structures than the learners can handle. Or they may talk too long, causing learners to lose track of what they are supposed to do. The suggested language in the Presentation section helps teachers avoid these pitfalls.

- Suggested activities or exercises. These activities—often introduced by "Have learners work in small groups to . . ." or "Using a semantic web, elicit from learners . . ." or the like—will help the flow of a lesson, though others can be substituted or added. You may need to adapt activities to the needs and proficiency level of the class, as well as to the characteristics of the learning site and your teaching style.

- Suggested teacher modeling and demonstration. Remember to model and/or give examples whenever possible. In activities such as completing interview grids, your asking a question first will make learners more comfortable in approaching their classmates.

4. Expansion/Extension.

By giving suggestions for additional classroom practice, this section answers the common teacher lament, "I've finished the Student Book, so what do I do now?" It functions as an idea bank both for whole-class exercises and for activities specifically geared to certain types of learners. The more advanced learners are challenged to be creative with the language they have acquired and to try out new language; slower learners are given opportunities for more work in problem areas. Some of the expansion exercises draw on the Teacher's Resource File, or TRF (see below). Others are variations of activities already done in class. Still others help move the language lesson from the classroom to the world outside, asking learners to do something new and immediately useful with the language they have acquired.

The Teacher's Edition also gives less experienced teachers insights into what might be going on when a student or a class is faced with learning a certain function or structure. These insights come both from research into second language acquisition and from classroom practice. It helps teachers to know that when learners continually make mistakes with a certain structure, it is not because they haven't presented the structure correctly or given enough practice with it, but because, as research and experience have shown, the structure is acquired late and will remain a problem even for advanced learners. Similarly, it is helpful to know that, according to classroom experience, a particular exercise works better in small groups than with the whole class, or that learners must be at an intermediate language level before they can be expected to be aware of certain features of language, such as register. The *LifePrints* Teacher's Edition is designed to be used effectively by both experienced and less experienced teachers.

Teacher's Resource File

The Teacher's Resource File (TRF) extends the Student Book by giving teachers a wide variety of reproducible complementary activities. Only so much text can fit in a Student Book, so the TRF for each level offers exercises, simulations, problem-solving activities, and games relevant to the themes of individual units, as well as generic games or game boards that can be used at any time. Because of the match between the Student Book and the TRF at each level, the Expansion/Extension sections in the Teacher's Edition often refer to specific TRF activities. Though an optional feature of *LifePrints,* the TRF is a resource that teachers can use over and over again, saving countless hours of planning and materials preparation.

Basic English Skills Test

The Basic English Skills Test (BEST), another optional feature of *LifePrints*, assesses listening, speaking, reading, and writing in life-skills contexts. It contains two distinct parts: a one-to-one structured oral interview, which uses picture stimuli, and an individual or group-administered reading and writing section. BEST can be used both as a placement tool and as a progress test. Its scores are correlated with the Student Performance Levels (SPLs) of the Mainstream English Language Training (MELT) Project's, as are scores on the California Adult Student Assessment System (CASAS). For a description of the SPLs, see pages 22–23.

V

Developing Literacy and Reading Skills at Level 1

Level 1 of *LifePrints* is designed for learners at Student Performance Levels 0–1, that is, learners who can function minimally in English, if at all. They may understand a few isolated words or formulas, such as *hello* and *good morning,* but their vocabulary is extremely limited, they have no control of English grammar, and they are likely to be nonliterate or barely literate in English. Some adults may be nonliterate in their native language as well.

Two features of Level 1 and its approach to developing literacy and reading skills warrant special mention. First, the Student Book is highly visual, relating pictures to meaning and stimulating students to connect their current lives with their past experiences. The pages are designed so that learners can focus on visual representations of thoughts or vocabulary, can relate what they are hearing on the tapes to clear pictures of situations or people, and can work with materials in charts and other graphic formats.

The second feature of Level 1 is that, from the beginning, literacy is taught and practiced in meaningful contexts. Learners are exposed to their names in an English-speaking environment, then their addresses and telephone numbers, then other vital emergency information. In the early lessons, literacy is limited to important sight words—for example, personal names; addresses, including street names and numbers; telephone numbers; days of the week; and names of Student Book characters. Traditional initial literacy lessons, which focus on such reading and writing readiness skills such as shapes discrimination, left to right/top to bottom progression, and learning the alphabet, are not included. Although such work may be important for some learners, we do not assume that all nonliterate and low-literate learners need it. For those who do, teachers can easily provide appropriate exercises or turn to one of many available workbooks. For those who don't, it is more important to use literacy for authentic purposes immediately—for example, picking one's name from a pile of name tags and pinning it on so others can read it; writing the names of family members in a family tree diagram that can be used as a visual aid when learners talk about their families; and simply lining up under alphabetical headings as one often does in social service offices.

All learners, whether literate or nonliterate, can participate in these authentic literacy activities. In reality, beginning level classes often mix learners from both groups. While the literate learner with little oral language can rely on chalkboard squiggles and note-taking as part of the learning process, the nonliterate learner cannot do so, and therefore may feel isolated from the literate learner in a mixed class. The Level 1 oral and written activities can accommodate both types, forming a community of learners. With nonliterate learners, the teacher will have to move more slowly, relying heavily on realia and other visual stimuli to elicit oral language and working with students individually and in small groups to teach and/or enhance literacy.

Beginning second language learners often perceive their new language as undifferentiated noise. Literate learners take comfort in being able to see words written, or to write them down, and then to look them up in a bilingual glossary or dictionary. For nonliterate or low-literate students, this is not possible, so such students must depend on short-term aural memory. Many will retain only a fraction of new material from one class to the next. Conventional ESL instruction, which delays reading instruction until such students gain some degree of oral proficiency, has frustrated many adult newcomers who realize that literacy is an important part of their new society. These learners expect to be taught to read and write, as well as to understand and speak, from their earliest classes, and Level 1 of *LifePrints* is designed to meet such expectations.

Two approaches to the teaching of reading are currently prominent: a skills-based model and a strategy-based model. In a skills-based model, the learner is asked to focus on pieces of language, for example, first sounds, then words, then phrases. Phonics-based instruction, such as decoding, is a skills-based model for teaching reading. In a strategy-based model, the focus is on both comprehension and production. "Whole language" is a strategy-based model. *LifePrints* draws on a whole language model, with reading, writing, and oral language being mutually supportive components of a communications system that focuses on meaning. Literacy that focuses on meaning gives adult learners new ways to understand and to control and participate in the new environments in which they find themselves. It also enables them to tap into their background knowledge and to express something from their past.

While *LifePrints* adopts whole language strategies, some phonics instruction may be of value. English does use an alphabet, which means there is a sound-symbol correspondence, and phonics may help learners visualize the written form of words they have already acquired orally. The important point to remember is that all skills must be a part of, not separate from, meaningful communication. The following section describes in more detail *LifePrints* activities that develop reading and writing, as well as listening and speaking, through a focus on meaning.

VI

Features of Student Book 1 Lessons

1. First and Last Pages

The first page of every lesson is a full-page visual that introduces a main theme. It also taps into previous knowledge and experience, and into the vocabulary learners might already possess. By asking questions such as "What do you see?" "Where do you think they are?" and "Do you have (name of objects) in (name of learner's native country)?" the teacher elicits or provides vocabulary, gives learners a chance to answer and ask questions about a visual stimulus, and "hooks" learners into the lesson. At this point, the teacher will want to write the vocabulary on the board and/or prepare a set of word and picture flash cards that can be used throughout the lesson.

The last page of every lesson gives learners a chance to look back at what they have learned in the lesson and to use their reading and writing skills by doing something authentic with language: completing a form, matching pictorial with written information, following written directions, categorizing information, and so on. It also gives learners a chance to review vocabulary, connect it with what they have learned, and extend it to new situations outside of class.

Between the first and last pages, a variety of language presentations and exercises introduce and give practice in listening, speaking, reading, and writing holistically, that is, as interacting parts of a complete system. There is no set pattern. Authentic language situations often call for one skill more than other. For instance, a visit to a doctor's office elicits listening and speaking practice primarily, while checking a bus schedule or peering at the small print on a bottle of cough medicine requires reading primarily. The flow of Level 1 follows the situation and the language needed to cope in that situation.

2. Activity and Exercise Types

The Student Book contains various exercise and activity types, including question-answer, matching, charts, identification, interview, fill-in, labeling, and alphabetizing. Other activities or exercises are suggested in the Teacher's Edition for each page—for example, using graphic organizers such as semantic webs and Venn diagrams; doing a Total Physical Response (TPR) activity; using a substitution drill; playing games such as Concentration; and creating a Language Experience Approach story. The following are short step-by-step instructions for many of the exercises and activities that appear either in the Student Book or in the Teacher's Edition. Instructions that are self-evident, as for matching and question-answer activities, are of course not included.

Listening/Speaking Activities

Until recently, listening was considered the passive skill and speaking the active skill in aural/oral communication. We now see that good language learners are active participants in the listening process, not just passive recipients. Level 1 listening activities, in which learners must respond with action or demonstrate comprehension, help learners start developing strategies for active listening. They are also effective lead-ins to the Level 1 speaking activities.

- **Total Physical Response (TPR)**
TPR refers to listening/action activities, which are excellent for a beginning class. The general objective of TPR is to teach the spoken language through the performance of actions in response to commands. Essential to TPR are concrete action verbs that can be used in the imperative form. However, the approach does not limit the teacher to simple physical commands, such as "Walk," "Jump," "Get up," and "Sit down." More complex commands can be used, for example, "Find Sandburg Park on the map," and "Find all the signs in the picture."

Steps for Using TPR
1. Say new vocabulary words or phrases in command form and model the meanings. (For example: "Touch your head." "Jump.") Learners respond by doing each action.
2. Command and model again. In a large class, first command and model with all the learners, then with a small group, then with an individual learner.
3. Command without modeling and have a large group, a small group, and/or one learner respond by doing the action.
4. Recombine old and new commands with and without modeling. Learners respond by doing each action. If they show any confusion during this or the previous step, immediately return to modeling the actions for them.

Variations
Change the order of commands to increase interest or change the kinds of groups being commanded (small group, large group, pairs, individual, etc.). Learners listen more carefully when they cannot anticipate what will be said or who is being addressed. If learners are comfortable, allow them to issue the commands or to be part of a whisper command chain, starting with you. As a challenge, you can turn TPR into a game of Simon Says.

- **Listen and Do**
Because listening is such a key skill at the beginning level, exercises that foster listening

and then responding by doing something are important motivating activities. In general, it is a good idea to ask learners to listen to each conversation on the audiotape at least three times.

Steps for Using "Listen and Do"

1. Play the taped conversation and have learners listen in order to understand the situation, identify the speakers, and gain overall meaning. At this point learners are not asked to take any action, only to listen and perhaps to look at a certain page in their book for contextual clues.
2. Ask learners *Yes/No* and *Wh-* questions about what they heard as a check on their literal comprehension, inferences, interpretation, and so on. Such questions as "Where does Arturo live?" "Is Anita talking to City Bus Service?" and "What does Lily want to buy?" will let you know if learners have a gist of the conversation. Ask learners if they have any questions about the conversation.
3. Tell learners that you will play the tape a second time. Ask them to listen for specific information that appears in their books, either in written or picture form (numbers, places, people, and headings on forms, for instance). Play the tape a second time and have learners do the activity called for in their book (or one that you create), perhaps circling, underlining, matching, checking, writing, or filling in.
4. Play the tape a third time, asking learners to check their answers. You should check for overall understanding of the conversation as well.

Variations

The second listening can be broken into two steps, the first time for honing in on the desired information and the second for doing the exercises in the book. A fourth listening then becomes the answer/comprehension check. You can also play only snippets of the conversation and have learners match descriptions with places or people; note certain vocabulary, such as descriptive terms; or have learners identify who is talking to whom.

While the audiotapes provide extensive listening opportunities, you can expand them even further. Here are suggestions for sharpening listening skills with a focus on Level 1 Student Book pages:

- Have learners look at a page that has several pictures. Compose and read a description of one of the pictures and have learners choose from the set of pictures the one that is being described.
- Have learners focus on the picture on page 1 of any unit. After you have done the activities suggested for this page, read learners a flawed description of the picture and have them mark the differences on the picture.
- Compose a description of each member of the Wilson or Lee families, read it to learners, and have them fill in the names on a family tree.
- Read route directions to learners and have them draw a map to neighborhood places. "Listen and do" exercises are limited only by your imagination. Just remember that, at the beginning level, learners cannot handle a very complex activity or very much language at one time.

- **Chain Drills**

Chain drills are good icebreakers for learners at the beginning level, because they are a form of finite and controlled communication. They should not be used too often or too long, because they can get very boring. They should be used with a meaningful communicative purpose. For example, one learner asks another, "Where are you from?" The second learner answers and then asks another learner the same question. This is a communicative activity the first few times, but if learners do the same drill ten times, or if forty students make up the chain, the drill is no longer communicative; you should therefore keep chain drills short and mix them with other activities.

Steps for Using Chain Drills

1. Model the activity by asking a question or greeting a learner, saying, for example, "Where are you from?" The learner answers you ("I'm from Haiti"), then turns to another learner to ask the same question you asked.
2. In groups forming a circle or line, the first learner greets or asks a question of the second learner.
3. The second learner responds and asks the question of the third learner.
4. The third learner responds and continues the chain.

Variation

Learners form a circle. One learner addresses a question to the whole circle and then tosses a ball to an individual learner. The catcher answers the question, asks the whole circle the original question, and tosses the ball to another person. And the game continues.

- **Structured Interviews**

  In many Level 1 activities, one learner asks another for information. Most of the time learners record the information on a chart or grid by making a check mark, writing *yes* or *no,* or writing a number or name. At first, little literacy is required, though learners do have to understand how to read and use charts and interview grids, as in grasping the function of headings across the top and down the left side.

  Steps for Using Structured Interviews

  1. Have learners form pairs, or pair the learners yourself. The interview process works best if the partners do not know each other well.
  2. One partner interviews the other.
  3. The partners reverse roles. Both partners record the results of the interview.
  4. The results of the interviews are shared, with either the whole class or with a group composed of three to six pairs. Each learner speaks for the person he or she interviewed.

  Variations

  Depending on his or her ability, one learner can interview from three to six classmates, not just a partner. Interviews are excellent activities for multilevel groups, because learners can give longer or shorter answers according to their ability. Higher-level learners can even create their own interview questions.

  An extension of the interviewing activity has learners lining up for various reasons. For example, Unit 2 presents an interview grid that asks learners if they are married or single. After the interviews are concluded, have all married learners form one line and all single learners form another line, counting the number in each. If an interviewer asks "What country do you come from?" have learners line up in alphabetical order by country.

- **Semantic Webbing**

  Semantic webbing is a form of graphic organizing in which learners and teacher work together to make connections between ideas they group together and the vocabulary inherent in those ideas. Besides being an excellent whole-class warm-up activity, semantic webbing builds vocabulary by asking learners for information and language they already possess, and it links that information and language with new vocabulary. Moreover, learners can use the webs throughout the unit for both oral and written work. An example of a semantic web appears below.

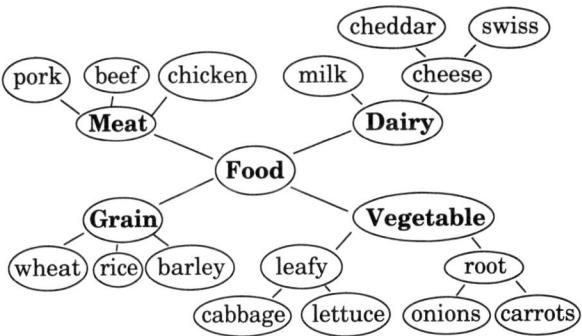

  Steps for Using Semantic Webbing

  1. In the center of the board, write a word referring to the topic of the unit. Be sure learners understand the word by asking them for an explanation, description, or examples.
  2. Ask learners for related vocabulary, trying to elicit the unit's key words. Organize the words into categories, as in the example above.
  3. Have learners copy the web in their notebooks. Keep a copy for class use.
  4. Refer to the web during the unit, adding vocabulary where appropriate.

  Variations

  Other graphic organizers can help learners store and categorize new information. For example, time lines not only allow learners to organize and sequence events chronologically but also give meaningful practice in the past and present tenses. Flowcharts show progression, sequencing, and cause and effect, and Venn diagrams are good for comparing and contrasting.

Venn Diagram

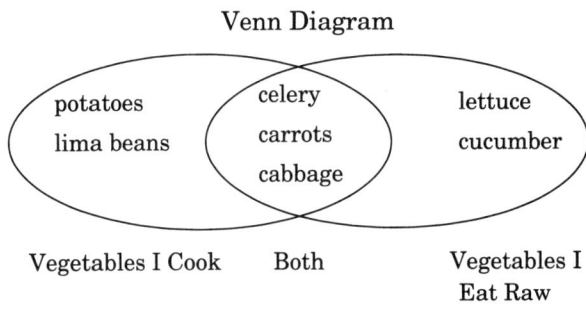

- **Substitution Drills**

  A major focus of Level 1 is the acquisition of vocabulary. New vocabulary is always introduced and practiced in meaningful contexts. At the beginning level, substitution drills can be helpful to reinforce vocabulary recognition and to add new words in similar semantic categories.

  ### Steps for Using Substitution Drills

  1. Tell learners you want them to replace a certain word in a sentence. Model by giving a sentence and saying the word you want learners to substitute. (For example: "Today I feel happy–*angry*.") The next sentence is "Today I feel angry," with another cue word coming after *angry*.
  2. You can lead the drill and have learners do the substituting, or you can have a learner lead the drill. Try to elicit authentic, relevant substitutions whenever possible.

  ### Variations

  You can combine substitution drills with other drills, starting with a chain drill. To make a drill harder, give two or more slots (words) that need substitutions, or use visual cues (pictures, photos) and have learners supply the vocabulary. To make a drill more communicative, have learners add a sentence, such as "Today I feel happy. I got a letter from my best friend."

- **Paired Exercises**

  Many exercises in *LifePrints* call for learners to work with a partner. The following technique, sometimes called "Think-Pair-Share," is a cooperative learning activity that allows learners to share information and ideas; it is also useful for tapping into prior knowledge and building vocabulary. It is an excellent way to deal with the first page of each unit or with other pages that contain large visuals.

  ### Steps for Using Paired Exercises

  1. With a visual stimulus (for example, a picture or realia), ask learners to think about vocabulary associated with the picture or item.
  2. Learners think to themselves and, if they can, list the vocabulary.
  3. Learners form pairs to compare and discuss their lists.
  4. Learners share their vocabulary with the class, while you list all the words on the board.

  5. During the unit refer to these words, making sure that by the end of the unit learners understand them when they hear them in context.

- **Role Play**

  In many instances the Level 1 Teacher's Edition suggests role-play activities. These activities put learners in situations similar to ones they have already practiced through activities involving the characters in the Student Book. Typically, one learner takes a role in a given situation, and another learner (or the teacher) takes the other role in the conversation. Role plays for Level 1 might consist of one learner calling for bus schedule information and another learner playing the part of a bus company employee. Or, one learner might pretend to be lost and ask another learner for directions to Sandburg Park.

  ### Steps for Using Role Play

  1. Tell learners to imagine themselves in a given situation. Be as explicit and descriptive as possible.
  2. Ask learners to play specific roles in this situation, or ask a learner to play one role while you play the other. (You will want to take part in role plays in situations where you think the language would be too difficult for learners to produce or where you think they might feel uncomfortable.)
  3. Ask learners to behave as if the situation were real and to have a conversation using language appropriate to their roles.

  ### Variations

  Effective role plays for adults are ones that also involve problem solving. The problem should be relevant to the learners and to the topic they have been studying. Set the scene by telling a story or narrating a situation. For example: "You are in downtown Chicago. You need to take the bus to Sandburg Park, but you don't know if the bus that stopped is the right bus. What can you say to the bus driver?" Have individual learners, pairs, or small groups prepare and then present what they would say.

Reading/Writing Activities

After learners go through the initial process of learning to read, they then read to learn or to do. Along the way they also learn to write, and the writing in turn helps them to read. As literate persons they will read for information, meaning, directions, and/or pleasure. Many learners in Level 1 will be just learning to read and write. The following activities will be helpful in that process.

- **Language Experience Approach (LEA) Stories**

    In creating LEA stories, the learners' own words are used as the material for reading and then writing. LEA stories are good for practicing not only literacy skills but also aural/oral skills. The advantage of language experience stories is that they are learner-generated materials; as such, they hold the learners' interest and are never too difficult or too easy. Learners will provide only stories that are within their language capabilities. All learners in the class can participate, adding what they can to the story. The word *story* can mean a narrative, but also a description, instructions, explanations, and the like. There are many ways to do LEA stories. This is one of them:

    Steps for Creating LEA Stories

    1. Using the visuals in the Student Book or any other pictures that evoke a story or situation that learners may find of interest, go around the room, giving each learner the opportunity to contribute to the story. Stimulus questions such as: "What do you think is happening?" "What is that?" and "Who is doing (some action)?" are helpful if learners do not respond spontaneously.
    2. On the board, write what the learners dictate. Do not correct at this point, as this would only serve to discourage and inhibit learners. The learners are expressing what they want to say in the way they know how to say it. However, it is acceptable for other learners to make corrections.
    3. When the story is finished, read it aloud to the learners and have them repeat it.
    4. Point out certain vocabulary for special practice and repetition.
    5. Sometime later, edit the story for corrections and type it up to make a copy for each learner.
    6. During a following class, distribute the story and review it in final form.
    7. Have learners keep a folder of all their LEA stories so they can always have reading materials they can understand.

    Variations

    Variations include doing a language experience story with each learner on the basis of picture stimuli or basing stories not on a picture but on learners' experiences (vacations, celebrations, coming to the United States, etc.). Many kinds of activities can be created from the learner-generated stories. For example, sentence strips can be made and the order of the story can be rearranged. Sentences can then be cut up and rearranged for practice with grammatical structures and word order. The vocabulary generated by the learners can be worked into new learner-written dialogues. And the stories can be made into cloze exercises.

- **Learner-Produced Picture Books: A Class Library Project**

    It is very important for beginning ESL learners who are new readers to realize that they can "write" as well as read. Having learners produce books that then become part of the class library is a good technique. Learners might produce books that go with the topics of the units (for example, neighborhoods here and in my native country; markets in my native country compared with U.S. shopping; and health remedies from my native country).

    Steps for Using Learner-Produced Books

    1. Distribute or have learners bring in "picture" magazines such as *National Geographic* or *Life*, as well as mail-order catalogs and the like, which can be cut up.
    2. Each learner finds a picture of interest, clips it, and mounts it on a sheet of paper.
    3. Ask learners to write something about the picture on another sheet of paper. They may write only one or two words, or they may ask you to write down what they say. More advanced learners may write more detailed pieces.
    4. Correct what the learners write to make it comprehensible; that is, do not necessarily correct every mistake, but enough so the message is clear.
    5. Have learners produce clear, neat, corrected copies of what they wrote.
    6. Repeat this activity throughout the course. Near the end, have learners assemble their pictures and written work into books for the class library.

Variations

Have learners develop a cultural resource library. Ask them to find pictures or bring in photographs from their native countries and then to write about those countries and about the visuals in particular. You might have learners write and illustrate folktales from their native countries. Developing books can also be a group project, with a learner at a higher level of language and literacy acting as the group leader.

- **Dialogue Journals**

  These journals are written "conversations" between learners and teacher. Though not necessarily tied to any specific unit, they will help your students become literate, getting reading as well as writing practice. Traditionally, the learner initiates the topic and the teacher responds. Sometimes beginning learners are reluctant to write, so you might prompt them by suggesting that they write about the topic of the lesson. Over time, both the quantity and the quality of learners' writing will increase. Learners will write more about themselves and their personal experiences or about their native countries. Even learners with very low literacy skills can participate in journal projects.

  Steps for Using Dialogue Journals

  1. Make sure learners have wide-rule notebooks or loose-leaf paper for their journals.

  2. Introduce the concept of the Dialogue Journal. Tell learners they can write to you and you will write back to them. Learners can write whatever they want; the information will be kept confidential. Even a word or two is good. Learners with low literacy skills should be encouraged to draw pictures as well as trying to write.

  3. Set aside class time (10–15 minutes) for learners to write in their journals.

  4. Let learners write (and/or draw) whatever they want, providing prompts if necessary.

  5. Respond soon afterward, on the same or similar topic and with the same amount of writing at the same language level. You too can draw pictures, if that is what the learner has done, and write a word or short sentence to go with each picture. Do not correct form. If you do not understand what the learner is trying to communicate, ask for clarification. (For example: "Are you telling me . . . ? "Did you say . . . ?")

  6. Return the journal to the learner for the next entry.

- **Process Writing**

  Anyone learning how to write, and along the way becoming a better reader, must be given the opportunity to write freely. As with oral language, the focus needs to be on communication and on the development of ideas, but in this case by means of the written word. Good writers produce many drafts before they consider their work final. Learners need to have the same opportunity and to have feedback from both their peers and their teacher. Particularly in the later lessons, which call for writing (as in writing a note in Unit 10), learners ought to realize that writing is a process and that, while the final product is important, so is the process.

  Steps for Using Process Writing

  1. Use the Student Book writing exercises or choose another topic. Group discussions are helpful in identifying potential topics.

  2. Write ideas related to the topic on the board, perhaps using a semantic web (see page 15). This *prewriting* activity helps learners to focus and recall vocabulary.

  3. Have learners write freely for a few minutes. This is the *drafting* part of the process. Encourage low-literate learners to draw a picture or to simulate writing as best they can.

  4. In pairs or small groups, have learners *share*, *read*, and *discuss* their drafts. At this time, circulate among the groups. You may provide other questions for learners to consider in their writing and help them expand or elaborate on what they have written. For learners who are new to literacy, you (or a peer) can help them put pictures into words or form their letters more precisely. However, at this stage the focus should be on content.

  5. Have learners *redraft and revise*, focusing specifically on the purpose of their writing and on the audience.

  6. Have learners *edit* their work for a final version, paying attention to form or whatever portions of the mechanics of writing they are capable of handling. At

this writing proficiency level, it is acceptable for the teacher to function as editor. You can change spelling and punctuation for and/or with the learners.

7. Have those learners who wish to do so read their work to the entire class, display it prominently where other learners can read it, or publish a class anthology. This final *publishing* step is important, because it establishes each learner as an author.

- **Strip Stories**

Strip stories can be done in pairs or small groups. Learners each have one piece or strip of a story, a set of instructions, or a conversation, and together they must put the pieces in their logical order. This exercise can be used with stories in the Student Book, from materials provided in the TRF, or from learner-generated texts.

Steps for Using Strip Stories

1. Cut a reading passage, a conversation, or a set of instructions/directions into parts. Parts may consist of a phrase, a sentence, or connected discourse.

2. Tell learners that they must reconstruct the whole by putting the parts in the right order.

3. Working in pairs or small groups, learners read their pieces to each other and reconstruct the story by numbering the pieces.

4. Have learners read their reconstructed work to the class, and have the class judge whether or not the task has been successfully completed.

Variations

A variation of strip stories is called Scrambled Sentences. On the board or on paper, write sentences in random order and ask learners to number them in the correct order. You can also set out cards or pieces of paper with words on them and have learners move around and put them in order.

This is by no means an exhaustive list of exercises and activities. You will find that, as you use them, some will be more comfortable to you and your learners than others. You will also find yourself inventing your own variations.

3. Structures

In *LifePrints,* grammar is a discovery process in which learners are exposed to and use structures in context in the thematic units and then, in Units 6 and 12, focus specifically on a portion of the grammar they have used in the preceding five units. Not all the structures presented in the thematic units are emphasized and practiced in *Discovering Patterns* (Units 6 and 12). Those that are selected are structures that learners should be able to use actively. If you feel that your learners need or want practice with other structures, you can of course add exercises. On the other hand, you may feel that your learners are not ready for overt grammar practice. If so, you can skip Units 6 and 12. Learners have more than one chance to practice structures as they practice functions. The index of structures on page 192 indicates where structures are recycled through the thematic units. In Level 1 the emphasis should be on communication over accuracy, on function over form.

The exercises in the *Discovering Patterns* units of Level 1 are not only contextualized but are as visual as possible, with the illustrations adding to meaning. You can extend and vary these exercises with transformation drills, that is, by asking learners to change utterances from one grammatical form to another. For instance, you can ask learners to change statements into questions or positives into negatives. The Teacher's Resource File also includes activities that focus on grammar. Do not expect the learners to have control over grammar at this stage. Control really begins at a higher performance level. (See the Student Performance Levels, pages 22–23.)

4. Vocabulary

Vocabulary is best taught in context, as part of communicative listening, speaking, reading, and writing activities. Isolated lists of vocabulary items that learners memorize do not lead to meaningful use. New words and phrases become internalized to the point where learners will use them in new situations after multiple opportunities for use. Vocabulary-building and internalizing activities include semantic webbing, matching words to pictures, labeling, TPR, and other types of exercises that require following directions. As learners progress through the unit, recycle vocabulary from previous lessons and help them start recognizing synonyms and antonyms. Keep on display in the room semantic webs and lists that learners have made, checking off vocabulary that learners seem to have mastered. This gives beginning learners a powerful tool for seeing how much they have learned. Prompt learners to use new vocabulary in LEA stories and to read those stories several times as you go through the units. As learners gain more and more vocabulary, have them see what "old" words they can identify in "new" words. There are many ways to exploit each activity for its potential to reinforce vocabulary.

5. Culture

Language and culture are integrally bound, so learning a new language means understanding a new culture. Culture is the institutions and shared behavior patterns of a society. But it is also the values, attitudes, and beliefs that underlie the institutions and behaviors. How we think about family is culture-bound. So is our attitude toward gender roles, competition, and medicine. All these factors are touched upon in Student Book 1. From the beginning units, learners are asked to reflect upon their experiences in the United States in terms of what things were like or how they did things in their native countries. You as the teacher are the guide in helping learners understand cross-cultural situations. Start from learners' native cultures to help them explore their new one. Both you and the other learners in the class can learn much.

6. Pronunciation

There are no overt pronunciation exercises at Level 1 of *LifePrints*. Like grammar, pronunciation deals with form, not function. Teachers can devise sound-discrimination listening activities or minimal-pair (*pat*/*bat*) speaking activities in limited situations where pronunciation gets in the way of meaning. In providing examples of natural speech, the audiotapes are good models of pronunciation. You may want to point out intonation patterns and have learners practice them, particularly when it comes to the difference between questions and statements. In general, however, attention is better devoted to fostering communication than to working on pronunciation.

VII

Testing and Assessment

Testing is a part of teaching, and while no formal end-of-unit tests are included in *LifePrints*, you should use performance-based techniques to see that learners have progressed in the outlined objectives. Checklists are an easy way of showing progress over time. The summary pages for each unit in the Teacher's Edition can be used as checklists. Additional items on an *aural/oral checklist* might include: nonverbally responds appropriately to spoken language; uses isolated words/phrases to respond verbally to spoken language; uses extended speech to respond verbally to spoken language; initiates conversation; and participates in small group/paired activities. A *reading checklist* might include: recognizes some words in context; recognizes isolated sight words; responds to comprehension questions; can read LEA stories aloud; and can retell those stories. For *writing*, portfolios that include learner writing over time can indicate progress by displaying a range of writing tasks, as well as growth in vocabulary, fluency, and mechanics of writing. At this level, it is more important for learners to be able to perform, to show you what they can do with language, than to pass formal tests.

In addition to checklists, learner-generated learning logs can be a form of self-assessment. Learners can keep separate pages in their notebooks labeled: Things I Learned This Month; Things I Find Easy in English; Things I Find Hard in English; Things I Would Like to Be Able to Do in English. Learners should make an entry on one or more pages every week. Every three months or so, go over the logs with learners, showing them how much they have learned and noting their ambitions so that, whenever possible, you can individualize instruction.

VIII

Classroom Management

Most of you will have multilevel groups or classes. Some will also teach in open entry/open exit situations. Others will have impossibly large classes. *LifePrints* strongly emphasizes pair and small-group work. While pairings and groupings will not solve all classroom management problems, they offer many advantages. When the entire class is actively engaged in pair or small-group work, everyone is communicating. For a learner who is uncomfortable speaking in front of the entire class, for instance, pair work offers an audience of one. Small-group work allows that same learner to contribute what he or she can, relying on others to both add and stimulate.

Pairings are of three types: random, voluntary, and assigned. It is a good idea to vary pairings so learners get to work with different members of the class. *Random pairs* are generally formed by asking two learners who are sitting next to each other to work together. Random pairs can work together for active listening practice, conversation, completing various exercises, cooperative writing, and reviewing each other's work. When learners form *voluntary pairs*, they are likely to gravitate toward a classmate with whom they feel comfortable. Often this is someone who speaks their native language, so expect to hear some non-English conversation in the classroom. You should use voluntary pairs when the task is such that English must be produced, as in the preparation and presentation of dialogues, the creation and ordering of strip stories, and interviews outside of class that require interaction with native speakers of English. *Assigned pairs* are usually based on proficiency levels. If you pair learners with similar abilities, they can work together at the same pace on various activities or they can correct each other's exercises. At other times, assigning partners of different levels is helpful, because the more advanced learners who are also in the process of language learning can quietly help the less advanced. Both learners benefit: the less advanced are generally not threatened, and the more advanced gain valuable practice and self-esteem. It should be noted that this type of informal peer tutoring is the normal practice in many educational situations around the world. It is part of many cultures for one learner to help another.

In moving from pair work to small-group work, you will be much more involved in forming the groups. Heterogeneous assigned groups usually stay together to complete a task, and if they are working well together they may remain together for the entire unit. Groups of four to eight work well for cooperative learning tasks. With the groups, specify roles that are required. There needs to be a leader to organize the group, to keep it on track, and to see that everyone participates; a recorder to write down the results of the group; and a reporter to report to the class. These roles can be assigned by you or self-assigned by the group. For a group to be heterogeneous, literacy level comes into play, especially for the role of recorder.

For a mixed class of low-literate and nonliterate learners, you will also want to have homogeneous groups of nonliterate learners so that you can work with them on special tasks. If pairings and groupings are the norm in your classroom, there will be no stigma attached to a group working on literacy-acquiring tasks.

In managing a pair or group activity, you will find that your role changes. First, in your lesson planning you will need to create reasons for the two or more learners to cooperate. Much of that has already been done for you in *LifePrints*. Second, you will need to move around the classroom, paying attention to what each pair or group is doing, rather than orchestrating from up front. Third, for assessment purposes, you will need to focus on what each learner in the pair or group is doing so you can provide appropriate feedback and evaluation.

Most of the exercises and activities geared to pairs and small groups can easily be converted into *one-to-one situations*. Wherever the ■ icon appears in this Teacher's Edition, you will find a suggestion for adapting group and pair work to a one-to-one exercise. In working with one learner, the tutor plays several roles: those of teacher, facilitator, *and* fellow learner. Classroom management per se is not a problem, but varying the learning situation is. The burden for performing must be shared by the tutor and the learner. If learners feel they must be talking all the time, their affective filter will be high. If teachers feel they must be in charge all the time, they will tire quickly. By doing exercises and conversation activities together—provided that learners have their own listening, reading, and writing time during the tutoring session—learners and tutors will set a comfortable learning/teaching pace.

In going through this Teacher's Edition as you teach the units, note on the TE pages or in a notebook what worked and what didn't work, and why. This will help you in teaching with *LifePrints* later on. Good luck to you and your learners.

Allene Guss Grognet
JoAnn (Jodi) Crandall

Note: *In the following pages, italicized sentences generally indicate suggested questions and other language for the teacher to use. Sentences in regular type (usually in parentheses) generally indicate responses and other language that learners can be expected to produce.*

Student Performance Levels

	GENERAL LANGUAGE ABILITY	LISTENING COMPREHENSION	ORAL COMMUNICATION	BEST SCORE	CASAS SCORE
0	**BOOK ONE** **No ability whatsoever.**	**No ability whatsoever.**	**No ability whatsoever.**	0–8	N.A.
I	• Functions **minimally, if at all,** in English. • Can handle only **very routine entry-level** jobs that do not require oral communication, and in which all tasks can be **easily demonstrated.**	• Understands only a few **isolated words,** and **extremely simple learned** phrases (What's your name?).	• Vocabulary limited to a few **isolated words.** • **No control** of grammar.	9–15	165–185
II	**BOOK TWO** • Functions in a **very limited way** in situations related to **immediate needs.** • Can handle only **routine entry-level** jobs that do not require oral communication, and in which all tasks can be **easily demonstrated.**	• Understands a **limited number** of **very simple learned** phrases, spoken slowly with frequent repetitions.	• Expresses a **limited number** of **immediate** survival needs using **very simple learned** phrases. • Asks and responds to very simple learned questions. • **Some control** of **very basic** grammar.	16–28	186–190
III	• Functions **with some difficulty** in situations related to **immediate needs.** • Can handle **routine entry-level** jobs that involve only the **most basic** oral **communication,** and in which all tasks can be **demonstrated.**	• Understands **simple learned** phrases, spoken **slowly** with **frequent repetitions.**	• Expresses **immediate survival** needs using **simple learned** phrases. • Asks and responds to simple learned questions. • **Some control** of **very basic** grammar.	29–41	191–196
IV	• Can satisfy **basic survival** needs and a few **very routine social** demands. • Can handle **entry-level** jobs that involve **some simple** oral communication, but in which tasks can also be **demonstrated.**	• Understands **simple learned** phrases easily, and **some** simple **new** phrases containing familiar vocabulary, spoken **slowly** with **frequent repetitions.**	• Expresses **basic survival** needs, including asking and responding to related questions, using both **learned** and a **few new phrases.** • Participates in basic conversations in **very routine social** situations (e.g., greeting, inviting). • Speaks with **hesitation** and frequent pauses. • **Some control** of **basic** grammar.	42–50	197–205

22 • STUDENT PERFORMANCE LEVELS

	GENERAL LANGUAGE ABILITY	LISTENING COMPREHENSION	ORAL COMMUNICATION	BEST SCORE	CASAS SCORE
V	**BOOK THREE** • Can satisfy **basic survival** needs and **some limited social** demands. • Can handle **jobs** and **job training** that involve following **simple oral** and **very basic written** instructions but in which most tasks can also be **demonstrated**.	• Understands **learned** phrases easily and **short new** phrases containing familiar vocabulary spoken slowly with **repetition**. • Has **limited** ability to understand on the telephone.	• Functions independently in most **face-to-face basic survival situations** but needs **some help**. • Asks and responds to direct questions on familiar and some unfamiliar subjects. • Still relies on **learned** phrases but also uses **new phrases** (i.e., speaks with **some creativity**) but with **hesitation** and pauses. • Communicates on the phone to express a **limited** number of **survival** needs, but with **some difficulty**. • Participates in basic conversations in a **limited number** of **social** situations. • Can occasionally clarify general meaning by simple rewording. • Increasing, but inconsistent, control of **basic** grammar.	51–57	206–210
VI	• Can satisfy **most survival needs** and **limited social** demands. • Can handle **jobs and job training** that involve following **simple oral and written** instructions and diagrams.	• Understands **conversations** containing some unfamiliar vocabulary on many everyday subjects, with a need for **repetition, rewording, or slower speech**. • Has **some** ability to understand without **face-to-face** contact (e.g., on the telephone, TV)	• Functions **independently** in most survival situations, but needs **some help**. • Relies less on learned phrases; speaks with **creativity**, but with **hesitation**. • Communicates on the **phone** on **familiar** subjects, but with **some difficulty**. • Participates with **some confidence** in **social** situations when addressed **directly**. • Can sometimes **clarify** general meaning by **rewording**. • **Control** of **basic** grammar evident, but **inconsistent**; may attempt to use more difficult grammar but with almost no control.	58–64	211–216

Information taken from the Mainstream English Language Training (MELT) Project, of the U.S. Department of Health and Human Services.

Scope and Sequence

UNIT	FUNCTIONS (• introduce ✓ recycle)	STRUCTURES (• introduce ✓ recycle)	CULTURE	LIFE TASKS
Preliminary Lessons	•Introducing oneself •expressing simple greetings •giving/getting personal information	•*My name is…* •*I'm from…* •subject pronouns	Greetings and introductions in the U.S.	Responding to personal information sight words; recognizing letters of the alphabet; numbers 1–100; writing/recognizing personal information
1. Neighborhoods	✓Giving/getting personal information •describing/observing physical surroundings •identifying places •dealing with phone numbers	•Simple present tense of regular verbs ✓subject pronouns •*yes/no* questions •*wh-* questions •prepositions: *from, in, at* •simple contractions •affirmative/negative forms •articles	Comparison of living in the U.S. and in native countries; nature of neighborhoods in the U.S.; accessing emergency phone numbers	Writing personal information; observing and recognizing environmental print; locating phone numbers in a telephone book/yellow pages; calling for help in an emergency; reading simple maps
2. Families	✓Giving/getting personal information •identifying family relationships •making introductions ✓expressing greetings	✓*Wh-* questions with contractions •possessives and possessive adjectives ✓simple present tense: *be, have* ✓negatives •present continuous tense	Celebrations; variations in family structure; name and personal title conventions; terms for marital status	Recognizing days, months, times; recognizing and writing dates
3. Keeping in Touch	•Requesting assistance •expressing needs •giving/getting information ✓dealing with phone numbers/area codes •clarifying ✓expressing greetings •dealing with numbers: time, money	•*Would like* + infinitive •politeness markers ✓present continuous tense	Accessing information: phone books, telephone operators, signs; using the U.S. Postal Service and telephone systems; conventions for addressing envelopes; time zones	Making long-distance phone calls; calling Information (Directory Assistance); recognizing time zones; addressing envelopes/packages; recognizing post office mail slots and signs; writing money orders; understanding the concept of insurance
4. Getting From Here to There	•Giving/following oral and written directions ✓clarifying •verifying ✓asking for/giving information ✓dealing with numbers: time	•Sequence words •preposition of direction: *by* ✓prepositions of place: *across, down, next to, on* •imperatives •*wh-* questions: *where, how*	Forms of transportation in the U.S. and in native countries	Using the yellow pages; reading a map; reading a schedule; reading street signs
5. Feelings	•Expressing emotions •sympathizing •expressing likes/dislikes	✓Present continuous tense ✓*yes/no* questions ✓*wh-* questions •*be* + adjective	Culture shock	Dealing with feelings; dealing with strangers

24 • SCOPE AND SEQUENCE

UNIT	FUNCTIONS	STRUCTURES	CULTURE	LIFE TASKS
6. Discovering Patterns		✓Pronouns and verb: *be* ✓questions: *yes/no* with *be* and *yes/no* with *do* ✓questions: *who, what, where, when, why, how* ✓verbs: present and present continuous ✓possessives		
7. What Did You Do Before?	•Expressing abilities, skills, responsibilities ✓expressing wants/needs ✓expressing likes/dislikes ✓asking for/giving information	•*Wh-* questions with *do/does* •past tense: regular verbs •past tense: verb *be* •adverbs of time ✓*would* + *like*	Work in native country compared to work in the U.S.; convention for presentation of dates	Reading job ads; filling out forms; identifying job preferences; finding employment; accessing community resources for job information
8. The Cost of Things	•Describing things ✓requesting assistance ✓expressing preferences ✓dealing with money •dealing with sizes	•*Wh-* questions: *how much* •intensifiers: *too, very* •*need/want* + infinitive •descriptive adjectives •modal: *can*	Methods of payment in the U.S.; U.S. money system	Reading sale ads; reading store directory signs; reading labels/price stickers; paying with cash; writing a check; reading receipts; understanding U.S. clothing sizes
9. Getting Well	•Describing symptoms ✓clarifying/verifying ✓expressing needs •identifying body parts ✓sympathizing •following written directions ✓asking for/giving information ✓giving personal information	✓Modals: *can/can't* •adverbs of frequency •prepositions of time	Health-care options in the U.S.; medical insurance; home remedies in native countries and in the U.S.	Reading medication labels; reading signs at a hospital/clinic; filling out simple medical forms; writing absence notes
10. Asking for Help	•Describing problems • expressing need for service ✓requesting assistance	•*Need* + passive infinitive ✓*wh-* questions: *when, how* •past tense: regular verbs •past tense: irregular verbs •imperatives	Community services in the U.S. and in native countries; understanding tenants' rights and responsibilities	Calling 911; calling for repair work; writing a note to a landlord regarding a problem
11. The Spice of Life	•Identifying/categorizing ✓understanding/giving oral directions ✓expressing likes/dislikes •comparing/contrasting ✓dealing with numbers ✓expressing needs	✓Imperatives •nouns: count/noncount ✓*wh-* questions: *how much/many, where* ✓present continuous tense •comparatives •superlatives	Diet in the U.S. and in native countries; shopping and cooking in the U.S.; meals as social gatherings	Reading food ads in the newspaper; reading signs in the supermarket; reading labels on food products; understanding U.S. weights and measures
12. Discovering Patterns		✓Prepositions of place ✓present tense: *have* ✓modals: *can/can't* ✓nouns: count/noncount ✓verbs: verb + *to be* + past participle		

SCOPE AND SEQUENCE • 25

Preliminary Lessons

Summary

The three preliminary lessons are designed to welcome learners to the classroom environment and to acquaint them with basic expressions in English before introducing the *LifePrints* lessons. The activities can be adapted for one or two class periods. Learners who are not familiar with the Roman alphabet or who have low literacy skills in their native language will need additional practice in letter and number recognition, handwriting, and basic reading skills. For these learners, the number and letter activities described in the preliminary lessons will need to be repeated or reviewed often throughout the *LifePrints* student book.

Objectives

Functions
- Introducing oneself
- Expressing simple greetings
- Giving and getting personal information

Life Tasks
- Responding to personal information sight words
- Recognizing letters of the alphabet
- Recognizing numbers 1–100
- Writing personal information

Structures
- *My name is* . . .
- *I'm from* . . .
- Subject pronouns

Culture
- Greetings and introductions in the United States

Vocabulary

address
name
(learners' native countries)
(letters A–Z)
(numbers 1–100)

Preliminary Lesson A

Purpose: To introduce giving and getting personal information; to introduce recognizing letters of the alphabet and numbers 1–10

Teacher Preparation and Materials

1. Map of the world, pushpins
2. Name tags: *Hello, my name is . . .*
3. Samples of simple forms asking for names
4. Copies of bingo grids with various letter combinations on each grid, pennies or small pieces of paper to cover letters, letter cards (or copies of TRF Handouts G.1 and G.2, *Alphabet Bingo 1* and *2*)
5. Number cards: 1–10 (or TRF Handout G.10, *Numbers*)
6. Inflatable globe or beach ball *(Expansion/Extension)*
7. Construction paper and markers for all *(Expansion/Extension)*
8. Alphabet cards (or TRF Handout G.11, *Letters*)*(Expansion/Extension)*
9. Newspapers, magazines *(Expansion/Extension)*
10. Deck of cards *(Expansion/Extension)*
11. Large rectangle of cardboard, markers *(Expansion/Extension)*

Presentation

1. Introduce yourself to the class. Point to a world map and place a pushpin on your native country. Say *My name is . . . ; I'm from . . . .* Have learners introduce themselves and place pins on their respective countries on the map. Be prepared to assist learners in locating their native countries.

2. Have learners introduce themselves and all the learners preceding them in the activity. FOR EXAMPLE: *My name is María. I'm from Colombia. Her name is Eva. She's from Mexico. His name is Gustav. He's from Germany.* Learners should be encouraged to help those who cannot remember. Divide a large class into groups of five or six for this activity.

3. Write each learner's first and last name on the board. If possible, distribute name tags to all class members. Have learners write or copy their names onto the tags. Assist or make name tags for learners who are not able to write. Give learners copies of simple forms asking for names. Have learners practice writing/copying their names.

4. Model and have learners repeat common forms of greetings and responses. Then model a sample dialogue with a volunteer. FOR EXAMPLE:
    A: Hello. (Shake hands.)
    B: Hi.
    A: How are you?
    B: Fine, thanks. And you?
    A: Fine.
   Have learners move around the room, shaking hands and greeting each other. ■ In a one-to-one situation, have the learner practice (or act out) greetings with other people, such as teachers, coworkers, other learners, and neighbors.

5. Model and have learners repeat exchanges used in simple introductions: *My name is . . . . What's your name? Nice to meet you.* Model a sample dialogue with a volunteer. Have learners move around the room, introducing themselves to each other. ■ In a one-to-one situation, have the learner practice (or act out) introductions with other people, such as teachers, coworkers, other learners, and neighbors.

6. Write the alphabet on the board. Introduce and give practice with letter names and letter recognition. Say letters and have learners come to the board and point to them. Point to letters and have learners respond with the letter names.

7. Play Alphabet Bingo. Give pairs of learners letter grids and pennies or pieces of paper to cover letters (or use TRF Handouts G.1 and G.2, *Alphabet Bingo 1* and *2*). Place the pile of letter cards upside down on the table. Turn them over one at a time and call out the letters. Learners work in pairs and cover letters on their grids as you call them out, until one pair covers all their letters. This winning pair reads out the letters and becomes the letter callers for the next round. ■ In a one-to-one situation, give the learner a grid and take one for yourself. Then take turns choosing letter cards and calling out the letters.

8. Introduce and give practice in counting from 1 to 10. Have learners count books, chairs, and other objects in the room; or bring in varying amounts of small objects to count, such as pencils, buttons, cups, and paper clips.

9. Write the numbers 1–10 on the board. Have learners practice saying the numbers as you

point to them, first in order and then randomly. Show number cards and have learners respond with the numbers.

Expansion/Extension

- Toss an inflatable globe or beach ball around the class and encourage learners to catch it and introduce themselves. If a globe is used, have the learners point to and say the name of their native countries. If a beach ball is used, have the learners say where they are from.

- On construction paper, write four to six lines of apparently random letters. Within each of the lines, spell out the last name of someone in the class (including your own). FOR EXAMPLE:

N	B	A	W	O	N	G	E
C	H	A	V	E	Z	P	L
K	R	T	R	A	N	S	D

Read aloud all the letters in a line while learners find the letters and practice left-to-right progression. Then, dictate the letters that spell the last name of someone in the class. FOR EXAMPLE: W-O-N-G, C-H-A-V-E-Z, T-R-A-N. Learners find and circle the group of letters. Repeat until all learners have found their own last names.

- Make a new grid, using the first names of those in the group, and repeat the procedure.

- Learners can practice listening and letter recognition. Say a letter name and have a learner find it in a pile of alphabet cards. Focus on letters needed to spell the learner's name. Then have learners dictate letters for you to find. Depending on learners' skills, dictate series of letters that spell common words or learners' names. Have learners find and arrange the letters in order. FOR EXAMPLE: N-A-M-E, R-I-T-A. Then have learners read or copy the words or names.

- Have learners practice finding and circling letters in reading materials, such as ads, newspapers, and magazines.

- Take out the picture cards (ace, jack, queen, king) from a deck of cards. Shuffle and deal the remaining cards to the learners. Say numbers from 2 to 10 and have learners hold up the appropriate cards.

- Use only pairs of numbers from a deck of cards (two 2s, two 3s, two 4s, etc.). Distribute one card to each learner. Then have each learner find the person with the same number card. (**Note:** Learners are matching the numbers on the cards, not the suits.)

- Use number cards and the ace from only one suit (all hearts or all clubs, etc.). Distribute one card to each learner. Then have learners line up in numerical order, the ace being 1. ■ In a one-to-one situation, use the numbers and ace from a suit and have the learner arrange that set of cards in numerical order.

- Explain the concept of a welcome mat to the class. Write the word *Welcome* on the board. Have learners give you the translation of the word in their native languages. Learners can practice saying the greeting in each other's languages. Using a large rectangle of cardboard, make a class welcome mat. Learners can write their names and their native expressions of welcome on the mat. Place the mat at the classroom door.

Preliminary Lesson B

Purpose: To introduce writing personal information and following directions

Teacher Preparation and Materials

1. Name tags with names of the learners used for Preliminary Lesson A or new set
2. Alphabet cards (or TRF Handout G.11, *Letters*)
3. List of learners' addresses
4. Blank index cards
5. Copies of a teacher-made bookplate, glue (see sample bookplate in *Presentation*)
6. *LifePrints* Student Books
7. Samples of forms asking for personal information, such as a Social Security card application, driver's license application, passport application, or welfare forms *(Expansion/Extension)*
8. Personal identification documents, such as a Social Security card, driver's license, passport, or alien registration card *(Expansion/Extension)*
9. Copies of a blank personal information form *(Expansion/Extension)*

Warm-up

1. Place a personalized name tag on each seat in the class. Have learners find their name tags, put them on, and then sit down.

2. Review the letters of the alphabet. Show alphabet cards in random order and have learners name the letters. Then give learners the cards. Dictate letters and have learners hold up the appropriate cards.

3. Briefly review oral questions and answers about names. *What's your name? How do you spell it?* If necessary, have learners arrange alphabet cards to spell their names.

4. Review numbers 1–10. Write the numbers in random order on the board. Say a number and have a volunteer come and erase or circle the number. Repeat for the rest of the numbers.

5. Introduce the question *What's your address?* If necessary, draw a house or apartment building on the board and write your address. Give learners a copy of their address if they do not have it written down. As necessary, help learners in pronouncing the number and street name and in copying their address on an index card. Then give practice with questions and answers about addresses. (*What's your address?* [My address is] eight twenty-three Charles Street, ten fifty-one Highland Avenue, and so on.) Learners need only say, read, and recognize their own addresses. (**Note:** Numbers in street addresses are not usually read as single digits. Although learners have not been formally introduced to the names of two-digit numbers, they can practice using them in their own addresses by repeating them as you model.)

Presentation

1. Draw a sample bookplate on the board:

This book belongs to . . . (or My Book)
Name _____
Address _____
_____
Phone Number _____

2. Have learners listen and watch as you demonstrate the following Total Physical Response (TPR) activity.
   1. Take some chalk.
   2. Find the word *Name*.
   3. Write your name.
   4. Find the word *Address*.
   5. Fill in your address.
   6. Read your name and address.
   7. Put down the chalk.

3. Have volunteers go to the board and perform the TPR steps, using the sample bookplate. Learners can copy their addresses from the index cards used in the *Warm-up*.

4. Have learners perform the TPR activity several times. Then change the order of some of the steps or leave out some steps. FOR EXAMPLE: *Find the word* Address. *Take some chalk. Fill in your address. Put down the chalk.* In this way, learners will practice listening actively and responding appropriately.

5. Have learners as a group give the instructions or key words for the various steps for you to perform at the board.

6. Give learners copies of the bookplate. Have them point to the words *Name* and *Address* on the bookplate.

7. Give appropriate instructions for learners to fill in the bookplate with their own information. (**Note:** Phone number is not filled in at this point. It will be covered in Unit 1.)

8. Distribute the Student Books. Have learners glue or tape the bookplate to the inside cover of their books. Then give learners time to look through their books.

Expansion/Extension

- Collect the learners' name tags and address cards. Place them all in two separate piles on a desk. Learners can come up and find their name tags and address cards.

- Bring in copies of forms such as applications for a Social Security card, driver's license, and passport. Have learners perform TPR steps that apply. FOR EXAMPLE: *Take your pencil. Find the word* Name. *Write your name. Find the word* Address. *Fill in your address. Read your answers. Put down your pencil.* This will give learners more practice in recognizing sight words and filling in appropriate information on a variety of real forms.

- Show various personal identification documents. Learners can identify the name and address on each. They can bring in copies of their own documents. Help learners find the sight words *name* and *address*.

- Distribute blank personal information forms (asking for name and address). Learners can practice writing or copying their names and addresses in the appropriate places.

Preliminary Lesson C

Purpose: To introduce using a table of contents and recognizing two-digit numbers

Teacher Preparation and Materials

1. Number cards: 1–20, 30, 40, 50, 60, 70, 80, 90, 100 (or TRF Handout G.10, *Numbers*)
2. Pictures of apartment/neighborhood, family group, telephone/post office, bus/car (or other common type of transportation), happy and sad people, workplace, department/clothing store, health clinic/medical checkup, fire or emergency situation, food/supermarket
3. *LifePrints* Student Books
4. Copies of bingo grids with different combinations of numbers (1–99) on each grid, pennies or small pieces of paper to cover numbers, number cards (or copies of TRF Handouts G.3 and G.4, *Number Bingo 1 and 2*) *(Expansion/Extension)*
5. Magazines with pictures related to topics in #2 above *(Expansion/Extension)*

Warm-up

1. Introduce and practice numbers 11–20. Write the numbers on the board. Have learners practice saying the numbers as you point to them, first in order and then randomly. Use the number cards to review the numbers in the same manner. Count learners, books, chairs, and other objects in the room.
2. Introduce and give practice in counting by 10s to 100. Write 1–10 on the board. Add a zero to each number. Have learners practice saying the numbers as you point to them, first in order and then randomly. Use the number cards to review the numbers.
3. On the board write:
   10 20 30 40 50 60 70 80 90 100
   Under 20, write in a column 21, 22, 23, 24, 25, 26, 27, 28, 29. Have learners practice saying the numbers as you point to them. Depending on the group, you may want to introduce the other numbers (31, 32, 33, . . . 100) in this preliminary lesson or later on in the Student Book lessons.
4. Write various two-digit numbers on the board in random order. Dictate one of the numbers. Have a volunteer come to the board, find the number, and circle it. Repeat with other numbers. It is not expected that learners will master all the numbers 11–100 in this lesson, but they need to master those that appear in their own addresses. (**Note:** Three-digit address numbers are usually read as a single digit followed by a two-digit group. FOR EXAMPLE: 427 is read as *four twenty-seven*. Four-digit address numbers are read as two two-digit groups. FOR EXAMPLE: 1427 is read as *fourteen twenty-seven*.)

Presentation

1. Tape the pictures of people and places on the board. Allow learners to identify people and places they already know. Point to pictures one at a time and ask learners about the people and places. *Do you go to (the supermarket)?* (Yes/No.) *Do you speak English at (the bank)?* (Yes/No.) *Do you see (happy) people?* (Yes/No.) *Do you see a (mother and father)?* (Yes/No.) *Do you speak English to people at (work)?* (Yes/No.) (**Note:** This lesson is designed not to teach vocabulary but rather to have learners indicate by pointing or responding *Yes/No* to people and places important in their daily lives.)
2. Depending on learners' skills, elicit words or information about the pictures and write learners' suggestions on the board.
3. Number the pictures on the board according to the appropriate units:
   Unit 1, apartment/neighborhood
   Unit 2, family group
   Unit 3, telephone/post office
   Unit 4, bus/car (or other common type of transportation)
   Unit 5, happy and sad people
   Unit 7, workplace
   Unit 8, department/clothing store
   Unit 9, health clinic/medical checkup
   Unit 10, fire or emergency situation
   Unit 11, food/supermarket.
4. Have learners turn to the table of contents in their books. Show how to use the table of contents by pointing to a picture and unit number on the board and asking *What page (is it on)?* Learners can say the page number and then find the page in the book.

5. Have learners practice finding other pages in the book. Say *Turn to page 26. What unit (number) is it in?* Learners can work individually or in pairs.

Expansion/Extension

- Play Number Bingo. Give pairs of learners number grids and pennies or pieces of paper to cover numbers (or use TRF Handouts G.3 and G.4, *Number Bingo 1* and *2*). Place the pile of number cards upside down on the table. Turn them over one at a time and call out the numbers. Learners work in pairs and cover numbers on their grids as you call them out, until one pair covers all their numbers. This winning pair reads out the numbers and then calls out the numbers for the next round. ■ In a one-to-one situation, give the learner a grid and take one for yourself. Then take turns choosing number cards and calling out the numbers.

- Learners can practice following two-step directions. FOR EXAMPLE: *Turn to page 47. Point to the word* name. *Turn to page 32. Find the number* twenty-two.

- Say unit numbers and have learners find magazine pictures associated with the unit topics.
  FOR EXAMPLE:
  (Unit) 11, food/supermarket/cooking;
  (Unit) 7, workers/machines or tools for work.

- Hold up pictures associated with the various unit topics and have learners use their table of contents to determine the appropriate unit and page number. FOR EXAMPLE: a car or van = (Unit) 4, page 38.

- Dictate two-digit numbers for learners to write.

- Many learners have difficulty distinguishing and pronouncing certain numbers. Write two lists of numbers on the board. FOR EXAMPLE:

15	50
14	40
18	80
16	60

  Have learners listen as you read list 1 (15, 14, 18, 16) and then list 2 (50, 40, 80, 60). Have learners continue listening as you read 15, 50; 14, 40; 18, 80; 16, 60. This will give learners a chance to focus on listening before trying to pronounce the different numbers. Next, pronounce a number at random from either list. Have learners indicate the column number. FOR EXAMPLE: If you say *80,* learners should say or point to column 2. Continue until you are sure that learners can hear the difference between the numbers. Then have learners practice pronouncing the different numbers.

- Give various commands, using the page numbers from the pronunciation drill above, and have learners find the correct pages. FOR EXAMPLE: *Turn to page 30. Find page 13. Turn to page 17. Now turn to page 70.*

PRELIMINARY LESSONS • 31

1 2 3 4 5 6 7 8 9 10 11 12 Summary
Neighborhoods

Objectives

Functions
- Giving and getting personal information
- Observing and describing physical surroundings
- Identifying places
- Dealing with phone numbers

Life Tasks
- Writing personal information
- Observing and recognizing environmental print
- Locating phone numbers in a telephone book/yellow pages
- Calling for help in an emergency
- Reading simple maps

Structures
- Simple present tense of regular verbs
- *Yes/No* questions
- Affirmative and negative forms
- Subject pronouns
- *Wh-* questions
- Prepositions: *from, at, in*
- Simple contractions
- Articles

Culture
- Comparison of living in the United States and in native countries
- Nature of neighborhoods in the United States
- Accessing emergency phone numbers

Vocabulary

Key words:

address
ambulance
apartment
bank
city
clinic
drugstore
fire
name
number
phone
police
post office
school
state
supermarket
telephone
zip code

Related words:

emergency
health
home
hospital
language
mailbox
neighborhood
(numbers 0–100)
street
telephone book
town
yellow pages

127 Center Street

Purpose: To give practice in giving and getting personal identification information (name, address, native country); to introduce characters in the book

Teacher Preparation and Materials

1. Number cards: 0–30
2. Refer to page 6 for names of characters introduced on page 5.
3. Map of the world (*Expansion/Extension*)

Warm-up

1. Orally review questions and answers about name, address, and native country. FOR EXAMPLE: *What's your name? What's your address? Where are you from?* Have learners practice in pairs or in a chain drill.
2. Review number recognition for 0–30. In pairs, have learners quiz each other with number cards.

Presentation

1. Have learners turn to page 5 and look at the picture.
2. Ask simple questions about the picture to determine vocabulary learners know. FOR EXAMPLE: *What do you see? What's the address?* List the words and comments on the board.
3. Point to the characters and say their names. (**Note:** Refer to page 6 for names of characters.) Have learners find the characters and repeat the names. (FOR EXAMPLE: *Her name is Anita Gómez. His name is Fred Wilson.*)
4. Have learners point to the characters as you say statements about them. *Point to Michael. Show me Anita Gómez.* and so on.
5. Point to characters and ask about their names and addresses. *What's his name? What's her name? What's his address? What's her address?*
6. Introduce the native countries of the characters. Model and have learners repeat. *Anita is from Mexico. Tom and May Lin are from China. Fred and Carol Wilson are from the United States.*
7. Ask questions about the characters' native countries. *Where is Anita from? Where are Fred and Carol Wilson from?* and so on.

127 Center Street

Expansion/Extension

- Learners can copy the words and comments from the board into a notebook or use the words to label the picture on page 5. Depending on the learners' skills, they can create their own sentences using the vocabulary words or, as a class, create a short Language Experience Approach (LEA) story.

- Give practice with subject pronouns and the verb *be*. Learners can make statements about themselves and a partner. (FOR EXAMPLE: *My name is Felicia. I'm from Chile. My address is 421 Perkins Street. His name is Tran. He's from Vietnam.*)

- Learners can draw pictures of their own houses/apartment buildings. In pairs or small groups, learners can talk about their pictures and ask or give information about their homes. (FOR EXAMPLE: *Where do you live? Who are your neighbors? Where are they from?*)

More *Expansion/Extension* on page 44

UNIT 1 • 33

At Home

Purpose: To give practice in giving and getting personal identification information (name, address, native country)

Teacher Preparation and Materials

1. Audiotape for Level 1
2. Ball *(Expansion/Extension)*
3. Magazines with pictures of houses and rooms, posterboard, glue, and scissors for all *(Expansion/Extension)*
4. Blank index cards *(Expansion/Extension)*

Warm-up

1. Introduce subject pronouns (*I, you, he, she, it, we, you, they*) and the verb *be* by asking questions about members of the class and having learners respond with complete sentences. FOR EXAMPLE: *His name is René. Where is he from?* (He's from Haiti.) *Their names are María and Rosa. Where are they from?* (They're from Puerto Rico.) *Where are you from* (asking two learners from the same country)? (We're from Poland.) *Where are you from* (asking one learner)? (I'm from . . . .)

2. Practice the question words *Who* and *Where* by asking about learners. FOR EXAMPLE: *Her name is Marie. Where is she from? Who is from Haiti?* On the board, you may want to draw a face or stick figure (or tape a picture of a person) to represent the question word *Who* and draw or tape a picture of a map to represent the question word *Where* to help clarify the meanings. Write the question words on the board.

Presentation

1. Have learners turn to page 6 and look at the pictures.
2. Ask questions about the pictures. *What is her name? their names? their address?*
3. Play the audiotape and have learners listen.
4. Ask questions. *What is the name of the street? What is the building number? What is the address? Who is from Mexico? China? Where is Anita Gómez from? Where is David Lin from? Who lives in Apartment 1A? 2A? 3A?* Depending on the learners' skills, ask one question and then

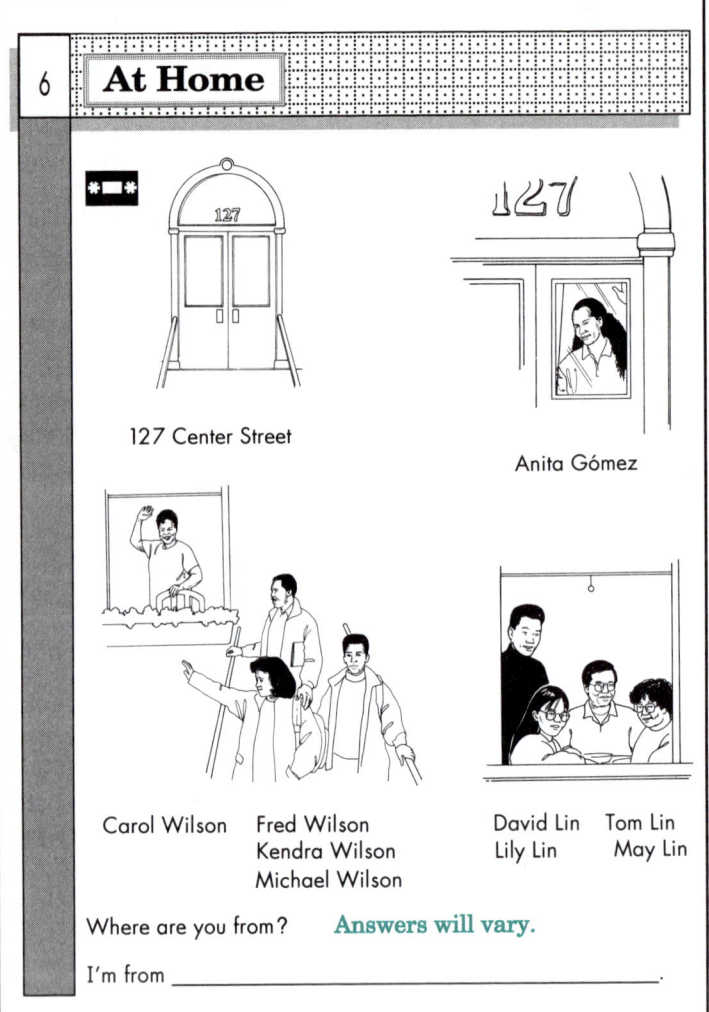

replay the audiotape so learners can listen for the answer. Then repeat the procedure with the other questions.

5. Review questions and answers about native countries in a chain drill. *Where are you from?* (I'm from . . . .)
6. Read the question at the bottom of page 6 to the learners. Have learners read the answer and give the names of their native countries. Have them write the names of their native countries. Assist learners with spelling. Learners can draw pictures of themselves next to their answers at the bottom of the page.

Expansion/Extension

- Learners can practice questions and answers in a circle game. One learner asks a question (from the lesson) and tosses a ball to another learner. The catcher answers the question, asks another question, and tosses the ball to another person. (**Note:** This activity can be recycled throughout the book as a way to practice and review questions and answers and other structures.)

More *Expansion/Extension* on page 44

Languages

Purpose: To introduce giving and getting personal identification information (languages spoken)

Teacher Preparation and Materials
1. Audiotape for Level 1
2. Copies of TRF Handout 1.1, *Interview Chart (Expansion/Extension)*
3. Copies of TRF Handout 1.6, *Focus on Pronouns (Expansion/Extension)*
4. Pictures of famous or important people from different countries *(Expansion/Extension)*

Warm-up
1. Review subject pronouns and the verb *be*. On the board, make a chart of the characters.

Name	From	Apartment	[blank]
Anita Gómez	Mexico	1A	
Fred & Carol Wilson	U.S.	2A	
Tom & May Lin	China	3A	

   Have learners practice making up sentences about the characters. (FOR EXAMPLE: Anita Gómez is from Mexico.)
2. Introduce *apartment* and the verb *live*. Model sentences and have learners repeat. *Anita lives in apartment 1A.* and so on. Have learners practice making up sentences about the characters, using the information on the chart. (**Note:** At this level, do not be concerned if learners do not pronounce the final *s* on verb forms in the third-person singular.)
3. Introduce the verb *speak* by modeling statements. Say *I'm from . . . . I speak English (and . . .). Anita is from Mexico. She speaks Spanish and English.* and so on.
4. Introduce *language* using questions and answers. Model *What language do you speak? I speak . . . .* Have learners repeat the question and answer it using the name(s) of their native language(s). Practice with a chain drill.
5. Add *Language* to the last column on the chart. Model sentences about the characters. FOR EXAMPLE: *Anita is from Mexico. She speaks Spanish and English.* Have learners practice forming sentences. Fill in the names of the languages on the chart.

Presentation
1. Have learners turn to page 7, look at the picture, and identify the characters. Say *Point to Anita. Show me the Lin family.*
2. Play the audiotape and have learners listen.
3. Ask *Who speaks Chinese? Spanish? What language does Fred Wilson speak? What languages does the Lin family speak? Does Tom Lin speak English?* Ask one question and then replay the audiotape so learners can listen for the answer. Repeat the procedure with the other questions.
4. Ask *What languages do you speak?* Have learners respond with the name(s) of language(s) they speak. (*I speak . . . .*)
5. Read the question at the bottom of page 7 and have learners respond orally. Then, individually or in pairs, have learners complete the answer with the languages they speak. Assist learners with spelling.

Expansion/Extension
See **TRF HANDOUT 1.1,** *Interview Chart*
TRF HANDOUT 1.6, *Focus on Pronouns*

More *Expansion/Extension* on page 44

Around Town

Purpose: To introduce names of places

Teacher Preparation and Materials

1. Pictures of places: bank, drugstore, post office, school, supermarket, clinic, bus stop, apartment, mailbox
2. Copies of TRF Handout 1.2, *Signs in My Neighborhood* (Expansion/Extension)
3. Copies of TRF Handout 1.3, *Who Am I?* (Expansion/Extension)
4. Newspapers and magazines, and scissors for all (Expansion/Extension)
5. Alphabet cards (Expansion/Extension)
6. Blank index cards, cut in half to make two smaller cards (Expansion/Extension)

Warm-up

1. Show pictures of places, model the names, and have learners repeat.
2. Tape the pictures on the board and number them. Say names of places and have learners respond with the numbers of the pictures. FOR EXAMPLE: *bank* (2), *school* (5)
3. Say a number and have learners give the name of the place. FOR EXAMPLE: *5* (school), *1* (clinic)

Presentation

1. Have learners turn to page 8 and look at the map.
2. Ask *What do you see?* Have learners identify places. Write the words and comments on the board.
3. Have learners practice finding the places on the map. FOR EXAMPLE: *Show me the post office. Where's the drugstore? Point to the bank.*
4. Write the following sign on the board: *Sam's Supermarket*. Have learners find the word that names the type of place. (supermarket) Demonstrate circling the key word. Write several other examples on the board (*Southside Health Clinic, First National Bank*) and have volunteers come up and circle the key word(s).
5. On page 8 have learners find the proper names of the places on the map. Then have learners circle or underline the key word(s) in each of the place signs.

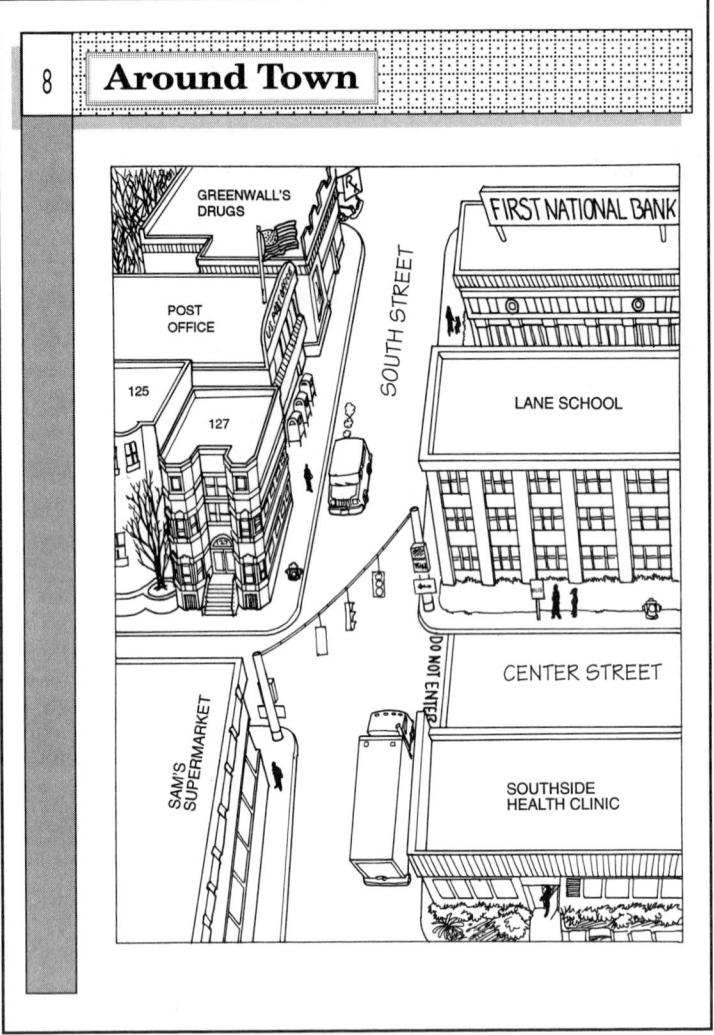

Expansion/Extension
See TRF HANDOUT 1.2, *Signs in My Neighborhood*
TRF HANDOUT 1.3, *Who Am I?*

- Have learners cut out examples of different styles and sizes of letters that they find in newspapers or magazines. The letters can be used to create signs for the classroom.
- Learners can review letter names using alphabet cards.
- Learners can practice writing uppercase letters on one half of an index card and lowercase letters on the other half. Learners can use the cards to practice matching upper- and lowercase letters.
- Learners can look at a page of a newspaper or magazine and circle examples of letters that you dictate. Alternatively, learners can cut out examples of letters. Learners can then arrange them to form the place names studied in the lesson, such as bank, school, and clinic.

36 • UNIT 1

In My Neighborhood

Purpose: To introduce observing and describing physical surroundings

Teacher Preparation and Materials

1. Pictures of places used for page 8
2. Large map of local area with learners' streets, or map of the city or town
3. Copies of TRF Handout 1.4, *Is There a . . .?* (Expansion/Extension)

Warm-up

1. Review the names of places, using the picture cues. Then tape the pictures on the board.
2. On a large map of the local area, have learners find their streets.
3. Introduce describing neighborhoods by modeling an example about your own. Point to the street on the map and then the general area and say *I live on Market Street. In my neighborhood, there is a bank. There is a supermarket. There is a bus stop and a mailbox. There isn't a post office.* (**Note:** The individual places may not be on the map, so learners are not expected to locate them. Learners should locate the streets where they live.)
4. Give practice in asking and answering questions about neighborhood places in a chain drill. FOR EXAMPLE: *In your neighborhood, is there a supermarket? Is there a school?* Learners should respond with short answers. (Yes, there is. No, there isn't.)

Presentation

1. On the board, make a large chart similar to the one on page 9. Talk about your own neighborhood again or the neighborhood around the school/learning center and check the correct columns.
2. Have several volunteers come up to the chart and put a check by places in their neighborhoods. Learners can talk about their neighborhoods, using the responses on the chart. (FOR EXAMPLE: *In my neighborhood, there is a mailbox. There isn't a bank.*)
3. Have learners turn to page 9 and look at the chart. Learners can add the name and/or draw a picture for line 7 of another place they go in the neighborhood.
4. Have learners complete the chart individually.
5. Use the chart on the board to summarize learners' responses. Add up the number of *yes* and *no* responses for each of the places. FOR EXAMPLE: bank—8 yes, 3 no; post office—2 yes, 9 no.

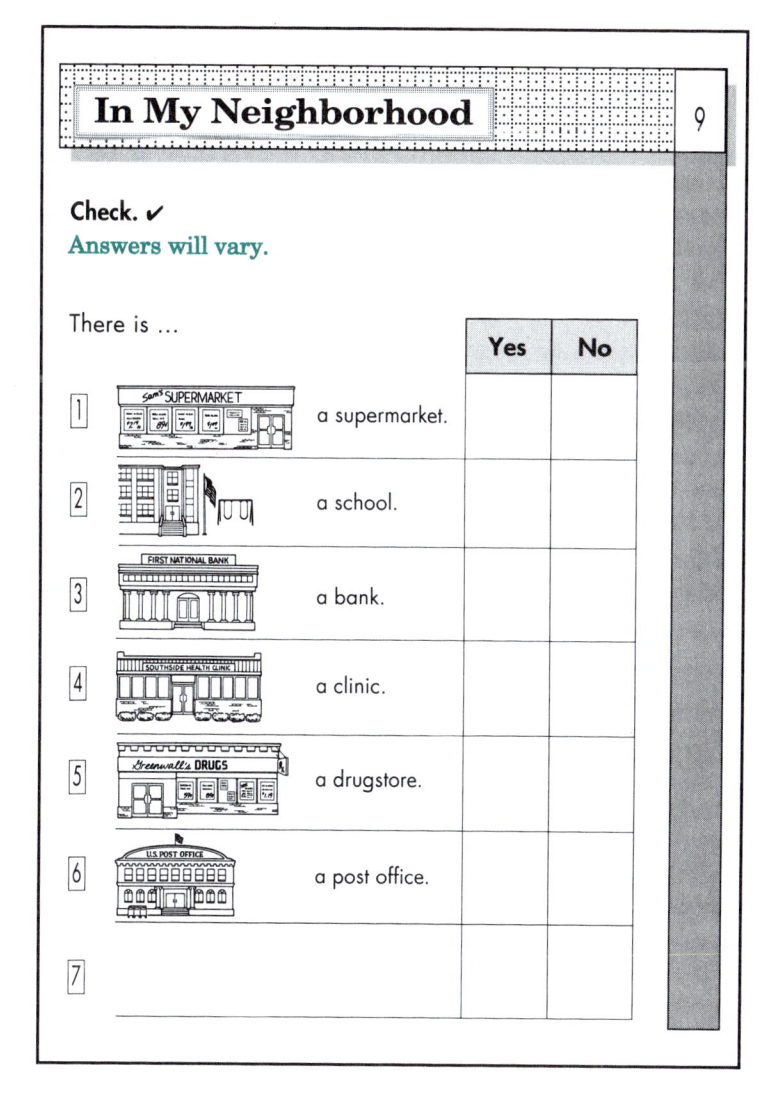

Expansion/Extension
See **TRF HANDOUT 1.4**, *Is there a...?*

- On the board, write an LEA story about places in the neighborhood. This can be done as a group about the local neighborhood, or individually. Learners can copy the story into a notebook and illustrate it or draw a map. (FOR EXAMPLE: In my neighborhood, there is one supermarket. There are two mailboxes. There isn't a bank.) Learners can expand the sentences to include street names. (FOR EXAMPLE: There is a supermarket on Franklin Street. There is a bank on Tenth Avenue.)

More *Expansion/Extension* on page 44

In My Neighborhood

Check. ✓
Answers will vary.

There is ...

		Yes	No
1	a supermarket.		
2	a school.		
3	a bank.		
4	a clinic.		
5	a drugstore.		
6	a post office.		
7			

UNIT 1 • 37

In Town

Purpose: To introduce observation and recognition of environmental print, including directional/informational signs and symbols

Teacher Preparation and Materials

1. Pictures of places used for page 8
2. Samples or pictures of items associated with the places: postage stamps, bank slips, checkbook, food ads and coupons, medicines and prescriptions, hospital/clinic brochures, school schedules, and so on
3. Copies of TRF Handout 1.5, *Concentration* (Expansion/Extension)
4. Copies of TRF Handout 1.7, *The Verb* Be (Expansion/Extension)
5. Local newspapers *(Expansion/Extension)*
6. Magazines or newspapers with pictures of places and buildings, posterboard, glue, and scissors for all *(Expansion/Extension)*

Warm-up

1. Review the names of places, using picture cues. Then tape the pictures on the board.
2. Write the place names under the pictures: *clinic, school, bank, supermarket, post office, drugstore,* and so on.
3. Give learners pictures or real items associated with the various places. Have learners look for the place names on the items or use their own experience to decide the places associated with each. (**Note:** Learners do not need to know the names of the items or what they are used for in the activity.) Ask *What do you see at the bank?* Ask learners to hold up or point to appropriate items. Repeat the question with other places.

Presentation

1. Have learners turn to page 10 and look at the pictures.
2. Ask questions about the pictures. FOR EXAMPLE: *Look at picture #1. Where is she? Is she at the bank? Is she at the supermarket?*
3. Have learners look at the proper names on the right. Say *Look at a. What kind of place is this? Is it a post office? Is it a clinic? Is it a school? Underline the word* school.
4. Have learners circle or underline the key word(s) in the other place names.
5. Individually or in pairs, have learners draw lines from the pictures to the names of the places associated with them.

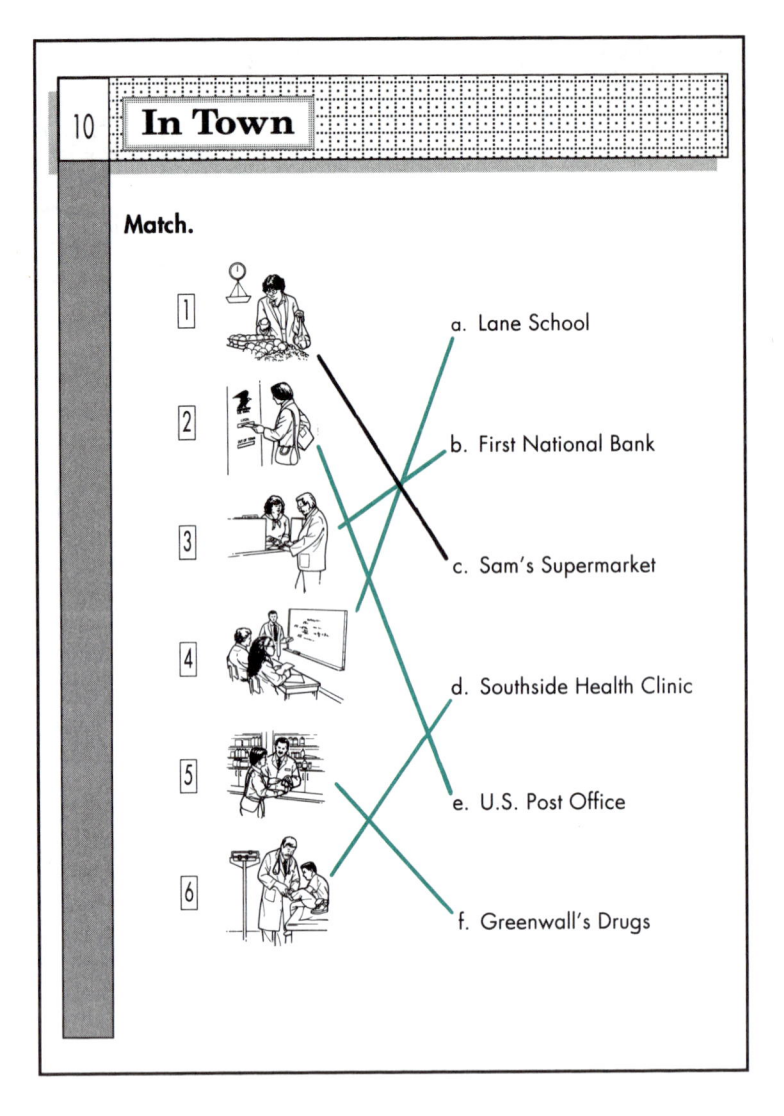

Expansion/Extension

See TRF HANDOUT 1.5, *concentration*
TRF HANDOUT 1.7, *the verb* Be

- Learners can look through newspapers for ads or information about various places. They can find and circle the key words. After looking through the newspaper, give practice with *Yes/No* questions. Ask *In this section of the newspaper, is there a bank? Is there a supermarket?* and so on.
- Learners can find the names and addresses of some places in the neighborhood where the class meets. As a group, visit some of the places and pick up information or materials about them. Write an LEA story about the trip.

More *Expansion/Extension* on page 44

38 • UNIT 1

In Your Neighborhood

Purpose: To introduce asking and answering questions about neighborhoods; to introduce using a chart to record interview information

Teacher Preparation and Materials

1. Pictures of places used for page 8
2. Collages of houses and rooms made in an *Expansion/Extension* activity for page 6; magazines with pictures of buildings, towns, and neighborhoods (*Expansion/Extension*)

Warm-up

1. Use pictures to review place names.
2. Have learners practice describing their neighborhoods. Say *Tell me about your neighborhood. What places are in your neighborhood?* Have learners respond with the structure *In my neighborhood, there is a . . . .*
3. Model and have learners repeat questions and answers. *Is there a bank in your neighborhood?* (Yes, there is.) *Is there a post office in your neighborhood?* (No, there isn't.) Have learners practice asking and answering the questions in a chain drill.

Presentation

1. Make a chart on the board similar to the one on page 11.
2. Ask for a volunteer. Write that person's name at the top of the first column. Then interview the person. According to the responses, write *yes* or *no* in the appropriate boxes. Alternatively, learners may use a check mark for *yes*. Use the question form *Is there a . . . in your neighborhood?*
3. Ask another volunteer to come up, to interview you or another learner, and to record the responses on the chart.
4. Have learners turn to page 11 and look at the picture. Read the questions and answers as learners follow along.
5. Have learners read the names of the places in the first column. Then, have them write the name of another place on line 7.
6. Have learners interview three people. Have them write each person's name at the top of a column, ask the questions, and record the responses. ■ In a one-to-one teaching situation, have the learner interview three people outside of class. These might be co-workers, other people in the building, neighbors, and so on.
7. Have learners report their findings to the class. (FOR EXAMPLE: There's a drugstore in Gustav's neighborhood. There isn't a bank.)

Expansion/Extension

- Learners can make a simplified map of their neighborhood. Have them label as much as they can, including major roads and some of the important places.
- Learners can bring in photos or add to their collages of houses and rooms in their native countries (made in an *Expansion/Extension* activity for page 6). Depending on learners' skills and interests, introduce vocabulary about climate, people, size of buildings and towns, and building materials.
- Depending on learners' abilities, discuss neighborhoods. Ask *What do you like about your neighborhood? What don't you like?*

On the Phone

Purpose: To introduce giving and getting personal identification information (telephone numbers); to give practice in dealing with numbers

Teacher Preparation and Materials

1. Number cards: 0–9
2. Index cards with sight words: *Telephone #, Phone, TELEPHONE, Phone No.*
3. Map of U.S. area codes, found in address books or local telephone books
4. Local telephone book *(Expansion/Extension)*
5. Toy telephones *(Expansion/Extension)*
6. Blank index cards *(Expansion/Extension)*
7. Index cards with sight words: *Name, Street, City, State, Zip Code, Address, Phone (Expansion/Extension)*

Warm-up

1. Review reading single-digit numbers by using the number cards.
2. Introduce telephone numbers. Show the sequence of local numbers. Dictate numbers for the learners to write. FOR EXAMPLE: *six-eight-nine, four-seven-two-seven.* Dictate phone numbers that learners may need, such as the school phone number. Write the numbers on the board so learners can check their work.
3. Ask *What's your phone number?* Say *My phone number is . . . .* Write learners' phone numbers on the board as they dictate them. (**Note:** Some learners may not have phones or do not want to give out that information.) Have learners either make up a number or respond with an appropriate answer. (I don't have one. I'd rather not say.)
4. Tape the index cards with the words *TELEPHONE, Phone, Phone No.,* and *Telephone #* on the board. Have learners compare the words and find the word *phone* on each of the cards.
5. Have learners turn to the bookplate made in Preliminary Lesson B and fill in their phone numbers in the proper place.

Presentation

1. Have learners turn to page 12 and look at the picture.
2. Ask *Who do you see? What is Anita doing? What is she looking at? Why?*
3. Have learners read the phone numbers on Anita's list. Ask *What's the phone number for the Lin family?* and so on.
4. Introduce area codes. Have learners find the phone number that is longer than the others. Explain the following: *Anita lives in Chicago. Janet and Richard do not live in Chicago. They live in California. The number 209 is the area code (or the part of the phone number that people who live far away use to call them).*
5. Ask learners to look at an area code map and find the area code for their city/town/state. Write the number on the board.
6. Have learners complete the missing phone numbers on page 12. Then, have them read the question and complete the sentence. (**Note:** See note in *Warm-up* #3.)

Expansion/Extension **on page 45**

40 • UNIT 1

In the Yellow Pages

Purpose: To give practice in dealing with telephone numbers

Teacher Preparation and Materials
1. Alphabet cards
2. Copies of local yellow pages
3. Toy telephones

Warm-up
1. Give practice with telephone number conventions. Dictate phone numbers for learners to write down. FOR EXAMPLE: *seven-six-three, eight-two-one-nine.* If necessary, show where to place the hyphen in telephone numbers.
2. Give practice in asking and answering questions about phone numbers. FOR EXAMPLE: *What's your phone number?*
3. On the board, write the letters of the alphabet in order. Hand out cards with the alphabet letters. Have learners arrange the cards in the same order.
4. Write learners' last names on the board and have learners help you rewrite the list in alphabetical order.

Presentation
1. Bring in copies of the local yellow pages. Let learners look through them. Ask learners to find pages that have listings that begin with *A*. Have them find pages for other letters.
2. Ask learners to find the pages for *C*. Write the word *clinic* on the board. Have learners look for the word *clinic* in the directory. Have learners count the number of clinics listed and read the phone numbers. Ask *What can you find in the yellow pages?* (names of places, phone numbers, and addresses)
3. Have learners turn to page 13 and find the names of the clinics. Have learners circle or underline the word *clinic* in the ads. Point out that some health-care agencies do not use *clinic* in the name. Use *Health Check* and *Midtown Hospital* on page 13 as examples.
4. Ask learners to find and read the phone numbers for each of the places.

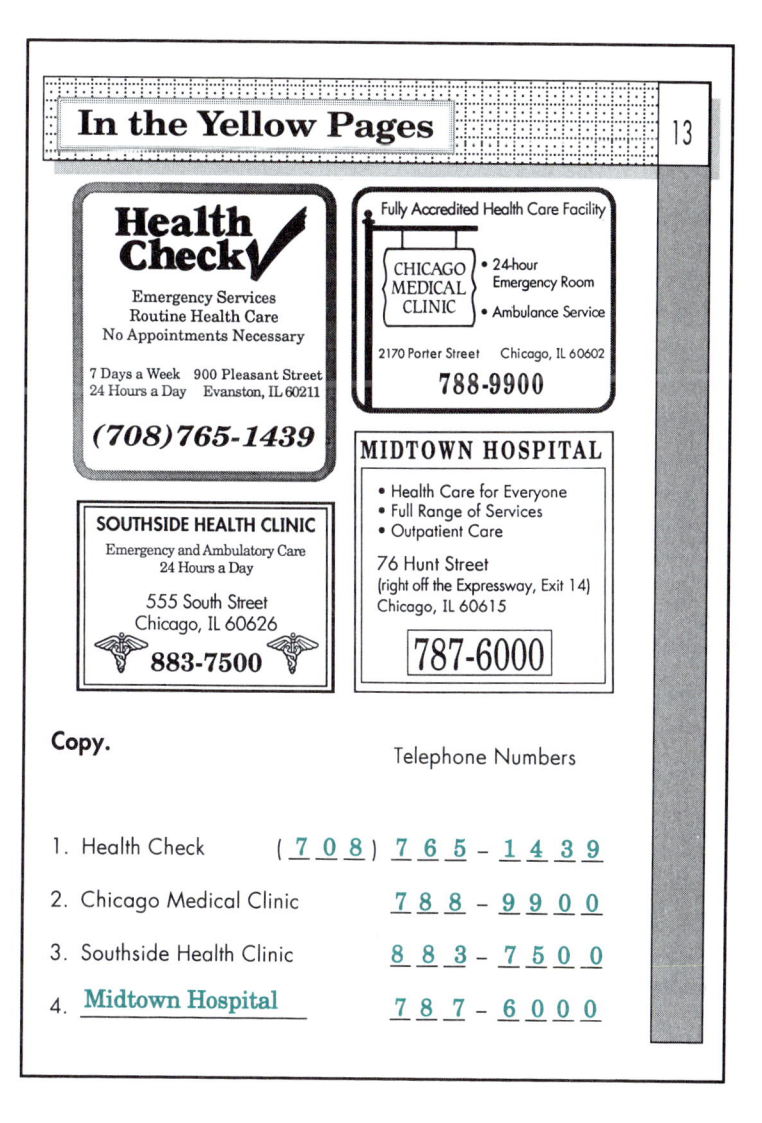

FOR EXAMPLE: *What's the phone number of the Chicago Medical Clinic? Health Check?*

5. On page 13, have learners circle or underline the phone numbers in the ads. Then, have them find and copy the phone numbers for the three clinics listed. Finally, have learners copy the name and phone number of the hospital.
6. In pairs, have learners role-play calling Directory Assistance to ask for phone numbers, using the toy telephones. Have one learner call to ask for a phone number. Have the other learner give the correct number from the yellow pages. FOR EXAMPLE:

   A: I need the phone number for Chicago Medical Clinic.
   B: The number is 788-9900.
   A: 788-9900. Thank you.

Expansion/Extension
- List places on the board, such as banks, schools, and hospitals. Learners can find listings of the types of places in the local yellow pages. Then, they can copy a proper name and phone number for each type of place.

More *Expansion/Extension* on page 45

In the Yellow Pages

Health Check ✓
Emergency Services
Routine Health Care
No Appointments Necessary
7 Days a Week   900 Pleasant Street
24 Hours a Day   Evanston, IL 60211
(708) 765-1439

Fully Accredited Health Care Facility
CHICAGO MEDICAL CLINIC
- 24-hour Emergency Room
- Ambulance Service

2170 Porter Street   Chicago, IL 60602
788-9900

SOUTHSIDE HEALTH CLINIC
Emergency and Ambulatory Care
24 Hours a Day
555 South Street
Chicago, IL 60626
883-7500

MIDTOWN HOSPITAL
- Health Care for Everyone
- Full Range of Services
- Outpatient Care

76 Hunt Street
(right off the Expressway, Exit 14)
Chicago, IL 60615
787-6000

Copy.   Telephone Numbers

1. Health Check   (7 0 8) 7 6 5 - 1 4 3 9
2. Chicago Medical Clinic   7 8 8 - 9 9 0 0
3. Southside Health Clinic   8 8 3 - 7 5 0 0
4. Midtown Hospital   7 8 7 - 6 0 0 0

In an Emergency

Purpose: To introduce preparing an emergency card; to introduce calling for emergency assistance

Teacher Preparation and Materials

1. Number cards: 0–9
2. Pictures of emergency situations: house on fire, injured person, car accident, robbery, and so on
3. Copies of emergency information from the first page of the local telephone book
4. Toy telephones
5. Plain white stickers small enough to fit on a telephone *(Expansion/Extension)*
6. Invite an emergency worker to visit the class or arrange a field trip to an emergency facility. *(Expansion/Extension)*

Warm-up

1. Review numbers 0–9 as necessary. Hold up number cards and have learners identify them.
2. Orally give practice in asking for and giving personal information, including name, address, and phone number. *What's your name? address? phone number?*

Presentation

1. Show pictures of emergency situations. For each situation, have learners decide which place(s) in their neighborhood(s) to contact.
2. On the board, write vocabulary that learners already know about emergencies. Be sure to include *Fire, Police,* and *Ambulance.*
3. Give learners copies of the emergency information from the first page of the local phone book. Have learners circle or underline the emergency numbers.
4. Show the emergency pictures again and have learners name the place and read the phone number that should be called for each situation.
5. Have learners recognize that the emergency people and places on the top of page 14 match the symbols on the bottom of the page.
6. Have learners fill in the emergency information cards with their own personal information (to be read over the phone) and real phone numbers to call. There is space for learners to fill in one other emergency number such as the Poison Information Center, sponsor, neighbor, doctor, and so on.
7. Role-play dialing and calling about emergencies using the information cards and toy telephones. One learner will role-play the emergency operator who asks questions. (FOR EXAMPLE: What's the problem? What's your address? What's your phone number?) The other learner will read the appropriate information from his or her emergency information card.

Expansion/Extension

- Learners can write the emergency numbers for their city or town on plain white stickers and attach them to their home telephones.
- Invite an emergency worker to visit the class or plan a class trip to one of the emergency facilities (police station, fire station, etc.). Learners can prepare questions ahead of time or an interpreter can assist with questions and answers.

More *Expansion/Extension* on page 45

42 • UNIT 1

Look Back

Purpose: To give practice in giving personal identification information and recognizing sight words

Teacher Preparation and Materials

1. Index cards with sight words: *Name, Address, City, State, Zip Code, Telephone Number*
2. Strips of paper for writing personal information
3. Blank copies of the form on page 15 *(Expansion/Extension)*
4. Blank samples of forms, such as Social Security card applications, school registration forms, driver's license applications *(Expansion/Extension)*

Warm-up

1. Review giving personal information in response to both oral questions and sight-word cards. *Name: What's your name? Address: What's your address?*
2. On the board, make an identification form similar to the one on page 15. On strips of paper, write a fictitious name, address, city, state, zip code, and telephone number. Hold up the strip of paper with the telephone number on it. Have a volunteer come up and tape the strip after the correct sight word on the identification form. Continue holding up the strips with personal information and have other volunteers tape them in appropriate spaces on the form.

Presentation

1. Using the identification form on the board, demonstrate copying the personal information from the strips of paper onto the form.
2. Ask learners to turn to page 15 and look at the form. If necessary, have learners point to the sight words. Ask them to point to the word *Name,* show you the word *State,* and so on.
3. Have learners complete the form individually, using the information about Lily. Ask them to cross off each piece of information after they have used it in the form.

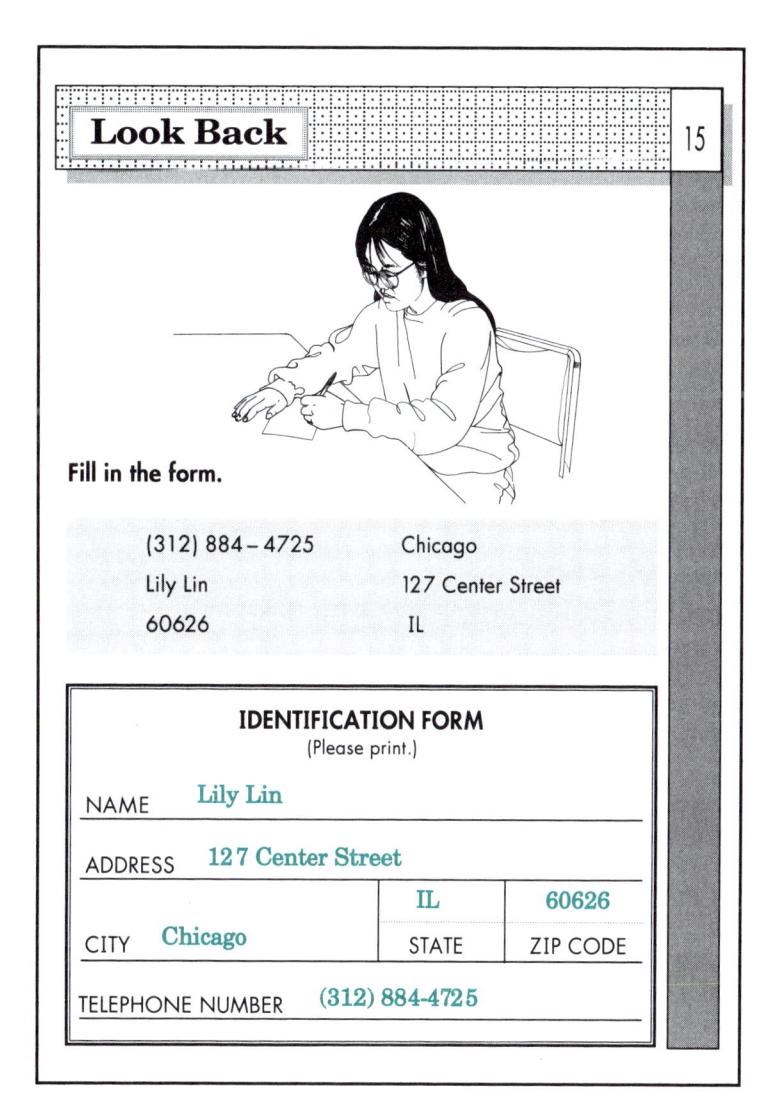

Expansion/Extension

- Give learners blank copies of the form on page 15. Learners can fill in their personal information.
- Bring in samples of forms, such as Social Security card applications, school registration forms, and driver's license applications. Learners can find the sight words on the forms and then fill in their information. Learners should determine if information needs to be written next to, over, or below the sight words, depending on the format of the form.

Look Back 15

Fill in the form.

(312) 884-4725   Chicago
Lily Lin   127 Center Street
60626   IL

IDENTIFICATION FORM
(Please print.)

NAME	Lily Lin
ADDRESS	127 Center Street

CITY	Chicago	STATE	IL	ZIP CODE	60626

TELEPHONE NUMBER	(312) 884-4725

UNIT 1: Neighborhoods
Expansion/Extension

127 Center Street
More *Expansion/Extension* for SB page 5

- On a world map, learners can find the countries mentioned in the story: Mexico, the United States, and China. They can also locate their own native countries.

At Home
More *Expansion/Extension* for SB page 6

- Learners can bring in photos or draw pictures of their apartments or houses. These can be labeled with learners' current addresses.
- Learners can make a collage of words, drawings, and pictures about the houses and rooms in their native countries. They will need magazines, posterboard, glue, and scissors. Learners can work individually or in pairs, selecting pictures and assembling their collages. Learners can show their pictures and talk about what they have written. Display the collages and allow time for learners to examine and talk about each other's work.
- For more advanced learners, write the story from the tapescript on a sheet of paper. Read the story as a group. Learners can underline all the words that they recognize. They can write new words on index cards. These can be used for individual practice or in peer teaching.
- Write the story again, leaving out some key words. In pairs, learners can read the story together and fill in the blanks as a cloze exercise.
- Learners can practice greetings and introductions. If there are other classes in your building, visit another class (if possible, a class with native English-speakers). Learners can walk around in pairs, meeting, introducing, and shaking hands. Encourage learners to remember names and faces by following the greetings with "Nice to meet you, (name)." If no group is available, use native English-speakers who may have regular contact with the learners, such as office staff, librarians, custodians, bus drivers, teachers, and so on.

Languages
More *Expansion/Extension* for SB page 7

- Bring in newspaper or magazine pictures of famous or important people from different countries. In pairs or small groups, learners can identify the people they know and their native countries. Then learners can write captions about them. (FOR EXAMPLE: Pelé is from Brazil. He speaks Portuguese and English. He lives in Brazil.) (**Note:** If possible, select pictures of people based on the learners' cultural and educational backgrounds.)
- Practice affirmative and negative statements with the verb *speak*. On the board, write the names of different languages represented in the class. Model sentences such as *I speak English. I speak French. I don't speak Chinese.* Learners can practice talking about languages, using the model sentences. Vary the subject pronouns by asking about other learners in the class. FOR EXAMPLE: *Does Olga speak Polish?* (Yes, she does.) *Does she speak Spanish?* (No, she doesn't.)

In My Neighborhood
More *Expansion/Extension* for SB page 9

- Learners can draw pictures of scenes in their neighborhoods. They can label them with the names of the streets and any important buildings or people they have included in the pictures.
- For more advanced learners, use other questions to help summarize and talk about the chart. FOR EXAMPLE: *Are there more banks or more post offices in our neighborhoods? What places do you want to have near your home? Are there places you don't want near your home? Why?*

In Town
More *Expansion/Extension* for SB page 10

- Learners can make a collage representing various places in their neighborhoods or towns, using magazine or newspaper pictures, posterboard, and glue. Learners can find and cut out pictures of things and activities associated with the various places. Depending on learners' skills, introduce vocabulary for the pictures gathered. Make a list of the words on the board. These can be used to label the collages.

- Depending on learners' experience and abilities, discuss the items used in #3 of the *Warm-up*. Ask questions about the items. FOR EXAMPLE: *What are these? Where do you get them? How do you get them? When might you get them? Why might you get them?*

On the Phone
Expansion/Extension for SB page 12

- Some learners may need to dial 1 before making calls to places outside the local calling area. Use the front pages of the phone directory to find out phone numbers in the local area.
- Learners can make a class phone directory. Give each learner a sheet of paper with two columns: *Name* and *Telephone*. Learners need to get the name and phone number of each class member. For learners who do not have a phone, instruct them to put "NA" (not applicable).
- ■ In a one-to-one teaching situation, the learner can make a directory of people and places, including the school. The learner can fill in the phone numbers (and addresses) at home.
- Practice basic telephone protocol: answering the phone, asking for someone, introducing yourself, and so on. Create some simple dialogues and have learners practice them with toy telephones. (FOR EXAMPLE: Hello, this is Lisa Patrone. May I speak to . . . ? Just a minute. She's/he's not here right now. I'll call later. Thank you. Good-bye.)
  Also, give practice with telephone dialogues needed for calling in sick and handling wrong numbers. FOR EXAMPLE:
  A: Hello, (name of school).
  B: Hello, my name is . . . .. I can't come to school. I am sick. My teacher is . . . ..
  A: Thank you. I'll give him/her the message.
  B: Thank you. Good-bye.

  A: Hello.
  B: Hello. May I please speak to . . . ?
  A: Who?
  B: (repeat name)
  A: I'm afraid you have the wrong number.
  B: Is this (phone number)?
  A: No, it's not.
  B: I'm sorry.
- Give learners blank index cards and have them write one piece of personal information (either a street address or telephone number). Collect the cards and redistribute them so that every learner now has a card written by another. Have learners walk around the room and question each other to find the card's original owner. Learners with phone numbers on the cards will ask "What's your phone number?" until they find the person with the same number as the one on the card. Learners with addresses will ask "What's your address?" After finding the person who wrote the card, a learner should then ask for and fill in other personal information so he or she has a card that is complete with the name, address, and phone number of the other learner.
- Review asking and answering personal information questions. Hold up one of the sight-word cards. Have learners respond orally with the appropriate information. FOR EXAMPLE: *Name* (María López), *Street* (Perkins Avenue), *City* (Chicago), *State* (Illinois), *Zip Code* (60609), *Phone* (455-6364), *Address* (23 Perkins Avenue, Chicago, IL 60609). Alternatively, have a learner write his or her personal information on the board. Have other volunteers tape or place the sight-word cards next to the appropriate information.

In the Yellow Pages
More *Expansion/Extension* for SB page 13

- Have learners find and read other numbers in the yellow pages. Learners can underline the address of each clinic. Introduce *city, state,* and *zip code* in the addresses. Then have learners identify their own city, state, and zip code.
- Give practice in alphabetizing words and names. Learners can arrange a class list or sight-word cards in alphabetical order.

In an Emergency
More *Expansion/Extension* for SB page 14

- Discuss emergency help in the learners' native countries. Ask *Who helps in* (name of native country) *when there is a fire/accident/problem?* Attitudes toward police and other public service people may vary, depending on the country and political situation. Make a chart comparing who is called for emergencies in learners' native countries and in the United States.

1 2 3 4 5 6 7 8 9 10 11 12 Summary
Families

Objectives

Functions
- Giving and getting personal information
- Identifying family relationships
- Making introductions
- Expressing greetings

Life Tasks
- Recognizing days, months, times
- Recognizing and writing dates

Structures
- Simple present tense: *be*, *have*
- Negatives
- Present continuous tense
- *Wh-* questions with contractions
- Possessives and possessive adjectives

Culture
- Celebrations
- Variations in family structure
- Name and personal title conventions
- Terms for marital status

Vocabulary

Key words:

April	March
August	married
brother	May
children	Monday
daughter	mother
December	November
family	October
father	parent
February	Saturday
first name	September
Friday	single
grandfather	sister
grandmother	son
husband	Sunday
January	Thursday
July	Tuesday
June	Wednesday
last name	wife

Related words:

date	Mr.
day	Mrs.
female	Ms.
friend	party
invite	place
lunch	relationship
male	time
meet	visit
Miss	

A Family Celebration

Purpose: To introduce family relationship terms; to give practice in giving and getting personal information about family members

Teacher Preparation and Materials
Photo of your own family or picture of a family group

Warm-up
1. Review questions and answers about names. Point to a learner and ask the question: *What's his/her name?* Have learners respond with the form *His/Her name is . . . .*

2. Show a photo of your family or a family group. Ask questions. *Who are they? Who is he/she?* Introduce the family members. FOR EXAMPLE: *Her name is Ana. She is my/the daughter.* Have learners repeat the family terms.

3. Depending on learners' skills, ask other questions about the pictures. *Where are they? What are they doing?*

Presentation
1. Have learners turn to page 16. Give learners time to look at the pictures.

2. Have learners identify people and relationships. Say *Show me the mother. Point to the children Who is she? Where is Fred Wilson?*

3. Write the family words on the board. Introduce other relationship words and write them on the board. Be sure to include *children, parents, grandparents, grandchild(ren), son, daughter, mother, father, husband, wife, brother, sister.*

4. In pairs, have learners practice asking each other the characters' names. Have one learner point to each character and ask, "What's his/her name?" The other learner answers with the name.

5. Have learners identify the people on page 16. Say *Fred and Carol have two children. What are their names? Michael has a sister. What is her name? Alma and Harold have two daughters. What are their names?*

6. Ask questions about the family relationships. *Find Carol. Is she Harold's mother?*

1 2 3 4 5 6 7 8 9 10 11 12
Families ▪ ▪ ▪ ▪ ▪ ▪ ▪ ▪ ▪ ▪ ▪ ▪

Janet and Richard Stevens

Alma and Harold Jones

Carol and Fred Wilson Kendra and Michael

A Family Celebration

Is she Fred's wife? Is she Janet's sister? Point to Harold. Is he Alma's husband? Is he Kendra's father? Is he Richard's brother? Who's Kendra's brother? Fred's daughter? Who are Harold's daughters? Who's Janet's sister? Michael's mother? father? Harold's wife?

Expansion/Extension
- Learners can copy the words from the board into a notebook. Depending on learners' skills, they can create their own sentences using the words. *Sokham is my wife. Sokhanno is my daughter.*

- Talk about the characters on page 16. Learners can speculate about what the people do at work, how old they are, etc.

- Learners can bring in family photos or draw pictures of their families and talk about the names of the various family members and their relationships.

- Give practice with possessive adjectives. Review *my, your, his,* and *her,* and introduce *their.* Ask *What's your name? his name? her name? their names?*

A Family Tree

Purpose: To give practice with relationship and family vocabulary

Teacher Preparation and Materials

1. Index cards with sight words: *First Name, Last Name*
2. Pictures of family groups
3. Index cards with sight words: *parents, mother, father, children, son, daughter, grandparents, grandfather, grandmother, grandchildren, granddaughter, grandson, husband, wife, brother, sister*
4. Copies of TRF Handout 2.1, *My Family (Expansion/Extension)*
5. Copies of TRF Handout 2.2, *My Family Tree (Expansion/Extension)*

Warm-up

1. On the board, write *First Name* and *Last Name*. Have learners write their first and last names under the appropriate columns. FOR EXAMPLE:

First Name	Last Name
Gina	López
Chan	Le

   (**Cultural Note:** In some cultures the family, or last, name is written first and then the given, or first, name.)

2. Hold up the sight-word cards with the words *First Name* and *Last Name*. Have learners respond. (FOR EXAMPLE: My first name is Pedro. My last name is López.)

3. Show pictures of family groups. Have learners find appropriate relationship words from the set of sight-word cards.

4. Have learners look at the pictures on page 16. Make a family tree on the board that looks like the one on page 17. Write the name *Janet* in the middle. Ask *Who's Janet's sister?* To the left, write *Carol*. Ask *Who are Janet's parents (father and mother)?* Write *Alma and Harold Jones* on the top. Ask *What is Janet's last name?* Write *Stevens*. Explain that before she was married, her last name was Jones. Ask questions about other family members and write their names in the appropriate places on the family tree.

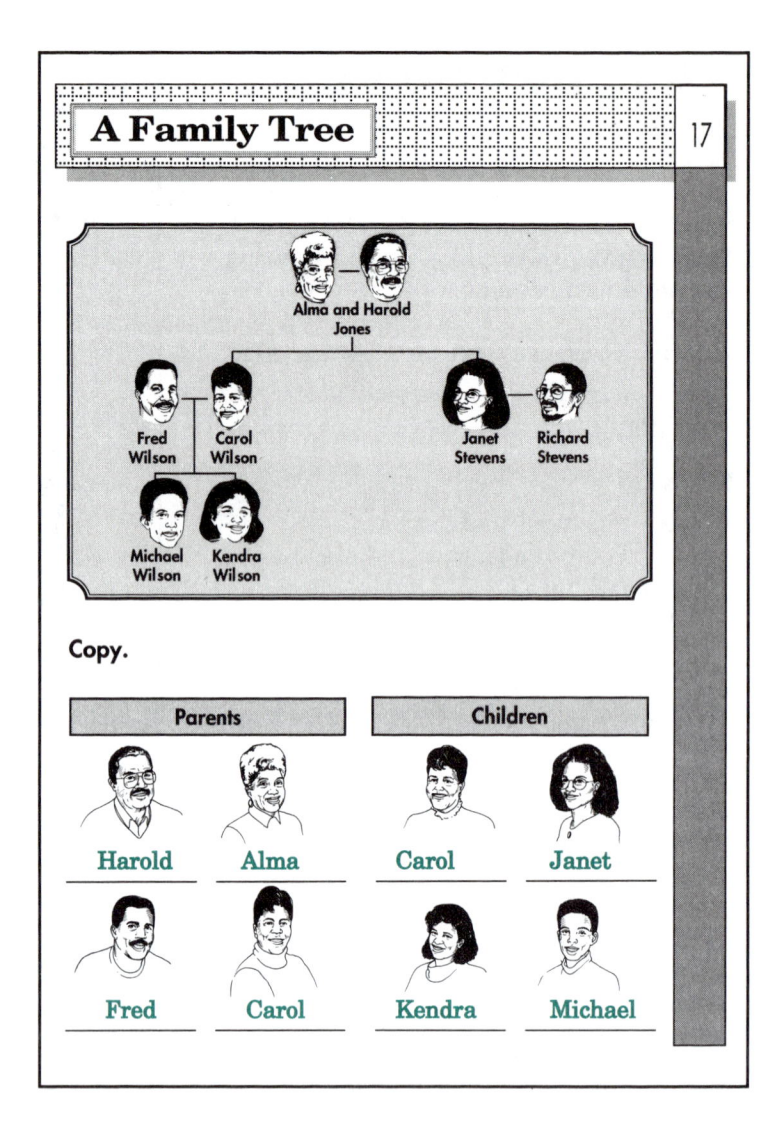

Presentation

1. Have learners turn to page 17 and find the names of the family members. Ask *Does Carol have a sister? Who's Carol's sister? husband?*

2. Using the family tree on the board, demonstrate multiple relationships. Go through the tree line by line. Write the relationship terms under the names of the people. (FOR EXAMPLE: Alma Jones: wife/mother/daughter; Carol Jones: wife/mother/daughter/sister)

3. Ask questions about the family tree. *Who are Alma and Harold's children? Who are Michael's parents?*

4. Have learners copy the names from the family tree on the lines below the pictures.

5. Ask learners about their own families. *Do you have a brother?* (Yes, I do. No, I don't.) *What's his name?* (**Cultural Note:** The topic of family may evoke strong feelings. Some learners may have lost family members and/or left their families in their native countries. Be aware of this possibility and help learners express their feelings.)

***Expansion/Extension* on page 58**

48 • UNIT 2

Family Members

Purpose: To give practice in explaining family relationships

Teacher Preparation and Materials
1. Family relationship sight-word cards used for page 17
2. 20–30 blank index cards *(Expansion/Extension)*

Warm-up
1. Review family relationships. If necessary, refer back to the family tree to illustrate relationships. Say *Fred and Carol are Kendra's father and mother. Who are Janet's mother and father? Who are Michael's mother and father? Alma and Harold are Michael's grandmother and grandfather. Are they Kendra's grandmother and grandfather? Richard's?* Continue with questions about brother and sister, and husband and wife relationships.
2. Have learners practice reading the relationship terms on the sight-word cards.

Presentation
1. Ask learners to turn to page 18, look at the pictures, and read the relationship terms. Ask *Who are the grandfather and grandmother? Are Fred and Carol the grandfather and grandmother?*
2. Have learners create sentences orally, using the pictures and words. (FOR EXAMPLE: Fred and Carol are the father and mother of Michael and Kendra. Alma and Harold are the grandfather and grandmother of Michael and Kendra.)

Expansion/Extension
- Individually, learners can label pictures of their own families with the family relationship terms.
- Make a matching game that uses index cards showing parts of simple sentences that describe the Jones family. Write the names of the people on one set of cards and the relationships on another set, then scramble them up. FOR EXAMPLE:

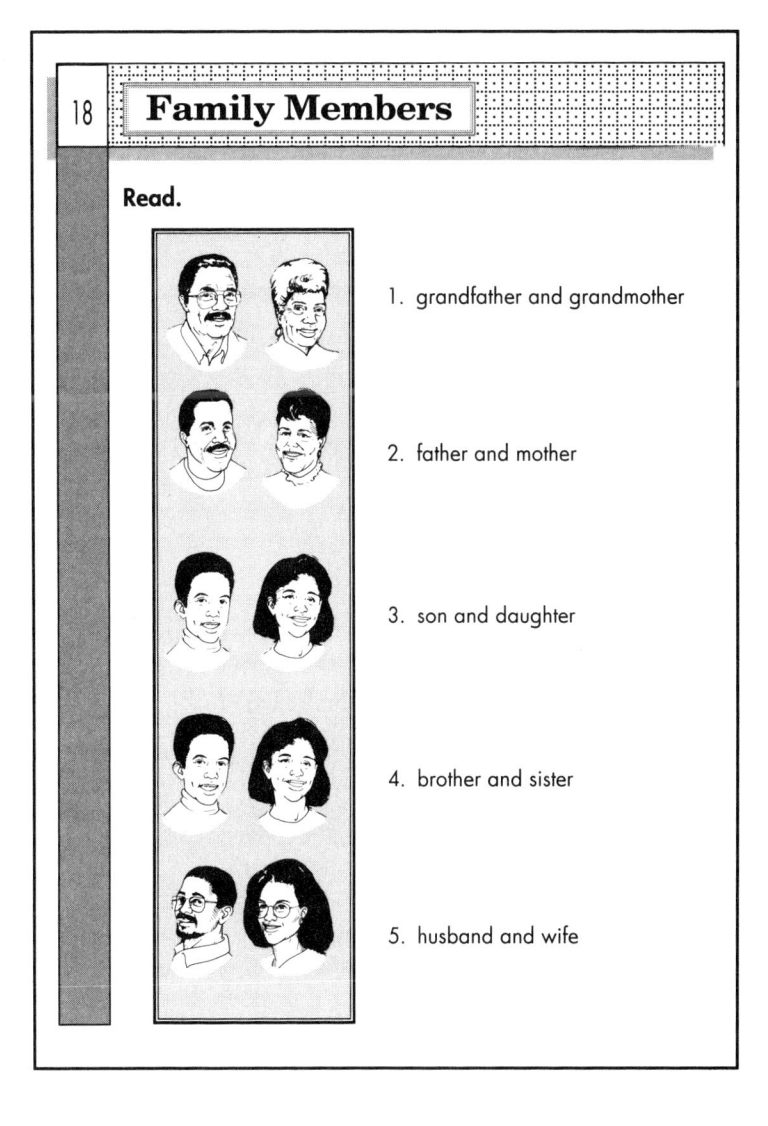

Fred and Carol	are father and mother.
Michael and Kendra	are brother and sister.
Alma and Harold	are grandfather and grandmother.
Janet and Richard	are husband and wife.

Learners can match the parts to create sentences that describe the family tree on page 17. Learners can create other sentences about the family tree to write on the cards. (FOR EXAMPLE: Carol and Janet are sisters. Fred and Kendra are father and daughter.) Learners can also play Concentration using the cards.
- In pairs or small groups, learners can practice asking for and giving information about their family members. (FOR EXAMPLE: Do you have a son/daughter/brother/sister/husband/wife? What is his/her name? How do you spell it? Does he/she go to school? What language(s) does he/she speak?)

---

18 Family Members

Read.

1. grandfather and grandmother
2. father and mother
3. son and daughter
4. brother and sister
5. husband and wife

UNIT 2 • 49

Male or Female?

Purpose: To introduce giving personal information (male/female)

Teacher Preparation and Materials
1. Family relationship sight-word cards used for page 17
2. Samples of forms and applications that include *Male/Female* or *M/F,* such as subsidized school lunch forms, health forms, and Social Security card applications *(Expansion/Extension)*

Warm-up
1. Have learners look at the pictures again on page 18 and identify the family members.
2. Tape the sight-word cards on the board. Point to a word. Have a volunteer use the word to make a sentence about the family pictures. (FOR EXAMPLE: *father*—Fred is Kendra's father. *wife*—Alma is Harold's wife.)
3. On the board, draw the generic symbols for women and men used on page 19. Demonstrate categorizing by taking one of the sight-word cards and taping it under the correct symbol. Ask volunteers to come up to the board and categorize the other words under male or female. Note for learners that *parents* and *children* can be in both columns.

Presentation
1. Erase the chart on the board. Have learners turn to page 19 and read the family relationship words in the box. Point to the symbol for women and ask *Which words belong with this symbol?* Have learners read the appropriate words from the box. Repeat the procedure with the symbol for men.
2. Have learners categorize the terms under the proper headings in the book. Learners can work individually or in pairs.

Expansion/Extension
- On the board, write the words *Male* and *Female* as headings. Learners can come to the board and write their names under the correct heading.

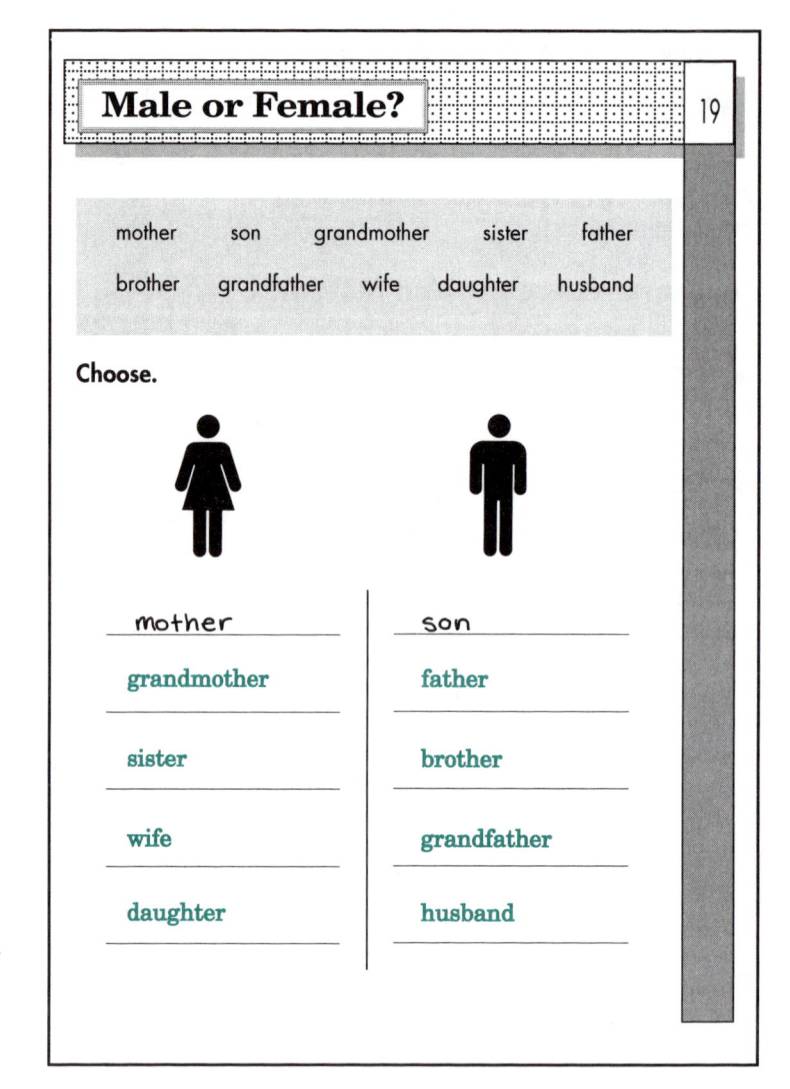

- Bring in forms listing *Male* and *Female* or *M* and *F*. Forms might include subsidized school lunch forms, health forms, and Social Security card applications. Have learners find the words *Male* and *Female* or *M* and *F*. Demonstrate various ways of filling in the information, such as checking a box and writing *M* or *F*.
- Make a chart for learners to fill in the names of their family members. Include columns for learners to list relationship and sex of family members. FOR EXAMPLE:

Name	Relationship	Male/Female
Monica Novak	daughter	female

- Introduce the sight words *Men* and *Women,* as used on rest rooms. If possible, have learners find them in the building. Depending on learners' skills, ask what other words they have observed, such as *Ladies* and *Gents*.

50 • UNIT 2

Who's in the Family?

Purpose: To give practice in explaining family relationships

Teacher Preparation and Materials

1. Photo of your family
2. Photos of learners' families *(Expansion/Extension)*
3. Blank copy of chart on page 20 *(Expansion/Extension)*
4. Magazines with pictures of people, posterboard, scissors, and glue for all *(Expansion/Extension)*

Warm-up

1. Review the Jones family picture and family tree on pages 16 and 17 and the names of the people and their relationships. Ask *Who is Kendra's brother? Who is Carol's son? Who is Harold's grandson? Who is Michael?* (He's Kendra's brother. He's Carol's son. He's Harold's grandson.) *Tell me about Janet.* (She's Carol's sister. She's Richard's wife.)

2. List the family relationship terms: *mother, father, sister, brother, grandfather, grandmother, husband, wife, son, daughter.* Then create three or four columns on the board to make a chart.

3. Write your name at the top of the first column. Show a picture of your family and talk about yourself. (FOR EXAMPLE: *I am a sister and a wife.*) Demonstrate how to fill in the chart by checking the appropriate relationship words about yourself.

4. Ask for a volunteer. Write the volunteer's name at the top of the next column. Ask questions about his or her family. *Do you have children?* or *Are you a father* or *mother? Do you have a sister or brother?* or *Are you a sister* or *brother?* Check the appropriate words. Do other examples as necessary.

Presentation

1. Have learners turn to page 20 and identify the people in the picture. Say *Show me Kendra. Point to Fred. Where's Carol?*

2. Review orally the example of Carol on page 20. Ask *Who is Carol? Is Carol a mother? Is she a father?*

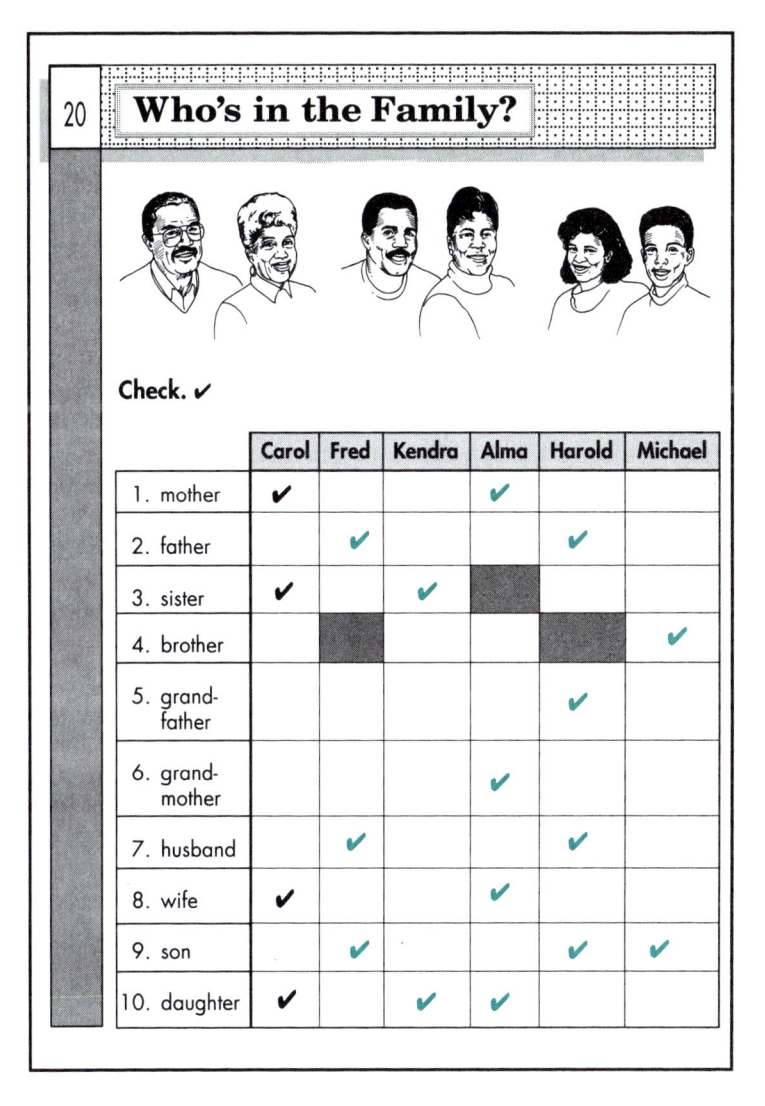

3. Ask learners which relationship terms apply to Fred. *Who is Fred? Is he a mother? Is he a father?* and so on. Have learners check the appropriate columns. (**Note:** Spaces that are shaded indicate that information is not available to determine the answer.)

4. Have learners complete the chart individually or in pairs. (**Note:** Some learners may need assistance in filling in the correct spaces on the chart. A ruler or blank sheet of paper can be used to help learners focus on one column at a time.)

Expansion/Extension

- Give practice with possessive nouns using the chart. FOR EXAMPLE: *Tell me about Carol. Whose mother is she?* (She's Kendra's mother.) *Whose sister is she?* (She's Janet's sister.)

- Learners can practice talking about relationships in their own families, using photos, if possible. (FOR EXAMPLE: *I'm Gina's mother/father. I'm Daniela's husband.*)

More *Expansion/Extension* on page 58

---

20 Who's in the Family?

Check. ✓

	Carol	Fred	Kendra	Alma	Harold	Michael
1. mother	✓			✓		
2. father		✓			✓	
3. sister	✓		✓	▓		
4. brother		▓			▓	✓
5. grandfather					✓	
6. grandmother				✓		
7. husband		✓			✓	
8. wife	✓			✓		
9. son		✓			✓	✓
10. daughter	✓		✓	✓		

Planning a Party

Purpose: To introduce days, months, time; to introduce recognizing and writing dates

Teacher Preparation and Materials

1. An oversized calendar page of the current month
2. Copies of a calendar page of the current month
3. 12-month calendar
4. Clocks with movable hands, can be made of cardboard, preferably one for each learner
5. Photos or pictures of celebrations (optional)
6. Magazines with pictures of holiday celebrations, posterboard, scissors, and glue for all *(Expansion/Extension)*
7. Blank index cards *(Expansion/Extension)*
8. Copies of TRF Handout 2.3, *Days of the Week (Expansion/Extension)*

Warm-up

1. Ask *What day is it today? What days do we study?* On the board, write:

    Su   M   T   W   Th   F   S

    Model and have learners repeat the days, first in order and then randomly. Write the whole word and have learners read the days as you point to them.

2. Tape the large calendar page on the board. Review the days. Then point to numbers and have learners say them. Model and have learners repeat ordinals in dates. FOR EXAMPLE: April first, April second, April third. Model and point to components of dates. FOR EXAMPLE: Monday, April fifteenth; Thursday, April fourth; Sunday, April twenty-first. Say dates and have volunteers circle them on the calendar page. Give each learner a calendar page and have them circle dates as you say them.

3. Show a 12-month calendar and read the months. Have learners repeat the months.

4. Introduce telling time (focus on hours). Dictate whole-hour times and have learners position the hands of a clock. Write times on the board and have learners position the clock hands.

Planning a Party

Read.

Janet and Richard Stevens are visiting Carol and Fred Wilson. Janet and Carol are sisters.

Carol is planning a party for Janet and Richard. She's inviting family and friends.

Come to a Party!

For: Janet and Richard Stevens
Date: Saturday, October 2nd
Time: 8:00 p.m.
Place: 127 Center Street, Apt. 2A

Carol and Fred Wilson

Presentation

1. Have learners turn to page 21 and ask them to look at the pictures. Ask *What do you see?* On the board, write the words that learners already know.
2. Have learners follow along as you read the story.
3. Say names of people and family words used in the story. Have learners point to the words. Say *Find the name* Carol. *Point to the word* family. and so on.
4. Read the story again. Ask questions in the present continuous tense. *Who is visiting Carol? What's Carol planning? What's she writing? What are the people doing?*
5. Read the invitation at the bottom of page 21 as learners follow along. Ask *Who's the party for? Where is the party? What date is the party? What time is it?*

Expansion/Extension
See **TRF HANDOUT 2.3,** *Days of the Week*

- Learners can suggest reasons for the party. Introduce vocabulary for various kinds of celebrations.

More *Expansion/Extension* on page 58

Hello!

Purpose: To give practice in expressing greetings

Teacher Preparation and Materials
1. Audiotape for Level 1
2. Index cards with sight words: *Mr., Mrs., Ms., Miss*

Warm-up
1. Review greetings from the Preliminary Lesson. Greet individual learners and have them respond appropriately. FOR EXAMPLE: *Hello.* (Hi.) *How are you?* (Fine, thanks.)
2. Introduce new greetings: *Nice to see you again. I'm happy to see you again.* Model greetings and have learners repeat. Then, have learners get up and practice greeting each other.
3. Introduce the titles *Mr., Mrs., Ms.,* and *Miss.* Tape sight-word cards on board. Ask *What's your name?* (Ricardo Vásquez) Point to the appropriate title. Then greet the person using a title. FOR EXAMPLE: *Nice to see you again, Mr. Vásquez.*

Presentation
1. Have learners turn to page 22, look at the illustrations, and identify the characters. *Who do you see? What is his/her name?*
2. Ask questions about the pictures. *Where are they? What are they doing? Why are they at the house?*
3. Play the audiotape while the learners look at the pictures. Learners will hear a variety of common greetings that go along with the illustrations. Some of the greetings are recycled from the Preliminary Lesson. Have learners repeat the various greetings as you point to characters in the pictures.
4. Have learners role-play each of the various parts: host/hostess, entering guests, friends, acquaintances, family members, and so on.

Expansion/Extension
- Practicing greetings should begin every lesson. Introduce other common idiomatic phrases associated with greetings throughout the course. FOR EXAMPLE: *How're you doing? What's new? How've you been? Not bad. Can't complain. So-so.*
- Depending on the learners, you may want to discuss party customs both in the United States and in learners' native countries. Ask *Do guests usually bring something for the host/hostess? flowers? some candy? How do you know when it is time to leave? Do you always help the host/hostess? How do you thank the host/hostess?*
- Discuss the titles *Mr., Mrs., Ms.,* and *Miss.* Ask *Which title is for a man? Which is used for married women? Which can be used for single or married women?*
- Depending on learners' skills, discuss the use of titles in the conversations. Anita calls Harold "Mr. Jones," but he calls her "Anita." Learners can think of various reasons for using titles instead of first names. Some reasons might be the age of a person (use title to show respect for older person), formality of a situation (use title on important or special occasions), familiarity (use title for a person you have just met).

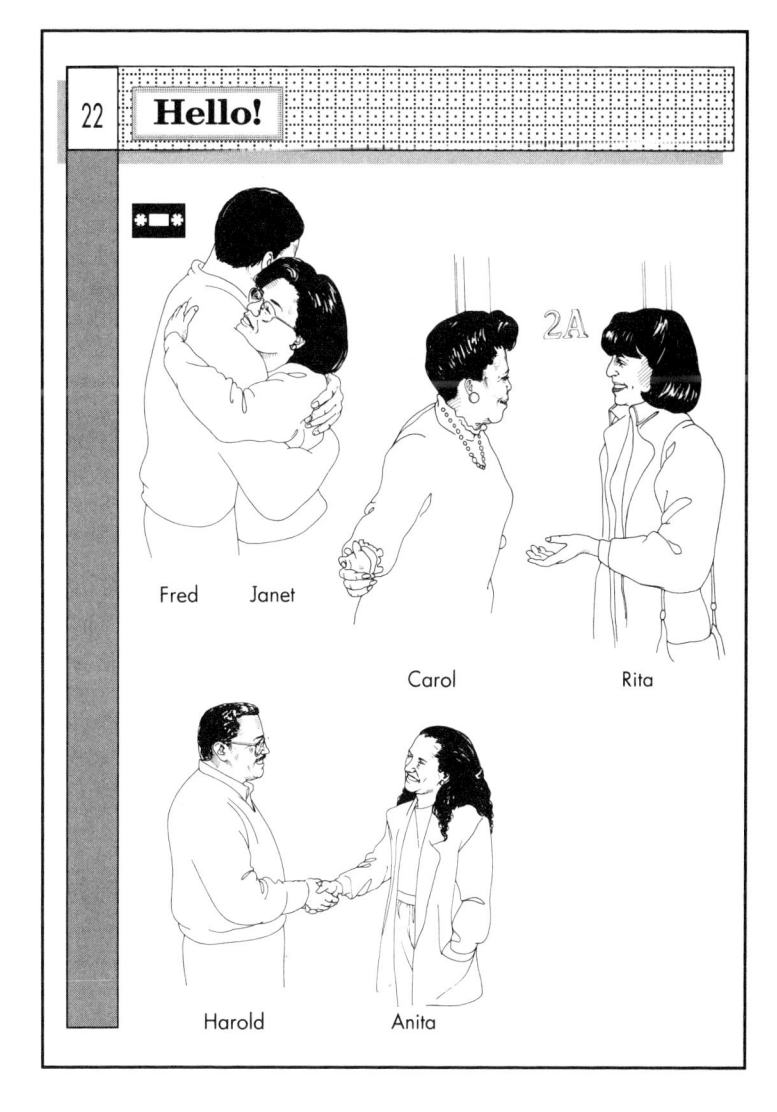

More *Expansion/Extension* on page 59

UNIT 2 • 53

Nice to Meet You

Purpose: To introduce new expressions in making introductions

Teacher Preparation and Materials
1. Audiotape for Level 1
2. Puppets (optional)
3. Copies of TRF Handout 2.6, *Mr., Mrs., Miss, and Ms. (Expansion/Extension)*

Warm-up
1. Review family relationships, friends, and neighbors of characters. Have learners turn to page 5 and page 16. Ask questions about the people to review character names and their relationships. *Who's she? What's her name? Who's her father?*
2. Review names of learners in class with questions and answers. *What's your name? What's his/her name?*
3. Introduce new expressions for introductions: *I'm glad to meet you. Nice to meet you. How do you do?* Have learners repeat the expressions.

Presentation
1. Page 23 continues the party from the previous page. The focus is on introductions. Have learners identify the characters in the illustrations on page 23. Ask questions about the pictures. FOR EXAMPLE: *What are they doing? What are they talking about?*
2. Play the audiotape. Have learners listen to the conversations introducing various characters that go along with the illustrations.
3. Have learners practice introducing classmates to each other. In a one-to-one situation, you may want to use puppets for role-playing introductions. In this way, you can practice introductions involving three or more people without having to play the role of more than one person at a time.

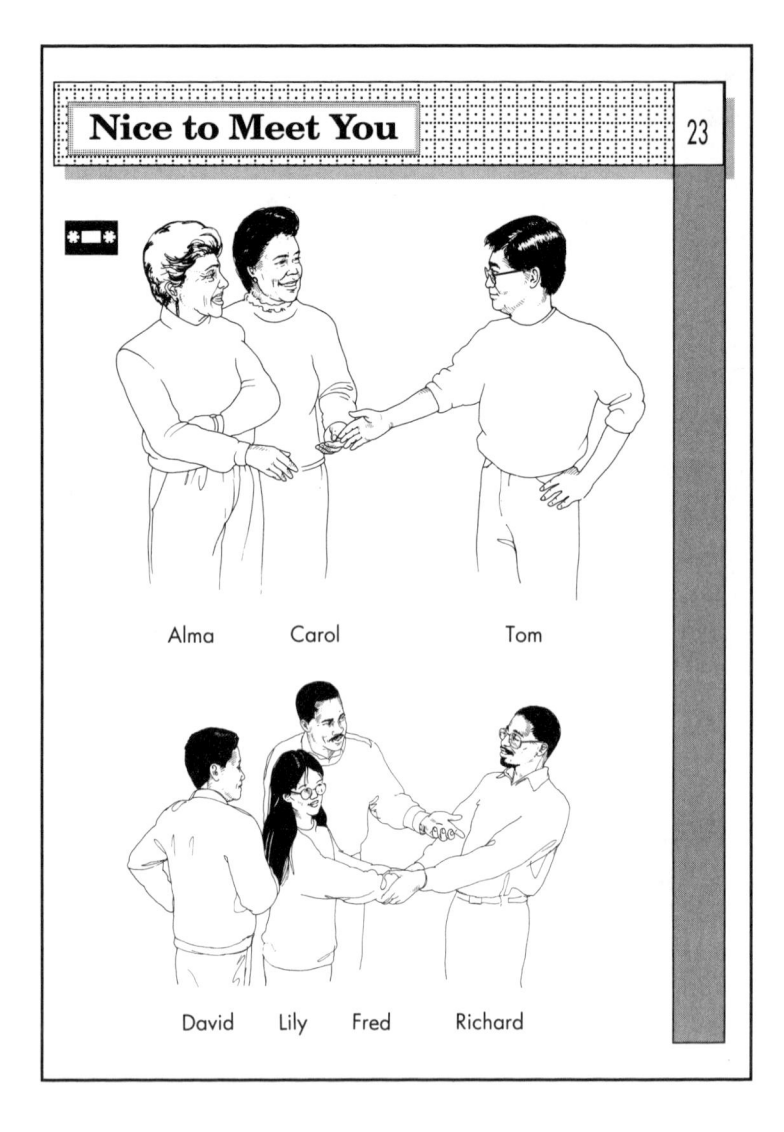

Expansion/Extension
See **TRF HANDOUT 2.6**, *Mr., Mrs., Miss, and Ms.*

- You may want to introduce learners to workers or other teachers in the building. Learners might also introduce you to friends studying or working in the building.
  If you are working with a learner in a home situation, the learner can practice introducing you to friends and family in their building/neighborhood.

- Give practice in asking for clarification in introductory situations. Say *Excuse me? I'm sorry. Could you repeat that? I'm sorry. I didn't get your name.*

- Discuss names used in introductions and greetings. Ask *Why does Tom say* Mrs. Jones? *Why does Alma say* Mr. Lin?

Nice to Meet You 23

Alma   Carol   Tom

David   Lily   Fred   Richard

Days of the Week

Purpose: To give practice in recognizing and writing days, months, time, and dates

Teacher Preparation and Materials

1. 12-month calendar (either a large wall calendar or enough small calendars for all)
2. Clocks with movable hands for all
3. Audiotape for Level 1
4. Blank calendar form *(Expansion/Extension)*
5. Copies of TRF Handout 2.4, *Class Calendar (Expansion/Extension)*

Warm-up

1. With a calendar, review the names of the days of the week. Have learners say them in order. Ask questions and have learners respond with the correct day. FOR EXAMPLE: *What day is the eighth?* (It's Friday.)
2. Use the calendar to review months. Have learners say them in order. Ask questions and have learners respond with the correct month. FOR EXAMPLE: *What month is it now? What was last month?*
3. Review finding dates on a calendar. Say sentences with dates and have learners find them on the calendar. (FOR EXAMPLE: *We started class on October 20th. I have to go to the doctor on June 6th.*)
4. Review time. Dictate a time, such as *8:00* or *3:00,* and have learners position the hands of the clock and then write the time. Introduce time on the half hour. FOR EXAMPLE: *9:30 (nine thirty).* Say sentences with times and have learners position the hands of the clock and write the time. (FOR EXAMPLE: *I go to work at 9:30. We finish class at 3:00.*)
5. Introduce the abbreviations *a.m.* and *p.m.* Illustrate the meanings with a person's daily schedule and times. (FOR EXAMPLE: *I get up at 6:30 a.m. I eat dinner at 6:30 p.m.*)

Presentation

1. Have learners turn to page 24, look at the picture, and identify the characters. Ask questions such as *Where are they? What are they doing? What times do you see written in the book? What dates are in the book? What days of the week have dates written in?*
2. Play the audiotape. Ask *What are they planning to do? Is Tuesday OK? Is Wednesday OK? What is the date next Wednesday? What time are they going to meet?* If necessary, ask one question and then play the audiotape again so learners can focus on that information. Repeat the procedure for other questions. Depending on the learners' skills, ask detailed questions, such as *Why can't they meet on Tuesday? Who is Janet staying with?*
3. Listen to the conversation again. Together read the questions at the bottom of the page. Have learners fill in the correct day and time in the spaces provided.

Expansion/Extension
See **TRF HANDOUT 2.4,** *Class Calendar*

- Give learners blank calendar forms. Have them fill in their schedules. First have them fill in the name of the month, the days, and numbers. Then learners can fill in places they need to go with the times on the proper dates. Learners can fill in dates and times for class, work, shopping, appointments, and so on. (They can be real or made up.)

More *Expansion/Extension* on page 59

---

24 Days of the Week

Janet   Anita

1. What day are Anita and Janet meeting for lunch?
   Wednesday

2. What time are they meeting? __12:30__

UNIT 2 • 55

Married or Single?

Purpose: To introduce giving and getting personal information (marital status)

Teacher Preparation and Materials

1. Pictures of married couples (wedding pictures) and single people
2. Samples of forms that require information about marital status, such as tax forms, welfare forms, health forms, housing or credit applications *(Expansion/Extension)*
3. Copies of TRF Handout 2.5, *Family Interview (Expansion/Extension)*
4. Copies of TRF Handout 2.7, *An International Family (Expansion/Extension)*

Warm-up

1. Review names of the characters and their relatives from page 17. Have learners identify the characters by name and relationship. (FOR EXAMPLE: *This is Carol. She's Fred's wife.*)
2. Review *Yes/No* questions with the verb *be*. (FOR EXAMPLE: *Is this Carol? Are you from China?*)
3. Show photos or pictures of married couples and single people. Introduce *married* and *single*. Provide sentences for each of the photos or pictures. FOR EXAMPLE: *This is Carol and Fred Wilson. They are married. This is George Ross. He is single.* Ask *Is he/she married or single? Are they married or single?* Have learners give the appropriate word: *married* or *single*.
4. Write *married* and *single* on the board. Have learners tape the pictures under the appropriate word.

Presentation

1. Have learners turn to page 25, look at the pictures, and identify the characters.
2. Together, read the descriptions of the pictures.
3. Give practice with questions and answers about marital status. *Is Janet married?* (Yes, she is.) *Is Anita married?* (No, she's single.) Have learners look at the family tree on page 17. Have learners ask and answer questions about other characters.
4. Give practice in asking and responding to questions about marital status in a chain drill. *Are you married?* (Yes, I am. No, I'm not.)
5. On the board, write the headings from the chart on page 25. Have learners give the names of the characters. Write them under the heading "Name." Ask about the marital status of the characters and demonstrate making a check mark in the correct column.
6. Add the names of learners to the chart. Ask these learners if they are married or single. Record the responses.
7. Have learners interview three other people about marital status and record the names and responses on the chart on page 25. ■ In a one-to-one situation, the learner can use the other characters in the lesson or record information about you, friends, or relatives.
8. Go over the interview responses orally. Total the number of people in each category. Summarize the class results.

Expansion/Extension
See **TRF HANDOUT 2.5,** *Family Interview*
TRF HANDOUT 2.7, *An International Family*

More *Expansion/Extension* on page 59

Married or Single?   25

Janet and Richard Stevens are married.

Anita Gómez is single. She's not married.

Interview.   *Answers will vary.*

Name	Married	Single
1. Anita		✔
2. Janet	✔	
3.		
4.		
5.		

Are you married or single?   *Answers will vary.*
I'm _____.

56 • UNIT 2

Look Back

Purpose: To give practice in giving personal information and explaining relationships

Teacher Preparation and Materials

1. A sample of an emergency contact card (with names of who to contact in an emergency)
2. Samples of forms that require information about family and relationships, such as school emergency information forms, subsidized lunch forms, health forms, and welfare forms *(Expansion/Extension)*

Warm-up

1. Review personal information questions and family relationship terms orally. *What's your name? What's your first name? What's your last name? What's your telephone number? Where are you from? Are you married or single? Who's in your family?*
2. Show an example of an emergency contact card. Talk about why people carry them. If necessary, act out a situation when the card might be needed, such as fainting on the subway. Also act out how it is used to contact the relative or person listed on it.
3. Have learners give examples of other emergencies when the card might be useful.

Presentation

1. Have learners look at the first form on page 26 and find the sight words: *name, telephone number, first, last.*
2. Ask questions about the form. *What is the name of this person? What is his first name? What is his last name? Who do you call if Harold is hurt? What's her phone number? Who is she? (How is she related to Harold?)*
3. Have learners individually fill in the bottom form with their own information.

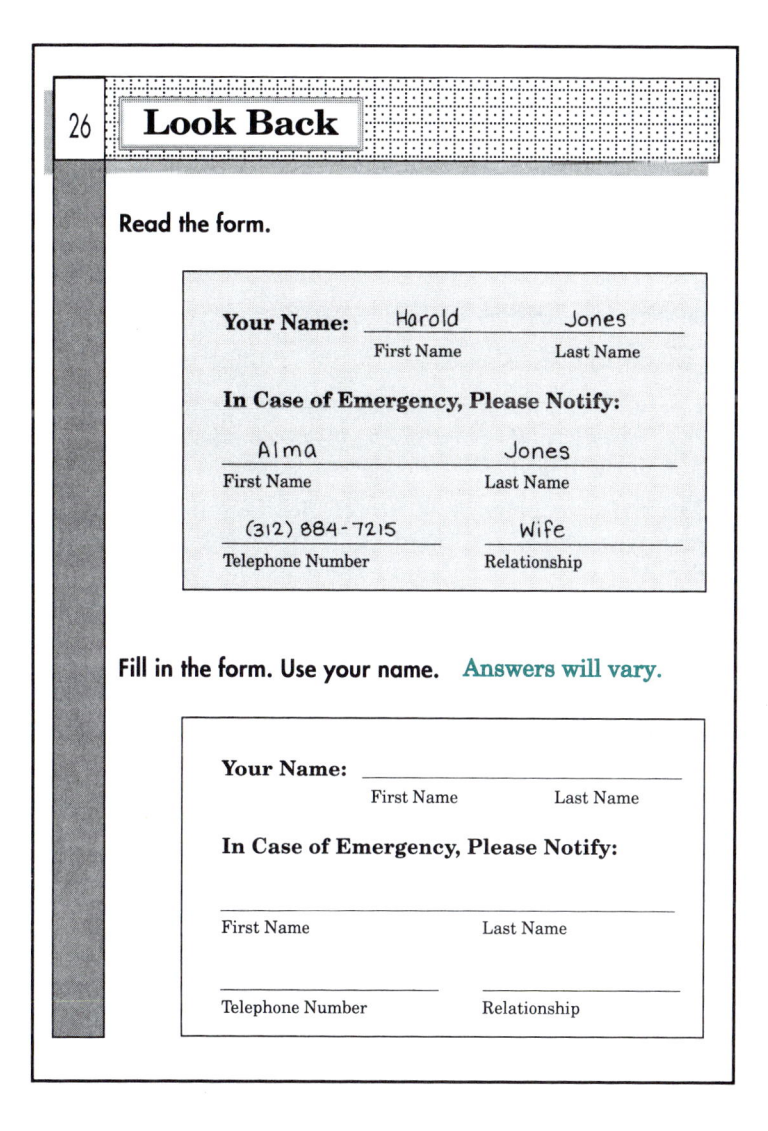

---

26 | **Look Back**

Read the form.

> Your Name: __Harold__   __Jones__
>   First Name   Last Name
>
> **In Case of Emergency, Please Notify:**
>
> __Alma__   __Jones__
> First Name   Last Name
>
> __(312) 884-7215__   __Wife__
> Telephone Number   Relationship

Fill in the form. Use your name.   **Answers will vary.**

> Your Name: _____   _____
>   First Name   Last Name
>
> **In Case of Emergency, Please Notify:**
>
> _____   _____
> First Name   Last Name
>
> _____   _____
> Telephone Number   Relationship

Expansion/Extension

- Bring in or ask learners to bring in samples of forms that require information about family members: name, address, sex, relationship, and so on. Some forms might be school emergency information forms, subsidized lunch forms, health forms, and welfare forms. Practice finding the sight words and then filling out those parts of the forms.
- On the board, make a chart of characteristics of the class members such as sex, country of origin, and number of children. Learners can count and tabulate the results and then mark them on the chart. In small groups, learners can write a report about the results of the survey. FOR EXAMPLE: *There are . . . learners in our group. There are . . . women. There are . . . men. There are . . . from Mexico.* Additionally, learners can ask and answer questions about the chart. (FOR EXAMPLE: *How many learners are in our group? How many women are there?*)

UNIT 2: Families
Expansion/Extension

A Family Tree

Expansion/Extension for SB page 17
See TRF HANDOUT 2.1, *My Family*
　　TRF HANDOUT 2.2, *My Family Tree*

- Learners can write the relationship terms under the family members on the family tree, as you did on the board.
- Learners can bring in photos of their families and practice talking about and introducing their family group. (In my family, there are five people. I have a father, a mother, two brothers, and a sister. This is my father. His name is . . . .) Learners can talk about where various family members live.
- Introduce other relationship terms such as *cousin, nephew, niece, aunt,* and *uncle*. These can be added to the Joneses' family tree on page 17 and/or to the learners' own family trees.

Who's in the Family?

More *Expansion/Extension* for SB page 20

- Prepare a similar chart but without the names. Learners can interview three to six others in the class to complete the chart. Learners can share their findings with the class. (FOR EXAMPLE: Inez is a sister and a wife.) ■ In a one-to-one situation, the learner can interview neighbors or friends to complete the chart.
- Learners can cut out and categorize magazine pictures (or draw their own) associated with the roles of various family members (FOR EXAMPLE: father—cook, work, take care of children, study). Learners can make a collage for each family word by gluing pictures to posterboard and labeling their work with the family relationship term. Depending on learners' skills, discuss family members' roles in the various cultures represented in the group.

Planning a Party

More *Expansion/Extension* for SB page 21

- Use calendars to introduce and practice other time concepts: *yesterday, today, tomorrow, next week, last week,* and so on.

- Learners can discuss roles in planning parties. Ask learners *Who cooks the food for parties in your family? Who invites the people?* Learners can speculate about Carol's role and Fred's role in planning their party.
- Learners can plan a class party and prepare some simple invitations.
- Learners can make a class calendar. Write in dates of holidays, learners' birthdays, school or program starting and ending dates, and other relevant dates.
- Create a matching exercise. Write the sight words *for, date, time,* and *place* on one set of index cards. Write the information from the invitation on page 21 on another set. Learners can match the sight words with the correct information. After matching the information, learners can create sentences using the present continuous tense. (FOR EXAMPLE: She's having a party for Janet and Richard. She's having a party on Saturday, October 2nd.)
- Talk about holidays and celebrations both in the United States and in learners' native countries. Compare holidays and celebration customs. Learners can bring in or make a picture of their favorite holiday to share with the class. Learners can find the dates on a calendar.
- Learners can cut out magazine pictures of things associated with various holidays and celebrations. They can make a collage on posterboard and label the pictures. Introduce holiday and birthday songs at times of the year when they are appropriate.
- Learners from the same country or religion can prepare a presentation about their most important or favorite holiday.
- Give practice with the present continuous tense by referring to actions in the class. Act out and model these sentences: *I'm writing. I'm listening. I'm reading. I'm talking.* Then, give practice with questions and answers about what learners are doing. FOR EXAMPLE: *Juan, what are you doing?* (I'm reading.) *Ana, what's Juan doing?* (He's reading.)
- On the board, write the contracted forms *I'm, she's, we're,* and so on. Model and write the long form for *I'm (I am)*. Ask learners what the other long forms are.
- Learners can look back at the story on page 21 and pick out the verbs with the ending *-ing*. Write them on the board and then circle or write the base forms of the verbs. Learners can categorize the verbs in three groups: verbs with no change, verbs that drop the silent *e*, and verbs

that double the last letter. Place other verbs learners know in the correct categories.

- Show pictures of various activities that learners do during the day: study, eat, sleep, work, cook, go to the store. Ask questions about when the actions are done. Learners can orally give the time or write the time. *What time do you go to work? What time do you eat lunch?* and so on.

- Give practice with ordinals with the names of the months of the year. Ask questions and learners can find the correct month name. FOR EXAMPLE: *What's the first month of the year? Find the fifth month.*

- Give practice with pronunciation of *t* and *th* with a minimal-pair drill.

Tuesday	Thursday
tin	thin
tank	thank
tan	than

Hello!
More Expansion/Extension for SB page 22

- Learners can compare the greetings used in the conversations with greetings in their native cultures. Talk about when it is appropriate to shake hands or to hug or kiss a person.

- Learners can categorize greetings as formal or informal. FOR EXAMPLE:

    Formal: Hello. Good afternoon.
              It's nice to see you again.
    Informal: Hi. How are you doing?
              Good to see you.

- Learners can make a chart of names or types of people for the different titles. FOR EXAMPLE:

First Name (only)	children, classmates, neighbors
Mr., Mrs., Miss, Ms. (Last name)	children's teachers, program director, older neighbors, and so on

Days of the Week
More Expansion/Extension for SB page 24

- In pairs, learners can role-play setting up appointments. (FOR EXAMPLE: *Can you come to a party on Thursday, March 15th?*) Learners can look at their calendar schedules from the previous Expansion/Extension activity and respond yes or no. (*Yes, I can. No, I can't.*)

- Give practice in answering questions about other dates. (FOR EXAMPLE: *When is your birthday? anniversary? When is your child's birthday?*) Learners can fill in this information on their calendar forms.

- Introduce other ways of saying times. (FOR EXAMPLE: *8:30—half-past eight, eight thirty; 8:00—eight sharp, 8 a.m., eight o'clock*) Learners do not need to be able to produce the variations, but they should be familiar with and understand them.

Married or Single?
More Expansion/Extension for SB page 25

- Introduce and give practice with other vocabulary related to marital status; FOR EXAMPLE: *widowed, separated, divorced.* Ask *Are you married or single?* (*I'm separated.*)

- Learners can look at forms that require information about marital status. FOR EXAMPLE: tax forms and health forms. Learners can find the sections about marital status and circle the words *married* and *single*.

- Discuss personal questions and when they are appropriate. Say *You are required to answer questions about marital status for welfare and tax purposes, but you are not required to answer them in job interviews.* Also talk about how to avoid answering personal questions in social situations. (FOR EXAMPLE: *I'd rather not say. That's personal.*)

- Learners can bring in pictures or talk about marriage customs and traditions in their native cultures. Ask questions such as *Where do you get married? How old do people have to be to get married? What do you do to celebrate? Is there a party or other celebration? How long does the celebration last? Who decides who you marry—you or your parents?*

1 2 **3** 4 5 6 7 8 9 10 11 12 Summary
Keeping in Touch

Objectives

Functions
- Requesting assistance
- Expressing needs
- Giving and getting information
- Dealing with telephone numbers/area codes
- Clarifying
- Expressing greetings
- Dealing with numbers: time, money

Life Tasks
- Making long-distance phone calls
- Calling Information (Directory Assistance)
- Recognizing time zones
- Addressing envelopes and packages
- Recognizing post office mail slots and signs
- Writing money orders
- Understanding the concept of insurance

Structures
- *Would like* + infinitive
- Politeness markers
- Present continuous tense

Culture
- Accessing information: phone books, telephone operators, signs
- Using the U.S. Postal Service and telephone systems
- Conventions for addressing envelopes
- Time zones

Vocabulary

Key words:

airmail
Central Time
closed
Eastern Time
foreign
letter
local
long-distance information
money order
Mountain Time
open
operator
out-of-town
Pacific Time
package
stamp
Stamps Only
telephone operator
time zone

Related words:

cents	nephew
dial	pay to
dollars	please
fee	postage
from	send
help	sign
holiday	thank you
hours	total
insurance coverage	window
live	

An International Call

Purpose: To give practice in dealing with telephone numbers; to introduce telephone protocol and requesting assistance

Teacher Preparation and Materials
1. Two real or toy telephones (optional)
2. Map of the world
3. Audiotape for Level 1
4. Copies of international pages from local telephone book *(Expansion/Extension)*

Warm-up
1. Review telephone numbers. Give practice with questions and answers. *What's your phone number?* Write the numbers on the board as learners say them. Tell learners they don't have to give a real number.
2. Place the two telephones on a desk. Hold one of the receivers and dial a learner's number listed on the board. Say the numbers as you dial. Have the learner whose number was dialed come and underline the number and then "answer" the other phone.
3. Use the phones or draw a push-button phone keypad on the board and have learners practice dialing phone numbers. Demonstrate dialing as you give a direction such as *Dial 567-4218.* Give various dialing instructions and have learners dial or point to the appropriate buttons. FOR EXAMPLE: *First dial 1, then dial 444-9237. You need to dial 467-3387.*
4. Introduce *operator*. Ask learners if they have ever dialed 0. Ask *Who answers when you dial 0? How can the operator help you?*
5. On the world map, find the United States and your state and/or city. (**Note:** Some learners may not have strong map-reading skills and may need assistance locating your state.) Explain that the operator (0) can help with phone calls in the United States. Have learners find their native countries on the map. Explain that the overseas operator (00) can help with calls to other countries. (**Note:** All calls are more expensive with operator assistance.)

Presentation
1. Have learners turn to page 27 and look at the pictures. Ask *What do you see? What do you think is happening?*

1 2 3 4 5 6 7 8 9 10 11 12
Keeping in Touch ■ ■ ■ ■ ■ ■ ■

Mrs. Wong

May Lin
Tom Lin   telephone operator

An International Call
What's happening?   **Answers may vary.**

2. Play the audiotape and have learners listen to the conversation.
3. Ask questions about the conversation. *Who do you think Tom is calling? What country does he want to call? What numbers should Tom dial first to call Mrs. Wong?* Depending on the learners' skills, ask one question and then have learners listen to the audiotape again for the answer to the question. Repeat the procedure with other questions.
4. Ask *What's happening?* Give learners time to talk about the pictures.

Expansion/Extension
- Ask learners if they have called overseas. *What numbers did you dial? Did you dial yourself or have help?* Together write an LEA story about experiences calling overseas.
- Learners can describe the pictures on page 27 using simple sentences or phrases. Write the learners' descriptions on the board and have learners copy them. More advanced learners can create their own sentences or phrases.

More *Expansion/Extension* on page 72

UNIT 3 • 61

Long-Distance Information

Purpose: To give practice in requesting information and dealing with phone numbers

Teacher Preparation and Materials

1. Map of the United States (or map on Student Book pages 126-127)
2. ▣ Audiotape for Level 1
3. Local telephone books or copies of necessary pages *(Expansion/Extension)*
4. Copies of TRF Handout 3.4, *Pay Phone* *(Expansion/Extension)*

Warm-up

1. Review writing phone numbers from dictation. Dictate phone numbers and have learners write them. FOR EXAMPLE: *six-seven-two, five-five-one-eight*. Learners can read them back to check their work. Review the use of a hyphen in writing phone numbers.
2. Review family relationship terms. Have learners look at the family tree on page 17 and identify the family members. Introduce *niece/nephew*. Ask *Who is Janet's nephew? Do you have a niece/nephew?*
3. Have learners turn to page 5. Have learners find Anita Gómez. Review information about her. Ask *What's her name? Where does she live? Is she married or single?* Explain *Anita has a nephew. His name is Arturo Soto. He lives in New York.* Write his name on the board. Help learners find Brooklyn, New York and Chicago, Illinois, on the map of the United States.

Presentation

1. Have learners turn to page 28 and look at the picture. Ask *What is Anita doing? What is she using the paper and pencil for?*
2. Together, read the description of the picture. Explain that Information is the same as Directory Assistance.
3. Ask comprehension questions about the reading. FOR EXAMPLE: *Who is Anita calling? Where does he live? What number is Anita dialing in the picture?*

4. ▣ Play the audiotape and have learners listen to the phone call. Together, read the question. ▣ Then, play the audiotape again. At the bottom of the page, have learners write the number they hear. ▣ Replay the audiotape if necessary. Have a volunteer write the phone number on the board.

Expansion/Extension
See TRF HANDOUT 3.4, *Pay Phone*

- Learners can look in the local telephone book for the numbers for local Directory Assistance and long-distance Directory Assistance. In most areas, local Directory Assistance can be reached at either 411 or 555-1212. Long-distance Directory Assistance is 1-(area code)-555-1212. Learners can also look for charges for calling local Directory Assistance. Long-distance Directory Assistance charges can vary and are not usually listed.

---

28 Long-Distance Information

Anita Gómez is calling her nephew, Arturo Soto. Arturo lives in Brooklyn, New York.

Anita is dialing long-distance information. She's dialing 1-718-555-1212.

▣

What's Arturo's phone number?

9 6 5 _ 2 0 2 9

More *Expansion/Extension* on page 72

62 • UNIT 3

Time Zones

Purpose: To introduce information on time zones

Teacher Preparation and Materials
1. Clocks with movable hands for all
2. Pictures of activities related to specific times of the day: getting up, going to school/work, going to bed, eating dinner, and so on
3. Map of the United States (or map on Student Book pages 126-127)
4. Local telephone books
5. Copies of TRF Handout 3.1, *Picture Strips 1* (Expansion/Extension)
6. Copies of TRF Handout 3.2, *Conversation Strips* (Expansion/Extension)
7. Copies of TRF Handout 3.3, *Long-Distance Operator* (Expansion/Extension)

Warm-up
1. Review time. Dictate times (*8:00, 8:30,* and so on) and have learners adjust the hands of the clock to the correct times.
2. Give practice with *a.m.* and *p.m.* Show pictures of various activities associated with morning and afternoon/evening. Say a sentence for each picture and have learners agree or disagree. FOR EXAMPLE: *I eat breakfast at 7:00 p.m.* (No.) *The children go to school at 8:00 a.m.* (Yes.)
3. Show the map of the United States. Have learners locate your state/city. Have learners locate other places they know on the map. If possible, have learners look through the beginning of local phone books for a map of the United States. Introduce and explain the four time zones (Eastern, Central, Mountain, and Pacific) using the maps. Have learners repeat the names.

Presentation
1. Have learners turn to page 29 and look at the map. Ask *What is this map for? What times are on the clocks? Why are they different?*
2. Have learners find and trace the heavy lines between Pacific and Mountain, Mountain and Central, and Central and Eastern time zones.
3. Have learners outline your state. Have them label their city/town and then identify the local time zone and copy its name on line 1.
4. Point out the cities on the map and identify each city's time zone. Use the map on Student Book pages 126-127 to talk about other states and major cities. FOR EXAMPLE: *In what time zone is Santa Fe, New Mexico? Washington, D.C.? Seattle, Washington? Cleveland, Ohio?*
5. Together, read the other questions at the bottom of the page. Have learners give the answers to the questions orally. If necessary, demonstrate adding or subtracting the correct number of hours to determine the time in another zone. FOR EXAMPLE: *You are in Chicago. It is 10:00 a.m. In New York, you add one hour, so it is 11:00 a.m. in New York.*
6. In pairs, have learners complete the exercise by drawing the hands of the clocks to indicate the times in the different cities.

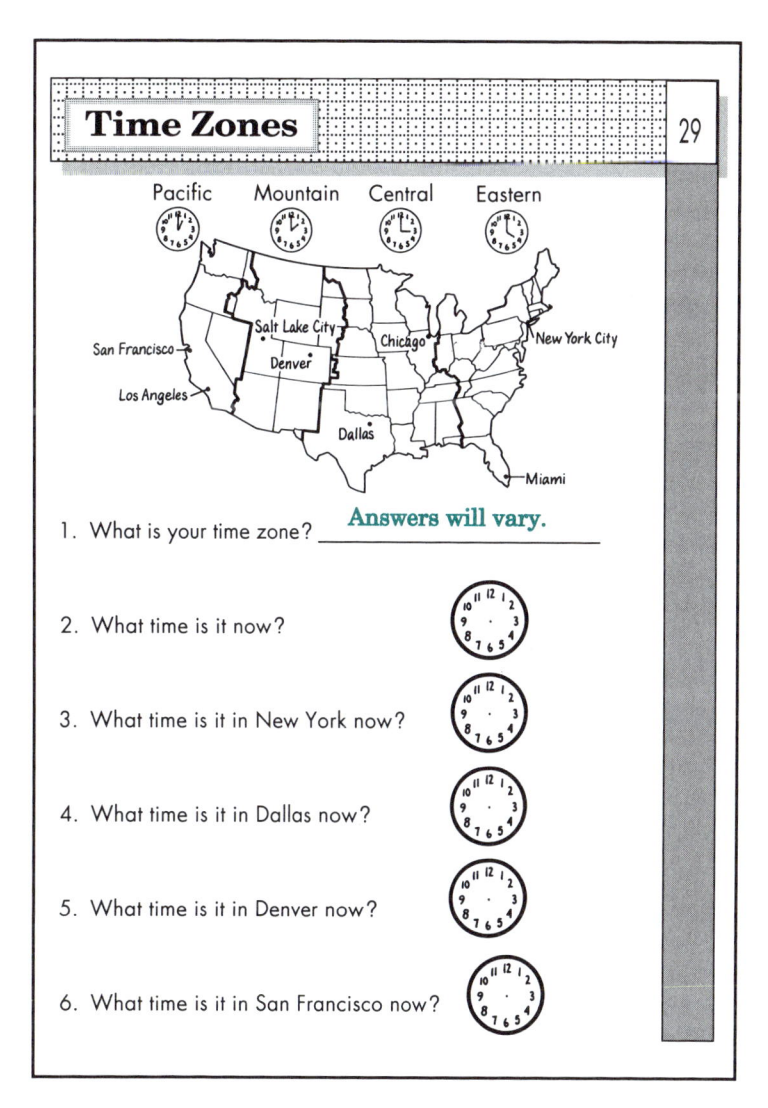

Expansion/Extension
See **TRF HANDOUT 3.1**, *Picture Strips 1*
  TRF HANDOUT 3.2, *Conversation Strips*
  TRF HANDOUT 3.3, *Long-Distance Operator*

More *Expansion/Extension* on page 72

UNIT 3 • 63

Sending a Package

Purpose: To give practice in addressing envelopes and packages

Teacher Preparation and Materials

1. Class sign-in sheet
2. Alphabet cards
3. A few photocopied pages from an address book with names and addresses
4. Blank labels used for packages (*Expansion/Extension*)
5. Blank envelopes, pens, postage stamps (*Expansion/Extension*)

Warm-up

1. Have learners write or copy their names and addresses on a class sign-in sheet at the start of the lesson.
2. Review questions and answers about addresses. Ask *What's your address? name? city? state? zip code?*
3. Review alphabetizing. Write the letters of the alphabet in order on the board. Have the group organize themselves in a line in alphabetical order by last names. Ask learners to write their names in order on the board and to check the list with the alphabet. If needed, have learners arrange alphabet cards in order.
4. Have learners look at samples of address book pages. Have learners find the pages for some letters of the alphabet. FOR EXAMPLE: *Find the page for the letter N. Find the last names that begin with the letter A.*

Presentation

1. Have learners turn to page 30 and look at the picture. Ask *What is May doing? Why is she wrapping a package?* (**Note:** Learners may mention the phone call from page 27.) Have them discuss what might be in the package. Write learners' comments on the board. Be sure to include the words *package* and *send*.
2. Ask learners if they have sent packages to relatives. *Who do you send packages to? What types of things do you send?*
3. Ask questions about the address book page. Ask *What is this? What names are on the page? What address and telephone numbers are there?* Point out that all names start with *W*.
4. On the board, make a sample package label. Point out *To* and *From* on the label. Demonstrate filling it in by asking for a volunteer's name, street address, city, state, and zip code. Use another learner's address for the return address. Ask questions about the label. FOR EXAMPLE: *Who is going to get this? Who is sending it? What goes on the first line?*
5. Have learners find Mrs. Wong's address in the address book. Ask questions about her address. *What is the name of the city? Is there a state? Where is the country written?* Have learners copy her address onto the package label at the bottom of the page. (**Note:** In Chinese, *liu* means *road*.) Explain that May Ling does not use the English word *road* in the address because the package is going to China.

***Expansion/Extension** on page 72*

64 • UNIT 3

At the Post Office

Purpose: To introduce post office vocabulary and signs

Teacher Preparation and Materials

1. Monthly or weekly calendar
2. Samples of postal items: postage stamps (local and airmail), aerograms, postcards, packages
3. Arrange a field trip to the post office. *(Expansion/Extension)*

Warm-up

1. Use a calendar to review the names of the days of the week. Ask questions about days. FOR EXAMPLE: *What day(s) do we have class? What days do you work? What days do your children go to school?*
2. Have learners look at the various postal items and identify those they know. Introduce other vocabulary. Be sure to include *stamps, package, postcard,* and *airmail.*

Presentation

1. Have learners turn to page 31 and look at the picture. Ask *Who do you see? Where are they? What does David have? Where is Anita?* List the words and comments on the board. Be sure to include *package, window, open,* and *closed.*
2. Have learners talk about what the characters are doing, using the present continuous tense. (FOR EXAMPLE: David and May are mailing a package. They are going to a window. The clerk is helping Anita.)
3. Have learners read the time on the clock and any other signs.
4. Ask *What's happening? Why can't the Lins mail the package from her window? Which window should they go to?*

Expansion/Extension

- Arrange a field trip to the post office. Together prepare a list of questions about the post office. (FOR EXAMPLE: What is the address of the post office? How much is a [first-class] stamp? How much is a postcard stamp? Is there a stamp machine?) Learners can get samples of forms. They can ask their questions and record the answers. Learners can also purchase stamps and aerograms. Some larger post offices give tours, which can be arranged by consulting the local postal chief.
- Together, write an LEA story about the field trip or about the picture in the book.
- Learners can locate the following signs in other buildings, such as stores, clinics, and banks: *Hours, Open, Closed, Pull, Push,* and so on. Learners can write down the names of the places where they see the signs.
- Learners can compare the costs of sending a postcard, a letter (in the United States), an airmail letter, and an aerogram. Learners can ask in the post office or ask friends and neighbors for the information. Learners can share their findings with the group.
- Introduce special delivery postal services, such as Express Mail and Priority Mail. Discuss differences in cost and delivery time.

At the Post Office 31

What's happening?   **Answers may vary.**

Post Office Sign

Purpose: To give practice in reading signs

Teacher Preparation and Materials

1. Index cards with sight words: *Sunday, Monday, Tuesday, Wednesday, Thursday, Friday, Saturday*
2. 12-month calendars for all
3. Copies of TRF Handout 3.6, *Post Office Conversation 1 (Expansion/Extension)*

Warm-up

1. Review the days of the week. On the board, tape the sight-word cards with the names of the days of the week in random order. Then, have volunteers come up and arrange them in the correct order.
2. Review times. Ask *What time do we start class? What time do we finish class? What time do you start work? What time do you finish work?* Introduce *hours*. Ask *What hours do you study? What hours do you work?* Have a volunteer answer the questions. Make a chart on the board using the information. FOR EXAMPLE:

	Start	Finish	Hours
Class	6:30 p.m.	8:30 p.m.	6:30–8:30 p.m.
Work	8:00 a.m.	4:30 p.m.	8:00–4:30 p.m.

3. Ask questions about the chart. *Is (volunteer) working at 9:00 a.m.? Is (volunteer) working at 9:00 p.m.?*
4. On the board write *12:00*. Introduce *12:00 noon* and *12:00 midnight*. Draw a sun and a crescent moon to clarify the distinction between noon and midnight.
5. Ask questions about holidays. FOR EXAMPLE: *What is a holiday? What holidays do you know?* On the board write the word *holiday*.
6. Have learners find the month of November on the calendars. Ask *What holiday do we celebrate in November? Why is it important in the United States?*

Presentation

1. Have learners turn to page 32 and look at the sign. Have them find the names of the days, the times, and the dates on the sign. Also have them find the words *closed*, *reopens*, and *holiday(s)*.

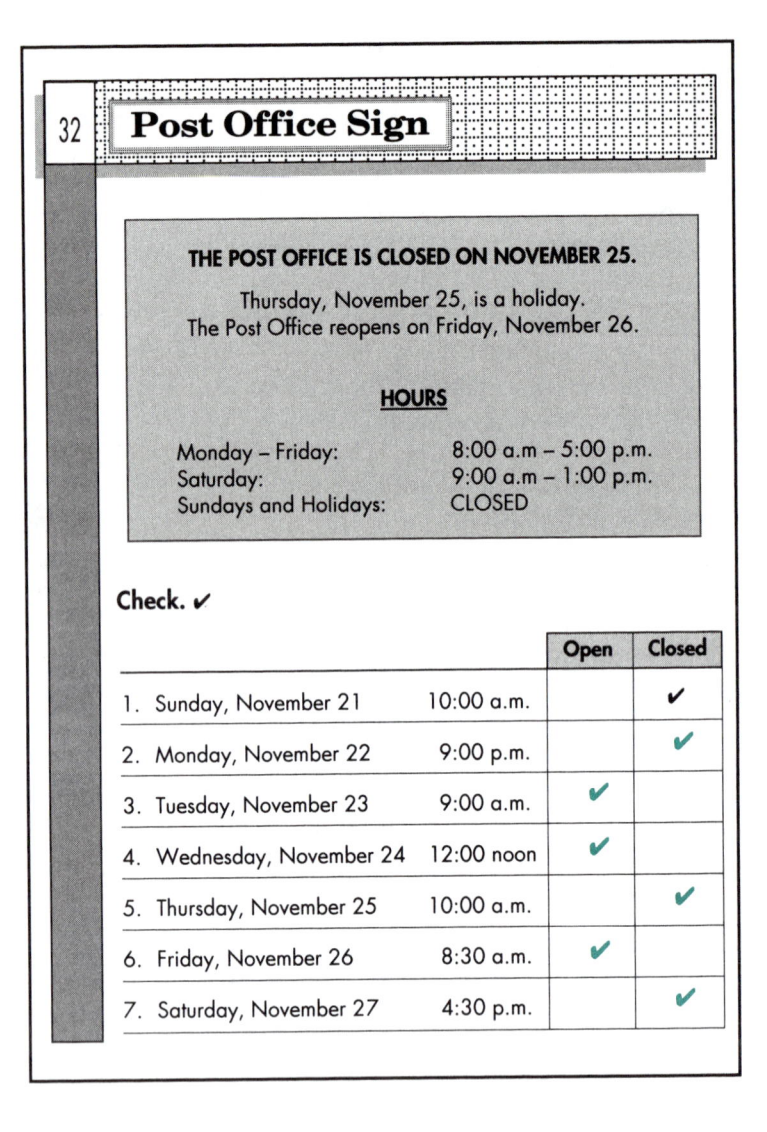

---

32 Post Office Sign

THE POST OFFICE IS CLOSED ON NOVEMBER 25.

Thursday, November 25, is a holiday.
The Post Office reopens on Friday, November 26.

HOURS

Monday – Friday:	8:00 a.m – 5:00 p.m.
Saturday:	9:00 a.m – 1:00 p.m.
Sundays and Holidays:	CLOSED

Check. ✔

		Open	Closed
1. Sunday, November 21	10:00 a.m.		✔
2. Monday, November 22	9:00 p.m.		✔
3. Tuesday, November 23	9:00 a.m.	✔	
4. Wednesday, November 24	12:00 noon	✔	
5. Thursday, November 25	10:00 a.m.		✔
6. Friday, November 26	8:30 a.m.	✔	
7. Saturday, November 27	4:30 p.m.		✔

---

2. Ask *Yes/No* questions. FOR EXAMPLE: *Is the post office open on Saturdays? Is it open on Sundays? Is the post office open on November 26? November 25? Is the post office closed on Friday? Is it closed on Sunday? Is it open on Monday at 10:00 a.m.?*
3. Ask *Wh-* questions. FOR EXAMPLE: *What time is the post office open on Fridays? What day of the week is the post office always closed? What hours is the post office open on Saturdays? Which day is a holiday?* (**Note:** Explain that this holiday is always on the fourth Thursday in November, but the date changes every year.)
4. Have learners complete the exercise in pairs or individually.

Expansion/Extension
See TRF HANDOUT 3.6, *Post Office Conversation 1*

- Learners can write a sign with the hours for the school, their workplaces, or some other public building.

More *Expansion/Extension* on page 72

Sending Money

Purpose: To give practice in dealing with numbers and money; to introduce using money orders

Teacher Preparation and Materials

1. Real or play pennies, nickels, dimes, quarters, and dollar bills
2. Samples of postal money orders *(Warm-up)* and bank money orders *(Expansion/Extension)*
3. Audiotape for Level 1
4. Newspaper and store ads *(Expansion/Extension)*

Warm-up

1. Introduce counting money. Give learners random numbers of pennies. Have them count and report the amounts. Say amounts and have learners gather the appropriate number of coins. FOR EXAMPLE: *Show me 15¢. Do you have 9¢?*
2. Introduce nickels and repeat the procedure, counting by fives (five cents, ten cents, etc.). Introduce dimes and quarters. (**Note:** Learners need to remember the values, not the names, of the coins.)
3. Give learners real or play dollar bills and introduce *dollars*. Show how dollars are written to the left of the decimal point and cents to the right of it. Say money amounts and have learners gather the correct coins and bills.
4. Have learners practice reading amounts. Write various amounts on the board. FOR EXAMPLE: *$13.25, $8.35, $11.95.* Say sentences and have volunteers come to the board and circle the amounts. FOR EXAMPLE: *I have $8.35. The book costs $13.25.*
5. Dictate amounts and have learners write them. FOR EXAMPLE: *It costs $25.50.*
6. Bring in postal money orders. Have learners find the words *post office, dollars, cents, to, from, address.* Ask *What is this? Where do you get money orders? Why do people get them? Do you use money orders?*

Presentation

1. Have learners turn to page 33 and look at the picture at the top of the page. Ask *Where is Anita? What's she doing?* Write responses on the board, making sure to include *letter* and *money order.*
2. Play the audiotape.
3. Ask *What does Anita want to buy? How much does a money order cost? How much is the money order for? How much money does she give the clerk? Why does she pay $25.75?* If necessary, ask one question and then play the audiotape again for learners to listen for the answer. Repeat the procedure with other questions.
4. Have learners look at the envelope and money order. Ask *Who is Anita sending the money order to? What is his address? What does Anita write on the money order? Why doesn't Anita send Arturo cash?*
5. On the money order, have learners circle the amount of the money order and the words *from* and *pay to*. Then have them fill in Arturo's name and address.
6. Ask *Why does the clerk tell Anita to "fill it out right away"?*

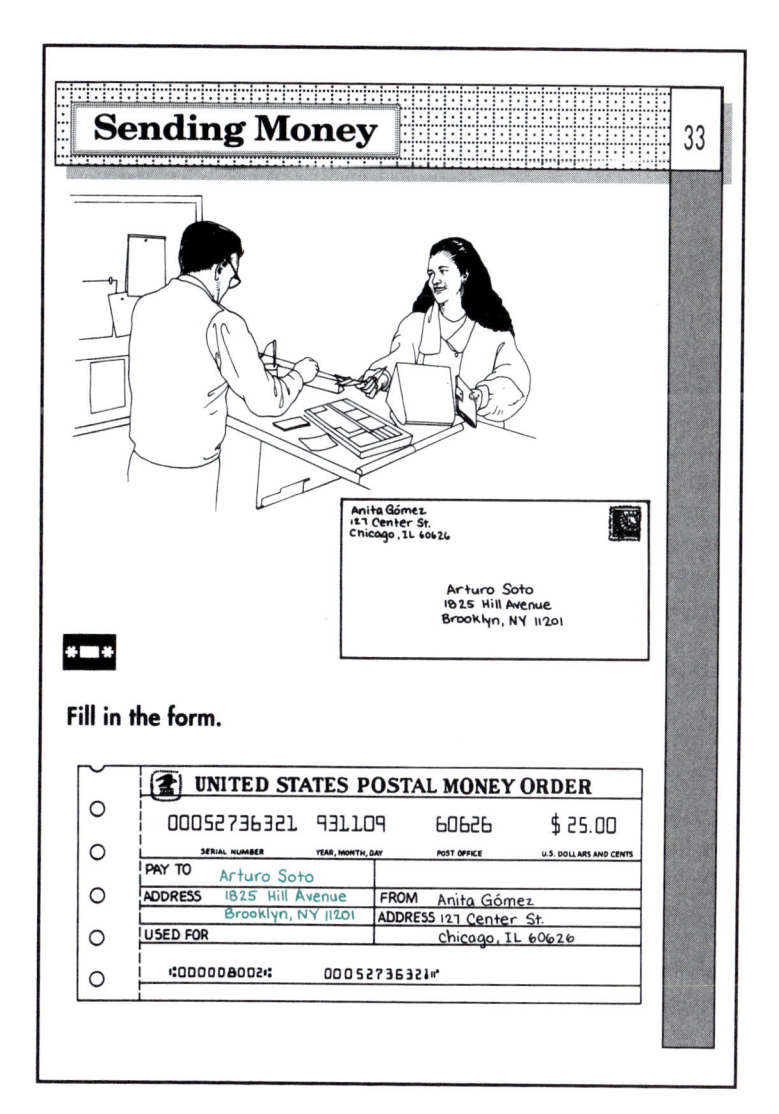

***Expansion/Extension* on page 73**

UNIT 3 • 67

Mailing a Package

Purpose: To give practice in reading post office signs

Teacher Preparation and Materials

1. Samples of postal items: postage stamps, packages, and money orders; play money
2. Index cards with sight words: *Open, Closed, Stamps Only*
3. Copies of TRF Handout 3.7, *Post Office Conversation 2 (Expansion/Extension)*
4. Blank index cards *(Expansion/Extension)*

Warm-up

1. Use the play money and postal items to act out postal activities. Model sentences in the present continuous tense. Have learners repeat. FOR EXAMPLE: *I'm buying a stamp. I'm sending a package.* Have learners choose items and act out the associated activities. Have others in the group identify the activities, using the third person. Ask *What's he/she doing?* (He's buying a money order. She's counting money.)
2. On the board, draw three boxes to represent the three windows in the post office. Make an *X* through the first one. Draw a smiling face in the second one. Tape or draw postage stamps around the third one. Say *These are windows in the post office.* Hold up the three sight-word cards: *Open, Closed,* and *Stamps Only*. Have volunteers tape the signs under the correct box. Take the signs down, shuffle them, and give them to other volunteers to place on the board. Repeat as necessary.

Presentation

1. Have learners turn to page 34 and look at the picture. Ask *Who do you see? Where are they? What are they doing? What sign is on the window? Are they going to the correct window?* Write the comments and words on the board. Be sure to include *package, window, Open, Closed,* and *Stamps Only.*
2. Have learners follow along as you read the passage. Ask *Who is sending a package? Who is she sending it to? Who is helping?*

Is he reading the sign? Are they in the correct line? Which window is the correct one?

3. Have learners decide which window David and May should go to and check the appropriate line.

Expansion/Extension
See **TRF HANDOUT 3.7**, *Post Office Conversation 2*

- Play charades. On blank index cards, write sentences in the present continuous tense about postal activities. FOR EXAMPLE: *You are buying a stamp. You're sending a package. You're writing a money order.* Have various corresponding postal items available for the activities. Demonstrate taking a card, choosing the appropriate postal item(s), and acting out the activity. Make sure that nobody else looks at the card. Learners can try to guess the action by giving a sentence in the present continuous tense. Ask questions such as *What is he doing?* (He's sending a package.) *What is she writing?* (She's writing a money order.)

More *Expansion/Extension* on page 73

Insuring a Package

Purpose: To give practice in dealing with numbers and money; to introduce insuring packages

Teacher Preparation and Materials

1. Real or play money
2. Store advertisements
3. Samples of postal insurance slips
4. Audiotape for Level 1
5. Blank samples of customs forms *(Expansion/Extension)*
6. Empty box(es), address labels for all, and various items that might be sent overseas; or scissors for all and magazines with pictures of items: clothing, electronic equipment, books, and so on *(Expansion/Extension)*
7. Blank index cards *(Expansion/Extension)*

Warm-up

1. Review money. Dictate amounts and ask learners to write the figures. FOR EXAMPLE: *two dollars and forty cents* ($2.40), *seven fifty* ($7.50). Have learners gather the correct amount of money for each price.
2. Practice adding money. Have learners look through store ads, select two items, and circle the prices. (**Note:** Learners do not need to know the names of the items.) Model a problem and write the calculations on the board. FOR EXAMPLE: Point to two items and write their prices on the board. *This is $10.50. This is $16.25.* Add the items and say *$26.75.* Have volunteers come to the board, show their items, write the prices, and calculate the total amounts.
3. Ask questions about mailing packages. FOR EXAMPLE: *Who do you mail packages to? Do you fill out papers for the packages?* Show samples of postal insurance slips. *What are these papers? Why do people use them?* If necessary, explain *insure* (to pay money in case something is lost or damaged).

Presentation

1. Have learners turn to page 35 and look at the picture. Ask *Who do you see? What are they doing?*
2. Play the audiotape and have learners listen to the conversation.
3. Ask *Where are David and May sending the package? How much is the postage? What's in the package? How much is David insuring the package for? How much does the insurance cost? How much does David pay to send and insure the package?* If necessary, ask one question and then play the audiotape again for learners to listen for the answer. Repeat the procedure with the other questions.
4. Have learners look at the insurance form at the bottom of the page and find the words *mail, insured, postage,* and *total.* In small groups, have learners decide where each sum of money belongs on the form and copy the amounts in the appropriate places. (**Note:** Explain that the *fee* in this case is how much David has to pay for the insurance.)

Expansion/Extension on page 73

Mailing Letters

Purpose: To give practice in using the post office and reading post office signs

Teacher Preparation and Materials
1. Map of the world
2. Index cards with sight words: *Local, Out of Town, Foreign/Airmail*
3. Local telephone directory/directories
4. Blank index cards and three boxes (big enough to hold index cards) *(Expansion/Extension)*
5. Copies of TRF Handout 3.5, *Picture Strips 2* *(Expansion/Extension)*
6. Two blank envelopes for each learner, or paper cut to envelope size *(Expansion/Extension)*

Warm-up
1. Review addresses. Ask *What's your address? What's your city?* On the board, write the address of the school or place where you meet. Have several learners write their addresses on the board. Ask questions about the addresses. FOR EXAMPLE: *What city are we in? Who lives in . . . ? Are all the cities the same?*
2. Introduce *local* and *out of town*. Read the address of the school or meeting place. Circle the name of the city and say *This is local*. Point to one of the learners' addresses. Ask if the city is the same. If it is the same, say *local*. If it is different, say *out of town*. Have learners decide if the other addresses are *local* or *out of town*.
3. Ask other learners about their addresses. Have them decide if they are in the local area or out of town.
4. Show the map of the world. Have learners find their native countries. Ask *Is Haiti local?* (No.) *How do you send letters there?* (airmail) *Is Haiti a foreign country?* (Yes.)
5. Show the three sight-word cards with the words *Local, Out of Town, Foreign/Airmail*. Read them and tape them on the board. Have learners give examples of places (cities, addresses, or countries) that belong in the categories.

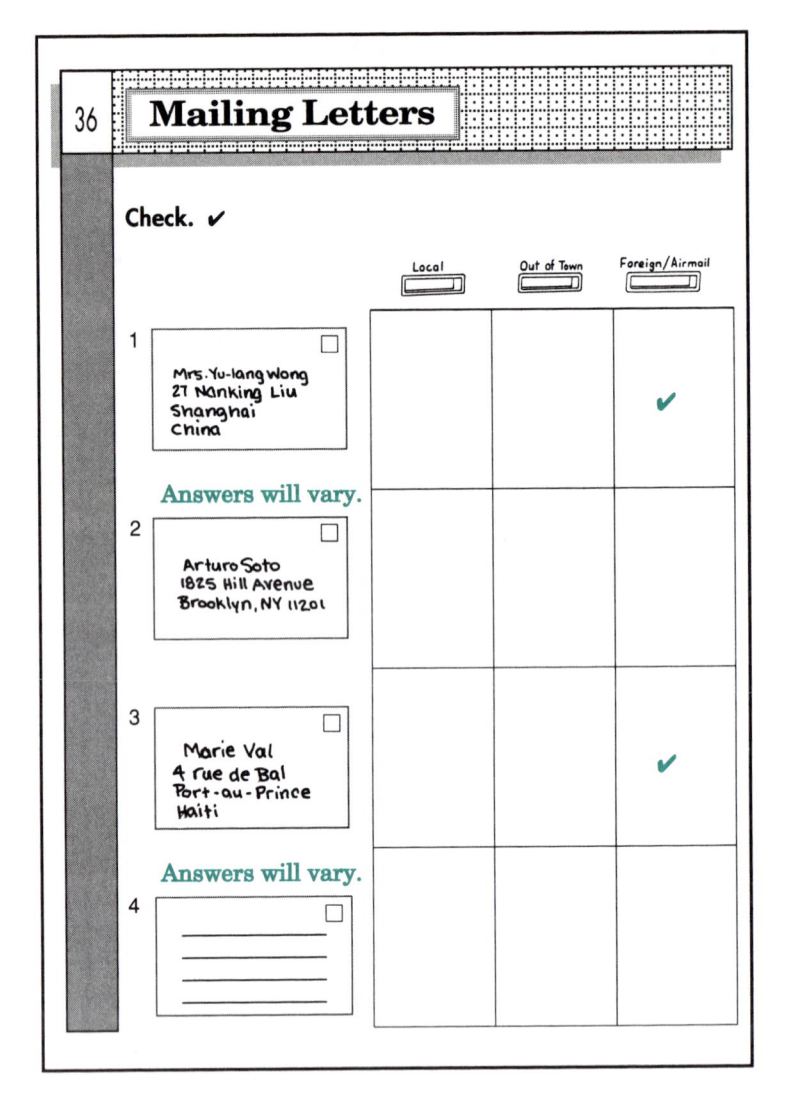

Presentation
1. Have learners turn to page 36 and look at the picture. Have learners find the three mail slot labels.
2. In pairs or small groups, have learners look at the addresses on the envelopes and decide which mail slot would be used if learners were mailing the letters themselves. Learners check the appropriate mail slot for each envelope.
3. Have learners look up a useful local address that they may actually use in a future activity. FOR EXAMPLE: City Hall or a local clinic. Write the complete address on the board.
4. Learners can copy the address from the board onto the fourth envelope on the page and then check the appropriate mail slot.

Expansion/Extension
See TRF HANDOUT 3.5, *Picture Strips 2*

More *Expansion/Extension* on page 73

Look Back

Purpose: To give practice with telephone and post office conventions

Teacher Preparation and Materials

1. Samples of postal items: money order, postage stamps, insurance form
2. Sight-word cards used for page 36, picture of a telephone operator
3. Calculator *(Expansion/Extension)*

Warm-up

1. Have learners identify the postal items and the sight words orally.
2. Say various phone and postal activities and have learners indicate the sight word or item needed to complete the activity. FOR EXAMPLE: *I'd like to send a letter to my friend in Mexico.* (Foreign/Airmail) *I'd like to find the phone number for the library.* (operator, 411 Directory Assistance, 1-555-1212) *I'd like to send a package to Poland.* (insurance slip) *I'd like to buy a money order.* (money order)

Presentation

1. Have learners turn to page 37. If necessary, demonstrate how to complete the matching exercise.
2. Depending on learners' literacy skills, you may want to read the sentences together. Learners can also find and circle the key word(s) in each sentence before doing the matching exercise. More advanced learners can complete the exercise individually.

Expansion/Extension

- Using the postal items, learners can practice asking for items at the post office using the structure *I'd like to . . . .* Have a volunteer act as the postal clerk. Other learners can be customers and then tell the postal clerk what they would like. (FOR EXAMPLE: *I'd like to mail this letter to Mexico. I'd like to insure this package. I'd like to buy an airmail stamp.*)

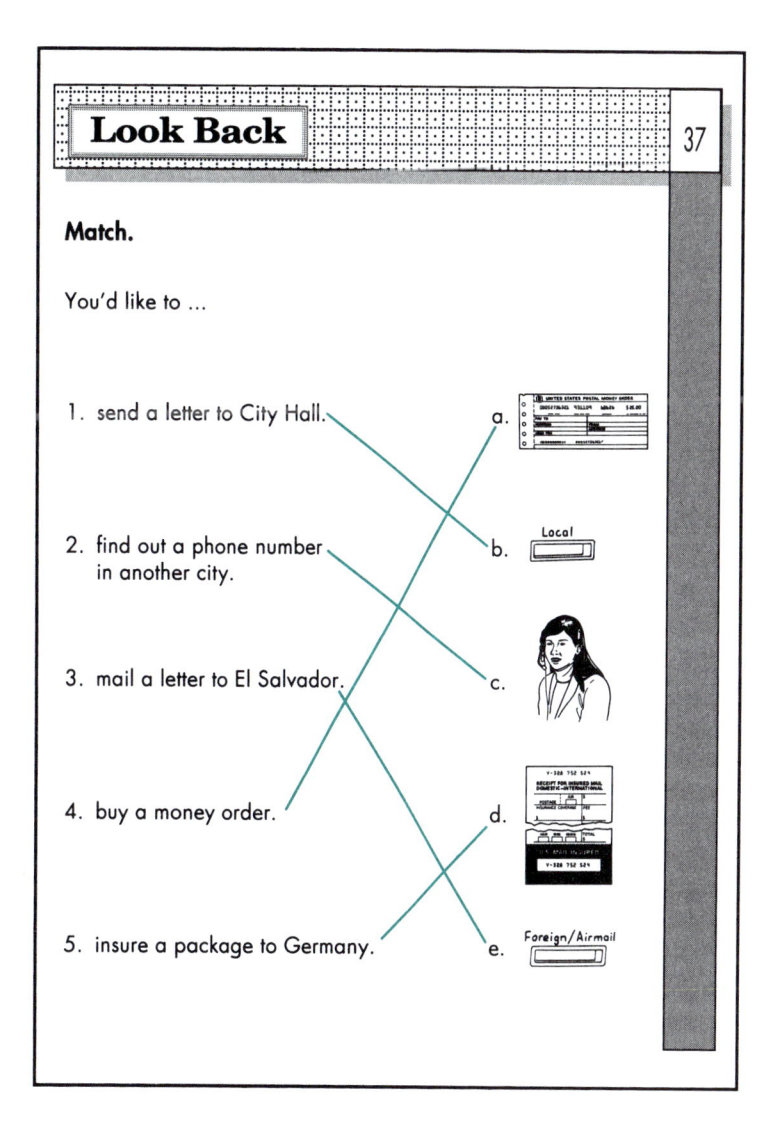

- Expand the role play. Give the postal clerk and customers play money. The postal clerk will need a list of prices for the various postal items. When the customers ask for items, the clerk can calculate the cost of the items and respond with an amount. Customers can give the appropriate amount and the clerk can calculate the change. Learners can practice suitable phrases. (FOR EXAMPLE: *That will cost $6.75. That will be $9.95. Here's your change. Thank you. You're welcome.*)

Look Back 37

Match.

You'd like to ...

1. send a letter to City Hall.
2. find out a phone number in another city.
3. mail a letter to El Salvador.
4. buy a money order.
5. insure a package to Germany.

a. (money order)
b. Local
c. (telephone operator)
d. (insurance receipt)
e. Foreign/Airmail

UNIT 3 • 71

UNIT 3: Keeping in Touch
Expansion/Extension

An International Call
More *Expansion/Extension* for SB page 27

- Learners can look up information on direct dialing and country and city codes in the local phone book. Discuss dialing 00 and the overseas operator. Explain that not every town or city will be listed in the phone book.
- Role-play calling the overseas operator. One learner calls to request a number. The other learner role-plays the overseas operator and uses the phone directory to find the correct country and city codes.

Long Distance Information
More *Expansion/Extension* for SB page 28

- Prepare an information gap exercise using people and places that are relevant to learners' interests and situations. Pair the learners. One learner can role-play the operator with a list of names, addresses, and phone numbers. The other learner has the same list with names and addresses only and asks the operator for phone numbers, and then writes them in the appropriate places on the list.
- Use a map from the local phone book to find which cities and towns are in the local calling area. Have learners name several places on the U.S. map that are in the long-distance calling area. Find area codes for the places that are long-distance calls.

Time Zones
More *Expansion/Extension* for SB page 29

- Write your local time on the board. Discuss what time it is in other parts of the country. Ask *Why is it important to know what time it is in other time zones?* List reasons on the board. Make up some problems involving time zones. Use a map and draw clocks to help learners solve them.
  FOR EXAMPLE: *Anita is calling from Chicago. Chicago is in the . . . time zone. She's calling Arturo in Brooklyn, New York. New York is in the . . . time zone. Anita is calling at 5 p.m. Arturo is answering at . . . p.m.*
- Have learners create their own time zone problems. (FOR EXAMPLE: You are calling . . . . It is 9 a.m. here. What time is it there? Your aunt is calling from Los Angeles. She's calling at noon. What time is it where you live?) Continue with other relatives or friends in other parts of the country.

- Introduce the time zone map and international code pages from the front of the local phone book. Ask learners what countries they might call. List the countries on the board. Have learners figure out what time it is in their native countries and in other countries on the list.
- Depending on the time of year, discuss daylight saving time and how and why the clocks should be adjusted. Learners can find out places in the United States and foreign countries that do not use daylight saving time. Discuss how daylight saving time affects the time differences for these places within the United States and in other countries.

Sending a Package
Expansion/Extension **for SB page 30**

- Bring in samples of package labels. Learners can find the places for the return address and the address of the person receiving the package and practice filling them in.
- As a group, prepare a short letter or request for information for learners to send to an American sponsor, agency, school, or business. The group should decide on the content of the letter. If this is done as an LEA, write the final version on the board for learners to copy. (One source for free booklets on a variety of topics is the Consumer Information Center, Pueblo, Colorado 81009.)
- Do a Total Physical Response (TPR) activity on addressing an envelope.
    1. Put your letter in the envelope.
    2. Seal the envelope.
    3. Take a marker or pen.
    4. In the center of the envelope, write the address.
    5. Write your name and address in the upper left-hand corner.
    6. Put a stamp on the upper right-hand corner.

Post Office Sign
More *Expansion/Extension* for SB page 32

- Learners can go to other places, such as banks, stores, clinics, and schools in the neighborhood, and find *Hours* signs. Learners can copy the names of the places and their hours and then report their findings to the group. Learners can also look for places that are open 24 hours a day.
- Go through the calendar and look for other holidays. Discuss on which holidays the post office and other government buildings are closed (federal holidays) and on which holidays they are open.
- Discuss Thanksgiving. Ask *Why do Americans celebrate that day? What do people do to celebrate*

Thanksgiving Day? Is there a Thanksgiving Day in your native country? When is it? How do you celebrate it?

Sending Money
Expansion/Extension for SB page 33

- Learners can write a sign giving the hours for the school, their workplaces, or some other public building that they use.
- Learners can look through newspapers and store ads for prices and practice reading the amounts. Compare the different ways that prices can be written. FOR EXAMPLE: 25¢ and $.25, $1.99 and 1⁹⁹.
- Bring in samples of bank money orders. Ask questions about them. FOR EXAMPLE: *Where else can you get money orders? Do you need a bank account to get a bank money order? What differences do you see between the bank and postal money orders?* (**Note:** Postal money orders only require filling in the names and addresses. Bank money orders often require filling in dates, amounts in numbers, name of receiver, signature and address of the sender.)
- Introduce writing dates by using numbers. Write the names of the months on the board and number them 1 through 12. Say a number and have learners respond with the name of the month. Write on the board *November 27, 1993*. Have learners tell you what number month November is. Write the date in numbers. (11/27/93) Provide other examples as necessary. Point out that the month comes first. Write other dates on the board and have learners rewrite them, using numbers.

Mailing a Package
More *Expansion/Extension* for SB page 34

- Role-play asking for assistance in the post office. Have one learner act as the postal clerk and calculate costs. Assign postal activities to other learners. Give practice in asking for items. (FOR EXAMPLE: *I'd like an airmail stamp. I'd like five first-class stamps. I'd like a money order for $50.00. That's $. . . .*) Learners can use play money to purchase items.
- If appropriate, discuss who helps learners cope with various daily tasks that require English, such as sending postal items, reading children's school papers, reading bills, and so on. Have learners look at the picture on page 34. Ask *Who is helping May? Do you think it is easy or difficult for children to help their parents? Do you think it is easy or difficult for parents to ask children to help them?*

Insuring a Package
Expansion/Extension for SB page 35

- Learners can get information from the post office and compare the costs of sending a 10-pound package by airmail and by surface mail.
- Customs forms are needed for shipping packages overseas. Bring in samples of the forms from the post office, or learners can go and ask for some. Find the place for filling in the contents of the package, the value, and so on. Learners can practice filling in the customs forms for a package they plan to send.
- Bring in items that are often sent overseas, or learners can cut out magazine or store ad pictures of items they send. Learners can select several items and place them in a box (can be simulated) to send. They can prepare an address label and then calculate the value of their package for insurance and customs forms.
- Role-play mailing a package, including paying for it and calculating change. Have learners check the change. Introduce language needed to question the change given. FOR EXAMPLE: *Excuse me, you only gave me $ . . . . I think it should be $ . . . .*
- For beginning literacy learners, write various sight words, using all uppercase letters, on a set of index cards. Write the same words in all lowercase letters on another set. Learners can practice matching them, using various methods, such as comparing the first letter of words, counting the number of letters in words, and so on. They can also use the cards to play Concentration.

Mailing Letters
More *Expansion/Extension* for SB page 36

- On blank index cards, write various local, out-of-town, and foreign addresses. Label three boxes *Local*, *Out-of-Town*, and *Foreign/Airmail*. Learners can sort the cards and place them in the appropriate boxes.
- Learners can address an envelope to themselves. Then, in pairs, one learner can read their address while the other listens and writes it down on the other envelope. Learners may need to ask for clarification. (FOR EXAMPLE: *How do you spell that? Is it 27 Main Street?*) Then learners can write their own return address in the proper place on the envelope with their partner's address.

1 2 3 4 5 6 7 8 9 10 11 12 Summary
Getting from Here to There

Objectives

Functions
- Giving and following oral and written directions
- Clarifying
- Verifying
- Asking for and giving information
- Dealing with numbers

Life Tasks
- Using the yellow pages
- Reading a map
- Reading a schedule
- Reading street signs

Structures
- Sequence words
- Prepositions of direction: by . . . (bus, train, etc.)
- Wh- questions: *where, how*
- Imperatives
- Prepositions of place: *across, down, next to, on*

Culture
- Forms of transportation in the United States and in native countries

Vocabulary

Key words:

across	plane
avenue	ride
bicycle	right
boat	second
bus	straight ahead
bus stop	street
car	subway
corner	take
down	then
drive	third
first	train
left	turn
next to	walk
on	

Related words:

arrive	leave
company	lobby
directions	minute
Do Not Enter	nursery
elevator	One Way
every half hour	park
every hour	room
fire station	schedule
floor	store
flowers	table
flower shop	taxi
hall	truck
hospital	window
information	work

Calling the Bus Company

Purpose: To introduce transportation vocabulary

Teacher Preparation and Materials

1. Pictures of places: bank, supermarket, school, drugstore, hospital, post office, fire station, restaurant, police station, computer store, laundromat, flower shop, park, bus stop . . .
2. Copies of the local yellow pages *(Expansion/Extension)*
3. Local transportation schedules *(Expansion/Extension)*

Warm-up

1. Use pictures to review the names of places. Hold up the pictures one at a time and have learners give the names of the places. If necessary, tape the pictures on the board and number them. Say a place name and have learners say what number it is. Then have learners practice pronouncing the names and finally, name the places in random order. If learners have difficulty with this, ask them yes/no and alternative questions. FOR EXAMPLE: *Is this a bank? Is this a fire station or a drugstore?*
2. Write the names of the places on the board. Have learners read them and/or match them with the pictures of the places.

Presentation

1. Have learners turn to page 38 and look at the picture.
2. Ask *What's happening? What do you see? Who do you see? Where is she? What is she doing? What is she thinking about?*
3. List responses on the board. Be sure to include *bus* and *flowers*.
4. Ask inference questions. *Who do you think she is calling? Where do you think she wants to go? What's she carrying? Why?*
5. Together, read the question on the bottom of the page. Then have learners talk about the answer.

1 2 3 **4** 5 6 7 8 9 10 11 12
Getting from Here to There ■ ■ ■ ■

Calling the Bus Company
What's happening?   **Answers may vary.**

Expansion/Extension

- Give each small group of learners a copy of the local yellow pages. Learners can practice looking up various places such as banks, clinics, hospitals, and so on.
- As a group, write an LEA story using the learners' predictions about the story.
- Learners can think of questions that Anita might be asking the bus company. Together, prepare a list of questions for her to ask, or create a short conversation between Anita and the bus company. (FOR EXAMPLE: What bus do I take? Where is a bus stop near Center Street? What time does the bus leave?)

Getting Information

Purpose: To give practice in asking questions; to introduce following oral directions

Teacher Preparation and Materials

1. Clocks with movable hands for all
2. 📼 Audiotape for Level 1
3. Local telephone book and/or yellow pages *(Expansion/Extension)*
4. Information about local public transportation: bus- or subway-route maps, schedules *(Expansion/Extension)*

Warm-up

1. Review time. Say times on the hour and half hour and have learners adjust the clock hands to the correct times. FOR EXAMPLE: *9:00, 1:30, 11:00, 5:30.*
2. Introduce other times by adjusting the clock, modeling the time, and having learners repeat. FOR EXAMPLE: *3:05, 3:10, 3:25, 3:35, 3:40, 3:55, 4:00.* Dictate times and have learners adjust the clock hands. Then have learners write the times on the board.
3. Draw a bus (rectangle with two circles on the bottom). Say *This is a bus. It leaves at 8:00.* Write *8:00* under the bus. Draw another bus and say *This bus leaves at 9:00.* Write *9:00.* Draw a third bus and ask *What time does this one leave?* (10:00) Write *10:00* under that bus. Point to the three buses and say *The buses leave every hour.* If necessary, repeat the process with different times.
4. Use the same procedure to introduce *every half hour.* FOR EXAMPLE: *1:30, 2:00, 2:30, 3:00.*
5. Say statements about bus departures and have learners calculate the correct times. FOR EXAMPLE: Adjust the clock to 5:00 and say *The bus leaves every hour. What time is the next bus?*

Presentation

1. Have learners turn to page 39 and look at the picture.
2. Ask *What do you see? What's her name? What time is it? What's she doing?*
3. Read the information under the picture as learners follow along in their books. Ask

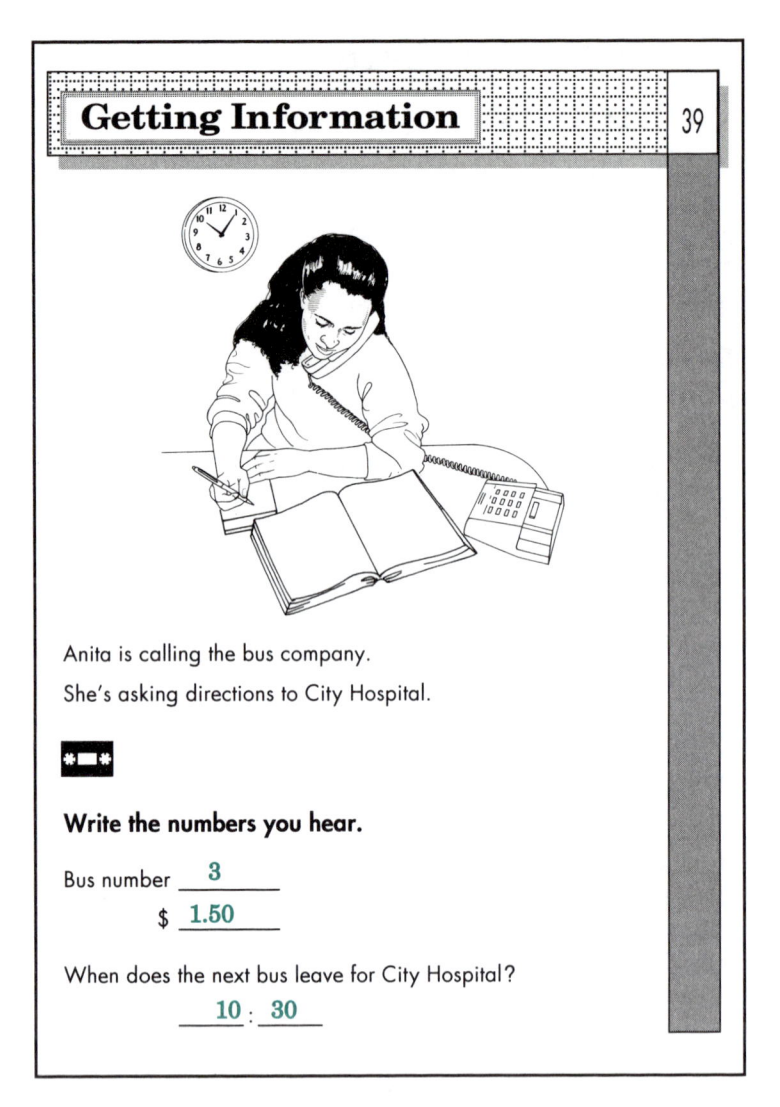

> ### Getting Information 39
>
> Anita is calling the bus company.
> She's asking directions to City Hospital.
>
> 📼
>
> **Write the numbers you hear.**
>
> Bus number ___3___
>
> $ ___1.50___
>
> When does the next bus leave for City Hospital?
>
> ___10___ : ___30___

Is Anita calling the hospital? Where is she calling? Is she asking directions to the store?

4. 📼 Play the audiotape and have learners listen to the phone conversation. Ask *Is Anita talking to City Bus Service? Does she live on Sandburg Avenue? Where does she want to go? Does Bus number 275 go to City Hospital? Which bus goes to the hospital? Does Bus number 3 leave every half hour? How much does it (the bus ride) cost?*
📼 If necessary, ask one question and then have learners listen to the audiotape for that information. Then repeat the procedure with the other questions.
5. 📼 Have learners listen to the audiotape again and fill in the bus number and fare on page 39. Then, have them determine what time the next bus will leave for the hospital, using the clock in the picture.

Expansion/Extension

- Learners can look up various transportation services in the local phone book or yellow pages and copy the phone numbers. Learners can call for information on schedules, routes, and fares.

More *Expansion/Extension* on page 86

76 • UNIT 4

To the Bus Stop

Purpose: To give practice in giving and following oral directions; to introduce map reading; to introduce prepositions of place and direction

Teacher Preparation and Materials

1. Pictures of places used for page 38
2. Copies of TRF Handout 4.2, *Find Your Way (Expansion/Extension)*
3. Blindfold or scarf *(Expansion/Extension)*
4. Neighborhood map or paper and markers for learners to make their own maps *(Expansion/Extension)*
5. Copies of TRF Handout 4.5, *Our Town (Expansion/Extension)*

Warm-up

1. Review place names using picture cues.
2. On the board, draw a simple grid showing the streets from the map on page 40. Point to the streets and say the names of them. Then say *The bank is on South Street.* Demonstrate finding the picture of the bank and taping it on South Street. Give other statements about places and streets and have learners tape the pictures of the places on the appropriate streets. Have learners repeat the statements.
3. Model and demonstrate directional phrases: *turn right, turn left, go straight.* (**Note:** Make sure you face in the same direction as learners.) Have learners follow your directions.
4. Model and demonstrate following directions on the map on the board, starting at Center Street. FOR EXAMPLE: *Where's the police station? Go straight. Then turn left on Elm Avenue. It's on the corner.* Have learners practice following directions and giving directions to places on the map.

Presentation

1. Have learners turn to page 40 and look at the map. Say *Where's Center Street? Point to Sandburg Avenue.* and so on.
2. Have learners find Anita's apartment building. Ask *What street is it on? What's her address?* Then have learners find the bus stop on Sandburg Avenue.
3. Introduce and practice prepositions of place and direction using the map on the board. Model statements and have learners repeat. FOR EXAMPLE: *The flower shop is next to the bank. The post office is across from the school. The bus stop is near the park.* Ask questions about locations of places and have learners respond with complete sentences.
4. Use the map on the board to demonstrate one possible route from Anita's apartment to the bus stop. Point as you give the directions. FOR EXAMPLE: *Turn left on South Street. Turn right on Sandburg Avenue. It's near the park. It's across from Union Bank.*
5. Have learners use the map in their books to follow the same route. Then, give alternative directions to the bus stop and have learners follow them on their maps.
6. Have learners mark the route that they think Anita should take. In pairs, have learners give their directions while their partners listen and follow them.

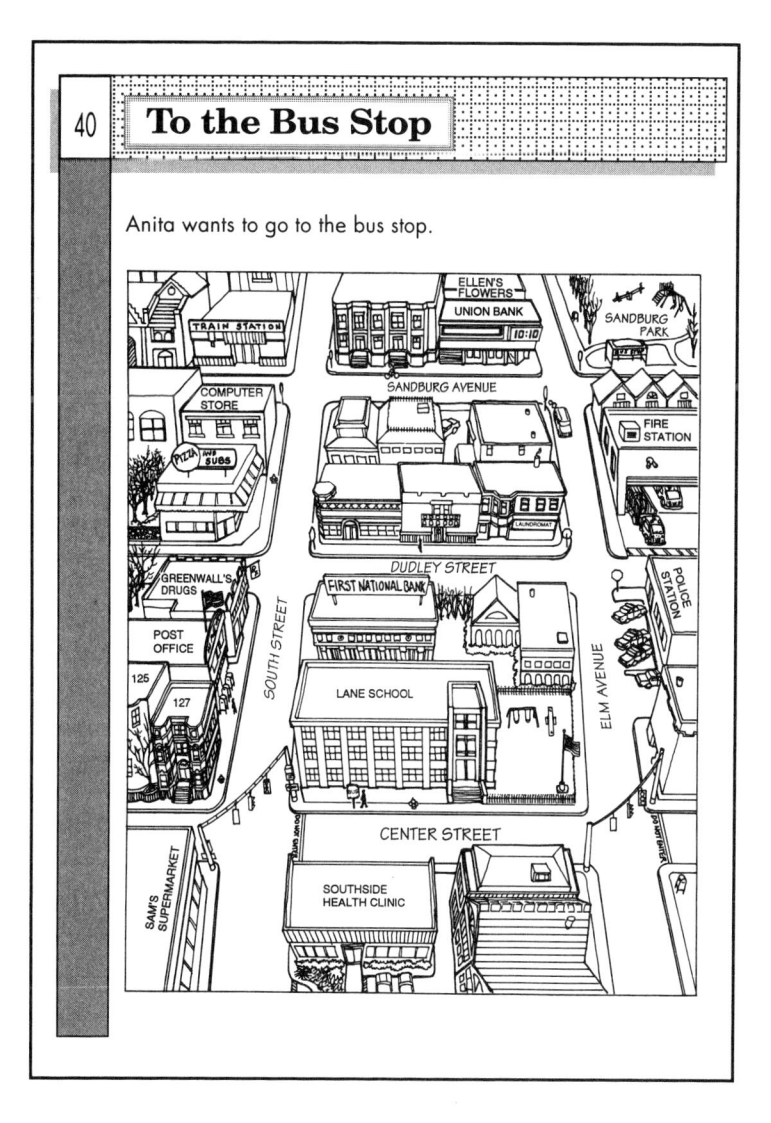

Expansion/Extension
See **TRF HANDOUT 4.2,** *Find Your Way*
TRF HANDOUT 4.5, *Our Town*

More *Expansion/Extension* on page 86

A Bus Schedule

Purpose: To give practice in reading time; to introduce chart reading

Teacher Preparation and Materials

1. Clocks with movable hands for all
2. Copies of TRF Handout 4.1, *Train Schedule* (Expansion/Extension)
3. Local bus schedules (Expansion/Extension)
4. Local bus- or subway-route maps (Expansion/Extension)

Warm-up

1. Have learners practice adjusting clock hands to match times you write on the board.
2. Use the clock to introduce math problems with hours. Adjust the clock to 8:00 and ask the time. Then adjust the clock to 9:00. Model *One hour.* Use the times 8:00 and 10:00 and model *Two hours.* Repeat with other times as necessary. Then introduce the math problems without the clock by writing times on the board. Have learners calculate the difference in hours.
3. Repeat the same procedure to introduce and give practice with math problems with minutes. Adjust the clock to 6:00 and then to 6:30.
4. On the board, write the following headings: *Sandburg Park, Roper Square, City Hospital.* Draw five buses (rectangles with two circles under them) under Sandburg Park and write times on them—*9:00, 9:30, 10:00, 10:30,* and *11:00.* Ask *How often do the buses leave Sandburg Park?* (every half hour) Draw an arrow from the first bus to the Roper Square heading. Write the time *9:15.* Ask *How many minutes does it take?* (15 minutes) Continue the arrow to City Hospital and write *9:30.* Ask *How many minutes does it take from Roper Square to City Hospital?* (15 minutes) *How many minutes does it take from Sandburg Park to City Hospital?* (30 minutes)
5. Draw an arrow from the second bus at Sandburg Park to Roper Square. Have a volunteer come and fill in the correct times for that bus under Roper Square and City Hospital. Have other volunteers draw the

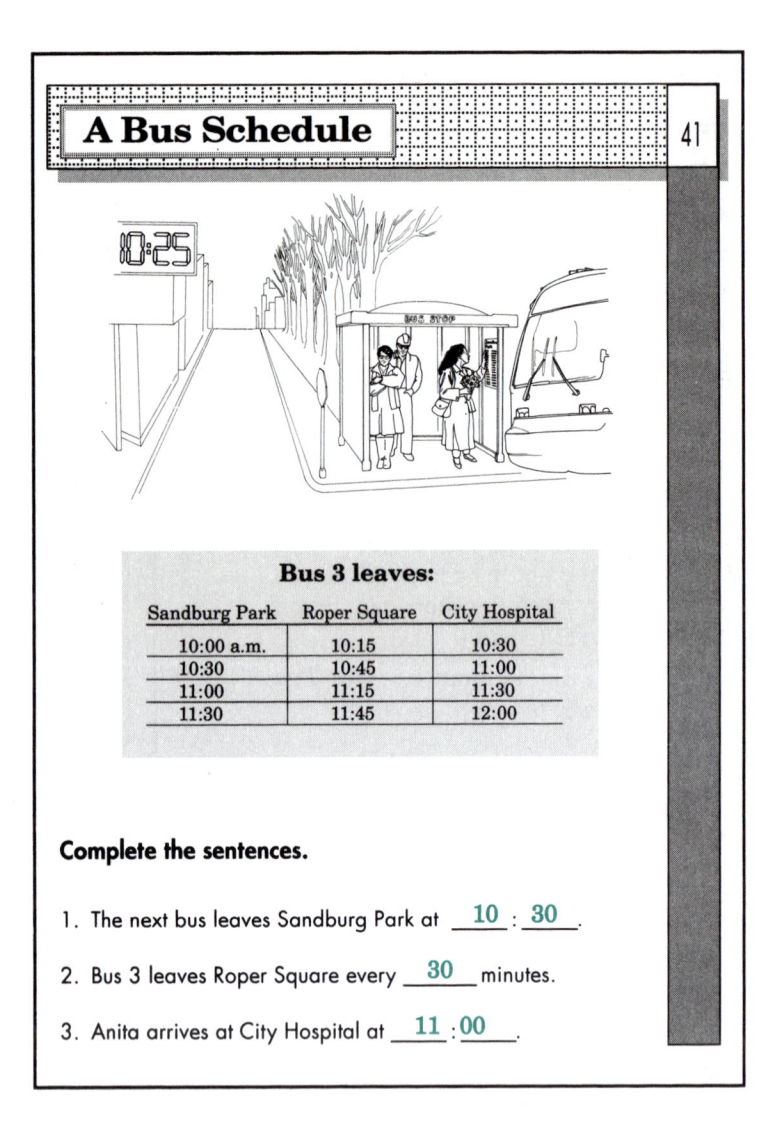

trips and write the times for the other buses. Explain *This is a bus schedule.* Then label it *Bus 3 Schedule.*

Presentation

1. Have learners turn to page 41 and look at the picture.
2. Ask *Where is Anita? What is she looking at? What is the number of the bus? What time is it?*
3. Have learners look at the bus schedule. Ask *What is the number of the bus leaving Sandburg Park? Where does Bus number 3 stop? What are the times that Bus number 3 leaves Sandburg Park? Does it leave every hour or every 30 minutes? What are the times that Bus number 3 arrives at City Hospital? What time will Anita get on the bus? What time will she get to Roper Square? What time will she get to City Hospital?*
4. Have learners use the schedule to complete the sentences at the bottom of the page.

Expansion/Extension

See **TRF HANDOUT 4.1,** *Train Schedule*

More *Expansion/Extension* on page 86

A Bus Schedule 41

Bus 3 leaves:

Sandburg Park	Roper Square	City Hospital
10:00 a.m.	10:15	10:30
10:30	10:45	11:00
11:00	11:15	11:30
11:30	11:45	12:00

Complete the sentences.

1. The next bus leaves Sandburg Park at __10__ : __30__ .
2. Bus 3 leaves Roper Square every __30__ minutes.
3. Anita arrives at City Hospital at __11__ : __00__ .

On the Bus

Purpose: To introduce modes of transportation

Teacher Preparation and Materials

1. Pictures of modes of transportation: bus, bicycle, car, taxi, truck, subway, plane, train, boat, walking
2. Blank index cards *(Expansion/Extension)*
3. Copies of TRF Handout 4.4, *Don't Do It!* *(Expansion/Extension)*

Warm-up

1. Use picture cues to introduce modes of transportation. Hold up pictures and have learners identify those they see and those they use. Model names and have learners repeat.
2. Have learners categorize the types of transportation. (FOR EXAMPLE: I like . . . ; I don't like . . . .)
3. If possible, take a walk around the neighborhood and look at various street signs. Note especially *Don't Walk, One Way, Do Not Enter*. Talk about the people who need the signs. Ask *Who needs (uses) this sign: the people who are walking or the people in the cars?*

Presentation

1. Have learners turn to page 42, look at the picture, and identify as many modes of transportation as they can.
2. Use a semantic web to introduce the vocabulary in written form. Start with the center word *Go*. Have branches leading out from the center word. On the branches, write the names for the vehicles. Be sure to include *car, bus, bicycle, train, taxicab, truck,* and *plane*. Depending on the learners' skills, you may want to add relevant verbs such as *drive, walk, ride,* and *fly*.
3. Ask questions about the picture. FOR EXAMPLE: *Where's the bus? How many cars do you see?*
4. Have learners copy the names of the vehicles near the appropriate places in the picture on page 42.
5. Have learners find and read the traffic signs in the picture.

Expansion/Extension
See TRF HANDOUT 4.4, *Don't Do It!*

- As a group, take a walk around the neighborhood and then write an LEA story about the types of transportation used in the area.
- Introduce descriptive adjectives related to the types of transportation. Learners can fill in a chart comparing the various types. They can summarize the results with simple sentences. (FOR EXAMPLE: The bus is cheap. The plane is expensive. The subway is slow. The car is fast.)

cheap	expensive	slow	fast	comfortable	uncomfortable

- Learners can find other street signs, copy them, and bring the information in to class. If appropriate, learners can copy the signs onto index cards and then hang them in the room. Put a *Do Not Enter* sign on a door that should not be used, and so on.

Getting to Class

Purpose: To introduce asking questions about transportation

Teacher Preparation and Materials
Pictures of modes of transportation used for page 42

Warm-up
1. Use picture cues to review names of types of transportation.
2. Show pictures, model statements, and have learners repeat statements about transportation use. FOR EXAMPLE: *I walk. I take the bus/the train/a taxi. I ride a bicycle. I drive my car.* Introduce and give practice with statements about other types of transportation that learners use.
3. Give practice with questions and answers about transportation. Ask questions and have learners respond with statements about themselves. FOR EXAMPLE: *How do you get to the store? How do you get to work? How do you go to class?* Have learners practice in a chain drill.

Presentation
1. Have learners turn to page 43 and identify the types of transportation in the box. On the blank line in the box, have learners write the name of another type of transportation often used in the local area.
2. On the board, make a chart similar to the one on page 43. Model interviewing several learners, writing their names, and checking the appropriate column. FOR EXAMPLE: *What's your name?* (Tesfai Gezzai.) *How do you get to class?* (I take the bus.)
3. Have learners look at the chart on page 43. Ask questions about Michael Wilson. *Does Michael get to class by subway? How does he get to class?* and so on.
4. Have learners write their name on line 2 and check the type of transportation they use to get to class.
5. Have learners interview four other people to find out how they get to class. ■ In a one-to-one situation, the learner can interview you and some friends or neighbors that take a class. Alternatively, the learner can use a different interview questions. (FOR EXAMPLE: How do you get to the store? bank? post office? work?) Have the learner choose a question, practice asking it, and then write it above the interview chart. The learner can then interview you and/or some friends with the new question.
6. Have learners report their findings to the class. (Tran rides a bicycle. Sonia takes a bus, etc.)

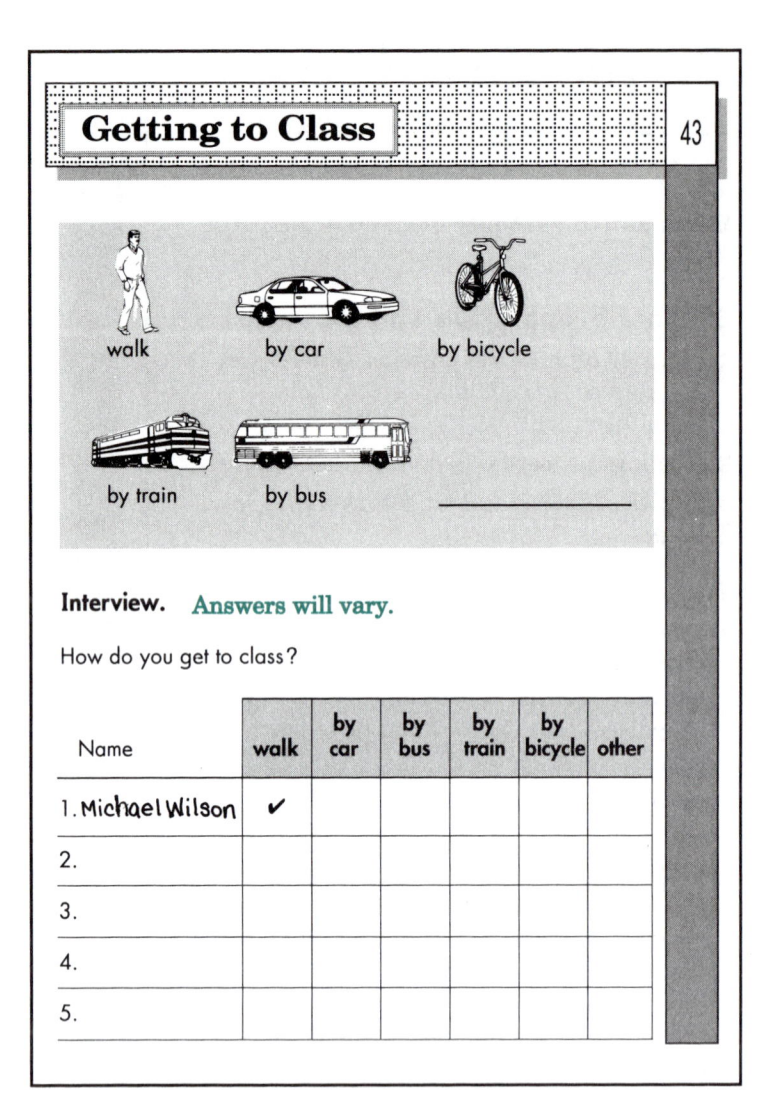

Expansion/Extension
- Use the large chart on the board to conduct a class survey. *How many people walk? How many drive a car?* and so on. Summarize the results in simple sentences. FOR EXAMPLE: *Five people get to class by bus. Five people get to class by bus/take a bus to class. Two people get to class by bicycle/ride bicycles. Three people walk to class.* Depending on learners' skills, you may want to write the results in percentages. FOR EXAMPLE: *Fifty percent of the people get to class by bus.*

More *Expansion/Extension* on page 87

Finding the Right Room

Purpose: To give practice with prepositions of place and direction; to introduce building features

Teacher Preparation and Materials

1. Various classroom items: book, pen, pencil, small box
2. Pictures of hospital lobby, nursery, hall, elevator, door labeled *305*
3. Audiotape for Level 1
4. Copies of TRF Handout 4.3, *From Start to Finish (Expansion/Extension)*
5. Copies of TRF Handout 4.6, *Help Me Get Out! (Expansion/Extension)*
6. Take learners to a building with a floor plan or directory. *(Expansion/Extension)*

Warm-up

1. Using classroom items, give practice with the prepositions of place and direction *across, on, down, next to, in*. Ask *Where's the book? Where's the pencil?* and so on.
2. Give directions for learners to follow. FOR EXAMPLE: *Walk across the room. Go stand next to the door.*
3. On the board, draw a large box to represent a hospital. Divide it horizontally into three sections. Introduce *floors* of a building by pointing to the appropriate sections and saying *This is a hospital. This is the first floor. This is the second floor. This is the third floor.* Point to different floors and ask *What floor is this?*
4. Use picture cues to introduce places in the hospital: *lobby, elevator, halls, nursery*. Model the names and have learners repeat. Write the names of places on the different floors. Say *The nursery is on the third floor.* Write *nursery* on the third floor.
5. Ask questions about places and have learners say the floor numbers. FOR EXAMPLE: *Where's room 305?* (It's on the third floor.) *Where's the lobby?* (It's on the first floor.)

Presentation

1. Have learners look at the pictures on page 44. Say *Point to the elevator. Show me a hall.* and so on. Have learners describe the pictures.

2. Play the audiotape and have learners follow the sequence of directions in their books.

3. Ask *Where is Anita? What room is Sonia in? Where does Anita go first? What floor does she take the elevator to? Does she turn left or right on the third floor? What is next to room 305?* If necessary, ask one question and then play the audiotape for learners to listen for that specific information. Repeat the procedure for the other questions.

4. Say parts of the directions in random order and have learners point to or say the numbers of the corresponding pictures. FOR EXAMPLE: *Turn left and go down the hall.* (3) *On the third floor, turn left.* (2) *First go across the lobby to the elevator.* (1)

5. Play the audiotape once again and have learners repeat the directions with books closed.

6. Finally, have learners give each other directions based on the pictures and prepositional phrases in the book.

Expansion/Extension on page 87

UNIT 4 • 81

In Room 305

Purpose: To give practice in naming classroom items and building features; to give practice with prepositions of place and direction; to give practice in giving directions

Teacher Preparation and Materials

1. Blank index cards
2. Copies of TRF Handout 4.7, *Mystery Message (Expansion/Extension)*
3. Various classroom items or pictures of items: pen, pencil, book, small box, notebook, marker, tape, and so on *(Expansion/Extension)*
4. Local yellow pages *(Expansion/Extension)*

Warm-up

1. Review visible classroom items and building features, including *window, hall, door, table, stairs*. Point to items or features and have learners identify them. Say commands involving items or features and have learners do the appropriate actions. FOR EXAMPLE: *Stand next to the window. Put the books on the table.*

2. On the board, write the names of the items and features. Have learners copy the words on index cards, one item/feature per card. Collect the cards. Hold up a card and have the learners read it aloud. Then, have a volunteer tape it to the appropriate feature or item in the room. Repeat until all cards are used up.

3. Review questions and answers involving prepositions of place and direction with room features and items. FOR EXAMPLE: *Where's the book?* (The book is/It's next to the window.) *Where's the bag?* (The bag is/It's on the table.) *Where's Alex?* (Alex is/He's next to the door.)

Presentation

1. Have learners turn to page 45 and look at the pictures.
2. Ask questions about the pictures. *Where are the flowers? Where is the nurse?* and so on.
3. Together, read the sentences under the pictures. If necessary, ask questions again to prompt learners to fill in the missing word.

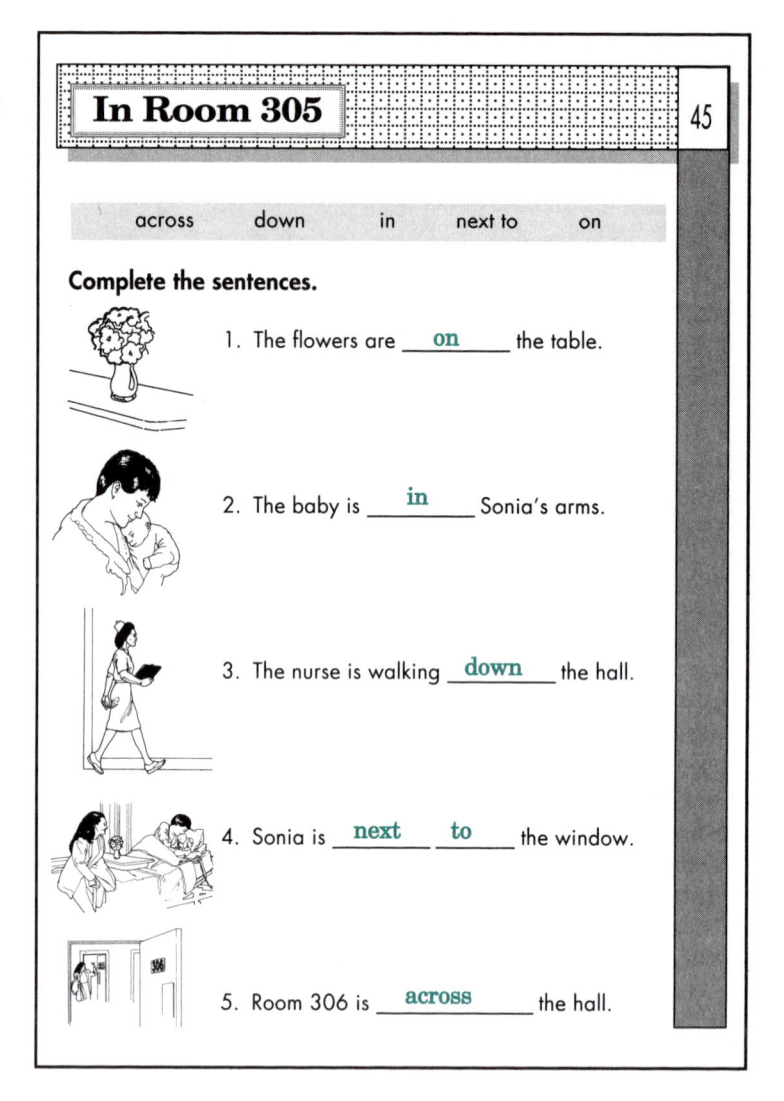

In Room 305 45

across   down   in   next to   on

Complete the sentences.

1. The flowers are ___on___ the table.
2. The baby is ___in___ Sonia's arms.
3. The nurse is walking ___down___ the hall.
4. Sonia is ___next to___ the window.
5. Room 306 is ___across___ the hall.

---

4. Have learners individually or in pairs read the sentences again and fill in the missing words from the box.

Expansion/Extension
See **TRF HANDOUT 4.7**, *Mystery Message*

- As a group, do an LEA about the classroom, focusing on locations of items and people.

- Learners can practice giving directions from the classroom to other parts of the building or vice versa. (FOR EXAMPLE: *The classroom is on the second floor. Go up the stairs. It's next to the library.*)

- Introduce and give practice with other common prepositions of place and direction, such as *up, under, over, below, above, beside, behind, in front of,* and *between*. Bring in classroom items or pictures of items and have learners take turns giving and following instructions about location of the items. (*Put the pen in the box. Place the box under the table,* etc.)

Getting Around

Purpose: To give practice with transportation vocabulary; to give practice in asking questions

Teacher Preparation and Materials

1. Pictures of places used for page 38
2. Pictures of modes of transportation used for page 42
3. Magazines with pictures of modes of transportation, scissors, glue, posterboard, and markers for all *(Expansion/Extension)*

Warm-up

1. Use the picture cues to review the names of places in the neighborhood.
2. Tape the transportation pictures on the board. Ask questions about how learners get to the various places. FOR EXAMPLE: *How do you go to school?* (I take the bus.) Have learners practice asking and answering questions about how they get around.
3. On the board, write the name of your town or city. Ask *How do people go to school and work in (name of your town/city)?* List the types of transportation that learners mention. Ask a volunteer *Where are you from?* Write the name of that country. Ask *How do people go to school or work in (name of country)?* List the types of transportation under the country heading. Repeat the procedure for other countries.
4. Have learners orally summarize the types of transportation that are common in the countries mentioned and the types that are different.

Presentation

1. Have learners look at the picture on page 46 and identify the types of transportation. Have learners add the name of another type of transportation that is used in their native countries, if appropriate.
2. Together, read the questions in the first column. Have learners add another place name for #6.
3. Together, read the other column headings. Have learners identify and write the names of their native countries above the second column and the name of their town or city above the third column.
4. Review types of transportation used in learners' native countries. FOR EXAMPLE: *How do you go to school in (name of country)?* (In [name of country], we walk to school.)
5. Ask about types of transportation used in learners' present town or city. Ask *How do you go to the supermarket in (name of town or city)?* (In [name of town or city], I take the bus.)
6. Have learners fill in their responses to the questions by copying transportation words from the picture. They can write "NA" for places they do not go.
7. In pairs or groups, learners can compare answers and report to the class. (FOR EXAMPLE: In Haiti, we walk to school. In Cambodia, they ride bicycles to school.)

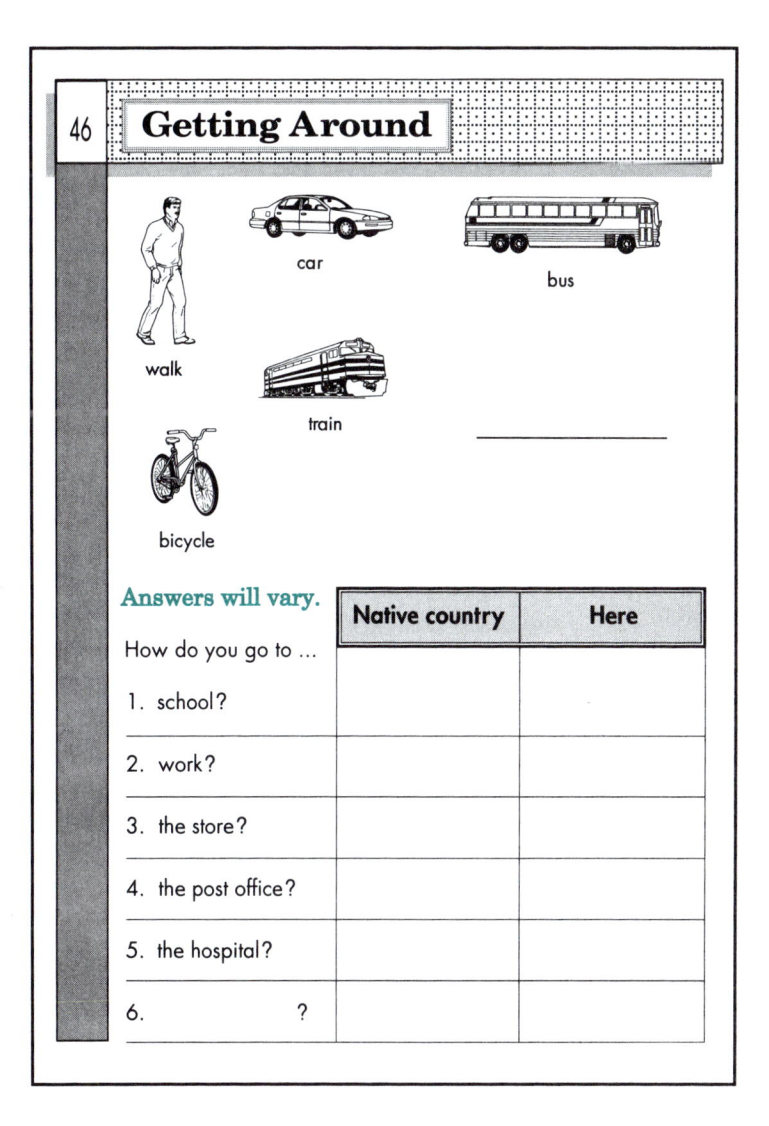

Expansion/Extension

- Learners can write sentences based on their charts. (FOR EXAMPLE: In my country, we ride bicycles to school. We usually walk to work. Here, I take a subway to school.)

More *Expansion/Extension* on page 87

UNIT 4 • 83

Coming to the United States

Purpose: To give practice in asking and answering questions; to give practice with transportation vocabulary

Teacher Preparation and Materials
1. Pictures of modes of transportation used for page 42
2. Map of the world, push pins or masking tape, colored yarns

Warm-up
1. Orally review questions and answers about native countries. FOR EXAMPLE: *Where are you from?* (I'm from . . ..) *Where's he from?* (He's from . . ..)
2. Use picture cues to review the modes of transportation.
3. Tape the pictures of the modes of transportation around a world map. Have a volunteer locate both the United States and his or her native country on the world map. Ask *How did you come from (name of native country) to the United States?* (By plane.) Use push pins (or tape) and colored yarn to trace the route of the trip. Repeat for other volunteers.

Presentation
1. Have learners look at the picture on page 47 and identify the characters. Ask *Who do you see?* (Learners can refer back to page 16 for the name of Harold Jones.)
2. Together, read the conversation.
3. Have learners look at the chart. Ask *Where is Anita from? How did she come to the United States? Where is Tom Lin from? How did he come to the United States?*
4. On the board, make a chart:

Name	What country . . . ?	How . . . ?

5. Interview one learner and demonstrate filling in the information on the chart. Ask *What's your name? How do you spell it? Where are you from? How did you come to the United States?* (**Note:** Some learners may have come by more than one type of transportation.) Refer back to the map and ask questions about parts of the trip.
6. Have a volunteer interview another person in the group and record the information on the chart.
7. Have learners interview four people and record the information on the chart. Ask questions and have learners report their findings to the group. FOR EXAMPLE: *Tell me about Hong. Where is she from?* (Vietnam) *How did she come to the United States?* (by boat and by plane)
8. ■ In a one-to-one situation, the learner can interview family and/or friends that came to the United States from other countries.
9. Depending on the size of the class, create a class chart. Summarize the results of the interviews. FOR EXAMPLE: *How many people came here by train?* (four people) *How many people came here by plane?* (one person)

***Expansion/Extension* on page 87**

Look Back

Purpose: To give practice in reading maps; to give practice with prepositions of place and direction

Teacher Preparation and Materials

1. Pictures of places used for page 38
2. Index cards with sight words: *Union Bank, Lane School, Ellen's Flower Shop, Greenwall's Drugs, Sandburg Park*
3. Pictures of modes of transportation used for page 42
4. Local yellow pages *(Expansion/Extension)*

Warm-up

1. Use picture cues to review the names of places in the unit.
2. Tape the pictures of the places around the board. Then, hold up a sight-word card showing one of the proper place names, such as *Lane School*. Point to the key word in the name as you read it. Then, tape the proper name under the picture of the place. Have learners take turns choosing one of the proper names, finding the key word, and then taping it under the correct picture.
3. On the board, draw a simple grid showing the streets from the map on page 40. Take one of the proper names and place it in the correct location. Model the question and answer *Where's the bus stop? It's on Sandburg Avenue.* As you place each proper place name on the map, have one learner ask the appropriate question and another give the answer, focusing on giving the street location. After all the place names are on the map, point to a place to cue a question. Then, point to the same place and a nearby location to cue an answer with a preposition of place and direction. FOR EXAMPLE: Point to the school and ask *Where's the school?* Then point to the school and bank and say *It's next to the bank.* Continue reviewing questions and answers with the prepositional phrases *next to, across from, down the street,* and so on.
4. Use picture cues to review the modes of transportation.

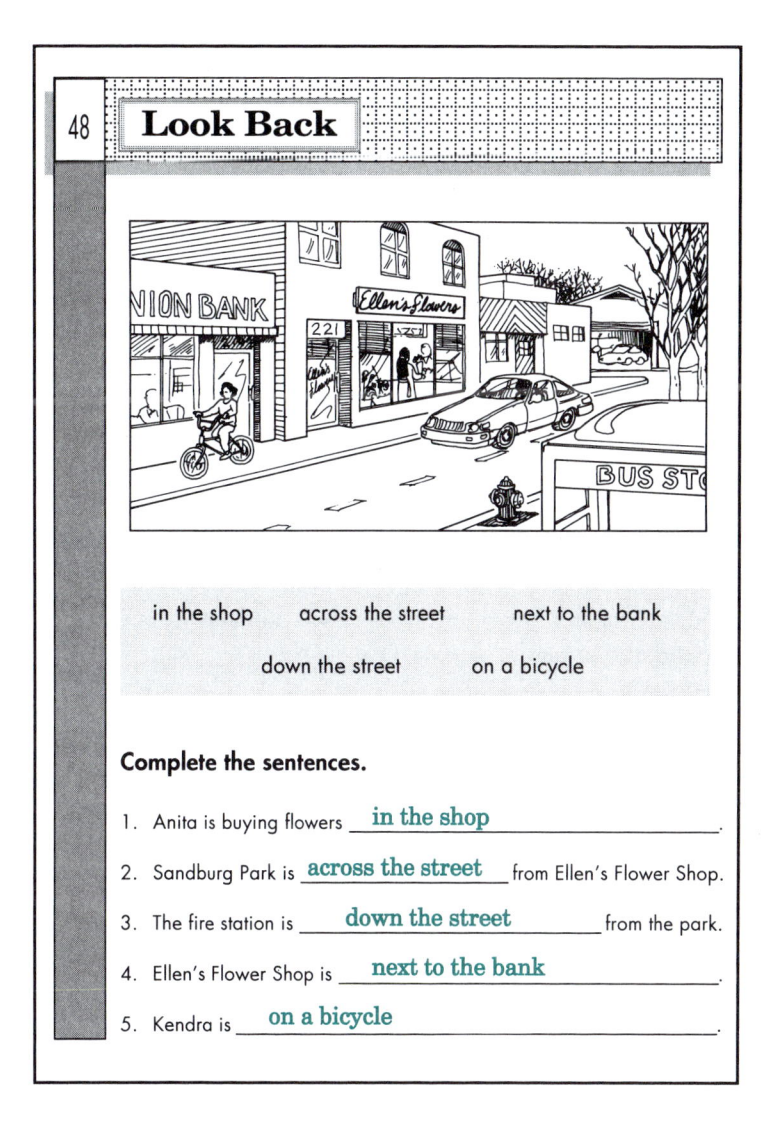

---

48 — Look Back

in the shop   across the street   next to the bank

down the street   on a bicycle

Complete the sentences.

1. Anita is buying flowers __in the shop__.
2. Sandburg Park is __across the street__ from Ellen's Flower Shop.
3. The fire station is __down the street__ from the park.
4. Ellen's Flower Shop is __next to the bank__.
5. Kendra is __on a bicycle__.

Presentation

1. Have learners turn to page 48 and look at the picture at the top of the page. Have learners identify the people, streets, and places in the picture. Say *Show me the flower shop. Point to Kendra.*
2. Ask questions about the picture. FOR EXAMPLE: *Where is Kendra? Where is Anita? Where is the bank?*
3. Together, read the phrases in the box. If necessary, learners can create questions and answers based on the phrases. (FOR EXAMPLE: *in the shop*—Who is in the shop? Anita is in the shop; *across the street*—What's across the street from the flower shop? The park is across the street from the flower shop.)
4. Individually, learners can read the sentences and fill in the blanks with the phrases from the box. Learners can refer to the map on page 40, if necessary, to find the fire station.

***Expansion/Extension* on page 87**

UNIT 4:
Getting from Here to There
Expansion/Extension

Getting Information
More *Expansion/Extension* for SB page 39

- Learners can find out information about buses or other transportation systems in their area. Learners can look at maps, schedules, signs at stations or on the vehicles and record information such as bus numbers, destinations, and fares. Together, learners can make a chart of the various bus (or other transportation) numbers, destinations, fares, and frequency. Learners can find out the time that service starts in the morning and ends at night.

- Learners can work in pairs to develop role plays about calling for transportation information. They can use the information they found about local transportation systems. One learner can call for information on how to get to a particular destination. The partner can give the bus number and fare.

- Bring in local bus-route maps (or subway-route maps, if applicable). Learners can work in pairs to locate their homes and places they want or need to go. Learners can trace the routes on the map.

- If transfers are used in the local bus system, introduce and practice asking for transfers, buying transfer tickets, and so on.

To the Bus Stop
More *Expansion/Extension* for SB page 40

- Use the furniture in the room to create a maze. Have a volunteer go through while you give directions. Then, blindfold volunteers and have them go slowly through the maze, following the directions. Learners can later give each other directions as they go through the maze.

- Introduce other directional phrases and prepositions commonly used. FOR EXAMPLE: *It's on the corner of . . . and . . . . When you get to (the) . . ., turn right. It's between (the) . . . and (the) . . . . It's just after (the) . . . . It's just before you get to (the) . . . . It's on the right. It's on the left.* Learners can practice giving directions with these phrases with the map on page 40.

- Learners can draw a new feature or building on their maps on page 40. In pairs, one learner can give directions to the new building for the other to follow and then to draw at the proper location on his or her map. Learners can switch roles. Then they can compare maps to check their work. (**Note:** Learners should not be able to see each other's maps until after completing the activity.)

- Bring in a map of the neighborhood. Have learners identify streets they know. Then, use the map to practice giving and following directions.

- Learners can draw their own neighborhood map. They can label streets and places that are important to them. They can also draw directions to their homes from another point. Depending on learners' skills, they can write the directions.

A Bus Schedule
More *Expansion/Extension* for SB page 41

- Practice other addition problems with time. Adjust the clock to 7:00. Ask *What time will it be in two hours? in five hours? in 30 minutes?* and so on.

- Introduce and practice time expressions. FOR EXAMPLE: *It leaves every 30 minutes/every half hour. It leaves every 60 minutes/every hour.* Compare the differences between the expressions *The bus leaves every 60 minutes (It leaves at 4:10, 5:10, 6:10, etc.)* and *The bus leaves every hour (It leaves at 4:00, 5:00, 6:00, etc.).*

- Bring in local bus schedules, or learners can call the bus service and ask for a schedule for a particular bus or find out where schedules can be picked up. Learners can find the times and destinations on the schedules. Depending on learners' skills, they can calculate how long (in terms of minutes or hours) various trips take.

- Give practice in asking for transportation information, using the schedules from the previous *Expansion/Extension* activity. (FOR EXAMPLE: What bus can I take to go to Central Square? What time is the next bus?)

- Bring in a map of local bus or subway routes. Have learners find information on the map about bus numbers, fares, routes, times, and so on.

- Learners can use bus maps and schedules to plan a bus trip that they would like to take.

Getting to Class
More *Expansion/Extension* for SB page 43

- Learners can talk about how they get to class by including information about bus numbers, time, cost, and so on. Together write an LEA story. This can be done individually or as a group. (FOR EXAMPLE: I take Bus Number 523. I get the bus at 5:45. The bus stop is on Main Street. I get off at Central Square. The trip is 30 minutes. It costs $1.50.)
- Practice and compare the first and third person singular forms of the present tense: *I walk to class. Michael walks to class. I ride a bicycle. David rides a bicycle.*
- Learners can categorize the modes of transportation by the appropriate verbs. FOR EXAMPLE:

ride	drive	take
a bicycle	a car	a bus
a motorcycle	a van	the train
		a taxi

Finding the Right Room
***Expansion/Extension* for SB page 44**
See TRF HANDOUT 4.3, *From Start to Finish*
TRF HANDOUT 4.6, *Help Me Get Out!*

- Go to a building, such as a library, store, or hospital, that has a floor plan or directory. Learners can look at it and find the names or numbers of rooms and the floors or places where they are located.
- Learners can make a directory and floor plan for the building where your class meets. Include various rooms, offices, rest rooms, public telephone, stairs, and elevators.
- Talk about fire safety and why it is important to know where stairs, fire extinguishers, and other items are located. If there is a fire-escape route for the building, use it to give practice with map reading and direction giving. If there is no planned route, learners can make their own.

Getting Around
More *Expansion/Extension* for SB page 46

- Learners can compare their charts and summarize the results on the board. (FOR EXAMPLE: In Haiti, people walk and go by bicycle. In Poland, people go by bus and by car.)
- Learners can make a collage with pictures about transportation in their native countries and transportation in the United States. Learners can look through magazines for pictures of modes of transportation or draw their own pictures. Pictures can be glued on posterboard and labeled with phrases or simple sentences.
- Learners can compare the cost, speed, and comfort of transportation in their native countries and in the United States.
- Some learners may want to use the past tense when talking about transportation that they used in their native countries. (FOR EXAMPLE: In my native country, I went to school by bicycle. Here, I go to school by bus.) Model the past tense if learners are interested.

Coming to the United States
***Expansion/Extension* for SB page 47**

- Learners can create an LEA story about their trips to the United States. Learners make a map to illustrate it, with places and types of transportation used.
- Learners can expand their stories to include dates, duration at certain stops, people who came with them, and so on. Ask questions to assist learners. FOR EXAMPLE: *When did you come? How long have you been here? How long did it take you to get from your native country to the United States? What other countries did you go to?*
- Learners can bring in memorabilia from their trips, such as pictures, ticket stubs, or other souvenirs. Learners can tell the group about the items or make a scrapbook about their trips.

Look Back
***Expansion/Extension* for SB page 48**

- Learners can say other simple sentences about places in the picture. Write the sentences on the board for learners to copy. (FOR EXAMPLE: Kendra is near the park. Kendra is riding her bicycle.)
- Write a list of places such as *bank, restaurant, park, school,* and the like. Learners can copy the list and find the proper names of some of the places in their neighborhood. This can be done by taking a walk around the neighborhood or by looking in the local yellow pages.

1 2 3 4 **5** 6 7 8 9 10 11 12 Summary
Feelings

Objectives

Functions
- Expressing emotions
- Sympathizing
- Expressing likes and dislikes

Life Tasks
- Dealing with feelings
- Dealing with strangers

Structures
- Present continuous tense
- *Yes/No* questions
- Wh- questions
- *Be* + adjective

Culture
- Culture shock

Vocabulary

Key words:

afraid	jealous
angry	joyful
bad	lonely
feel	proud
feeling	sad
glad	scared
good	unhappy
happy	upset

Related words:

answer	rain
can't stand	report card
cheer up	sorry
cry	strangers
door	study
good news	understand
grades	wait
learn	wet
mail carrier	What's wrong?
miss	

Feeling Good, Feeling Bad

Purpose: To introduce vocabulary about emotions and feelings number

Teacher Preparation and Materials

1. Index cards with faces, one face on each card portraying a feeling: happy, sad, angry, afraid
2. Magazine or other pictures of people portraying various feelings (*Warm-up* and *Expansion/Extension*)

Warm-up

1. On the board tape the index cards with the faces portraying happy, sad, angry, and afraid. Point to the happy face and say *He/She is . . . .* Give learners time to complete the sentence. If learners do not know the word *happy*, model and have learners repeat *He/She is happy*. Follow the same procedure with the other faces.
2. Number the faces on the board. Say a sentence and have learners give the number of the corresponding picture. FOR EXAMPLE: *They are sad today.* (2) *My friend is very angry.* (3) Say a number and have learners give the name of the feeling. FOR EXAMPLE: *1* (happy) *4* (afraid).
3. Bring in pictures of people showing different feelings, such as someone elatedly winning a race, someone crying, someone cowering in fear, someone angrily fighting, and so on. Have learners identify the feelings. (**Cultural Note:** Facial expressions for emotions are not universal; for example, in some cultures, people smile when they are angry or nervous.)

Presentation

1. Have learners turn to page 49 and look at the picture.
2. Ask *What do you see? Who do you see? Where are they? What is Anita doing? How do you think she feels?* List responses on the board. Be sure to include *happy, sad, angry,* and *afraid*.
3. Have learners guess the causes of the feelings. Ask *Why is Fred happy? How do you think May feels? Why does (do you think) she feel(s) that way?* Encourage learners' ideas on things not clearly seen or explained in the illustrations, such as Anita's photograph and the person outside May's door.
4. Together, read the question at the bottom of the page. *What's happening?* Have learners use their own words to describe the picture.

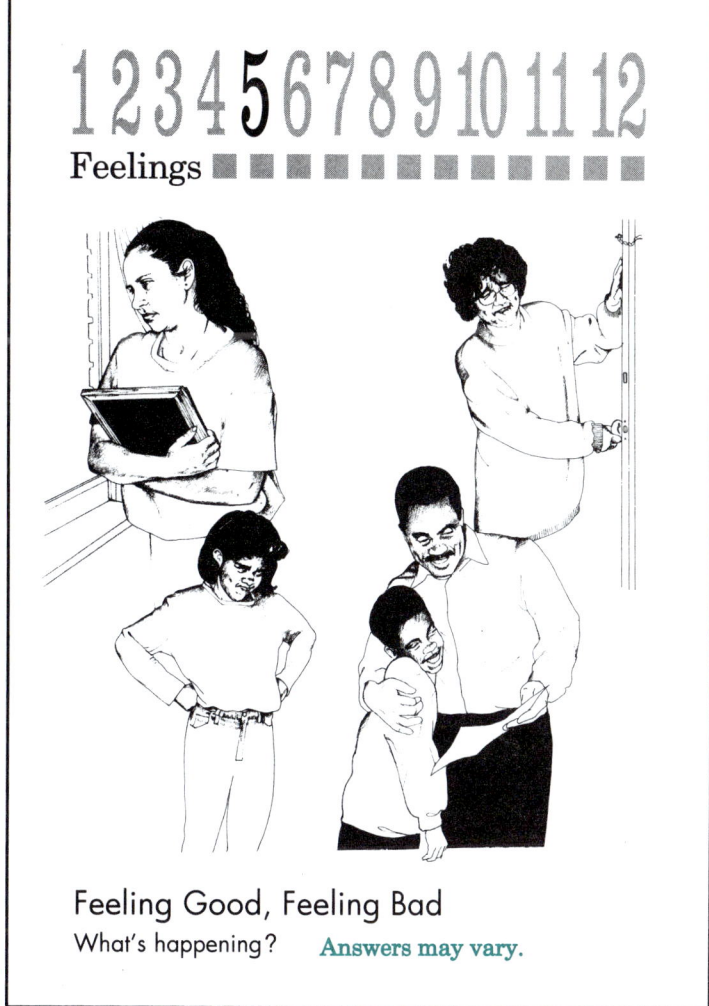

Expansion/Extension

- Learners can talk about the people, actions, and feelings on page 49 using the present continuous tense. Based on what learners say, write sentences on the board for them to copy. FOR EXAMPLE: Anita is looking at a photo. She is sad.
- Learners can look through magazines for pictures of people showing the four emotions: sad, happy, afraid, and angry. Say *Find someone who is happy. Show me someone who is angry.* and so on.
- Play charades. One learner can pick an index card with one of the four faces and can mime the feeling for the others to guess.

UNIT 5 • 89

Our Feelings

Purpose: To introduce additional vocabulary about feelings; to give practice with vocabulary about feelings

Teacher Preparation and Materials
1. Pictures of people used for page 49
2. Copies of TRF Handout 5.2, *How Do You Feel? (Expansion/Extension)*

Warm-up
1. Mime the four feelings sad, happy, angry, afraid. Have learners identify them. Then, say them and have volunteers act them out.
2. Write the four words as column headings on the board: *Sad, Happy, Angry, Afraid*. Have learners categorize the pictures of people portraying the different feelings by taping them under the proper headings.
3. Point to pictures one at a time and model sentences about them. FOR EXAMPLE: *He/She feels sad. He/She feels happy.* Have learners repeat. Then, point to pictures one at a time and ask *How does he/she feel?* Have learners respond with complete sentences.

Presentation
1. Point to the column of pictures for the word *happy*. Ask *What other words mean happy?* Have learners express other words they know, such as *glad, smiling, laughing, joyful* and *proud*. If learners do not suggest any words, introduce two or three. Model the new words and have learners repeat. Use the pictures or act them out to clarify meanings. Then write the words under the appropriate pictures.
2. Repeat the procedure for the three other feelings: *sad—lonely, crying, unhappy; angry—upset, mad, jealous; afraid—scared, confused, worried.* (**Note:** Be sure to include the words *scared, unhappy, proud, upset,* and *joyful.* They will be used later in the unit.)
3. Have learners make sentences about the pictures using the new words. Use questions as necessary. Ask *How does he/she feel?* (He/She's sad. He/She feels lonely. He's/She's crying.)

4. Have learners turn to page 50 and identify the four feelings. Then, have learners copy some of the new vocabulary items under the appropriate words and faces.

Expansion/Extension
See **TRF HANDOUT 5.2**, *How Do You Feel?*

- Learners can look through the book for pictures of the characters, describe how the characters feel in the different situations, and tell what the characters are doing.

- Learners can make a chart or time line of important dates and events in their lives. Learners can talk about how they felt at those times and events. Write what the learners say to make individual LEA stories. Depending on learners' skills, they can write their own sentences/stories about their lives. (FOR EXAMPLE: In 1972, I finished school. I was happy. In 1980, I left my country. I was sad, afraid, happy, and confused.)

This Makes Me Feel …

Purpose: To review vocabulary about feelings; to introduce adverbs of frequency

Teacher Preparation and Materials

1. Pictures of people used for page 49
2. Index cards with sight words: *happy: glad, smiling, laughing, proud; sad: lonely, crying, unhappy; angry: upset, mad, jealous; afraid: scared, confused, worried*
3. Magazine or other pictures of scenes, events, or items that evoke emotions (*Warm-up* and *Expansion/Extension*)
4. Scissors, glue, posterboard, and markers for all (*Expansion/Extension*)

Warm-up

1. Review feelings using picture cues. Ask *How does he/she feel? How do they feel?*
2. Tape the pictures on the board. Hold up the sight-word cards one at a time. Ask learners to read them aloud and then to tape them under the appropriate picture on the board. They may want to put more than one word under a picture.
3. Show pictures of scenes that evoke emotions. Ask learners to identify the feelings that they associate with the pictures. FOR EXAMPLE: Hold up a picture of a family celebration and ask *What is the family doing? How do you feel when your family has a party/celebration?* (I feel happy/glad.) (**Note:** The scenes will evoke different feelings in different people. There are no right or wrong answers in this activity.)

Presentation

1. Have learners turn to page 51 and look at the pictures.
2. Ask *What do you see (in picture 1)? How does this (do the flowers) make you feel?* and so on. Encourage learners to give words, phrases, or sentences about their reactions to the pictures or scenes.
3. Together, read the words in the box.
4. Individually or in pairs, have learners copy several feelings below each of the pictures.
5. As a group, compare the results. FOR EXAMPLE: Point to the picture of the flowers and ask *How do you feel? How many people feel …?* Record the number of responses for each picture on a chart. FOR EXAMPLE:

	Happy	Sad	Angry	Afraid
1. Flowers	12	2	0	0
2. Police Officer	5	3	1	5

6. Summarize the results. Introduce the use of adverbs of frequency: *sometimes, usually, always, never*. FOR EXAMPLE: *Flowers usually make us feel happy. Flowers never make us feel angry. Flowers sometimes make us feel sad.*

Expansion/Extension

- Learners can make collages or posters based on the following categories: These Make Me Feel Happy, These Make Me Feel Sad, These Make Me Angry, These Make Me Afraid. Learners can find pictures in magazines or draw their own pictures of things that evoke the different feelings.

More *Expansion/Extension* on page 100

Thinking of Home

Purpose: To give practice with vocabulary about feelings

Teacher Preparation and Materials
1. Map of the world
2. Magazines with pictures of international food, foreign places, various weather conditions; scissors, glue, posterboard, and markers for all *(Expansion/Extension)*

Warm-up
1. Review questions and answers about native countries. *Where are you from?* (I'm from . . . .) Have learners find their native countries on the map of the world.
2. Have learners review the names of the characters in the book and where they are from. They can look back at page 5 for pictures of the characters. Ask *What's his/her name? Where is Anita from? Where are the Lins from?* Have learners locate these countries on the map.
3. Have learners review family relationships. They can look at the family tree on page 17. Ask *Who is Kendra's brother? Who is Kendra's mother?* and so on.

Presentation
1. Have learners turn to page 52 and look at the picture.
2. Ask *What is Anita looking at? How does she feel? Who is in the picture/photo? Is Anita sad or happy in the photo? Is the picture of her home in the United States or her home in Mexico? Where do you think her family is now?*
3. Have learners discuss what Anita is thinking about. Then discuss possible actions for Anita. *Anita is sad/lonely. What can she do?* Some possible actions are to write a letter, call home, talk to a friend. Write the responses on the board.
4. Together, read the questions at the bottom of the page. Have learners answer the questions orally.
5. As a group, write an LEA story about Anita.
6. Ask *Do you miss people (family or friends)? What do you do when you feel sad/lonely/homesick?*

Expansion/Extension
- Learners can make up a story about Anita's life: where she is from, what family members are still there, why she came to the United States, how long she has been here, and so on.
- Learners can discuss their experiences of coming to the United States. Collect their ideas and write an LEA story together.
- Learners can write about their feelings in a journal or write a letter to an English-speaking friend about times when they feel homesick. (FOR EXAMPLE: Sometimes I feel lonely. I miss my family in . . . .. I want to see my friends.)
- Learners can make a collage using magazine pictures or drawings of things that they miss from their native countries. They can include pictures of foods, people, weather conditions, and so on. Pictures can be glued on posterboard. Learners can label them and then share their work with others in the group.

---

52 Thinking of Home

Answer the questions. Answers may vary.

1. How does Anita feel?
2. Why?
3. What can she do?

Who's at the Door?

Purpose: To give practice with vocabulary about feelings

Teacher Preparation and Materials

1. Pictures of a package, mail carrier, post office
2. Picture of a person who looks afraid
3. Pictures of scenes or events that make people afraid
4. Hat or uniform, identification card, clipboard *(Expansion/Extension)*

Warm-up

1. Review postal vocabulary related to the illustration on page 53 using pictures of a package, mail carrier, and post office. Ask *Do you get letters or packages in the mail? Where do you get them? Do you go to the post office to get them or does someone bring them to your home? Who brings them to your home?*

2. On the board, draw a scared face or tape a picture of a scared person. Ask *How does he/she feel? Why? What makes you feel scared?* Show a picture of something that scares you or talk about a time when you were afraid. Show other pictures of things that can scare people. Have learners choose/draw a picture of something they are afraid of or share a scary experience.

Presentation

1. Have learners turn to page 53 and look at the picture.

2. Ask *Who is at the door? What does he have? Does Mrs. Lin open the door? How do you think she feels? Why is she upset? Does she know the mail carrier? How do you think the mail carrier feels?*

3. Have learners suggest reasons why May Lin does not open the door. (She doesn't understand English. She doesn't understand the mail carrier. She doesn't know what he wants. The uniform is frightening. He's a stranger.)

4. Have learners guess what Mrs. Lin might be thinking.

5. Together, read the questions at the bottom of the page. Have learners

Who's at the Door? 53

I have a package for Tom Lin.

Answer the questions.   Answers may vary.

1. How does May feel?
2. Why?
3. How does the mail carrier feel?
4. Why?

---

discuss their answers orally. Write their responses on the board.

6. Discuss possible actions for Mrs. Lin. Ask *What can she do?* (She can ask for an identification card; she can call Anita; she can learn to say "I don't speak English" or "Please talk to the super.") (**Cultural Note:** Point out that there are times when Mrs. Lin's response is appropriate. Children should be warned about opening the door to strangers. Tell them to first look to see whether or not they know the person at the door. Then tell them to ask strangers to come back later or to see the building superintendent.)

Expansion/Extension

- Ask what other people in uniforms might appear at the door. (**Note:** This might be a sensitive issue for some learners.) Learners can role-play other characters responding to a gas-meter reader knocking on the door. Other uniformed people might be a delivery person or an electric-company worker. Learners can use a uniform or hat, clipboard, and identification card as props.

More *Expansion/Extension* on page 100

Talking to Friends

Purpose: To give practice with vocabulary about feelings; to introduce sympathizing and giving suggestions

Teacher Preparation and Materials

1. Picture of something that makes people sad
2. 📼 Audiotape for Level 1
3. Brochures and information about local adult education programs *(Expansion/Extension)*
4. Records or audiotapes of music that evoke various emotions, record player or audiotape player *(Expansion/Extension)*
5. Copies of TRF Handout 5.4, *Feelings* *(Expansion/Extension)*

Warm-up

1. On the board, write the following emotions as headings: *Happy, Sad, Afraid, Angry.* Have learners give examples of things that evoke these feelings. List their ideas on the chart.
2. Use the chart for asking about negative feelings and sympathizing. Have learners ask each other questions. FOR EXAMPLE:

    A. What's wrong? You look sad/scared/angry.
    B. I am sad/scared/angry. (Give a reason.)
    A. I'm sorry to hear that.

3. Show a picture of something that makes you feel sad or describe an experience that was sad. Tell how something happened that helped you feel happy again. Have volunteers share their own experiences.

Presentation

1. Have learners turn to page 54 and look at the top picture.
2. Ask *Who is at the door? What does he have? Is Anita afraid? Why is he giving Anita the package?*
3. 📼 Play the audiotape and have learners listen to the conversation between Anita and Joe, the mail carrier.
4. Ask *Who is the package for? What is the mail carrier's name? Who is sad? Why is she sad? What is Anita going to do to feel better? Does Anita know Joe?*

📼 If necessary, ask one question and then play the audiotape for learners to listen for that information. Repeat the procedure for the other questions.

5. Compare Mrs. Lin's and Anita's reactions to the mail carrier. Ask why Anita opens the door and Mrs. Lin doesn't. (She understands English. She knows the mail carrier.)
6. Have learners look at the bottom picture. Ask *Who is in the picture? What are they doing?*
7. 📼 Play the audiotape and have learners listen to the conversation between Anita and Tom. Ask *Is the package for Tom? Did May open the door? Does May know the mail carrier? What is Anita's idea? (What should May study?) Where can she learn English?*

Expansion/Extension
See **TRF HANDOUT 5.4**, *Feelings*

- In pairs or small groups, learners can re-create the conversations for the two pictures and then act out their conversations for the whole group.

More *Expansion/Extension* on page 100

94 • UNIT 5

A Wet Ride

Purpose: To give practice with vocabulary about feelings

Teacher Preparation and Materials
1. Index cards with faces used for page 49
2. Pictures of people riding bikes, looking at photos, arguing
3. Picture of people waiting at a bus stop
4. Copies of TRF Handout 5.3, *Customs Line: How Do They Feel? (Expansion/Extension)*

Warm-up
1. Give practice with the present continuous tense. On the board, make a chart using names of characters from the book and pictures for feelings and actions. FOR EXAMPLE:

	(Use cards/pictures noted)	
Kendra	happy face	riding a bike
Anita	sad face	looking at photos
Fred and Michael	angry face	arguing
(your name)	blank face	blank

If necessary, model statements based on the chart and have learners repeat. FOR EXAMPLE: *Kendra is happy. She's riding a bike. Anita is sad. She's looking at photos.* Point to *your name* on the chart and model statements about yourself. *I'm . . . . I'm . . .ing.* Have learners make up their own personal responses. Ask questions about the people and have learners respond with complete sentences. FOR EXAMPLE: *What's Kendra doing?* (She's riding a bike.) *How does she feel?* (She is happy.) *What are you doing?* (I'm . . .ing.) *How do you feel?* (I'm . . ..) Point to the various people and have learners practice creating their own questions and answers using the information on the chart.

2. Show the picture of the people waiting at a bus stop. Have learners describe the picture and the people. If necessary, use questions to guide the learners. Ask *Where are these people? What are they waiting for? Where do you think they are going? Do you think they will wait a long time for the bus? Is it a nice day or is it raining (in the picture)?*

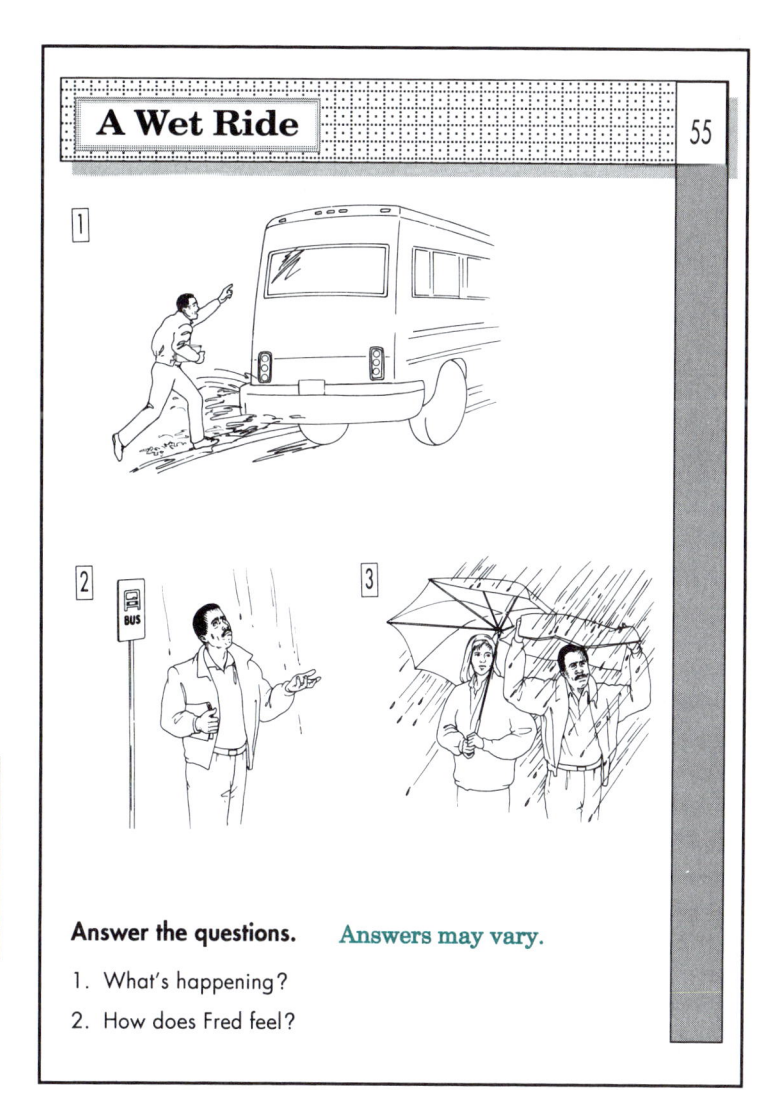

3. Ask learners about their personal experiences of using buses. *Do you take/use the bus? Do you wait a long time? Does the bus wait for people who are late?* and so on.

Presentation
1. Have learners look at the picture story on page 55.
2. Ask questions about the pictures. *What do you see? In picture 1, what is Fred doing? In picture 2, what is he doing?* and so on. List the words and comments on the board. Be sure to include *running, miss (the bus), raining, waiting, wet.*
3. Ask *How do you think Fred feels? Why?*
4. Together, read the questions at the bottom of the page. Have learners answer the questions orally.

Expansion/Extension
See **TRF HANDOUT 5.3**, *Customs Line: How Do They Feel?*

- Together, write an LEA story about the pictures of Fred. On the board, write the story that learners dictate. Then learners can copy it.

More *Expansion/Extension* on page 100

UNIT 5 • 95

Good News

Purpose: To give practice with vocabulary about feelings

Teacher Preparation and Materials

1. Pictures of people used for page 49; should include people portraying feelings: proud, jealous, and unhappy
2. An elementary school report card
3. Audiotape for Level 1
4. Copies of TRF Handout 5.5, *Why Do You Feel That Way? (Expansion/Extension)*
5. Copies of TRF Handout 5.6, *Impressions (Expansion/Extension)*

Warm-up

1. Have learners use simple sentences to identify feelings shown in various pictures of people. (FOR EXAMPLE: He is happy. She is sad. They are happy.) Review the words *proud, jealous,* and *unhappy*, using picture cues. Be prepared to give examples of each. (FOR EXAMPLE: proud—My son is finishing high school. I am proud. I will tell my friends and have a party for him. jealous—My neighbor has a new car. I want a new car, too. I'm jealous.)
2. Show an elementary school report card. Ask questions about it. *What is this? Who gets them? Why do teachers give them to the children? What grades are good? What grades are bad?* If necessary, explain report cards and grades.

Presentation

1. Have learners turn to page 56 and look at the picture.
2. Have learners identify the characters and discuss their feelings. Ask questions. *How does Fred feel? Why? How does Carol feel? Why?* and so on.
3. Play the audiotape and have learners listen to the conversation.
4. Ask questions about the conversation. *Do you think Fred had a good day or a bad day? Why is he wet? Does Carol have good news or bad news for Fred? Who's report card is good—Michael's or Kendra's?*

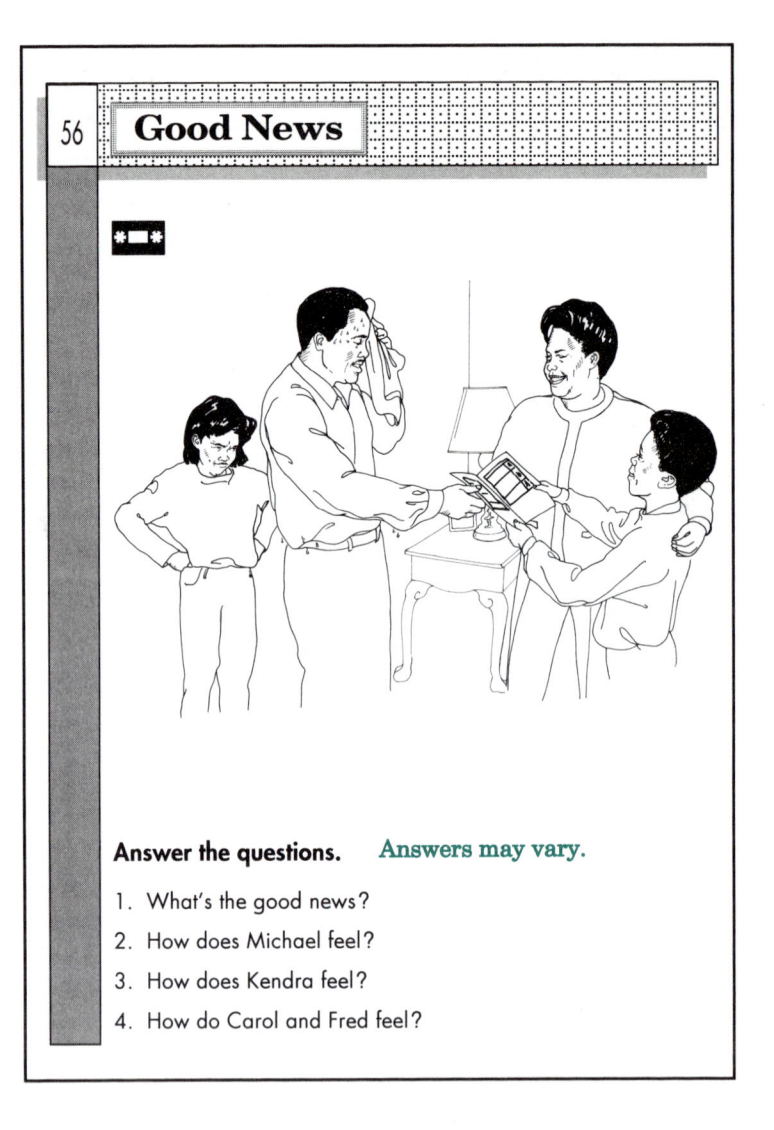

---

56 Good News

Answer the questions. Answers may vary.

1. What's the good news?
2. How does Michael feel?
3. How does Kendra feel?
4. How do Carol and Fred feel?

What grades does he have? Does Fred feel better now?
If necessary, ask one question and then have learners listen to the audiotape for that answer. Then repeat the procedure with the other questions.

5. Together, read the questions at the bottom of page 56 and have learners discuss their answers.

Expansion/Extension
See **TRF HANDOUT 5.5**, *Why Do You Feel That Way?*
TRF HANDOUT 5.6, *Impressions*

- Talk about parents and how they can help their children. Ask *When are you proud of your children? How do you tell or show them that you are proud?*
- Introduce and practice responses to good news: *Isn't it great? That's terrific! Wow! I'm so happy for you! Congratulations!* Learners can tell about something good that happened to them. Others in the group can respond with some of the new expressions.

More *Expansion/Extension* on page 100

Good Days and Bad Days

Purpose: To give practice with vocabulary about emotions

Teacher Preparation and Materials

1. Magazines with pictures of things that might make people feel good or bad, scissors, glue, and posterboard for all (Expansion/Extension)
2. Copies of TRF Handout 5.7, *Conversation Endings* (Expansion/Extension)

Warm-up

1. On the board, make two columns with the headings *Good Day* and *Bad Day*. Have learners look back through the unit and describe how the various characters feel. Ask learners which characters are having a good day and which are having a bad day. Have learners explain why.
2. Ask learners about their day and their feelings. *How do you feel today? Is today a good day or bad day for you? Why?*
3. Ask learners about things that make them feel good, such as nice music, someone saying hello, good food, or a present. Ask about things that make them feel bad, such as a rainy day, housework, children fighting, or being sick.

Presentation

1. Have learners turn to page 57 and look at the pictures.
2. Ask questions about the pictures. *How does Michael feel? Is he having a good day or a bad day? Why? How does Anita feel? Is she having a good day or bad day? Why?*
3. Together, read the sentences. Ask questions about them. *Who feels good today? How does he feel? Why is it a good day? Who feels bad? How does she feel? Why is it a bad day for her?*
4. On the board, make a chart similar to the one on page 57. Model the question and answer *What makes you feel good?* (Talking with my friend.) Record the information on the chart. Ask a learner *What makes you feel good?* Record the answer. Have learners practice asking and answering the question in a chain drill while you record the responses on the board. (**Note:** If learners have difficulty expressing their ideas, they can find or draw pictures to illustrate their responses, or they can act them out.) Introduce vocabulary as necessary for learners to express their ideas.
5. Model the question and answer *What makes you feel bad?* (Getting a cold.) Give practice with and record responses on the board in the same manner as above.
6. Have learners interview each other and record the responses on the chart at the bottom of page 57.
7. As a group, summarize the results from the interviews. Ask *What are some good things? How many people like ...? What are some bad things? How many people don't like ...?*

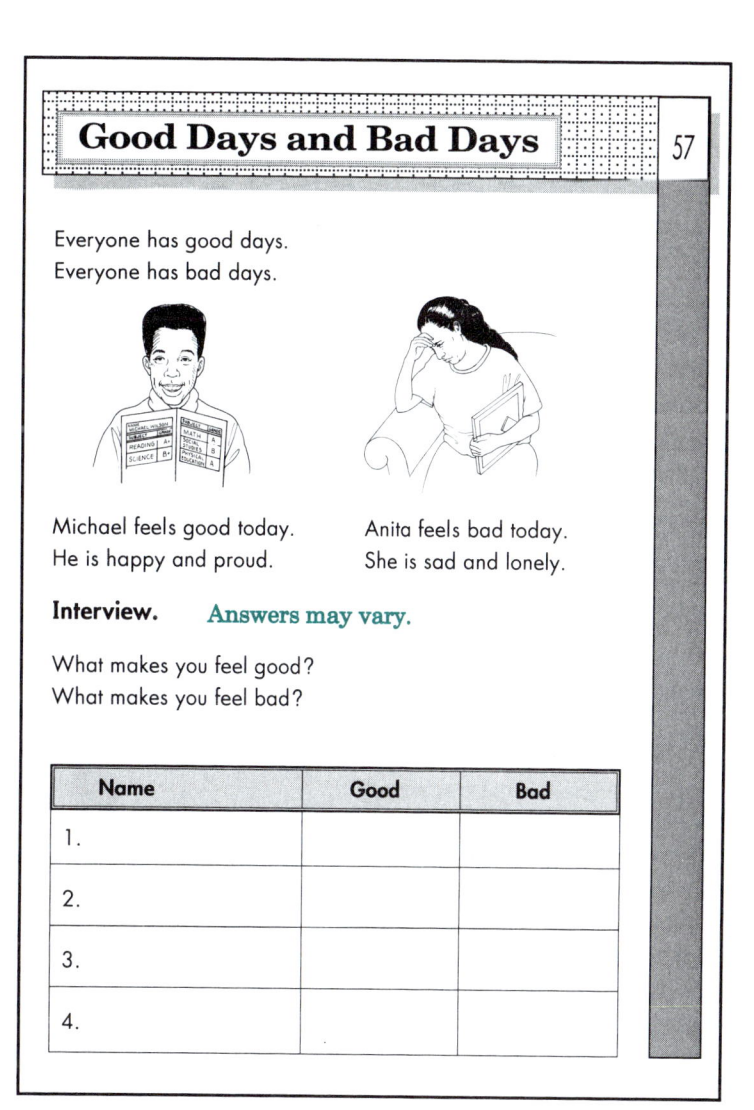

Expansion/Extension
See **TRF HANDOUT 5.7,** *Conversation Endings*

- Learners can make a collage of pictures from magazines and/or their own drawings of the types of things that make them feel good or bad. Learners can glue the pictures on posterboard and label them.

More *Expansion/Extension* on page 101

What's the Matter?

Purpose: To give practice with vocabulary about feelings; to introduce expressing likes and dislikes

Teacher Preparation and Materials

1. Pictures of foods, sports, or other items and activities that can be used for discussing likes and dislikes
2. Audiotape for Level 1
3. Magazines with a variety of pictures of foods, sports, or other items and activities that can be used for discussing likes and dislikes *(Expansion/Extension)*
4. Copies of TV program guides *(Expansion/Extension)*
5. Copies of TRF Handout 5.1, *What Do You Like?* *(Expansion/Extension)*

Warm-up

Show learners pictures of types of foods, sports, or other items and activities. Model your personal reaction to some of them. *I like this* (or say the name of the item/activity if learners know the vocabulary). *I don't like this. I can't stand this!* Have learners repeat the different reactions. Then hold up other pictures and have learners express their own likes and dislikes. Ask *Do you like this? What do you think of this?*

Presentation

1. Have learners turn to page 58 and look at the picture. Ask questions. *Who do you see? How does Kendra feel? Why do you think she feels angry? How does Carol feel?*
2. Play the audiotape and have learners listen to the conversation.
3. Ask questions about the conversation. *Is Kendra upset? Why is she upset? Who had good grades on the report card today? Is today a special day for Kendra or for Michael? Last month did Kendra have a special day? How did the family celebrate? Does Carol like Michael more than Kendra?* If necessary, ask one question and then play the audiotape. Have learners listen for that answer. Then repeat the procedure with the other questions.
4. Together, read the questions at the bottom of the page and have learners answer the questions orally.

Expansion/Extension
See TRF HANDOUT 5.1, *What Do You Like?*

- Together, write an LEA story about the picture and conversation. Learners can copy it into their notebooks.
- Learners can look through magazines and find pictures of things they like and dislike. Then, together make two lists: *Things about the United States that I like* and *Things that I don't like*.
- Distribute TV program guides. Learners can look through and pick out programs that they like and do not like. They can share and explain their choices to the group.
- Depending on learners' interests, they can talk about their likes and dislikes of music, movies, actors and actresses, famous personalities, and so on.

More *Expansion/Extension* on page 101

---

58 **What's the Matter?**

Answer the questions. Answers may vary.

1. How does Kendra feel?
2. Why?
3. What makes you feel angry?

Look Back

Purpose: To give practice with vocabulary about feelings

Teacher Preparation and Materials

1. Pictures of people used for page 56
2. Index cards with sight words used for page 51

Warm-up

1. Use picture cues to review the different emotions. Ask *How does he/she feel? Why do you think he/she feels that way?*
2. Tape the pictures on the board and number them. Then show the sight-word cards. Have learners tape them under the appropriate pictures.
3. Have learners identify the pictures and words that are associated with feeling good. Point to the picture and word for *upset* and say *He's/She's upset. Is he/she feeling good or bad?* (He's/She's feeling bad.) Repeat the procedure with the other pictures.

Presentation

1. Have learners turn to page 59. Together, read the words in the box and then the directions.
2. Have learners work individually to categorize the words under the proper columns.

Expansion/Extension

- Learners can look back through the book or their notebooks for other words to add to the chart on page 59.
- Learners can write sentences using the words. They can include reasons for the feelings. (FOR EXAMPLE: I'm glad when . . . . I'm afraid when . . . .) Learners can illustrate their sentences.
- Discuss how and when people show feelings. Ask *Do you let others know if you are happy? sad? angry? afraid? When? How do you show or tell people that you are happy? afraid? angry?*

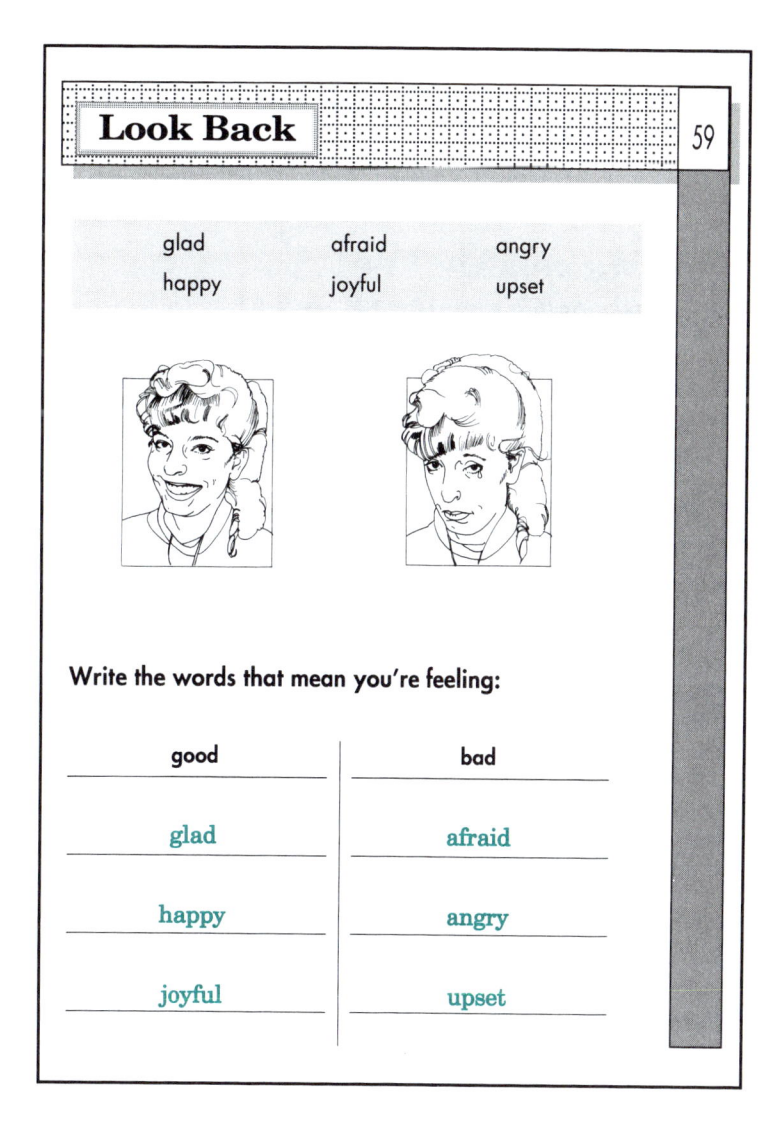

- Practice a short conversation asking about feelings and sympathizing.
    - A: That makes me so angry!
    - B: What does?
    - A: The noise outside the apartment.
    - B: Oh, I know what you mean.

    Introduce other phrases such as *I'm sorry to hear that* and *That's too bad.*

- Learners can fill in a chart about different feelings they felt during the past day or week. They can check different feelings and then fill in what made them feel that way. FOR EXAMPLE:

	Feelings	Why?
✔	happy	letter from home
	sad	
✔	angry	noisy dog
	afraid	

- Learners can compare how feelings are expressed in different countries.

UNIT 5 • 99

UNIT 5: Feelings
Expansion/Extension

This Makes Me Feel...
More *Expansion/Extension* for SB page 51

- Using adverbs of frequency, learners can complete sentences about feelings and what causes them. (FOR EXAMPLE: I always feel angry when.... I usually feel sad when.... I sometimes feel happy when....)

Who's at the Door?
More *Expansion/Extension* for SB page 53

- Role-play other situations when it is questionable to open the door: a salesperson selling something, a person wanting to use the phone, a religious organization.
- In pairs, learners can develop and present scenes/conversations about situations in which they were afraid. Then, other learners can make suggestions on how to handle the situations.

Talking to Friends
More *Expansion/Extension* for SB page 54

- Bring in or have learners find brochures or information about adult education programs in the local area. Look through the brochures and find courses offered, times, places, and so on.
- Have learners think about their own reasons and goals for studying English. Ask *What do you want to be able to say or do in English?* (ask questions when shopping, understand instructions at work, get into job training, read bills, get a driver's license, and so on) *Why do you want to study English?* (to know more things, to understand Americans) Have learners list three goals for their language study and how long they think it will take to attain them.
- As a group, make a list of things you can do when you are sad or afraid. Learners can illustrate it. FOR EXAMPLE:
    When I am sad, I can... write a letter.
    call a friend.
    listen to music.
    When I am afraid, I can... lock the door.
    take a walk.
    go to the neighbors.
- Bring in various types of music that evoke emotions. Ask learners what feelings they associate with the different types of music. FOR EXAMPLE: polka: happy; bugle blowing taps: sad. Reactions will vary. Learners can bring in samples of music from their native cultures that make them feel happy or sad.

A Wet Ride
More *Expansion/Extension* for SB page 55

- Encourage learners to discuss a "bad day." Record learners' comments and write an LEA story.

Good News
More *Expansion/Extension* for SB page 56

- If learners have children in school, expand the discussion of report cards. Ask *What kind of school are your children in? How often do they get report cards? What kind of grading system does the school use? Do the children bring them home or does the school send them to you? Do you have to sign the cards? Do you return the cards to the school? Do you talk to the teacher? What does your child study?* (ESL, spelling, math, art, science, and so on.) Learners can bring in samples of their children's report cards and find the names of the subjects or skill areas that are graded. (**Note:** Elementary schools do not always use letter grades. Some grading systems use marks, such as check marks, pluses, and minuses [✓, +, -]; others use letters, such as *S* [satisfactory], *NI* [needs improvement], *U* [unsatisfactory].) Learners can find the key on the report card to help decipher the meaning of the grades.
- Give practice with *Yes/No* and *Wh-* question formation. Make a chart using pictures of people portraying various emotions and the names of characters from the book.

Kendra	[picture: angry face]
Fred and Carol	[picture: happy face]
Michael	[picture: proud face]
May	[picture: afraid face]

Point to and say a character's name and an emotion: *Kendra, happy*. Then, model a *Yes/No* question that uses those two components: *Is Kendra happy?* Have a volunteer give the appropriate answer. (No, she isn't.) Provide other examples as necessary. Then, learners can create their own questions as you give the character's name and an emotion. Other learners can give the responses. Use the same chart to practice *Wh-*question formation. Say a question word and a feeling: *Who, happy*. Model a question that uses those two components: *Who is happy?* Have a volunteer give the appropriate answer. (Fred and Carol are happy.) Provide other examples as necessary. Then, learners can create their own questions as you give the question word and a feeling. Other learners in the group can give the responses.

- Practice forming negative sentences. Place four pictures on the board of people with different emotions. Describe one of the pictures, using negatives. Learners can guess the correct picture. FOR EXAMPLE: *She isn't smiling. She isn't feeling good. She isn't happy.* (She's sad.) Volunteers can describe other pictures using negatives for the class to guess.

- Learners can discuss who they talk to when they feel angry, when they feel sad, and when they feel happy. On the board, make a chart and have learners interview one another and record responses. FOR EXAMPLE:

Who do you talk to when you are . . . ?

	(Draw pictures as indicated)		
Name	happy face	sad face	angry face

Good Days and Bad Days
More *Expansion/Extension* for SB page 57

- Learners can write their responses to the questions. (FOR EXAMPLE: English class makes me feel good. My children make me feel good. Letters from home make me feel good and bad. Work makes me feel bad.)

- Learners can write about feelings in a daily journal. Encourage learners to include reasons for their feelings and ways of expressing or resolving negative feelings. (FOR EXAMPLE: Today is Friday, September 3rd. Today I had a good day. I was happy. I was in English class. Today is Saturday, September 4th. Today I had a bad day. I was angry. My children did not help. I . . ..)

What's the Matter?
More *Expansion/Extension* for SB page 58

- Discuss sibling rivalry. Ask *Are children always happy? Are they angry at each other sometimes? How do/did you get along with your brothers and sisters?* and so on.

- Discuss parent-child relationships and discipline. Ask *Do you get angry with your children sometimes? Why? Do children always listen? What do you want them to do? What do children want to do?*

  (**Note:** Parent-child relationships are often difficult. Immigrant parents may feel their children are becoming too Americanized. Children may feel embarrassed about their backgrounds or may rebel against their parents' cultural traditions. Forms of discipline for children may vary.)

- Introduce talking about likes and dislikes and then relate them to feelings. FOR EXAMPLE: *I like flowers. They make me feel happy. I don't like dogs. They make me feel afraid. I like my family, but they make me feel sad (because they are far away).*

1 2 3 4 5 6 7 8 9 10 11 12 Summary
Discovering Patterns

Objectives

- To help learners discover grammatical patterns
- To teach and give practice with those patterns

The structures covered are:
- pronouns and verb *be*
- questions: *Yes/No* with *be* and *Yes/No* with *do*
- questions: *Who, What, Where, When, Why, How*
- present and present continuous tense
- possessives.

About the Structures

• Pronouns and Verb: *Be*

The verb *be* has three forms in the present tense, which makes it different from other verbs. Learners will often omit the verb. Some pronouns are acquired more easily than others. Learners may have difficulty differentiating between *he* and *she* or *he/she* and *it*.

• Questions: *Yes/No* with *Be* and *Yes/No* with *Do*

In the exercises, the verb *be* is used both as a full verb and as an auxiliary (for the present continuous tense). The verb *do* is used only as an auxiliary. Learners may have problems with the word order for questions. Question formation requires a lot of practice; mastery is not expected at this level.

• Questions: *Who, What, Where, When, Why, How*

These exercises use the question word *What* to ask about a thing and *How* to ask about a way to do something. Learners may ask about other uses of those words: *What a beautiful dress! What time is it? How much? How many? How do you feel?* As with *Yes/No* questions, the word order will present problems. Learners will need a lot of practice.

• Verbs: Present and Present Continuous

This page compares the tenses in form: present tense with a one-word verb and present continuous tense with *be* + verb + *-ing*. Learners are not expected to master when to use which tense, although learners can begin to understand that the present continuous tense is used for actions that happen right now.

• Possessives.

This structure is easier on paper than in conversation. Learners may have trouble with *his/her* (both third-person singular) and *your/my*.

102 • UNIT 6 • SUMMARY

Pronouns and Verb: *Be*

Purpose: To give practice with subject pronouns and the present tense of the verb *be*

Teacher Preparation and Materials
Index cards with pronouns: *I, you, he, she, it, we, they*

Warm-up
1. Ask questions about languages spoken and native countries. Have learners respond with appropriate pronouns. FOR EXAMPLE: *Where are you from?* (I'm from Haiti.) *Where are Sophal and Peng from?* (They're from Cambodia.) *What language does Ivan speak?* (He speaks Polish.)
2. Practice a substitution drill with the verb *be*. Model the sentence *I am happy today*. Hold up sight-word cards as cues for learners to substitute in the sentences.

Presentation
1. Have learners turn to page 60 and look at the "Pronouns" chart. Have learners find the pronouns that are for one person. Learners can give an example of each in sentences. Ask learners to find the pronouns that are used for two or more people and then to give an example of each in sentences.
2. Point out how pronoun use changes depending on who is being addressed. Also, point out that *you* is the same in singular and plural forms.
3. Have learners look at the "Verb: *Be*" chart. *Which word (pronoun) uses* am? *Which words use* is? *What is another way to say* I am? *and so on.*
4. Have learners complete the two exercises.

Expansion/Extension
- Learners can circle the verb *be* in the sentences in the first exercise. (Anita Gómez *is* from Mexico. Fred Wilson *is* from the United States. Tom and May Lin *are* from China.)
- Learners can rewrite the first sentence, using subject pronouns. (FOR EXAMPLE: Anita Gómez is from Mexico. *She* is from Mexico.) Learners can use contracted forms of the subject pronouns and the verb *be*. (*She's* from Mexico.)
- Give practice with negative statements about the characters and their native countries. FOR EXAMPLE: *Anita Gómez is from Mexico. She isn't from China.* (or *She's not from China.*)
- Learners can circle examples of the verb *be* in the second exercise.
- Learners can rewrite appropriate sentences, using the contracted forms of *be*. (FOR EXAMPLE: *He's* Anita's nephew. *I'm* coming next month.)
- Learners can write sentences for each member of the class and for you about native countries and languages. (FOR EXAMPLE: This is Lev. *He's* from Russia. He speaks Russian and English.)
- Learners can write additional sentences for the first exercise about the characters' addresses. (FOR EXAMPLE: Anita—She lives at 127 Center Street. She's in apartment 1A.)

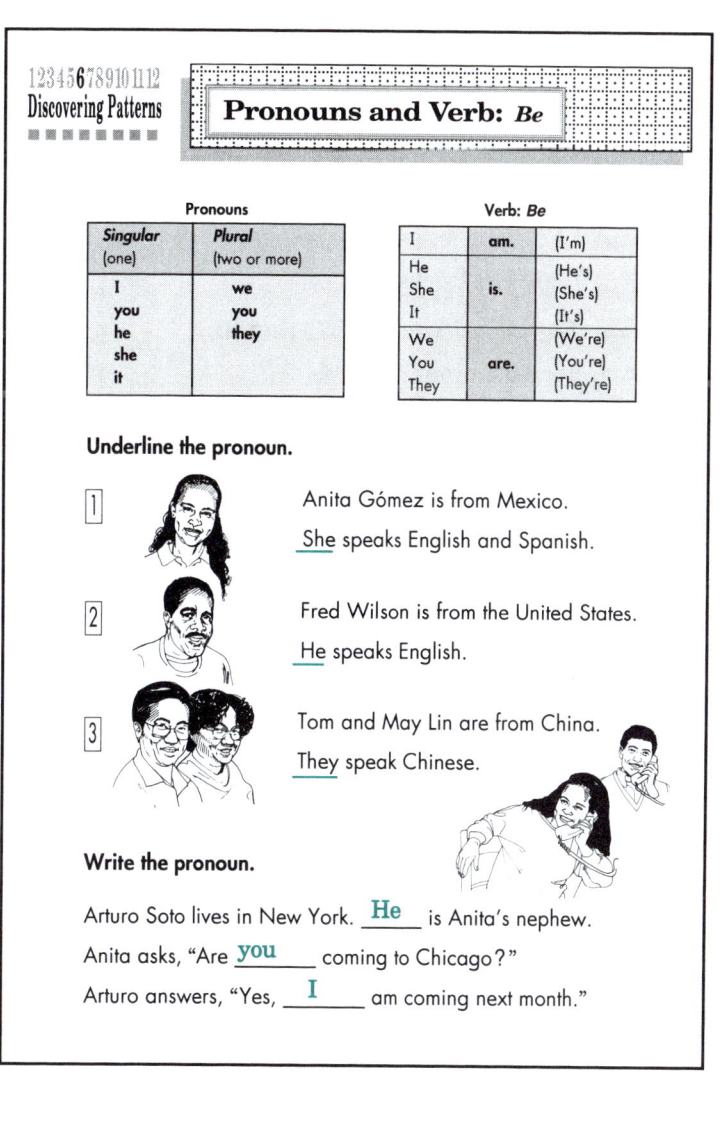

Discovering Patterns
Pronouns and Verb: *Be*

Pronouns

Singular (one)	Plural (two or more)
I	we
you	you
he	they
she	
it	

Verb: *Be*

I	am.	(I'm)
He / She / It	is.	(He's) (She's) (It's)
We / You / They	are.	(We're) (You're) (They're)

Underline the pronoun.

1. Anita Gómez is from Mexico.
   <u>She</u> speaks English and Spanish.

2. Fred Wilson is from the United States.
   <u>He</u> speaks English.

3. Tom and May Lin are from China.
   <u>They</u> speak Chinese.

Write the pronoun.

Arturo Soto lives in New York. **He** is Anita's nephew.
Anita asks, "Are **you** coming to Chicago?"
Arturo answers, "Yes, **I** am coming next month."

UNIT 6 • 103

Questions: *Yes/No* with *Be* and *Yes/No* with *Do*

Purpose: To give practice with *Yes/No* questions with *be* and *do*

Teacher Preparation and Materials

1. Index cards with pronouns used for page 60
2. Index cards with sight words and punctuation: *am, is, are, do, does, work, working,* ? (question mark), . (period)

Warm-up

1. Ask *Yes/No* questions about native countries and actions using the verb *be*. Have learners respond with short answers.
   FOR EXAMPLE: *Is Tuan from Vietnam?* (Yes, he is./No, he isn't.) *Are you studying now?* (Yes, I am./No, I'm not.)
2. Ask *Yes/No* questions about languages and addresses using *do/does*. Have learners respond with short answers.
   FOR EXAMPLE: *Do you speak Spanish?* (Yes, I do. No, I don't.) *Does Rita live in New York?* (Yes, she does. No, she doesn't.)
3. On the board, tape the sight-word cards to form the sentence *He is working*. Have learners make a *Yes/No* question by rearranging the cards. Add the appropriate punctuation card.
4. On the board, tape the sentence *They work*. Tape an additional card *do*. Have learners make a *Yes/No* question by rearranging the sight-word cards.

Presentation

1. Have learners turn to page 61 and look at the "*Yes/No* with *Be*" chart. Have them find the subject pronouns and the verb *be*. If necessary, ask questions about the question format. *In a question, is the verb before or after the word* he? *In the answer* "Yes, he is," *is the verb before or after the word* he? *and so on.*
2. Have learners look at the "*Yes/No* with *Do*" chart. Ask questions as necessary. *Which pronouns make questions with* do? *Which use* does? *Is the word* work *before or after the pronoun?* and so on.
3. Avoid explaining the difference between verb tenses. Point out that *working, read-*

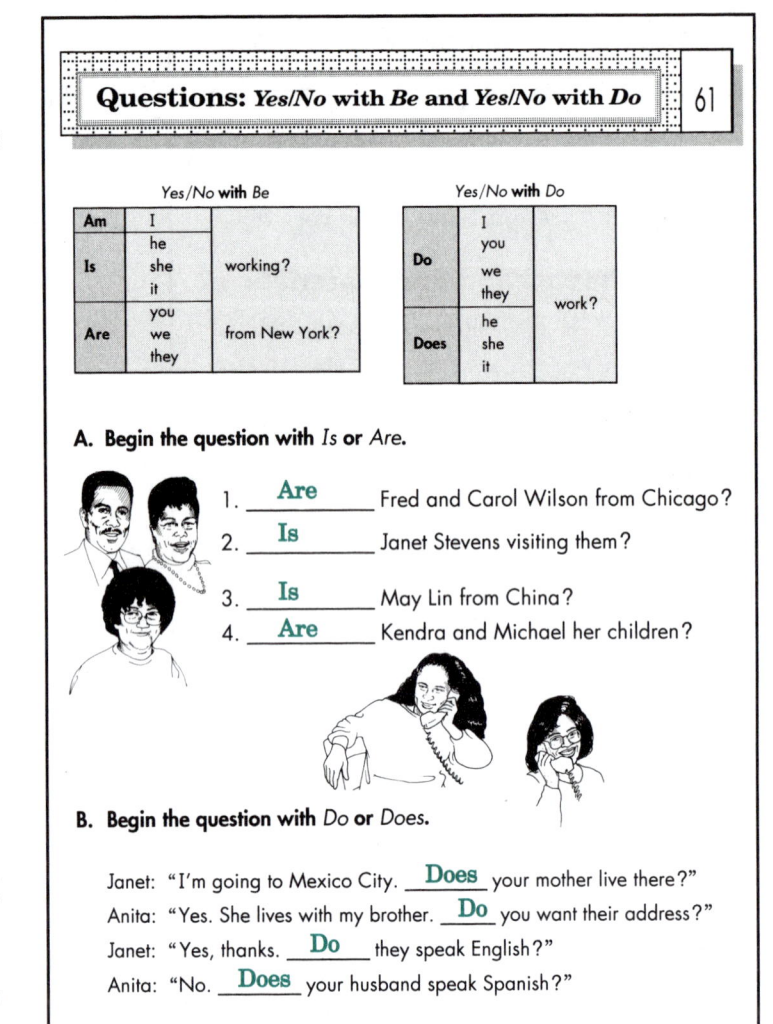

Questions: *Yes/No* with *Be* and *Yes/No* with *Do*   61

	Yes/No with Be	
Am	I	
Is	he / she / it	working?
Are	you / we / they	from New York?

	Yes/No with Do	
Do	I / you / we / they	work?
Does	he / she / it	

A. Begin the question with *Is* or *Are*.

1. __Are__ Fred and Carol Wilson from Chicago?
2. __Is__ Janet Stevens visiting them?
3. __Is__ May Lin from China?
4. __Are__ Kendra and Michael her children?

B. Begin the question with *Do* or *Does*.

Janet: "I'm going to Mexico City. __Does__ your mother live there?"
Anita: "Yes. She lives with my brother. __Do__ you want their address?"
Janet: "Yes, thanks. __Do__ they speak English?"
Anita: "No. __Does__ your husband speak Spanish?"

---

ing, speaking, and *visiting* use *am, is,* or *are*. Point out that verbs without *-ing* use *do* or *does* in questions and short answers.

4. Point out the use of a capital letter at the start of both sentences and questions. Also, point out the use of a question mark to end a question.
5. Have learners complete the two exercises. If necessary, learners can write the appropriate subject pronoun over the names of the people in the first exercise before choosing the verb form.

Expansion/Extension

- Learners can write *Yes/No* answers for the questions in the first exercise. (FOR EXAMPLE: Yes, they are. No, they aren't.)
- Learners can write other *Yes/No* questions from the exercises on page 60. (FOR EXAMPLE: Is Anita from Mexico? Does she speak English?)
- Learners can write other questions about personal information, using pronouns *you, I,* and *we*.
- Compare intonation of statements and *Yes/No* questions. Point out the rising intonation of *Yes/No* questions.

Questions: *Who, What, Where, When, Why, How*

Purpose: To give practice with *Wh-* questions in the present tense

Teacher Preparation and Materials
Blank index cards *(Expansion/Extension)*

Warm-up
Ask *Wh-* questions about personal information. FOR EXAMPLE: *Where are you from? What language does Ivan speak? Who speaks Spanish? When do we have class? How do you get to class? Why do you study English?* Have learners respond with the appropriate information.

Presentation
1. Have learners turn to page 62 and find the question words in the box.
2. If necessary, have learners give examples of answers for each question word. FOR EXAMPLE: *Where* (at school, in New York, in apartment 1A); *When* (8:00, tomorrow, after class); and so on.
3. Together, read the examples of questions and answers.
4. Explain question formation. The question words *what, where, when, why,* and *how* use the same formation as *Yes/No* questions. The question word *who* does not usually require *do* or *does*. Avoid complex explanations.
5. Learners can read the questions and match them to the answers.
6. Have learners make up their own questions for the pictures on the bottom of the page.

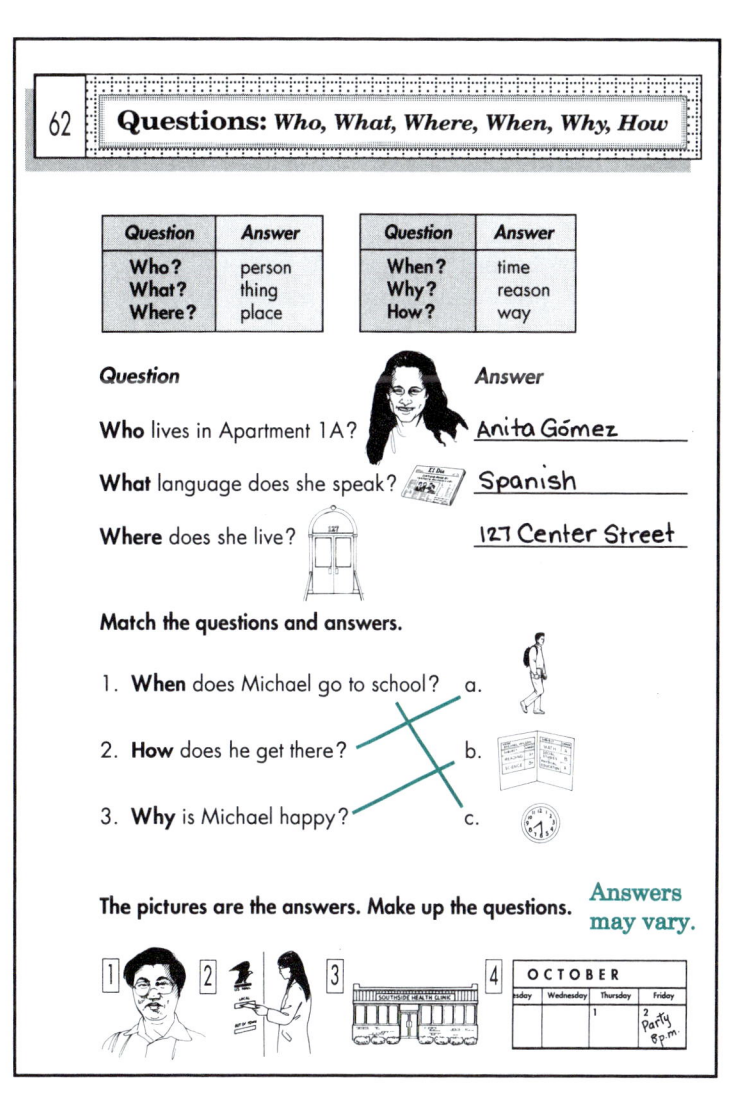

Expansion/Extension
- Learners can write additional questions for the question words based on the pictures on page 62. (FOR EXAMPLE: *Where does he go to school? What is his name? What time is it? What does he take to school?*)
- Learners can write the questions on a set of index cards and the answers on another set. They can match the questions and answers. They can also play Concentration.
- Learners can write *Wh-* questions for the pictures on the first page of each unit.

Verbs: Present and Present Continuous

Purpose: To give practice with the present tense and the present continuous tense

Teacher Preparation and Materials
Pictures of actions: work, study, read, watch (TV), talk, and so on

Warm-up
1. Give oral examples comparing the present and present continuous tenses. Show pictures to illustrate. FOR EXAMPLE: *Every day I work. At night I study a little and I watch TV. But right now, I'm talking. Every day my friend reads. She works at night. But right now, she's watching TV.*

2. Using picture cues, have learners create sentences about their usual activities. Ask *What do you do every day?* (I work. I study.)

3. Using picture cues, have learners create sentences about what they are doing right now. Ask *What are you doing now?* (I am talking. I am studying.)

Presentation
1. Have learners turn to page 63 and look at the "Present" chart. Ask *Which words (pronouns) use* work? *Which words (pronouns) use* works?

2. Have learners look the "Present Continuous" chart. Point out that there are two parts to the verb: *am, is, are,* and another word (verb) with *-ing.* Ask *Which words (pronouns) use* is working? and so on. **(Note:** Learners need to recognize that the present tense is made up of one word, and the present continuous is made up of two words, the verb *be* and another verb with *-ing.* Learners do not need to master when the tenses are used. They should recognize that a question in the present tense is usually answered in the present tense and a question in the present continuous tense is usually answered in the present continuous tense.)

3. Learners do not need to learn all the rules about adding *-ing* to verbs (*plan: planning; dance: dancing;* and so on).

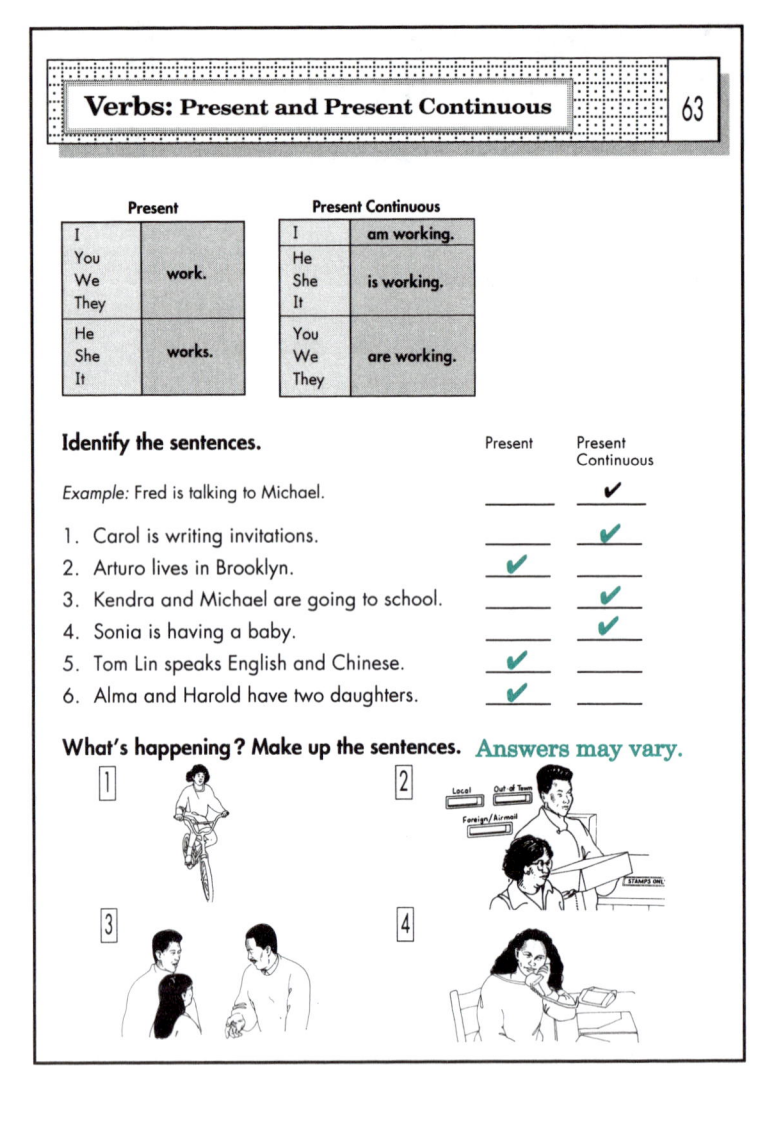

4. Have learners identify the tenses used in the first exercise. If necessary, have learners underline the verb(s) in each of the sentences before checking the correct tense.

5. Together, read the question at the bottom of the page. Have learners decide if sentences should be in the present tense or present continuous tense. Have learners make up sentences about each picture, using the present continuous tense.

Expansion/Extension
- Learners can write *Yes/No* questions in the present and present continuous tenses for the sentences. FOR EXAMPLE: *Carol is writing invitations.* (Is Carol writing invitations?) *Arturo lives in Brooklyn.* (Does Arturo live in Brooklyn?)

- Learners can write the negative forms for each of the sentences. FOR EXAMPLE: *Carol is writing invitations.* (Carol is not/isn't writing invitations.) *Arturo lives in Brooklyn.* (Arturo does not/doesn't live in Brooklyn.)

Possessives

Purpose: To give practice with possessive adjectives

Teacher Preparation and Materials
None

Warm-up
1. Ask questions about personal information. Have learners respond using appropriate possessive adjectives. FOR EXAMPLE: *What's your name?* (My name is Bernard Santos.) *Do you have a wife? What's her name?* (Her name is Florien.)
2. Model sentences about addresses. FOR EXAMPLE: *Theresa lives at 31 Park Street. Her address is . . . . Olga and Anton live at 102 Main Street. Their address is . . . .* Give other sentences about people in the group. Have learners respond by substituting the appropriate possessive adjectives for the names in the sentences.

Presentation
1. Have learners turn to page 64 and find the "Possessives" chart.
2. Together, read the sentences about the Lin family. Point out the possessive adjectives used and the possessive nouns to which they refer. If necessary, do other examples with objects in the room. FOR EXAMPLE: *This is Nina's book. This is her book. These are Manuel's and Tomas's chairs. These are their chairs.*
3. Have learners match the phrases in the first exercise.
4. Have learners look at the picture and identify the characters. If necessary, ask questions about the relationships.
5. Together, read the conversation in the second exercise. Have learners fill in the appropriate possessives.

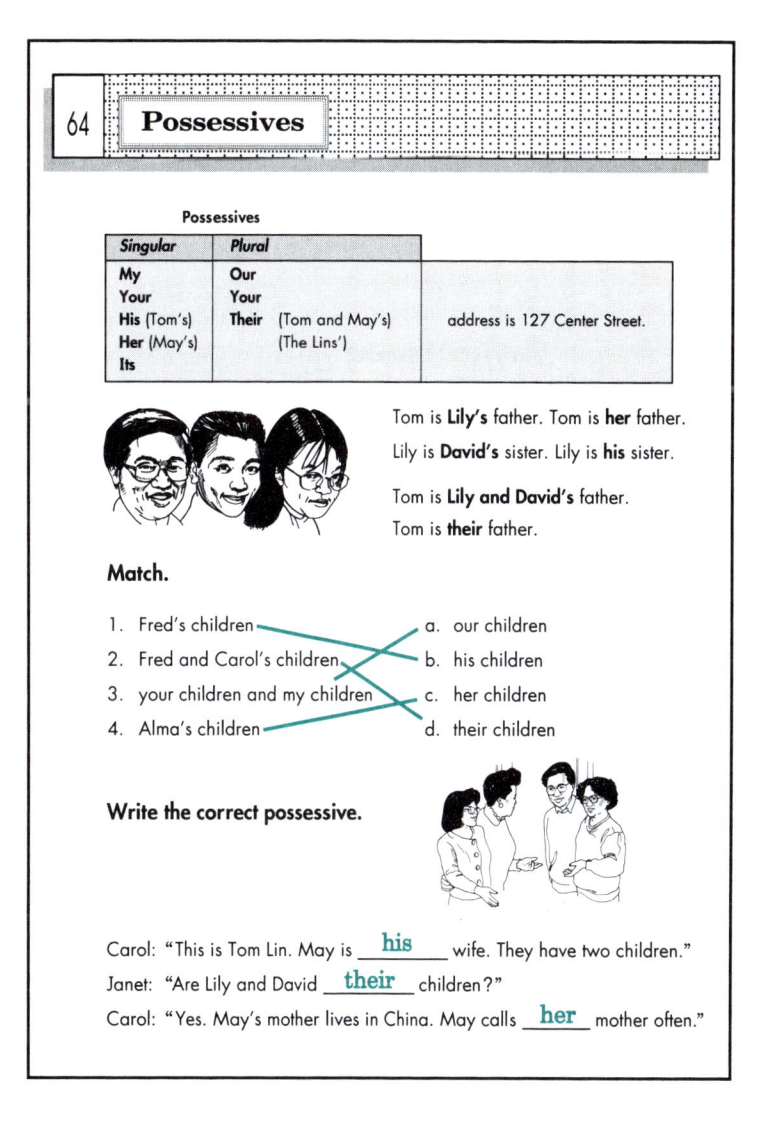

Expansion/Extension
- Learners can write questions and answers using the phrases from the first exercise. (FOR EXAMPLE: Who are Fred's children? His children are Kendra and Michael. Who are Fred and Carol's children? Their children are . . . .)
- Learners can write additional sentences about the Lin and Wilson families. (FOR EXAMPLE: This is May Lin. Tom Lin is . . . husband. Lily and David are . . . children. These children are Lily and David Lin. Tom Lin is . . . father. May Lin is . . . mother.)
- Learners can talk about or write about their own families, using possessive adjectives.

1 2 3 4 5 6 7 8 9 10 11 12 Summary
What Did You Do Before?

Objectives

Functions
- Expressing abilities, skills, responsibilities
- Expressing wants and needs
- Expressing likes and dislikes
- Asking for and giving information

Life Tasks
- Reading job ads
- Filling out forms
- Identifying job preferences
- Finding employment
- Accessing community resources for job information

Structures
- *Wh-* questions with *do/does*
- Past tense: regular verbs
- Past tense: verb *be*
- W*ould* + *like*
- Adverbs of time

Culture
- Work in native country compared to work in the United States
- Finding employment
- Convention for presentation of dates

Vocabulary

Key words:

assembly worker	manager
bank teller	nurse's aide
cashier	owner
electrician	receptionist
factory	student
farmer	superintendent
maintenance worker	work

Related words:

a.m.	hours
benefits	indoor
college	job title
company	jr. high school
country of origin	night
date of birth	outdoor
day	part-time
elementary school	p.m.
employer	salary
full-time	shift
graduate school	Social Security Number
high school	U.S. citizen
hourly	weekly

Looking for Work

Purpose: To introduce names of jobs and professions

Teacher Preparation and Materials

1. Pictures of workplaces: store, restaurant, factory, hospital, hotel, gas station, bank
2. Pictures of jobs: bank teller, maintenance worker, nurse's aide, receptionist, assembly worker, cashier
3. Audiotape for Level 1
4. Magazines with pictures of workplaces and jobs, posterboard, scissors, and glue for all *(Expansion/Extension)*
5. Index cards with sight words: *bank teller, maintenance worker, nurse's aide, receptionist, assembly worker, cashier (Expansion/Extension)*
6. Copies of TRF Handout 7.1, *People at Work (Expansion/Extension)*

Warm-up

1. Use picture cues to practice workplace names. Include *hospital, restaurant, store, bank*, and *factory*.
2. Tape pictures of jobs on the board: *bank teller, maintenance worker, nurse's aide, receptionist, assembly worker, cashier*. Number the pictures. Then show the picture of the hospital. Ask *Who works at a hospital?* Have learners point to or identify the job by number. Repeat with pictures of other workplaces.
3. Introduce and practice the names of the jobs. Point to the job pictures and say *He's/She's a cashier; He's/She's an assembly worker* and so on. Have learners repeat.
4. Ask questions about the pictures on the board. FOR EXAMPLE: *Who works in a bank?* (bank teller, cashier) *Where does a nurse's aide work?* (hospital)
5. Write the names of the occupations under the pictures.

Presentation

1. Have learners look at the picture on page 65. Prompt discussion by asking questions such as *Who do you see? Where are they?*
2. Ask learners to point to specific things and words in the picture. FOR EXAMPLE: *board, ads, nurse's aide*. List the words on the board. Be sure to include the occupations *bank teller, maintenance worker, nurse's aid, receptionist, assembly worker,* and *cashier*.
3. Have learners say what they know about Carol. Ask *Where does she live? Who is in her family?* Then, have them speculate about Rita. *Who is she? Where do you think she is from?*
4. Play the audiotape. Ask questions about the story. *What are Carol and Rita looking for? What does Carol want to do? be? What does Rita want to do?*
5. Replay the audiotape to verify comprehension.
6. Have learners answer the question *What's happening?* at the bottom of page 65. Depending on learners' skills, they can write the answers in their books.

Expansion/Extension

See TRF HANDOUT 7.1, *People at Work*

More *Expansion/Extension* on page 120

UNIT 7 • 109

Different Jobs

Purpose: To give practice with jobs and professions; to give practice with *Wh-* questions with *do/does*

Teacher Preparation and Materials

1. Number cards: 10, 20, 30, 40, 50, 60, 70, 80, 90, 100, 200, 300, 400, 500
2. Clock with movable hands (optional)
3. Pictures of jobs used for page 65
4. Sight-word cards used for page 65 (*Warm-up* and *Expansion/Extension*)
5. Pictures of workplaces used for page 65; new pictures: department store, clinic, supermarket, office setting
6. Index cards with sight words: *store, restaurant, factory, hospital, hotel, gas station, bank, department store, clinic, supermarket, office*
7. Help Wanted ads from newspapers (*Expansion/Extension*)

Warm-up

1. Use number cards to give practice in reading numbers.
2. Review money vocabulary. Say sentences using various amounts and have volunteers write the correct amounts.
   FOR EXAMPLE: *The pay is $6.25 an hour.* Repeat the procedure with larger amounts.
3. Give practice with time vocabulary by saying sentences about time and having learners write the times in numbers. If necessary, use a clock with movable hands to illustrate.
4. Have volunteers match pictures of jobs with job titles written on sight-word cards. Then have volunteers match pictures of workplaces with the appropriate place names.
5. On the board, write *benefits*. Explain various benefits and then list them on the board: *health plan* (pays the doctor or hospital), *dental plan* (pays the dentist), and *paid vacations* (pays for time you take off from work).

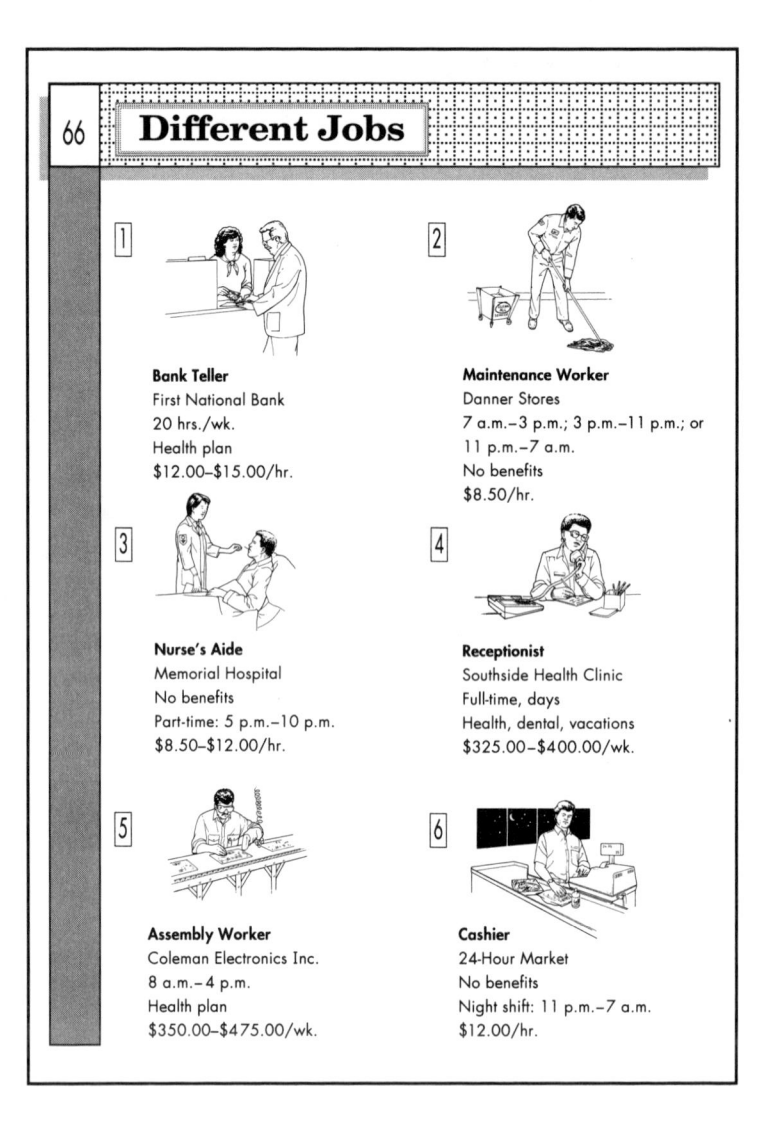

---

66 Different Jobs

1 Bank Teller
First National Bank
20 hrs./wk.
Health plan
$12.00–$15.00/hr.

2 Maintenance Worker
Danner Stores
7 a.m.–3 p.m.; 3 p.m.–11 p.m.; or 11 p.m.–7 a.m.
No benefits
$8.50/hr.

3 Nurse's Aide
Memorial Hospital
No benefits
Part-time: 5 p.m.–10 p.m.
$8.50–$12.00/hr.

4 Receptionist
Southside Health Clinic
Full-time, days
Health, dental, vacations
$325.00–$400.00/wk.

5 Assembly Worker
Coleman Electronics Inc.
8 a.m.–4 p.m.
Health plan
$350.00–$475.00/wk.

6 Cashier
24-Hour Market
No benefits
Night shift: 11 p.m.–7 a.m.
$12.00/hr.

Presentation

1. Have learners turn to page 66 and look at picture 1. Ask *What job is this about?* (bank teller) *Where is the job?* (bank)
2. On the board, write the first job listing. Read it together.
3. Ask *How many hours does the bank teller work? What benefits does the job have? How much is the pay/salary? What does* hr. *mean?*
4. Repeat the procedure for each of the listings but omit writing them on the board. Explain *day shift* and *night shift* by drawing a sun and listing day-shift hours below (7 a.m.–3 p.m.) and a moon with night-shift hours below (11 p.m.–7 a.m.). If necessary, explain *full-time* and *part-time*.
5. Ask a volunteer to go to the board and follow directions as you give them. Say *Circle the job title in listing 1. Put a check next to the name of the company. Underline the salary. Put an X next to the benefits. Draw a box around the hours.* If necessary, model the first one.
6. Have learners follow the directions with the other job listings in their books.

***Expansion/Extension* on page 120**

Comparing Jobs

Purpose: To give practice in reading job listings; to give practice with *Wh-* questions with *do/does*

Teacher Preparation and Materials

1. Index cards with sight words: *job title, employer, salary, hours, benefits, weekly, hourly, full-time, part-time*
2. Strips of paper, marker
3. Help Wanted ads from newspapers *(Expansion/Extension)*

Warm-up

1. Review *a.m.* and *p.m.* Ask learners questions about what they do in the morning, in the afternoon or evening, and at night. FOR EXAMPLE: *When do you come to class? When do you eat dinner?* Write their responses on the board and label them *a.m.* or *p.m.* as appropriate. Ask questions about other activities. FOR EXAMPLE: *Do you get up at 6 a.m. or 6 p.m.?*
2. Point to the picture of the cashier on page 66. Ask *What job is this? Where does he work?* Then make up a story. FOR EXAMPLE: *This is Marcel. He's a cashier. He works at 24-Hour Market. He works at night from 11 p.m. to 7 a.m. His salary is $9 per hour. There are no benefits.* Write the story on the board.
3. Show the *job title* sight-word card and ask *What's his job?* Have a learner come to the board and tape the card next to the word *cashier*. Repeat the procedure for the other sight-word cards.

Presentation

1. On strips of paper, write the different parts of the first job listing on page 66: *Bank Teller, First National Bank, 20 hrs., Health plan, $12.00–$15.00/hr.* Tape them in random order on a wall.
2. On the board, write the following as column headings for a chart: *Job Title, Employer, Salary, Hours, Benefits.* Have volunteers tape the strips of paper in the proper columns.
3. Ask *Is the salary weekly or hourly? Are the hours full-time or part-time?* Add the

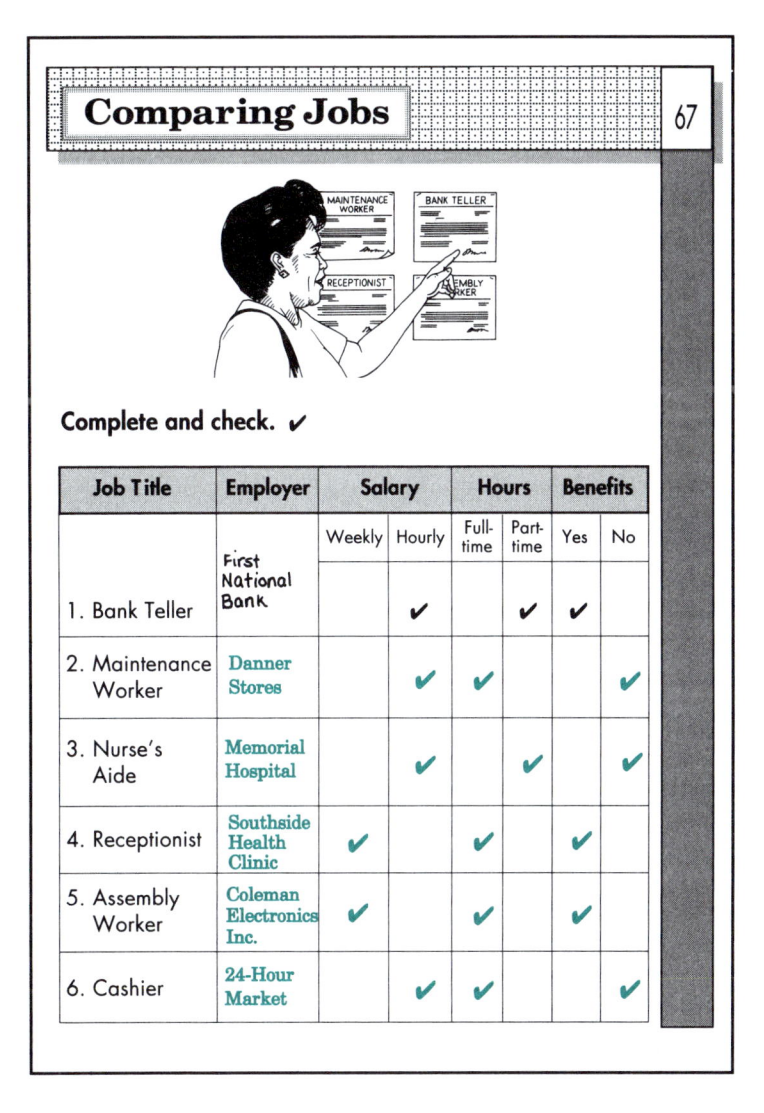

Comparing Jobs

Complete and check. ✓

Job Title	Employer	Salary		Hours		Benefits	
		Weekly	Hourly	Full-time	Part-time	Yes	No
1. Bank Teller	First National Bank		✓	✓		✓	
2. Maintenance Worker	Danner Stores		✓	✓			✓
3. Nurse's Aide	Memorial Hospital		✓	✓			✓
4. Receptionist	Southside Health Clinic	✓		✓		✓	
5. Assembly Worker	Coleman Electronics Inc.	✓		✓		✓	
6. Cashier	24-Hour Market		✓	✓			✓

words *weekly, hourly, full, part, yes, no* under the column headings as follows:

Job Title	Employer	Salary		Hours		Benefits	
		Weekly	Hourly	Full	Part	Yes	No

Have a volunteer come to the board and check the correct column for *salary, hours,* and *benefits.*

4. Have learners look at the chart on page 67. Together, read the information on the first job listing. Ask *What's the job title?* (bank teller)
5. Have learners look on page 66 for the information on the second job. Ask specific questions.
6. Individually or in pairs, have learners complete the chart using the information from the listings on page 66.

Expansion/Extension

- Summarize the chart. Ask *Which jobs are full-time? Which jobs have benefits? Which have weekly salaries?*

More *Expansion/Extension* on page 120

In Line

Purpose: To give practice in filling out forms; to introduce job-related sight words

Teacher Preparation and Materials

1. Index cards with sight words: *Full Name, Address, Telephone Number, Date, Date of Birth, Signature, U.S. Citizen, Social Security Number, Country of Origin, Elementary School, Jr. High School, High School, College, Graduate School*
2. Class calendar showing birthdates (see TRF Handout 2.4, *Class Calendar*)
3. Samples of Alien Registration cards and Social Security cards
4. Pictures of five school buildings
5. Local telephone book and/or yellow pages *(Expansion/Extension)*

Warm-up

1. Ask personal information questions and use sight-word cards to cue responses. *What's your address? What's your phone number?*
2. Use the class calendar to practice birthdays. Ask *When is Ming's birthday?* and so on.
3. Ask *What's your date of birth or birthdate?* Show the sight-word card *Date of Birth*.
4. Show samples of Social Security cards. Ask *Do you have this card? Why is it important? What is the number on it?* Use the sight-word card to cue responses to the following question: *What is your Social Security Number?* (**Note:** Some learners may also have Alien Registration cards. Discuss legal issues only if learners ask about them.)
5. Introduce *U.S. Citizen* using a sight-word card. Ask *What does U.S. mean? Are you a U.S. citizen?*
6. Tape pictures of five school buildings on the board. Write ages under the buildings as follows: *5–12 years old, 12–15 years old, 15–18 years old, 18–22 years old, 22 years old–...* Say the names of the various schools: *elementary, jr. high, high school, college, graduate school*. Ask learners how old their children are and the names of their schools. Write the types of schools over the pictures.
7. Ask *Did you go to school in your country? Did you finish high school?* (**Note:** Help learners determine the U.S. equivalent of their educational background.)

Presentation

1. Have learners turn to page 68 and look at the picture. Ask *Who do you see? Where are they? Why is Rita in this line and Carol in the other line? What is Carol's last name? Why are they at the employment office?*
2. Have learners find sight words on the form. Ask *What is Rita's address? What is her native country? What level of school did she finish?*
3. Point out the differences in Rita's full name, her signed name, and the name her friends use.
4. Ask additional questions. FOR EXAMPLE: *Why is Rita filling out the form?*

Expansion/Extension

See **TRF HANDOUT 2.4**, *Class Calendar*

More *Expansion/Extension* on page 120

112 • UNIT 7

Filling Out Forms

Purpose: To give practice in filling out forms

Teacher Preparation and Materials
1. Index cards with sight words used for page 68
2. Blank and varied sample forms, such as job applications *(Expansion/Extension)*
3. Copies of TRF Handout 7.4, *Personal Data Sheet (Expansion/Extension)*

Warm-up
1. Give practice in giving personal information by asking questions using the sight-word cards: *What's your name? What's your Social Security Number?*
2. Give practice in asking and answering questions about schooling. *Did you go to school in your native country? Did you finish elementary school? Did you finish high school?*
3. On the board, make three signs: *A–H, I–P,* and *Q–Z.* Ask learners *Which line would you go to?* Learners can write their last names under the correct sign.

Presentation
1. Have learners write their last names under the correct sign at the top of the page.
2. Draw a blank form (similar to the one on page 69) on the board or on a large piece of paper.
3. Tape sight-word cards on the board.
4. Ask personal information questions such as *What's your address? What's your phone number? Where are you from?* Have volunteers go to the board and point to the sight word(s) related to each question and fill in the information on the form on the board.
5. In pairs, have learners practice asking and answering questions based on the form.
6. Have learners fill in the form on page 69 with their personal information.

Expansion/Extension
See TRF HANDOUT 7.4, *Personal Data Sheet*

- In small groups, learners can practice reading sight words and giving information. Shuffle the sight-word cards and put them in a pile upside down on the table. Learners take turns drawing a card, reading the sight word, showing it to the others in the group, and then giving the appropriate personal information.
- Compare educational systems in the United States and learners' native countries: types of schools, cost, who attends, and so on.
- Discuss other types of schools and educational programs in the United States, such as technical schools and vocational schools.
- Bring in samples of forms that require educational background information such as job applications and school applications. Compare the different formats and the responses required. Learners can practice finding the sight words and filling in the appropriate information.
- Make signs on the board: *A–H, I–P,* and *Q–Z.* After learners have completed TRF Handout 7.4, they can place the forms under the correct sign.

Filling Out Forms 69

| A–H | I–P | Q–Z |

Fill in the form. Use your name.   Answers will vary.

Department of Employment and Training

Full Name: _____   Date of Birth: _____
Address: _____

Telephone Number: _____

U.S. Citizen: Yes ____ No ____
Country of Origin: _____
Social Security Number: _____

Check Highest Grade Completed:
____ Elementary   ____ Jr. High School   ____ High School
____ College   ____ Graduate School   ____ Other _____

Date: _____   Signature: _____

Getting Advice

Purpose: To introduce giving information about work experience and educational background

Teacher Preparation and Materials
1. 📼 Audiotape for Level 1
2. Blank index cards *(Expansion/Extension)*

Warm-up
1. Introduce the past tense of regular verbs by making the following chart on the board:

Daniel	When?	Where?
finish high school	1985	Haiti
work in a factory	1986–1989	Haiti
learn English	1993	Lane School

   Model past-tense statements by pointing to the appropriate parts of the chart and saying *Daniel finished high school in 1985. He finished high school in Haiti. He worked in a factory from 1986 to 1989. He didn't work in 1985.* Have learners form statements based on the chart.

2. Give practice with *Yes/No* questions in the past tense using the chart. Model questions and answers and have learners repeat. *Did Daniel work in a hospital?* (No, he didn't.) *Did he work in a factory?* (Yes, he did.) Have learners form *Yes/No* questions based on the chart.

3. Model *Wh-* questions and answers in the past tense while pointing to appropriate parts of the chart. Have learners repeat. *When did Daniel work in a factory?* (He worked from 1986 to 1989.) *Where did he learn English?* (He learned it at the Lane School.) Finally, have learners work in pairs asking and answering *Wh-* questions based on the chart.

4. Give practice in giving and getting information about work experience and educational background. First model with a volunteer. *Did you work in your native country?* (Yes, I did/No, I didn't.) Continue in a chain drill. Give practice with other questions. FOR EXAMPLE: *Did you like your work? Did you finish high school/elementary school? Did you study English?*

Presentation
1. Have learners turn to page 70 and look at the picture. Ask *Who do you see? Where are they?* Introduce *employment counselor.* Talk about what employment counselors do.
2. Ask *What are they talking about? Why are they talking? What questions will he ask Rita?* List learners' ideas on the board.
3. 📼 Play the audiotape. Ask questions like *What kind of work did Rita do before? Was it noisy and hot?*
4. 📼 If necessary, replay the audiotape so learners can listen for answers.
5. Together, read the questions on page 70.
6. Have learners underline or circle the correct response individually.

Expansion/Extension
- Learners can write Rita's story using the past tense.
  📼 Learners may want to listen to the audiotape again.

More *Expansion/Extension* on page 120

114 • UNIT 7

What Did They Do?

Purpose: To introduce past tense of verb *be;* to give practice in talking about work experience

Teacher Preparation and Materials

1. Pictures of jobs used for page 65; new pictures: farmer, factory worker, student, and other jobs learners might have had in their native countries
2. Copies of TRF Handout 7.2, *Occupations and Tools (Expansion/Extension)*
3. Copies of TRF Handout 7.6, *Interview (Expansion/Extension)*
4. Magazines with pictures of jobs, posterboard, scissors, and glue for all *(Expansion/Extension)*
5. Invite a job developer or counselor to speak to the class. *(Expansion/Extension)*

Warm-up

1. Use picture cues to review names of jobs. Use pictures to introduce vocabulary for other jobs. Be sure to include *farmer, student, factory worker,* and jobs that learners had in their native countries.
2. Make a chart on the board with a column for learners' names and one for their former jobs. Ask learners to draw pictures that show jobs they had in their native countries. Have each learner hold up the picture and say the name of the job. Fill in the job name in the chart next to the learner's name.
3. Model asking and answering questions about work experience using the chart. *What did Eva do in her native country?* (She was a bus driver.) Then have a volunteer model with you about his or her work experience. *What did you do in your native country?* (I was a farmer.) Continue in a chain drill.
4. Use the chart to give learners practice making affirmative statements using the past tense. (FOR EXAMPLE: Roger was a mechanic. Gina was a teacher.) Follow with practice forming questions and answers. (Was Roger a farmer in his country? Yes, he was. No, he wasn't.)

What Did They Do? 71

1. Tom was a farmer.

2. Anita was a student.

3. Rita was a factory worker.

What did you do in your native country? **Answers will vary.**

I was a _____.

Presentation

1. Have learners turn to page 71 and look at the pictures. Ask questions like *What do you see in picture 1? Where is Tom? What is he doing?*
2. Together, read the sentences. Ask *Who was a student? What did Tom do in China?* and so on.
3. Together, read the question at the bottom of the page. Have learners answer orally and then fill in their answers. Learners can draw pictures for their answers. (**Note**: Some learners may have worked in several countries before coming to the United States. Give them an opportunity to describe their complete work experience.)

Expansion/Extension
See TRF HANDOUT 7.2, *Occupations and Tools*
TRF HANDOUT 7.6, *Interview*

- Learners can talk about other aspects of the characters' (and/or their own) work experience. Depending on learners' skills, they can write sentences or phrases describing their work experience.

More *Expansion/Extension* on page 121

UNIT 7 • 115

Making Choices

Purpose: To introduce *would* + *like* and adverbs of time; to give practice in expressing likes/dislikes

Teacher Preparation and Materials

1. Pictures of jobs: indoor and outdoor occupations; pictures of workplaces: indoor and outdoor locations
2. Index cards with sight words: *night, day, full-time, part-time, outdoors, indoors*
3. 📼 Audiotape for Level 1
4. Pictures of activities associated with jobs: cooking, driving, typing, and so on *(Expansion/Extension)*
5. Copies of TRF Handout 7.5, *My Experience (Expansion/Extension)*
6. Copies of TRF Handout 7.3, *My Skills (Expansion/Extension)*
7. Magazines with pictures of people and various activities *(Expansion/Extension)*

Warm-up

1. Use picture cues to review names of jobs and workplaces.
2. Review sight-word vocabulary by writing the words *night, day, full-time,* and *part-time* on the board, in chart form.
3. Introduce the words *outdoors* and *indoors* with pictures. Ask *Is this indoors or outdoors?* Write the words on the board.
4. Classify your work. *I am a teacher. I work full-/part-time, days/nights, indoors.* Have learners say what they do (or did) and where they work(ed). Have volunteers write other jobs under the correct columns on the board.
5. Begin a chain drill about languages. FOR EXAMPLE: *What language(s) do you speak? I speak . . . .* Begin another chain drill using the third person. FOR EXAMPLE: *What languages does Carlos speak? He speaks . . . and . . . .*
6. Draw a weekly calendar on the board. Ask *What days do we have class this week?* and circle the days as learners say them. As you point to the days say *Some days we have class.* Ask a volunteer *What days do you work?* Ask learners *Do we have class every day or sometimes?*

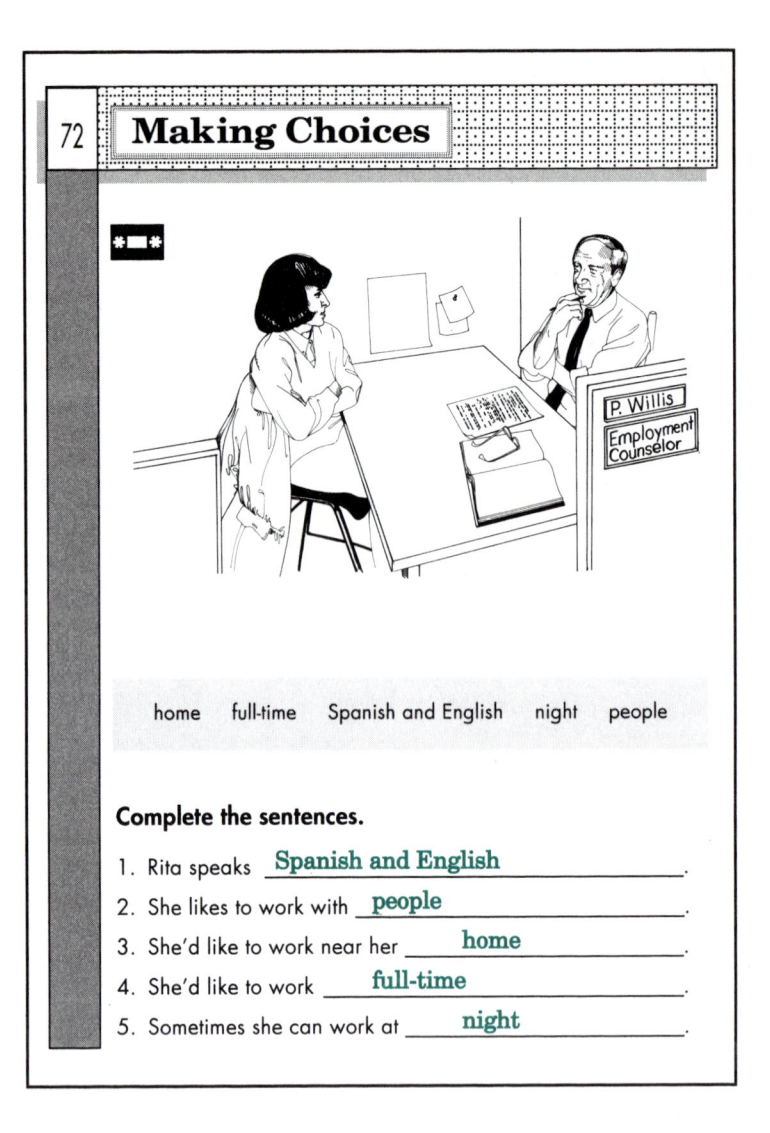

---

72 | Making Choices

home   full-time   Spanish and English   night   people

Complete the sentences.

1. Rita speaks __Spanish and English__.
2. She likes to work with __people__.
3. She'd like to work near her __home__.
4. She'd like to work __full-time__.
5. Sometimes she can work at __night__.

Presentation

1. Have learners turn to page 72 and identify the characters in the picture. Ask *Who do you see? What questions do you think Mr. Willis asked Rita?*
2. Have learners think of questions Mr. Willis might ask to find out about Rita's job needs. Use the sight-word cards to help learners form questions. (FOR EXAMPLE: *Does she need to work part-time?*) Write the questions on the board.
3. 📼 Play the audiotape. Ask *What languages does Rita speak? Where does she want to work? Does she want to work full-time or part-time? Can she work at night? Where is there a job?*
4. 📼 If necessary, replay the audiotape.
5. Together, look at the questions that were listed on the board and identify those that were asked in the conversation.
6. Together, read the exercise. 📼 Then, replay the audiotape. Have learners fill in the responses individually.

***Expansion/Extension* on page 121**

116 • UNIT 7

Your Choice

Purpose: To give practice with *would + like;* to give practice in expressing likes/dislikes

Teacher Preparation and Materials
1. Sight-word cards used for page 72
2. Blank index cards *(Expansion/Extension)*

Warm-up
Review vocabulary words by holding up the sight-word cards and asking learners for examples of jobs or shifts for each of the words. FOR EXAMPLE: *part-time*—9:00 to 1:00; *outdoor*—farmer.

Presentation
1. Tape sight-word cards on the board or wall in three groups and pronounce them with the term *work* as you point to them: *full-time work, part-time work; outdoor work, indoor work; day work, night work.* Say *What kind of work would you like: full-time work or part-time work?* Have learners repeat. Ask the question and have learners give their preferences. Repeat the procedure for the other sets of choices.
2. Ask *What kind of work would you like?* Model the answer by pointing to appropriate sight-word cards as you say *I'd like full-time work. I wouldn't like part-time work.* Have learners work in pairs forming sentences about their work preferences using the affirmative and negative forms.
3. Make a chart on the board similar to the one on page 73. Together, read the vocabulary words. Then, read the question and column headings. Ask a volunteer if he or she would like full-time work. Have him or her go to the board and record the response in the proper column. Repeat the procedure with the other vocabulary words.
4. Ask more advanced learners to explain their answers. (FOR EXAMPLE: *I'd like outdoor work. Why? Because I like to work in the sun. I wouldn't like full-time work. Why? Because I have children to take care of after school.*)
5. Have learners turn to page 73 and individually complete the chart. As a group, summarize the results on the board.

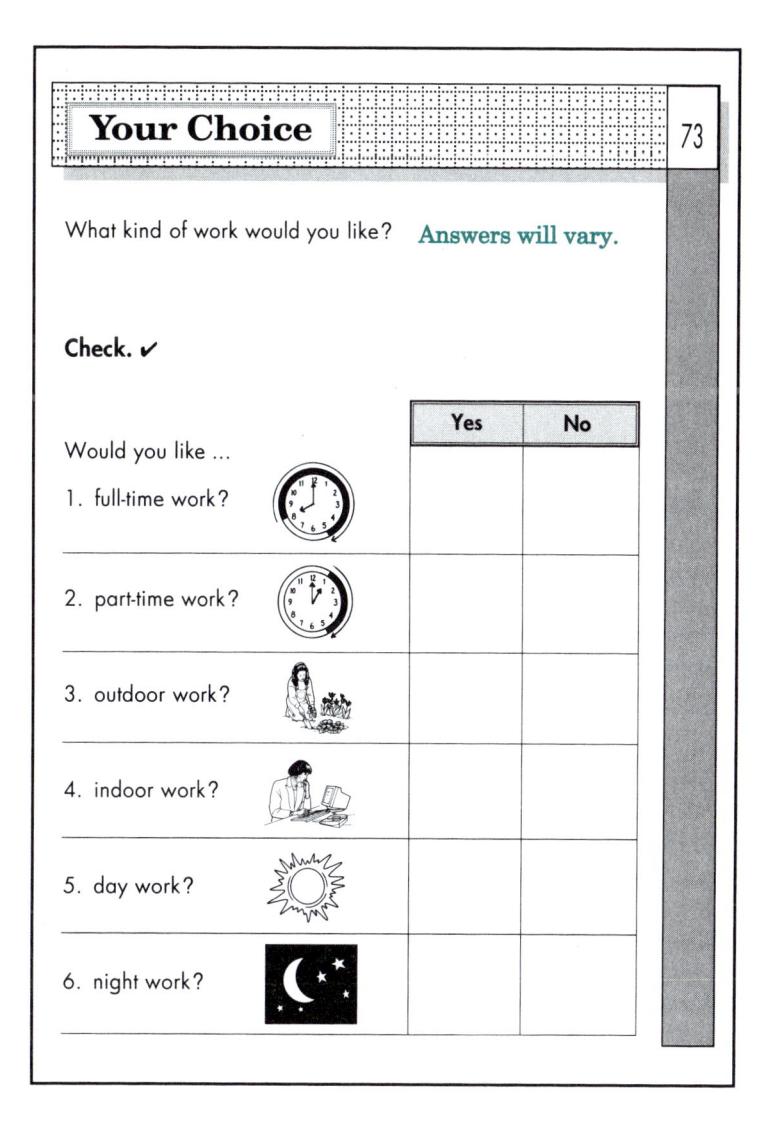

Your Choice 73

What kind of work would you like?   **Answers will vary.**

Check. ✔

Would you like ...

		Yes	No
1. full-time work?			
2. part-time work?			
3. outdoor work?			
4. indoor work?			
5. day work?			
6. night work?			

FOR EXAMPLE: *How many would like full-time work? How many would like part-time work?* (Ten people would like full-time work. Two would like part-time work.)

Expansion/Extension
- Have learners think of other categories, such as jobs working with food, with machines, with children, with cars, with computers, with numbers, with plants, with animals, with people who speak . . ., in a large company, or in a small business. Make a chart and have learners interview each other or people they know about their job preferences and then share the findings with the group.
- Learners can list jobs that go with each type of category. (FOR EXAMPLE: *nights*—factory workers, maintenance workers, waiters)
- Write the job categories on index cards. Learners can sort them according to what they would like and what they would not like. Learners can make up a sentence for each card.

More *Expansion/Extension* on page 121

UNIT 7 • 117

Your Past, Present, and Future

Purpose: To give practice in conveying information about past work; to give practice in expressing likes/dislikes

Teacher Preparation and Materials

1. Pictures of jobs used for page 71; new pictures: store manager, store owner, electrician, building superintendent, and other jobs learners might have or want to have
2. Sight-word cards of job titles used for pages 65 and 66; new cards: *farmer, student, store manager, store owner, electrician, superintendent*
3. Copies of TRF Handout 7.7, *Role Play: Interview (Expansion/Extension)*

Warm-up

1. Use picture cues to introduce new jobs: *store manager, store owner, electrician, superintendent.*
2. Tape sight-word cards with job titles on the board or wall. Ask questions about the jobs and have learners give the title. FOR EXAMPLE: *Who works in a factory?* (factory worker)
3. Introduce *I used to be . . . .* by modeling the sentences *I was a cashier. I used to be a cashier.* On the board, write *used to be = was*. Learners can practice talking about past work experience using *used to be* in a chain drill. FOR EXAMPLE: *What did you do in your country?* (I used to be a bus driver.)
4. In a chain drill, practice using the third-person singular. Have the first learner talk about his or her past and present jobs. The second learner talks about the first learner and then his or her own past and present jobs. (FOR EXAMPLE: Learner 1 says "I used to be a bus driver. Now I'm a factory worker." Learner 2 says "Tuan used to be a bus driver. Now he's a factory worker. I used to be a student. Now I'm not working.")

Presentation

1. Draw a chart on the board similar to the one on page 74. Fill in Carol Wilson's name. Ask about her past and present

---

74 | Your Past, Present, and Future

Interview. *Answers will vary.*

Name	I was ...	Now I am ...	I'd like to be ...
1. Carol Wilson	a cashier.	not working.	a bank teller.
2. Tom Lin	a farmer.	a store manager.	a store owner.
3. Anita Gómez	a student.	a superintendent.	an electrician.
4.			
5.			
6.			
7.			

---

work situation and fill in the chart. Then ask what she would like to be and fill in that information. Learners can look back at page 65 for the answer.

2. Have learners turn to page 74. Together, read about Tom Lin and Anita Gómez. Ask *What was Tom's job in his country? What does he do now?* and so on.
3. Demonstrate interviewing a learner and filling in the chart. Ask *What did you do in your native country? What do you do now? What would you like to do?*
4. Have a volunteer interview you or another learner and record the information on the board.
5. Have learners interview four other learners and fill in the chart. ■ In a one-to-one situation, have the learner interview friends or neighbors.
6. Have learners report their findings to the group using the third person. (FOR EXAMPLE: *Tuan used to be a fisherman. Now he's a factory worker. He'd like to be a machinist.*)

Expansion/Extension
See TRF HANDOUT 7.7, *Role Play: Interview*

More *Expansion/Extension* on page 121

118 • UNIT 7

Look Back

Purpose: To give practice in reading job titles

Teacher Preparation and Materials
1. Pictures of jobs used for page 74
2. Sight-word cards of job titles used for page 74
3. Newspapers with Help Wanted ads (Expansion/Extension)

Warm-up
1. Use picture cues to practice the names of jobs including *assembly worker, cashier, receptionist, maintenance worker, bank teller, nurse's aide.*
2. Hold up the sight-word cards one by one and have learners identify the written job titles.
3. Shuffle the cards. Have a volunteer choose one and act out the job. Have other learners guess the job title. Repeat with other learners acting out jobs.

Presentation
1. Tape the job pictures on the board. Hold up one of the sight-word cards with the name of one of the pictures. Have a volunteer tape it under the appropriate picture. Repeat with the other job titles.
2. Have learners turn to page 75. Have learners individually match the job titles with the appropriate pictures.

Expansion/Extension
- Learners can write the job site and/or job duties under each of the pictures on page 75.
- Learners can find Help Wanted ads in newspapers or some other postings for the jobs listed on page 75.
- Have learners choose one of the jobs listed and explain why they might like it. (FOR EXAMPLE: I'd like to be a bank teller. I'd like to work indoors and I'd like to work with people.)

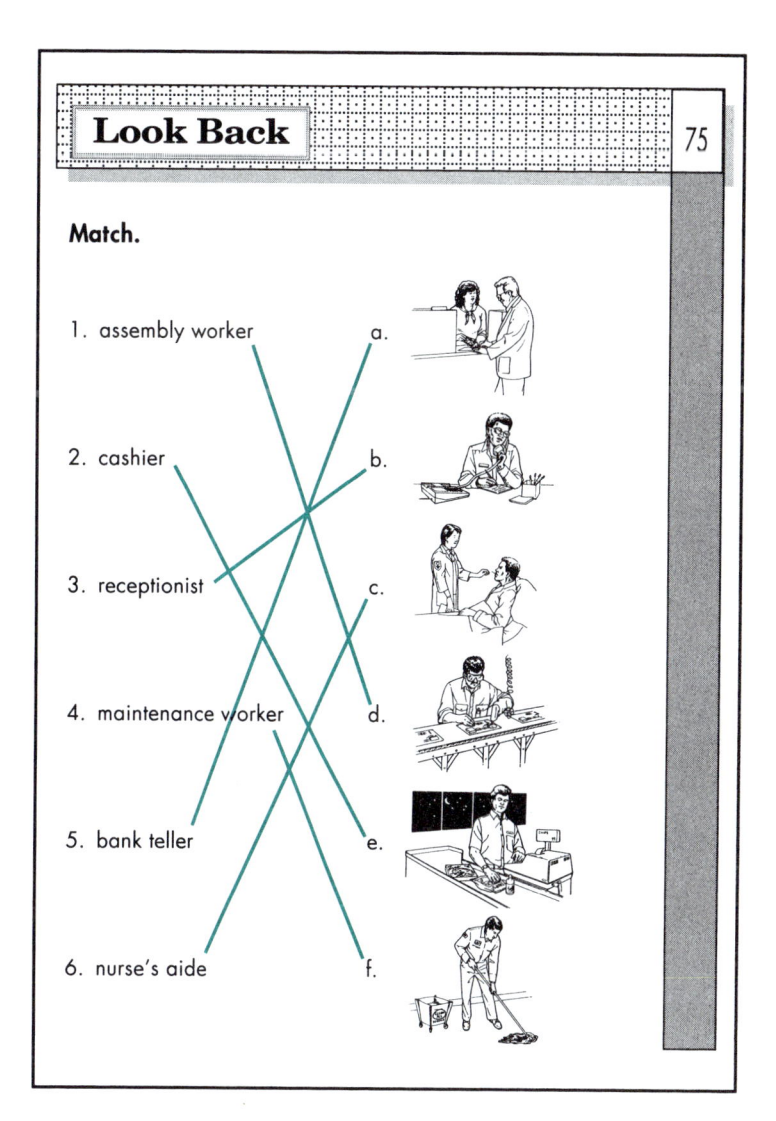

UNIT 7 • 119

UNIT 7:
What Did You Do Before?
Expansion/Extension

Looking for Work
More *Expansion/Extension* for SB page 65

- If learners work, ask them what kind of jobs they have and how they found their jobs. Learners can find pictures of their jobs in magazine illustrations. Help with vocabulary as necessary.
- Use the sight-word cards with names of jobs. Have a learner pick a card and mime the job for others to guess.
- Make a chart or collage of a workplace and the various jobs associated with it. Alternatively, make a collage of a job and the various workplaces associated with it. Learners can draw or cut out magazine pictures of jobs and workplaces, glue them on posterboard, and label the pictures. (FOR EXAMPLE: cook—in a restaurant, in a hospital, in a fast food restaurant.) Learners can write sentences about the collage. (FOR EXAMPLE: A cook can work in a restaurant. A cook can work in a hospital.)

Different Jobs
***Expansion/Extension* for SB page 66**

- Learners can look at Help Wanted ads from newspapers and circle the job titles, check the employer or location, and so on.
- Learners can look for job listings at schools, employment and unemployment offices, supermarkets, libraries, and so on. Learners can copy job titles and company names.
- Take one set of sight-word cards with abbreviations used in job listings and another set of with the whole word and have learners match the cards. Some abbreviations might be *hr., wk., co., a.m., p.m.,* and *dept.* Learners can also play Concentration.
- Learners can practice asking and answering *Yes/No* and *Wh-* questions with *do/does* about the job listings. FOR EXAMPLE: *Does the receptionist get vacations?* (Yes, he/she does.) *Does the bank teller get vacations?* (No, he/she doesn't.) *Where does the bank teller work? When does the cashier work? Does he/she get benefits? What benefits does he/she get?*

Comparing Jobs
More *Expansion/Extension* for SB page 67

- Bring in Help Wanted ads from newspapers. Compare how the jobs are listed. *Are they listed alphabetically? by categories? What categories are there?* (business, medical, professional, general, etc.) *Where would you find the job titles listed on page 67?* Find an ad for each of the job titles listed on page 67.
- Compare the weekly and hourly salaries for the job listings on page 67 by using multiplication and division. Ask *Which job has more pay—the cashier or the receptionist?* and so on.

In Line
More *Expansion/Extension* for SB page 68

- Discuss the differences between a state employment office and an unemployment office. Ask *When do you go to an employment office? When do you go to an unemployment office? How do they help people?* (**Note:** In some states, the employment and unemployment offices are located in the same building. In other areas, they may be at different sites. State employment offices do not charge fees for helping people find jobs.)
- Learners can look in the yellow pages or local phone book for phone numbers and addresses of the employment and unemployment offices. Learners can visit the offices and get information or brochures about the services offered at each.

Getting Advice
More *Expansion/Extension* for SB page 70

- Make a chart of the past tense of regular verbs. Group them according to pronunciation of the endings. FOR EXAMPLE:

/t/	/d/	/id/
finished	lived	needed
worked	learned	visited

Learners can look through the book for other verbs. Pronounce past tense forms and have learners check the appropriate column for each (or write the corresponding number in the appropriate column).

- Learners can write Rita's story using the past tense. Learners may want to listen to the audiotape again.
- Using the form on page 69, learners can write conversations or develop role plays between an employment counselor and a person looking for a job.

- Learners can write about their own work experience and educational background in the past tense.
- Make a matching game using the questions and answers on page 70. Write the questions on one set of index cards. Write the answers on another set. Then have learners match them.

What Did They Do?
More Expansion/Extension for SB page 71

- Some learners may not have had jobs outside the home. Help them describe chores and work around the house that they did or types of craft items they made. Learners can bring in samples of their crafts.
- Learners can make collages of their former jobs using magazine pictures or their own drawings of items, equipment, and activities related to their former jobs. Pictures can be glued to posterboard. Introduce vocabulary and language needed to describe the pictures so learners can label their collages.
- If possible, have a job developer or counselor come and talk about services offered to job seekers. They can also help learners describe their work experience. Learners may need someone from their field to help clarify job titles and duties.

Making Choices
Expansion/Extension for SB page 72
See TRF HANDOUT 7.5, *My Experience*
TRF HANDOUT 7.3, *My Skills*

- Learners can use the sentences on page 72 as a model to write about their job wants and needs. (I speak . . . . I'd like to work in a . . . . I'd like to work . . . . Sometimes I can work at . . . .)
- Partners can role-play an interview with an employment counselor and practice asking and answering questions about their skills and experience.
- Learners can practice talking about goals or dreams using the structure *I'd like to . . . .* or *I wouldn't like to . . . .* Learners can look through magazines for pictures to complete the following types of statements:

    I'd like to go to . . ..   I wouldn't like to go to . . . .
    I'd like to meet . . . .   I wouldn't like to meet . . . .
    I'd like to see . . . .   I wouldn't like to see . . . .

    In pairs or small groups, learners can share their responses.
- Give practice with the modal *can*. Use a picture showing various job activities. Model the question and answer form: *Can you cook?* (Yes, I can./No, I can't.) Learners can practice asking and answering questions about their job skills and abilities.

Your Choice
More Expansion/Extension for SB page 73

- Practice contractions. Learners can find examples and compare them to the full forms. Depending on learners' skills and interest, explain that some auxiliary verbs can be contracted with *not*. (Exceptions: *am, shall, may*; Irregular contractions: *can't, won't*) Some forms of the modals *be, have,* and *will (should/would)* can be contracted with subjects (FOR EXAMPLE: *she's, I've*).

Your Past, Present, and Future
More Expansion/Extension for SB page 74

- Compare the types of jobs learners used to have and have now. Talk about changes in job status. Point out that some people may be doing the same thing they used to do. Others may be doing different things than they used to do. Discuss what learners may need to do in order to make changes in their job status, such as get more training or education, learn new skills, pass certifying exams, talk to others in their fields, take out bank loans. Talk about frustrations involved with taking a lower-level job than you used to have.
- Learners can make lists of things to do to reach their job goals. Learners can share information or check local papers and phone books for organizations to contact. Help learners set realistic time frames for their goals.
- Discuss "men's work" and "women's work." Ask *What kinds of jobs do men do in your native country? What kinds of jobs do women do?* Compare their responses to kinds of jobs that men and women do in the United States.
- On the board, write:

1	2	3
Past (or Before)	Present (Now)	Future (Someday)

Give statements using the past or present tense or *would like to*. Have learners respond with the number of the tense. FOR EXAMPLE: *I'm a line cook.* (2) *I'd like to be a manager.* (3) *I was a mechanic.* (1) Repeat the procedure with questions. *What did you do?* (1) *What do you do?* (2) *What would you like to do?* (3)

1 2 3 4 5 6 7 8 9 10 11 12 Summary
The Cost of Things

Objectives

Functions
- Describing things
- Requesting assistance
- Expressing preferences
- Dealing with sizes
- Dealing with money

Life Tasks
- Reading sale ads
- Reading store directory signs
- Reading labels and price stickers
- Paying with cash
- Writing a check
- Reading receipts
- Understanding U.S. clothing sizes

Structures
- Wh- questions: *how much*
- Modal: *can*
- Intensifiers: *too, very*
- Descriptive adjectives
- *Need/want* + infinitive

Culture
- Methods of payment in the United States
- U.S. money system

Vocabulary

Key words:

accessories	medium
basement	pants
blue	pink
boot	price
check	second (2nd) floor
clothes	shirt
coat	shoe
color	size
cost	slipper
dress	small
glove	sneaker
hat	suit
home appliances	sweater
housewares	T-shirt
jewelry	third (3rd) floor
lamp	toys
large	umbrella
linens	watch
main floor	white

Related words:

amount	pay to the order of
birthday	present (noun)
cash tend.	sale
change	salesclerk
department store	tax
dollars	total
half (1/2) price	usually

Mrs. Lin's Birthday

Purpose: To introduce shopping vocabulary

Teacher Preparation and Materials

1. Gift-wrapped box
2. 12-month calendars for all
3. Picture of a birthday party
4. Magazines or store ads with pictures, posterboard, and glue for all *(Expansion/Extension)*

Warm-up

1. Introduce *present* by showing a gift-wrapped box and asking *What is this? What's inside?* Write *present* on the board. Ask *When do you give presents? What do you give?*
2. Together, look through the calendar. Give practice with *date of birth* by having learners find their birthdays. Ask *When is your birthday?* Point out that in the United States, people often give presents or send greeting cards on birthdays.
3. Show the picture of a birthday party. Ask *What do you do on your birthday? on your children's or friends' birthdays?*

Presentation

1. Have learners turn to page 76 and look at the picture. Ask *Who are these people? What person in the family is not in the room?*
2. Have learners identify things in the picture. Ask *What do you see?* List the words and comments on the board. Be sure to include *sale, birthday, ads.*
3. Have learners use the words on the board to guess what the characters are doing. Ask *What month is it? When is Mrs. Lin's birthday? Why are they looking in the newspaper?* If necessary, explain that some stores use newspapers to tell people about things for sale.
4. Have learners orally answer the question *What's happening?* at the bottom of the page, using words and phrases on the board.

1 2 3 4 5 6 7 **8** 9 10 11 12
The Cost of Things ■ ■ ■ ■ ■ ■

Mrs. Lin's Birthday
What's happening?   **Answers may vary.**

Expansion/Extension

- Together, create an LEA story about the picture. Ask *What could the Lins do for Mrs. Lin's birthday?* Learners can copy the story in their notebooks.
- Learners can make collages of gift ideas for various occasions or age groups. They can cut out pictures from magazines or store ads, glue them to posterboard, and label the pictures.
- Learners can bring in ads for their favorite stores. They can explain why they like the store. (FOR EXAMPLE: It is near my house. It has good prices.)
- Depending on learners' skills, talk about other occasions for gift giving, such as weddings, births, and graduations.
- Learners can discuss gift-giving practices in the United States and in their native countries. Ask *When do you give presents in your country? When do people give presents in the United States? What things are good presents for women? men? children? What things are not good presents for women? men? children?*

Department Store Sale

Purpose: To introduce clothing vocabulary; to give practice with *Wh-* questions and *how much* questions; to give practice in reading prices and newspaper ads; to give practice in dealing with money

Teacher Preparation and Materials

1. Pictures of clothing: shirt, pants, skirt, dress, hat, shoes, sneakers, slippers, socks, coat, jacket, watch
2. Index cards with prices: *$8, $10,* and so on; straight pins
3. Copies of TRF Handout 8.1, *Fashion Matches* (Expansion/Extension)
4. Copies of TRF Handout 8.2, *Clothing Names and Prices* (Expansion/Extension)
5. Store ads with pictures of clothing (Expansion/Extension)

Warm-up

1. Bring in pictures of clothing. Ask *What is this?* Introduce new items by holding up the picture, modeling the name, and having learners repeat. Put all the pictures on a desk in front of the class. Have a volunteer select and give you the proper clothing item as you ask for it. FOR EXAMPLE: *I need a jacket. I'm looking for a shirt and socks.*
2. Practice reading prices. Hold up index cards with prices and have learners read the amounts aloud.
3. Pin the price cards onto the clothing pictures. Hold up an item and model *How much are the sneakers?* ([They're] $12.) *How much is the shirt?* ([It's] $8.) Ask learners about the various items and have them find the item and say the price. Have learners practice asking and answering questions about clothing prices.
4. Introduce *1/2* by drawing a circle with a line through the middle. Shade half of the circle. Point to the shaded part as you say *one-half*. Write the fraction on the board.

Presentation

1. Use semantic webbing to give practice with items of clothing. Start with the word *clothes*. Make branches for *men, women,* and *children*. Have learners suggest appropriate clothing for each branch to add to the web. FOR EXAMPLE: *What clothes are for men?* (T-shirt, pants, sneakers) (**Note:** Some items may appear in more than one place.)
2. Have learners turn to page 77 and identify clothing items by answering questions about the ads. *What clothes are on sale for men?* and so on.
3. On the board, write *$30.00* crossed out and *$15.00* to the side. Point to the prices and say *Before—$30.00, Now—$15.00.* Say *half-price sale* and write *1/2 price sale* above *$15.00.* Ask *How much are the pants? What was the price before?* and so on.
4. Have learners ask each other what they want to buy and the price. (FOR EXAMPLE: *What do you want to buy? [I want] a T-shirt. How much does it cost? [It's] $6.*)
5. Together, read the question at the bottom of the page. Have learners fill in their answers individually.

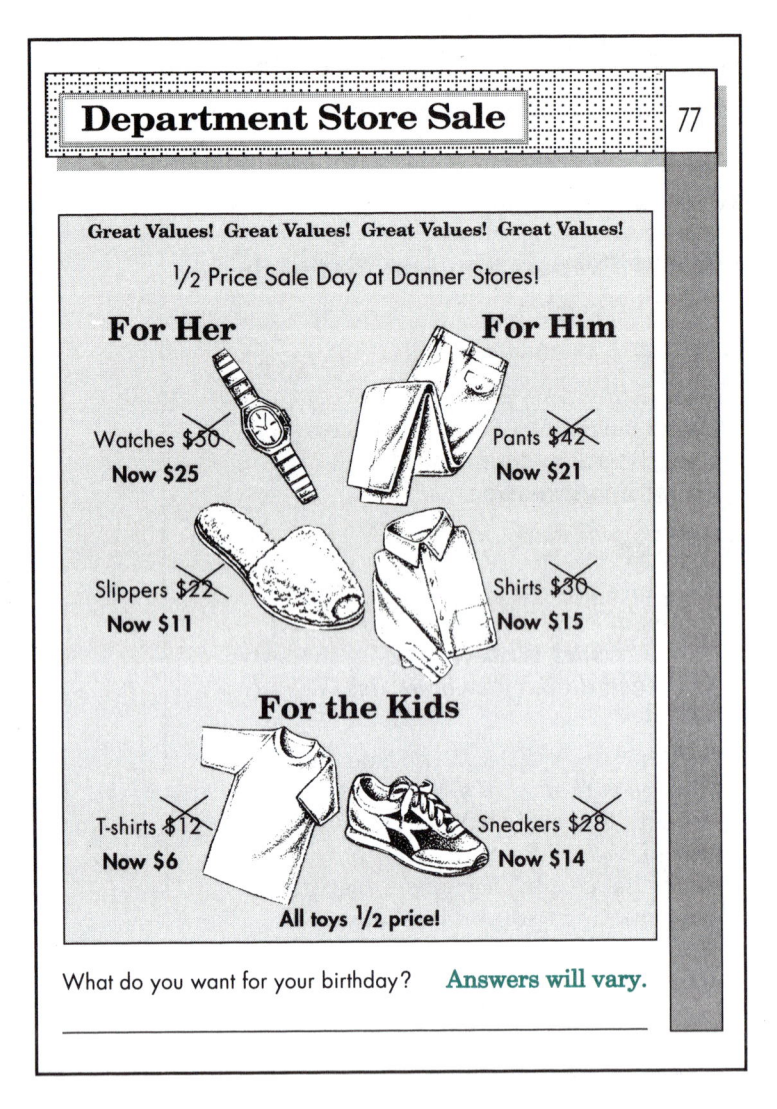

Department Store Sale   77

Great Values! Great Values! Great Values! Great Values!

1/2 Price Sale Day at Danner Stores!

For Her
- Watches ~~$50~~ Now $25
- Slippers ~~$22~~ Now $11

For Him
- Pants ~~$42~~ Now $21
- Shirts ~~$30~~ Now $15

For the Kids
- T-shirts ~~$12~~ Now $6
- Sneakers ~~$28~~ Now $14

All toys 1/2 price!

What do you want for your birthday?   **Answers will vary.**

***Expansion/Extension* on page 134**

The Store Directory

Purpose: To give practice with ordinal numbers; to introduce reading store signs and department names; to give practice with the modal *can*

Teacher Preparation and Materials

1. Pictures of clothing used for page 77; new pictures: suits, sweaters, jewelry, accessories, toys, housewares, kitchen appliances, lamps, linens
2. Department store ads with items featured in lesson
3. Index cards with sight words: *shirt, pants, skirt, dress, hat, shoes, sneakers, slippers, socks, coat, jacket, toys, suits, jewelry, sweaters, watch, home appliances, lamps, linens, accessories, housewares*

Warm-up

1. Use picture cues to ask about names of clothing. *What is this?* Use pictures to introduce the new items. Have learners repeat. Write the words on the board.
2. Use picture cues to introduce other new vocabulary: *housewares, kitchen appliances, lamps, linens.* Follow the above procedure.
3. Give learners department store ads and have them find various items in the ads as you point to the words on the board. FOR EXAMPLE: *I'm looking for home appliances. I need a new suit.*
4. Hold up the sight-word cards. Have learners look through their ads for the same words.

Presentation

1. Introduce ordinal numbers by drawing a large three-story building on the board. Identify the floors. Say *This is the first floor. This is the second floor.* Add a basement under the building and introduce the term *basement.* Have learners identify floors as you point to them. Ask *What floor is this?* Label the floors *basement, 1st floor, 2nd floor, 3rd floor.* Explain that the first floor can also be called the *main floor.* Write *main floor* near *1st floor.*
2. Have learners turn to page 78 and find the categories: Children, Men, Women, Housewares. Ask questions about categories. FOR EXAMPLE: *What things are for children?* (clothes, shoes, toys)
3. Ask learners to identify where items are located. *Where are men's coats?* (on the third floor) Have learners tape pictures or sight-word cards of items on the proper floors of the building on the board. Explain that the directory is not complete, so some cards won't fit anywhere.
4. Give practice with *Yes/No* questions about location. FOR EXAMPLE: *Are appliances in the basement?* (Yes, they are.) *Are men's coats on the second floor?* (No, they aren't.) Learners can use both the drawing on the board and the store directory in the book.
5. Together, review the examples in the book. Have learners work in pairs to fill in the chart.

Expansion/Extension

- Take a class trip to a department store. If the store has a directory, use it to find several departments.

More *Expansion/Extension* on page 134

---

78 | The Store Directory

Children		Men	
clothes	2nd floor	coats	3rd floor
shoes	2nd floor	shirts	3rd floor
toys	basement	shoes	main floor
		suits	3rd floor

Housewares		Women	
home appliances	basement	accessories	main floor
lamps	basement	dresses	2nd floor
linens	2nd floor	jewelry	main floor
		shoes	main floor
		sweaters	main floor

What can you buy ...

in the basement?	on the main floor?	on the 2nd floor?	on the 3rd floor?
Children: toys	Men: shoes	Children: clothes	Men: coats
Housewares: lamps	Women: shoes	shoes	shirts
home appliances	accessories	Housewares: linens	suits
	jewelry	Women: dresses	
	sweaters		

In the Store

Purpose: To give practice in dealing with money; to introduce intensifiers: *too, very;* to give practice with the modal *can*

Teacher Preparation and Materials

1. Pictures of items used for page 78; new pictures: gloves, umbrella, two different sweaters
2. Sight-word cards used for page 78; new sight words: *gloves, umbrella*
3. Department store ads with pictures of clothing, accessories, appliances, housewares, lamps, linens
4. Copies of TRF Handout 8.6, *No, You Can't!* (Expansion/Extension)
5. Local telephone book or yellow pages (Expansion/Extension)

Warm-up

1. Use picture cues to give practice with names of clothing and accessories and to introduce new items. *What is this?* (gloves, hat, umbrella) Have learners repeat.
2. Tape the pictures on the board. Ask learners to help each other read the sight-word cards and then to tape them under the correct picture.
3. Give practice in reading prices by drawing a price tag for each of the pictures on the board and filling in a price. Model a question and answer drill. *How much are the gloves?* ([They're] $6.50.) *How much are the sweaters?* ([They're] $18.95.) Have learners ask each other about prices.
4. Introduce the intensifiers *too* and *very* by showing pictures of two different sweaters. Talk about the price of each. *This sweater is $12. This other sweater is $50.* Point to the $50 sweater and model *It's very expensive.* Have learners repeat. Model *Do you want to buy it?* (Yes, I do./No, I don't. It's too expensive.)
5. Give learners department store ads. Have them find several items that they think are *too* or *very* expensive. Have learners share their findings with the group. (This . . . is $ . . . . It's too expensive. It's very expensive.) (**Note:** The distinction between *too* and *very* is subtle. It is not essential that learners master it at this point.)

Presentation

1. Have learners turn to page 79 and look at the picture. Ask *Who's in the store? What are they looking at? Why are they at the store? What floor are they on?*
2. Working in pairs, have learners ask each other questions about the prices of items. (FOR EXAMPLE: How much are the gloves?)
3. Together, read the sentence and question at the bottom of page 79. Ask *How much money do David and Lily have? Can they buy a sweater? Why or why not? Can they buy gloves?*
4. Have learners complete the exercise individually or in pairs. They should write in the names of three items that David and Lily can buy.

Expansion/Extension
See **TRF HANDOUT 8.6**, *No, You Can't!*

- Take a class trip to a nearby store. Learners can record prices for items and then share their findings with the group.

More *Expansion/Extension* on page 134

In the Shoe Department

Purpose: To introduce descriptive adjectives; to give practice in expressing preferences; to introduce requesting assistance; to introduce describing articles of clothing

Teacher Preparation and Materials

1. Pictures or store ads of shoes and footwear (*Warm-up* and *Expansion/Extension*)
2. Colored pieces of paper: red, white, blue, pink, and so on
3. Audiotape for Level 1
4. Copies of TRF Handout 8.5, *At the Department Store (Expansion/Extension)*

Warm-up

1. Bring in ads or pictures of footwear to practice vocabulary: *shoes, slippers, boots, sandals, sneakers.* Say *These are boots.* and so on. Have learners identify the items. Ask *What are these?* (boots)
2. Give practice with colors by holding up pieces of colored paper and having learners repeat the colors. Ask learners wearing a particular color to raise their hands. *Who is wearing something white? Who has on something blue?* Have learners find different colors in the room. Say *Show me something red. Find something yellow.*

Presentation

1. Have learners turn to page 80 and look at the first picture. Ask *Where are Lily and David? What are they looking at? Who is helping them? What types of shoes do you see?*
2. Play the audiotape and have learners listen to the first part. Ask questions as necessary. *What does David want to buy? Are the slippers very expensive? How much do they cost? Does David want to buy them?* Replay the audiotape to verify comprehension.
3. Together, read the first question. Have learners fill in the correct amount.
4. Ask questions about the second picture. *What are David and Lily looking at now? Are they looking at men's or women's slippers?*
5. Play the audiotape and have learners listen to the second part. Ask questions as necessary. *What size does Lily want? Do they have size 7 slippers? What color does Lily want? Do you think Lily and David will buy some slippers?* Verify comprehension by replaying the audiotape.
6. Have learners find the word *sale* on the sign in the second picture. Ask *What kind of a sale is it? What colors are written on the sign?*
7. Together, read the question at the bottom of page 80. Have learners complete the exercise.

Expansion/Extension

See **TRF HANDOUT 8.5,** *At the Department Store*

- Learners can find pictures of various types of footwear in ads. They can categorize footwear by season or weather, and by use (work, dress, etc.). Learners can compare footwear used in the United States and in their native countries.

More *Expansion/Extension* on page 134

Using Cash

Purpose: To give practice in dealing with money; to give practice in paying for things in cash

Teacher Preparation and Materials

1. Real/play bills and coins
2. Photocopied samples of store receipts
3. ▭ Audiotape for Level 1
4. Copies of TRF Handout 8.7, *Cash and Change (Expansion/Extension)*
5. Sales tax table or calculator *(Expansion/Extension)*

Warm-up

1. Give practice in dealing with money. Give pairs or small groups of learners real/play bills and coins of various denominations. Say amounts and have learners find possible combinations of coins and bills totaling the amounts. FOR EXAMPLE: *That will be twelve dollars and fifty cents. The total is twenty-three ninety-five.*
2. Show a receipt. Ask *What is this?* (It's a receipt.) Ask *Where do you get receipts? When do you get receipts?* Distribute receipts and have learners practice reading the amounts on them. Have learners find the dates and store names on the receipts.

Presentation

1. Have learners turn to page 81 and look at the picture. Ask *Where are Lily and David? What are they buying? What are they doing now?*
2. ▭ Play the audiotape and have learners listen. Ask questions as necessary. *What are they buying? How much do the slippers cost? What is the total with tax?* ▭ Replay the audiotape to verify comprehension.
3. Have learners look at the receipt on page 81. Ask *What is the name of the store? What is the date? Find the word* slippers. *How much do they cost? Why do stores give receipts?* If necessary, explain that receipts are needed if an item is returned or exchanged.

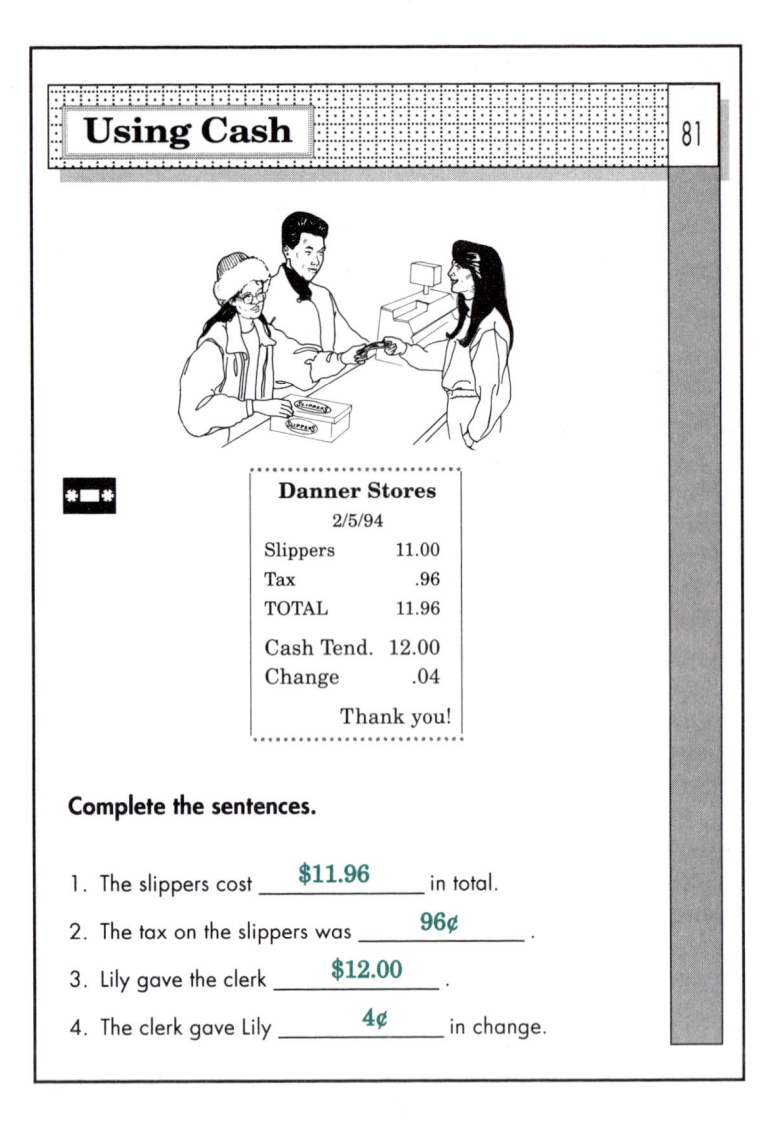

4. Give practice in identifying the parts of the receipt (*tax, total, cash tend.,* and *change*) by first reviewing with learners the information they already know. Ask *How much money did Lily give the salesclerk?* ($12.00) Write some calculations on the board to help clarify: *$11.00 (cost) + $.96 (tax) = $11.96 (total); $12.00 (cash tend.) – $11.96 (total) = $.04 (change).* If necessary, point out that the money Lily gave the salesclerk is the *cash tendered*. (**Note:** Tax is calculated here at 8.75%.)
5. Together, read the sentences at the bottom of page 81. Ask learners to work in pairs filling in the amounts from the receipt.

Expansion/Extension
See TRF HANDOUT 8.7, *Cash and Change*

- Ask learners if they have ever been given the wrong change. *What did you do? What are other possible things to do or say?* Give practice with things to say, such as *Excuse me, you only gave me $1. I think you gave me the wrong change.*

More *Expansion/Extension* on page 134

Using Cash — 81

Danner Stores
2/5/94

Slippers	11.00
Tax	.96
TOTAL	11.96
Cash Tend.	12.00
Change	.04

Thank you!

Complete the sentences.

1. The slippers cost __$11.96__ in total.
2. The tax on the slippers was __96¢__.
3. Lily gave the clerk __$12.00__.
4. The clerk gave Lily __4¢__ in change.

Sizes

Purpose: To introduce dealing with sizes; to introduce reading labels

Teacher Preparation and Materials

1. Clothing or pictures of clothing in sets of three sizes: small, medium, large
2. Copies of TRF Handout 8.3, *What Are Your Measurements? (Expansion/Extension)*
3. Copies of TRF Handout 8.4, *Just My Size (Expansion/Extension)*
4. Clothing with sizes marked on labels *(Expansion/Extension)*
5. Store ads with pictures of clothing *(Expansion/Extension)*

Warm-up

1. Use pictures or real clothing to give practice with clothing vocabulary.
2. Give practice with colors by asking questions about clothing and colors. *Who has a yellow shirt and blue pants? Who is wearing a green sweater and white blouse?* and so on.

Presentation

1. On the board write *S, M,* and *L*. Show three items of clothing or pictures of clothing of varying sizes. Ask learners *What is different?* If necessary, introduce the words *small, medium,* and *large*. Place pictures or items of clothing under the proper letter.
2. Practice the word *size*. Show other sets of clothing or pictures and ask *What size is this?* Have learners put them under the proper size category. Write the complete words (*Small, Medium, Large*) near the appropriate letters.
3. Have learners turn to page 82. Together, look at the first set of items. Ask learners to identify the type of clothing and sizes. Ask *What are these? Which boots are small? Which ones are large? Which boots are medium? Which size is circled?* Have learners find the check under the "Large (L)" column.
4. Individually or in pairs, have learners complete the exercise by checking the size of the article that is circled. Then, ask *Which size skirt is circled?* (small) *Which size glove is circled?* (medium)
5. Ask a learner *What size boot do you wear?* Then, working in pairs, have learners practice asking for various sized items. (FOR EXAMPLE: *Can I help you? Yes, I need a sweater. What size? Large.*)

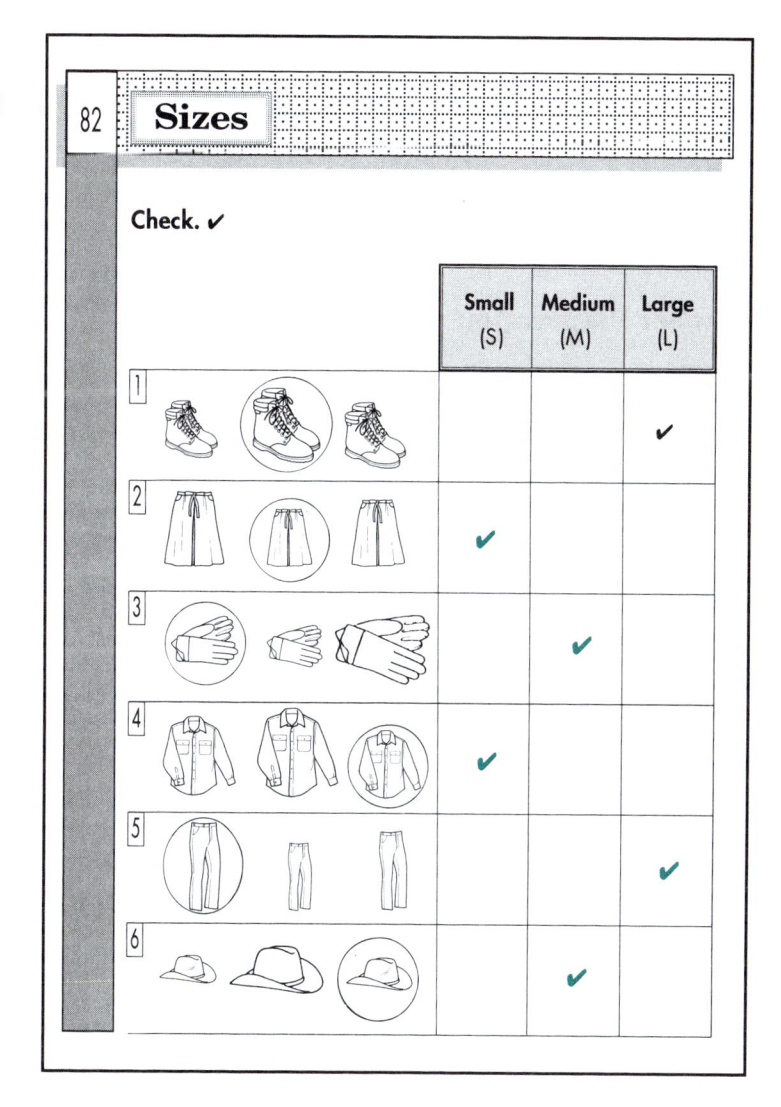

Expansion/Extension
See **TRF HANDOUT 8.3**, *What Are Your Measurements?*
TRF HANDOUT 8.4, *Just My Size*

- Bring in a selection of clothing. Learners can find the labels and sort the clothing according to the sizes (small, medium, and large).
- Introduce number sizes for various age groups. FOR EXAMPLE: Infants (6 mos., 18 mos.), Toddlers (2T, 3T), Girls (4, 6X), Boys (4, 14).
- Learners can look through clothing and store ads for various items and sizes. Learners can choose items they like and then circle or write in the size they would need. Learners can share their findings in small groups. (FOR EXAMPLE: *I like this dress. I need a size 6. I like this sweater. I need a medium.*)

More *Expansion/Extension* on page 135

Looking for a Present

Purpose: To give practice in requesting assistance and dealing with money; to give practice with *want/need* + infinitive

Teacher Preparation and Materials

1. Pictures of items used for page 79; new picture: T-shirt
2. Weekly calendar
3. 🔲 Audiotape for Level 1
4. Store ads with pictures of a variety of merchandise *(Expansion/Extension)*

Warm-up

1. Tape pictures of clothing and accessories on the board or wall. Model the question and answer *What do you want to buy? I want to buy a T-shirt.* Take the picture of the T-shirt. Ask learners *What do you want to buy?* (I want to buy a . . . .) Then give them the pictures of the items.

2. Introduce the past tense of the verb *go* with a weekly calendar. Point to (today) and say *On (Mondays) I go to class.* Point to (yesterday) and say *Yesterday I went to the supermarket.* Then ask a volunteer *Where do you go on (Mondays)? Where did you go yesterday?* Write what day it was yesterday on the board and the word *went* below it. Write what day it is today and the word *go* below it.

3. Introduce the past tense of the verb *tell*. Use *Warm-up* #2 as a model. Write the words *told* and *tell* under *went* and *go*. (**Note:** Learners are not expected to master *told* and *went*, but they need to recognize them.)

Presentation

1. Have learners turn to page 83 and look at the first picture. Ask *Where is Mr. Lin? What is he looking at?*

2. Together, read the first part. Ask *What does Mr. Lin want to buy? Who is the present for?* Have learners find examples of regular and irregular past-tense verbs.

3. 🔲 Play the audiotape and have learners listen to the first conversation. Ask questions. *Is Mr. Lin buying something now? What is he doing?* 🔲 Replay the audiotape to verify responses.

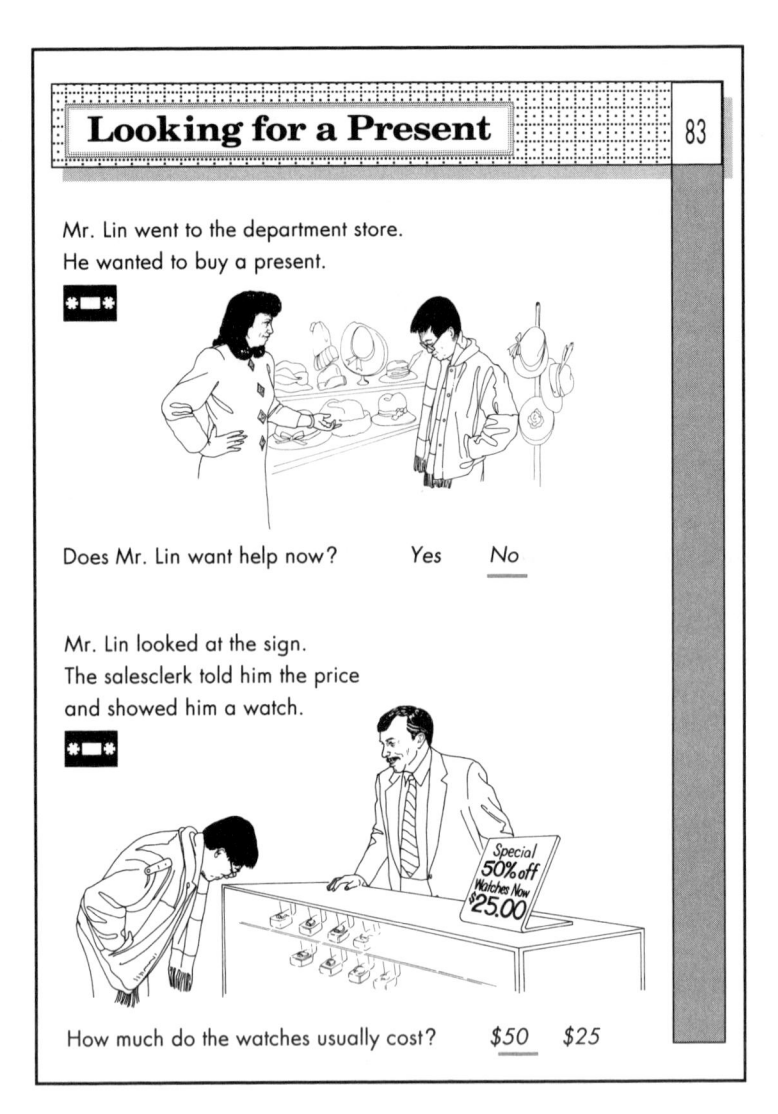

4. Together, read the question in the first part and have learners underline or circle the answer.

5. Ask questions about the second picture. *What is Mr. Lin looking at now? How much do the watches cost now?*

6. Together, read the second part. Ask *What did Mr. Lin look at? Who told him the price?* Have learners find examples of past-tense verbs.

7. 🔲 Play the audiotape and have learners listen to the second conversation. Ask *What is Mr. Lin looking for? How much do the watches cost now?* 🔲 Replay the audiotape to verify comprehension.

8. Together, read the question in the second part and have learners underline or circle the answer.

Expansion/Extension

- Give practice in offering and refusing assistance. *What can you say if you want to help someone?* (Can I help you?) *How do you answer?* (Yes, please. I need . . . . No, thanks. I'm just looking.)

More *Expansion/Extension* on page 135

130 • UNIT 8

Writing Checks

Purpose: To introduce ways to pay for things in the United States; to introduce writing checks; to give practice in dealing with money

Teacher Preparation and Materials

1. Index cards with these numbers written in word form as sight words:
   1–20, 30, 40, 50, 60, 70, 80, 90, 100
2. Sample of a personal check
3. Samples of identification used when paying by check in a store
4. Audiotape for Level 1

Warm-up

1. Dictate various prices. Have learners write them. *That's ten dollars and thirty-five cents* ($10.35) *It comes to nine seventy-five.* ($9.75)

2. On the board, write the numbers *1–20, 30, 40, 50, 60, 70, 80, 90, 100.* Next to each number, write the number in words. Give the sight-word cards to learners. Say a number and have learner with that card show it. Repeat with other numbers.

3. Introduce how to write prices that include a hyphen and amounts under $1.00 by writing on the board various prices: *$24.92 = twenty-four and 92/100 dollars.* Write a column of prices in numbers on the board such as $88.73, $12.13, $37.93. Ask learners to read each price and then write the price in words. (*Eighty-eight and 73/100 dollars*)

4. Show a sample of a personal check. Ask learners about their experiences using checks. *Did you ever get a check? What did you do with it? Did you ever write a check? What did you use it for?*

5. Show samples of identification such as a driver's license, employee ID, student ID, and passport. Have learners identify personal information on the samples. Ask *What are these? What are they used for? When do you need identification? Why do you need an ID like these to pay by check?*

Presentation

1. Have learners turn to page 84 and look at the picture. Ask *Where is Mr. Lin? What's he doing? Is he using money to buy the watch?*

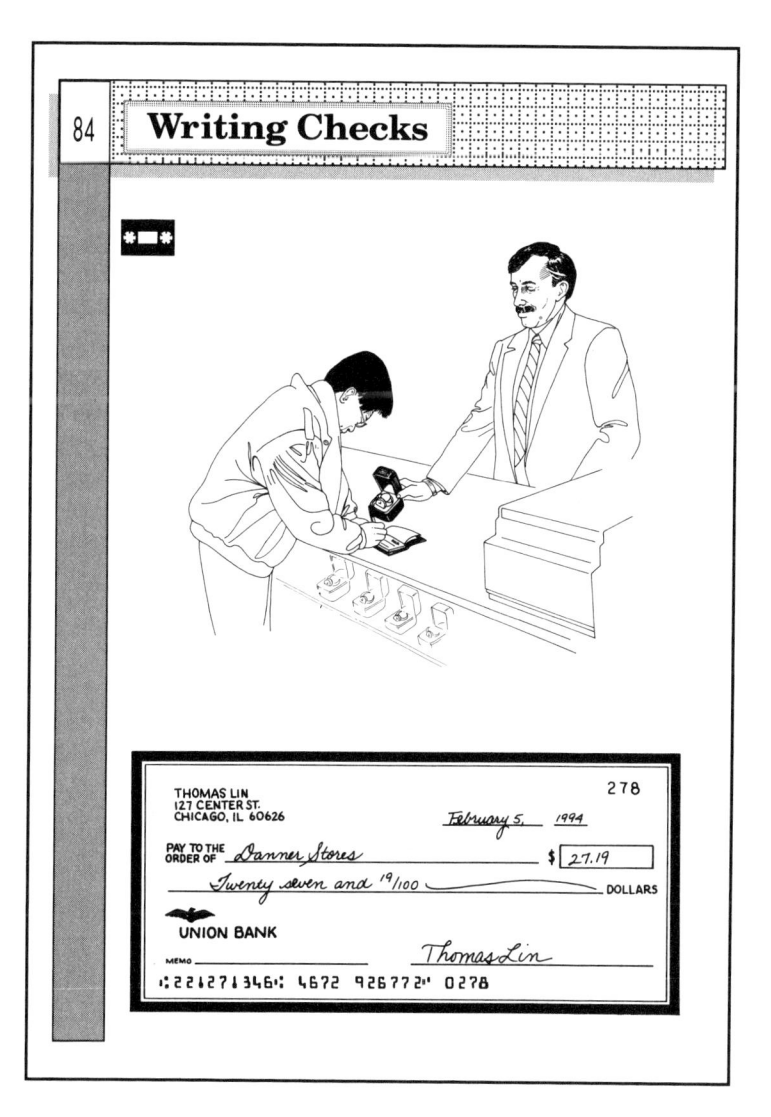

2. Play the audiotape and have learners listen. Ask *What is Mr. Lin buying? How much is the watch? How is he going to pay? What identification does he have?* Replay the audiotape to verify comprehension.

3. Have learners identify and explain information on the check at the bottom of page 84. Ask *What is the date? What is the name of the store (that Mr. Lin is paying)? How much is the check for? Who signed the check? The watch costs $25.00. Why is Mr. Lin's check for $27.19?*

Expansion/Extension

- Take a trip to several stores and find out their check policies. Many stores and offices have signs near the cash register. Ask *Do all places take personal checks?* Talk about reasons why some places may not take checks. *What happens if you write a check and there is no money in your bank account?*

- Compare various methods of paying for things, such as by cash, check, charge card, credit card, and layaway plan. List some advantages and disadvantages of each.

UNIT 8 • 131

Paying by Check

Purpose: To give practice in paying for things in the United States, writing checks, and dealing with money

Teacher Preparation and Materials

1. Pictures or store ads with pictures of linens: towels, sheets, blankets, tablecloths, napkins
2. Sight-word cards with numbers written in words used for page 84
3. Copies of a store receipt for all, showing date, store name, and total
4. Clothing or other items with price tags; sales tax chart *(Expansion/Extension)*
5. Blank check forms and receipts for all *(Expansion/Extension)*
6. Tax chart or calculator *(Expansion/Extension)*
7. Checking account application forms and signature cards, bank statement, check register *(Expansion/Extension)*

Warm-up

1. Use picture cues to practice housewares vocabulary: *linens, towels, sheets, blankets, tablecloths, napkins.* Ask *In what department can you find these things? Are they in men's clothes? shoes? housewares?*
2. Give practice with numbers by writing the numbers *1–20, 30, 40, 50, 60, 70, 80, 90, 100* in random order on the board. Have learners find and tape the correct sight-word cards under the correct numbers.
3. As a group, have learners practice filling out a check by drawing a large blank check similar to the one on page 85 on the board. Ask a volunteer to come to the board and fill in his or her name and address on the three lines in the upper left-hand corner. Give all learners a copy of a store receipt. Ask *What date is it?* and have learners circle the date on their receipt. Ask *What store are you paying?* and have learners underline the name of the store on the receipt. Ask *How much is the total amount?* and have learners make a box around the amount. Have learners spell out the total amount on their receipts. Ask volunteers to fill in date, store name, and total amount paid in the appropriate places. Point out that the total amount is written in two places. Ask the learner whose name and address is on the "check" to come and sign in the appropriate place.

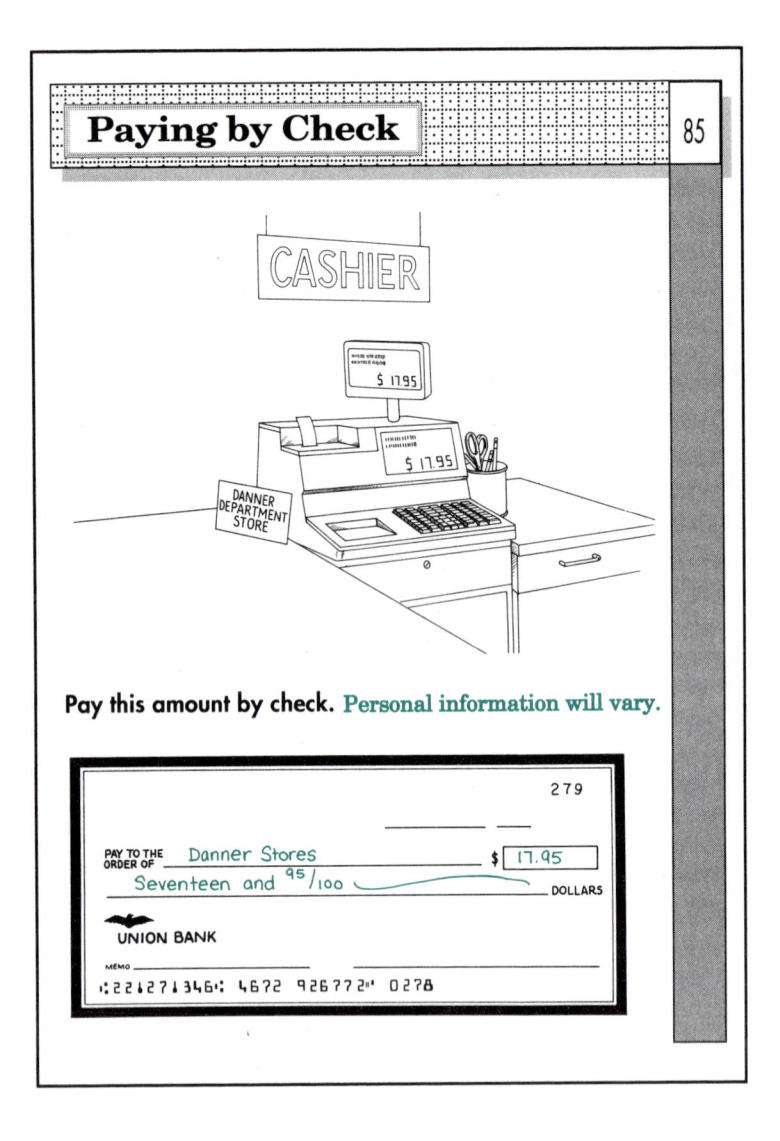

Presentation

1. Ask learners to turn to page 85 and to pretend they are in the picture. Ask *What do you see? What store are you in?*
2. Have learners imagine what was purchased. Ask *What does this store sell? What did you buy? Who is it for? How much do you have to pay?*
3. Have learners imagine that they will pay by check. Have them fill out the check in the book. Learners should fill in their own name and address and the current date on top of the check. (**Note:** This is one of the few times learners need to know how to spell numbers.)

Expansion/Extension

- If learners have checking accounts, they may want to write 1–20, 30, 40, 50, 60, 70, 80, 90, 100 in word form to keep for reference in their checkbooks.

More *Expansion/Extension* on page 135

Look Back

Purpose: To give practice in naming and describing items

Teacher Preparation and Materials

1. Pictures of clothing items and accessories used throughout unit
2. Small box
3. Store ads with pictures of a variety of merchandise *(Expansion/Extension)*
4. Boxes, gift-wrapping paper, tape, and ribbon for all *(Expansion/Extension)*
5. Local yellow pages *(Expansion/Extension)*

Warm-up

1. Use picture cues to review names of clothing items and accessories.
2. Introduce the past tense of the irregular verb *get*. Put pictures of clothing items in a box. Take a picture from the box and pass the box around for each learner to take a picture. Then model the question and answer *What did you get? I got a shirt.* Have learners practice asking and answering the question in a chain drill.
3. Give practice with questions and answers in the third person based on the activity above. Ask the first learner in the chain what the second learner got. *What did (Sonia) get?* (*She got . . ..*) Write a sample question and answer on the board. (FOR EXAMPLE: *What did Sonia get? She got sandals.*) Model and have learners repeat.

Presentation

1. Have learners turn to page 86 and look at the picture. Ask *What do you see? What did she get? Why did she get presents?* Together, read the sentences below the picture. Ask *What presents did May like?*
2. Have learners answer the first question on their own. If necessary, point out the similarity between that question and the question on the board.
3. Have learners look at the picture again and compare the presents they checked off in the first question. Ask *How many presents did May get in the picture?* (four) *How many presents did you check at the bottom of the page?* (three) *What else did May get?* Have learners write the answer to the last question on the page.

Expansion/Extension

- Model and give practice with language associated with giving and receiving gifts. (FOR EXAMPLE: Thank you. It's very nice. I really like this, etc.)
- Introduce and give practice giving and receiving compliments about clothing items. (FOR EXAMPLE: That's a beautiful bag you have. Thank you. My friend gave it to me. I like your hat. Thanks.)
- Have learners write their names on small pieces of paper. Place all the papers in a box. Then have each learner draw a name from the box and not show it to anyone (first checking that they did not draw their own name). Learners then look through store ads for a picture of something they think the other person would like. Learners exchange their "gifts" and then report what they got.

More *Expansion/Extension* on page 135

UNIT 8 • 133

UNIT 8: The Cost of Things
Expansion/Extension

Department Store Sale
Expansion/Extension **for SB page 77**
See TRF HANDOUT 8.1, *Fashion Matches*
TRF HANDOUT 8.2, *Clothing Names and Prices*

- Learners can categorize clothing pictures or store ads by season, adult/child, gender, work/dress, and so on.
- Practice demonstratives. Learners can look through store ads and find several articles of clothing that they like. They can share their findings with the group using simple sentences. (I like this dress. I like these shoes. I don't like this shirt. I don't like these boots, etc.)
- Bring in store ads from several local stores. Choose several items and compare the prices at the various stores. Also learners can find the dates on the ads for when the prices are in effect.
- Learners can find the sale price for various amounts. On the board, write some prices and ask learners what the 1/2-off sale prices are. FOR EXAMPLE: *$40* ($20), *$14* ($7). Practice calculating other types of discounts such as 1/4 off, 1/3 off. Also introduce 50% off, 25% off, 10% off, and so on.
- Discuss types of sales such as going-out-of-business sales, clearance sales, white sales, buy-one-get-one-free sales, and so on.
- Learners can bring in pictures of clothing worn in their native countries, such as traditional costumes, everyday clothing. Learners can talk about their pictures.

The Store Directory
More *Expansion/Extension* **for SB page 78**

- Give practice in forming and pronouncing plurals by adding *-s* and *-es*. List clothing items according to the endings used. Form a rule for plural endings based on the lists. FOR EXAMPLE:

    hat/hats   dress/dresses
    shoe/shoes   watch/watches

- Look through department store ads for other departments such as stationery, automotive, gardening, health and beauty, pets, music, and sports. Learners can list items found in each of the departments.

In the Store
More *Expansion/Extension* **for SB page 79**

- Discuss various types of discount stores: outlet stores, wholesale clubs, consignment shops/second-hand clothing stores, and so on. Talk about advantages and disadvantages of each. Learners can look through local phone book and yellow pages for names of stores in their area.
- Give practice with indefinite articles: *a, an*. List items of clothing according to the articles used. Help learners create a rule for the use of indefinite articles. Give practice in using the articles in simple sentences. (FOR EXAMPLE: I need an umbrella. She wants a sweater. He'd like gloves.)

In the Shoe Department
More *Expansion/Extension* **for SB page 80**

- Introduce other adjectives. Learners can practice asking for different types of items. (FOR EXAMPLE: Do you have anything less expensive/more inexpensive? less fancy? more fancy? more comfortable? more practical? more sturdy?)
- Learners can role-play customer and salesclerk. Customers can ask for help and then ask for less expensive items or for a particular color, size, style, and so on.
- Use the various categories of footwear to give practice with demonstratives: *this/that, these/those*. FOR EXAMPLE.: *These shoes are for work. Those shoes are for dress. These boots are for winter. Those boots are for summer.*
- Learners can talk about colors on the flags of their native countries. Learners can bring in pictures or make pictures to be displayed around the room.

Using Cash
More *Expansion/Extension* **for SB page 81**

- Write fill-in sentences on the board that are similar to the ones on page 81. FOR EXAMPLE: *The . . . cost(s) . . . in total. The tax on the . . . was . . . .* Give learners sample receipts and have them find the amounts and write them in the appropriate places.
- Ask learners if they have ever returned or exchanged an item. Discuss how to use receipts for returns or exchanges. Ask *Where do you go in the store? Who do you talk to? What do you need? Is there a time limit on returns?* Practice role plays about exchanges and returns.

- Ask learners if they have ever noticed an error on a receipt. Discuss various ways of handling the situation.
- Explain sales tax. Ask *What types of things are taxed? What types of things are not taxed? How much is the tax?* Depending on learners' skills, bring in a sales tax chart or calculator, or practice calculating and/or estimating tax by hand.

Sizes
More *Expansion/Extension* for SB page 82

- Learners can look on clothing labels for information on care. Introduce vocabulary such as *machine wash, dry-clean only, hand wash in cold water, do not bleach, do not use detergent,* and *iron*. Some clothing labels use symbols for clothing care. Learners can find them and try to guess the meanings.
- Introduce and give practice with other ways of talking about clothing fit and sizes. Give learners various items of clothing such as a hat or coat to try on and then talk about the fit. *How does it fit?* (It's too tight/loose/short/long. I think I need a smaller/larger size. It fits just right.)

Looking for a Present
More *Expansion/Extension* for SB page 83

- Learners can look through various store ads for ideas and make lists of things they need to buy and things they want to buy. (FOR EXAMPLE: I need to buy some boots. I want to buy skates.)
- Take a trip to a greeting-card store. Learners can look for birthday cards for various family members or appropriate holiday cards for the season.
- Depending on learners' skills, they can role-play a salesclerk offering assistance and a customer refusing or accepting.

Paying by Check
More *Expansion/Extension* for SB page 85

- Learners can practice writing checks for other items. Bring in receipts and blank check forms. Learners can find the totals and fill in the appropriate information.
- Set up a mock store. Learners can role-play a salesclerk and a customer paying by check. Customers can select clothing or other items with prices on them. The salesclerk(s) can total the items and use a sales tax chart to figure out the total amount. The salesclerk(s) should also ask for identification.
- Learners can go to a bank and find out how to open a checking account. Or, alternatively, bring in samples of application forms and cards that need to be filled out. Discuss the difference between having name and address or name, address, and phone number printed on the check.
- Depending on learners' skills and interests, discuss other information related to checking accounts such as keeping a check register, balancing an account, and reading a bank statement. Also discuss what to do if you make a mistake in writing a check.

Look Back
More *Expansion/Extension* for SB page 86

- Do a TPR activity on wrapping a present.
    1. You need to wrap a present.
    2. Put the paper upside-down on the table.
    3. Place the box on the paper.
    4. Pull up opposite sides of the paper and tape them.
    5. Fold one end and tape it.
    6. Fold the other end and tape it, too.
    7. Put a ribbon around the box.
    8. Tie a bow on top.
- Discuss options to buying presents. Ask *Are there things that you can make? Are there places you can go with the person?*
- Discuss specialty stores such as bookstores, flower shops/florists, stationery stores, bakeries, jewelry stores, camera stores, and video stores. Match stores with pictures of things sold. Look in a local yellow pages for names and addresses of specialty stores in your area.

1 2 3 4 5 6 7 8 **9** 10 11 12 Summary
Getting Well

Objectives

Functions
- Describing symptoms
- Asking for and giving information
- Clarifying/verifying
- Expressing needs
- Identifying body parts
- Sympathizing
- Following written directions
- Giving personal information

Life Tasks
- Reading medication labels
- Reading signs at a hospital or clinic
- Filling out simple medical forms
- Writing absence notes

Structures
- Modals *can/can't*
- Prepositions of time
- Adverbs of frequency

Culture
- Health-care options in the United States
- Medical insurance
- Home remedies in native countries and in the United States

Vocabulary

Key words:

absence note	health insurance
arm	hurt
body	knee
broken	leg
chest	medicine
directions	mouth
ear	nose
earache	pill
elbow	sick
eye	sore
fever	stomach
finger	stomachache
flu	tablet
foot	teaspoon
hand	throat
head	toe
headache	tooth

Related words:

amount	nurse
antibiotic	once
apply	over-the-counter
aspirin	patient
clinic	policy or group number
daily	prescription
doctor	receptionist
employee	refill
examination	rest
health problem	runny/running
infection	stethoscope
insurance	stuffy/stuffed-up
label	teacher
liquids	twice
no smoking	waiting room

In the Waiting Room

Purpose: To introduce health-care options in the United States

Teacher Preparation and Materials

1. Pictures of hospital/clinic/doctor's office and people who work there
2. Local telephone book or yellow pages *(Expansion/Extension)*
3. Local maps *(Expansion/Extension)*
4. Arrange a trip to a local clinic. *(Expansion/Extension)*

Warm-up

1. Use picture cues to review names of places and people associated with health care.
2. Have learners turn to page 13. Ask learners to find the names and phone numbers of clinics listed.
3. Ask learners if they have ever been to a clinic or hospital. If so, have them share their experiences. Ask *When do people go to a clinic? Do they go when they feel OK or when they are sick? Do people go when they are hurt? When do they go to a hospital?*

Presentation

1. Have learners turn to page 87 and look at the picture. Ask *What do you see? Where are these people? Who works here?* List the words and comments on the board. Be sure to include *receptionist, clinic, waiting room, sick, hurt.*
2. Have learners find the various signs in the waiting room. Say *Show me the sign that says* No Smoking. *Point to the sign that says* Pharmacy. *Where is the chart of the body?*
3. Have learners identify the characters and think about what they are doing in the waiting room. Ask *Why are Fred and Kendra at the clinic? Who is sick? Who is hurt? Who needs help? What are the people doing? What is the receptionist doing?*
4. Have learners answer the question *What's happening?* at the bottom of the page, using the words on the board.

1 2 3 4 5 6 7 8 **9** 10 11 12
Getting Well ▪ ▪ ▪ ▪ ▪ ▪ ▪ ▪ ▪

In the Waiting Room
What's Happening?   **Answers may vary.**

Expansion/Extension

- Write an LEA story about the picture or about learners' experiences in waiting rooms and clinics.
- Learners can look in the local yellow pages for names, addresses, and phone numbers of clinics and hospitals in the local area. Using local maps, help them find the clinic(s)/other health-care facilities nearest their homes.
- Take a trip to a local clinic. Learners can get clinic brochures and health information brochures.
- Discuss how to find a good doctor or clinic (referral from another doctor or other health-care worker, from a friend, etc.).

UNIT 9 • 137

The Human Body

Purpose: To introduce the identification of body parts

Teacher Preparation and Materials

1. Full-length picture of a person, which clearly shows body parts (can be drawn on board)
2. Index cards with sight words: *head, eye, ear, nose, mouth, throat, chest, stomach, elbow, arm, hand, finger, knee, leg, foot, toe*
3. Magazines with pictures of people *(Expansion/Extension)*

Warm-up

1. Introduce names of parts of the body by pointing to yourself as a model. Allow time for learners to name parts they know. Model new items and have learners repeat. Be sure to include *head, eye, ear, nose, mouth, throat, chest, stomach, elbow, arm, hand, finger, knee, leg, foot, toe.*
2. Give practice with body parts by having the group stand up and respond by pointing to the appropriate parts as you give various instructions. FOR EXAMPLE: *Put your hand on your knee. Show me your elbow. Point to your eye. Where's your foot?*

Presentation

1. Ask learners to turn to page 88 and to find the various parts of the body. Say *Point to the head. Where's the arm?*
2. Ask *Do you know any other parts?* Write additional words on the board. Learners can copy them in their books.
3. Post the full-length picture of a person on the board and have learners tape the sight-word cards to the appropriate parts of the body.

Expansion/Extension

- Give practice with *left* and *right* in relation to body parts. Say *Raise your left hand. Put your right foot out. Touch your left elbow.*
- Play Simon Says or teach a song such as "The Hokey Pokey" or "Head and Shoulders, Knees and Toes."
- Learners can draw a picture of themselves or cut out a picture from a magazine and then label the parts of the body.
- Categorize parts of the body. Learners can sort sight-word cards under the appropriate headings: Head, Upper Body, Lower Body.
- Learners can choose a sight-word card and mime a problem with that part of the body. Others in the group will guess the part and the problem. (FOR EXAMPLE: leg—His/Her leg hurts.)
- Introduce additional body parts, such as *thumb, neck, back, shoulder, tooth (teeth), wrist, ankle,* and *jaw.*
- Introduce names of internal parts, such as *heart, lungs, liver, kidneys, bones, blood,* and *muscle.*
- Introduce the plural forms of parts of the body. Point out the irregular plural form of *foot (feet)* and *tooth (teeth).*

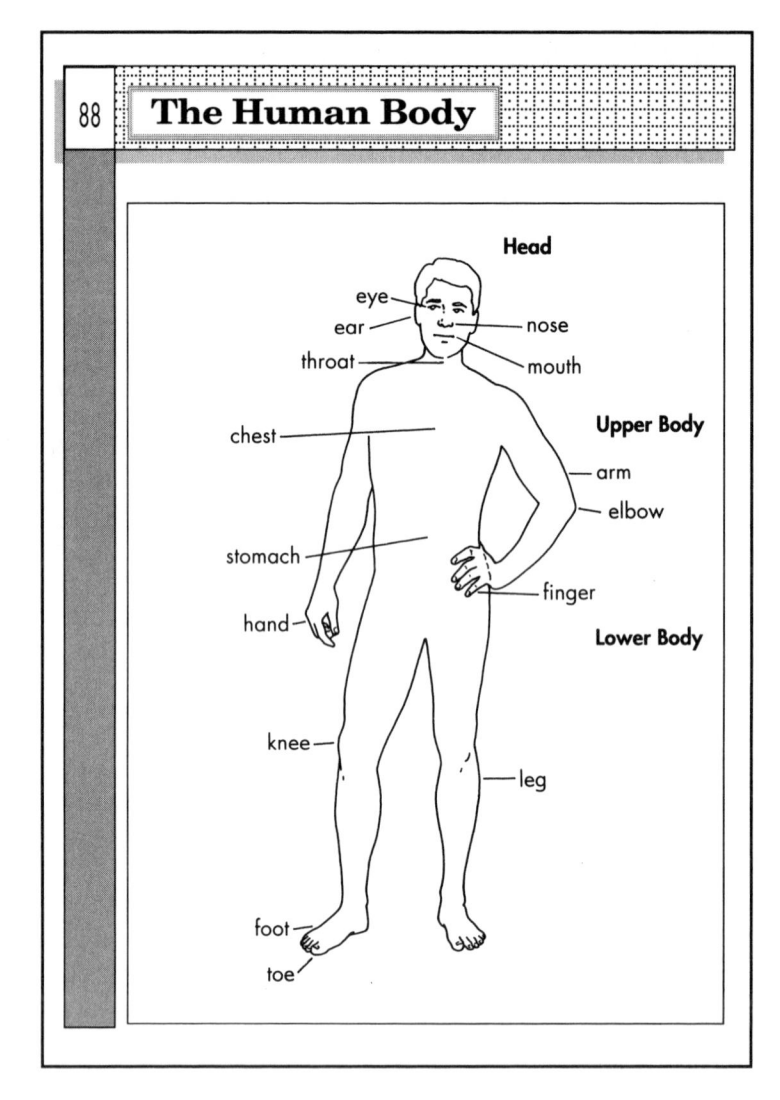

What Hurts?

Purpose: To give practice in identifying body parts; to introduce describing symptoms; to introduce expressing need

Teacher Preparation and Materials

1. Full-length picture of a person
2. Index cards with sight words used for page 88
3. Audiotape for Level 1
4. Toy telephones *(Expansion/Extension)*
5. Blank index cards *(Expansion/Extension)*
6. Magazines with pictures of people with health problems *(Expansion/Extension)*

Warm-up

1. Give practice with names of parts of the body by miming a problem and having learners say the name of each part. FOR EXAMPLE: Hold your knee as if it hurts. Ask *What's the matter?* (Your knee hurts.) Alternatively, point to various parts of the body on the full-length picture for learners to identify.
2. Give practice in reading sight-word cards with the names of parts of the body. Have learners respond by pointing to the appropriate parts of the body on themselves or the picture.
3. Give the sight-word cards to the group and have them find the appropriate card as you describe a health problem. FOR EXAMPLE: *I have a problem. My leg hurts.* (Learners find the sight-word card *leg.*) *I don't feel well. My throat is sore. My stomach has been bothering me for two days. There's something wrong with my eye.*
4. Model sentences about health problems and have learners repeat. *My . . . hurts.* Then, point to various parts of the body and have learners describe the problems.

Presentation

1. Have learners turn to page 89 and look at the picture. Ask *Who is talking on the phone? What are they talking about?*
2. Together, read the headings on the chart. Explain to the group that they will hear people calling the doctor. Each person will talk about a problem or problems.
3. Play the audiotape and have learners check the body part or parts that hurt for each person. (**Note:** Some callers mention more than one health problem.) Replay the audiotape to verify responses.
4. After the group completes the chart, have them give answers using the third person. (FOR EXAMPLE: *Her nose is stuffed up.*)

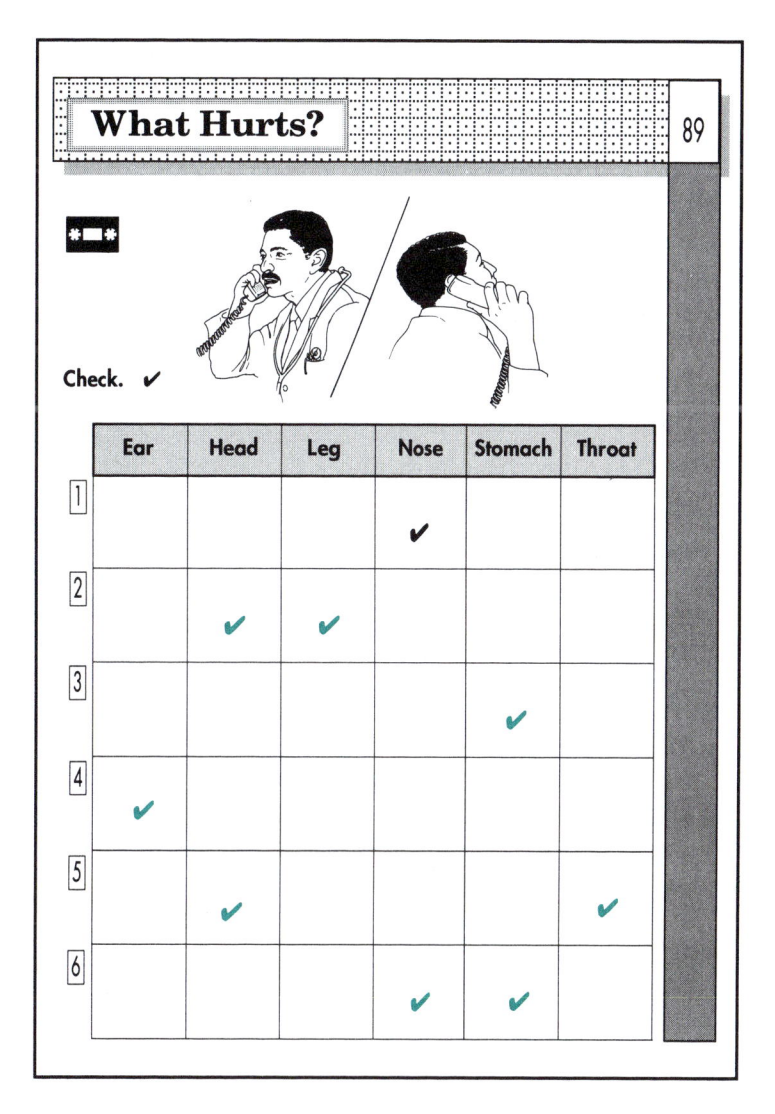

Expansion/Extension

- Learners can listen to the audiotape again and identify different ways to express health problems. Write the expressions on blank index cards. Learners can use the cards to practice explaining health problems.
- Role-play calling for an appointment at a clinic. One person can be the receptionist and ask questions, such as "What's your name?" "Can you spell that, please?" "Can you come in at 10:30 this morning?" The other person can ask for an appointment, give his or her name, and describe the problem.

More *Expansion/Extension* on page 148

UNIT 9 • 139

Health Insurance Form

Purpose: To give practice in asking for/giving information; to introduce medical insurance; to give practice in filling out a simple medical form

Teacher Preparation and Materials

1. Index cards with sight words: *name, address, date, telephone, health insurance, policy or group number, patient*
2. Copies of health insurance, Medicare, and/or Medicaid cards for all
3. Copies of blank clinic registration forms for all *(Expansion/Extension)*
4. Information on types of health insurance plans *(Expansion/Extension)*

Warm-up

1. Give practice in reading sight words by showing learners the sight-word cards *name, address, date, telephone*. Have learners respond with their personal information. (FOR EXAMPLE: *name*—[My name's] Hernando López.)
2. Pass out copies of health insurance, Medicare, and/or Medicaid cards. Ask *Do you have cards like these? What are these cards for? When do you use them? How do you get them? What do they help pay for?* Have learners look at page 66 to find the jobs that have health benefits or insurance. Briefly explain insurance plans.
3. On the board, write the words *health insurance, policy or group number, employee*. Have learners find the appropriate words on the sample cards.
4. Introduce the word *patient* by giving examples of medical situations and asking learners to say who is sick or hurt. FOR EXAMPLE: *Tom Lin hurts his leg. His wife takes him to the clinic. Who is the patient—Tom Lin or his wife? Anita Gómez does not feel well. Her friend drives her to the clinic. Who is the patient—Anita or her friend?*

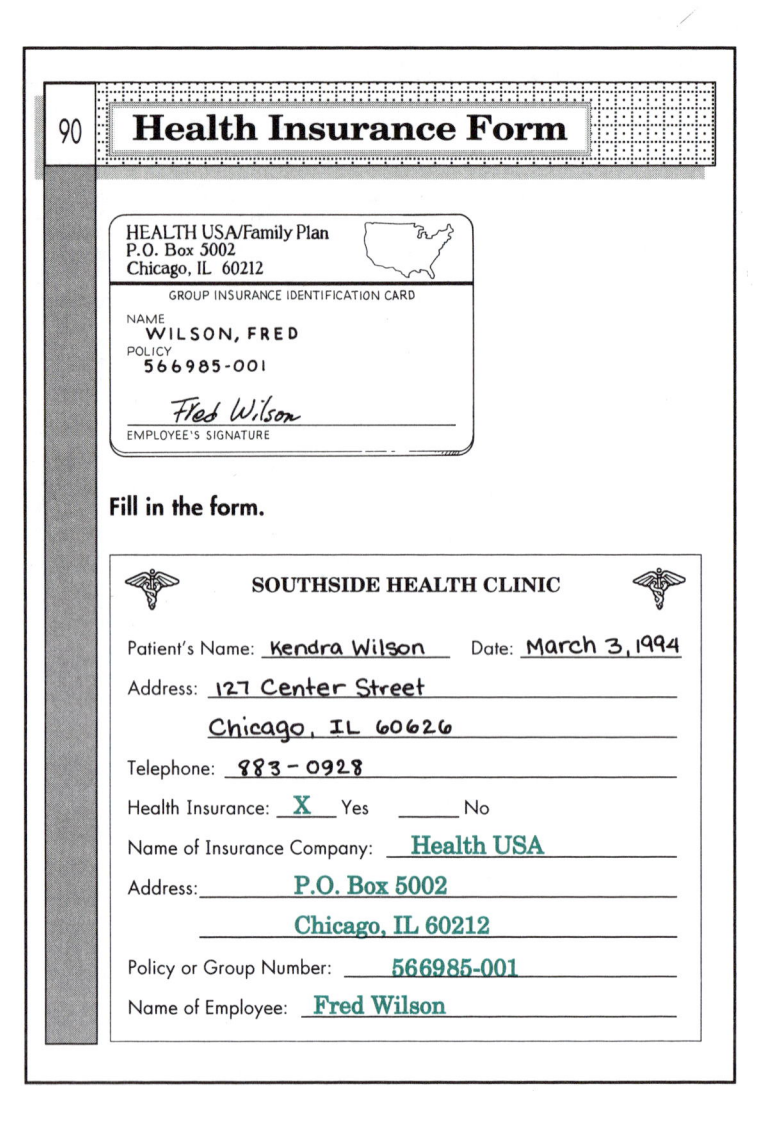

Presentation

1. Have learners turn to page 90 and find as many sight words as they can on the ID card.
2. Ask *What is the policy number? Whose name is on the card? What is the name of the insurance company? Who is the employee? Who signed the card?*
3. If learners have their own insurance cards, compare them to Fred's card.
4. Have learners find the word *family* on Fred's card. Explain *When Kendra is sick, her father's insurance plan helps pay the doctor.*
5. Have learners look at the clinic registration form on page 90 and find the words *patient's name, date, address, telephone, health insurance, policy or group number, employee*.
6. Ask *Who is the patient? What is the date? What's her phone number? Does Kendra have health insurance?*
7. Have learners fill in the form at the bottom of the page with the information from Fred's insurance card.

***Expansion/Extension* on page 148**

140 • UNIT 9

The Examination

Purpose: To give practice in describing symptoms and asking for/giving information; to introduce sympathizing

Teacher Preparation and Materials

1. Pictures of people with health problems: sore throat, headache, stomachache, earache, fever, cold (stuffed-up nose)
2. Audiotape for Level 1
3. Pictures of medical equipment: thermometer, blood pressure cuff, eye chart, stethoscope *(Expansion/Extension)*
4. Copies of TRF Handout 9.2, *Check-up (Expansion/Extension)*
5. Copies of TRF Handout 9.3, *In the Doctor's Office (Expansion/Extension)*

Warm-up

1. Give practice with names of body parts by having learners follow directions: *Raise your hand. Cover your eye. Open your mouth. Shut your eyes.* and so on.
2. Give practice in talking about health problems by showing pictures of people with various problems. Model and have learners repeat *My . . . hurts.*
3. Introduce other ways to talk about health problems using the pictures as cues. Model and have learners repeat *I have a sore throat/arm/foot. I have a headache/stomachache/earache. I have a fever/cold/stuffed-up nose.*
4. Give practice in talking about health problems by taping the pictures on the board, numbering them, and saying statements like *Monica doesn't feel well. She has an earache. Tom is sick. He has a fever.* Have learners say which number matches the health problem(s) you describe.

Presentation

1. Have learners turn to page 91 and look at the picture. Ask *What do you see? Where are Fred and Kendra? What is in the room? What is Kendra/the doctor doing? What do you think they are talking about?* List the words and comments on the board. Be sure to include *examination room, thermometer, stethoscope.*

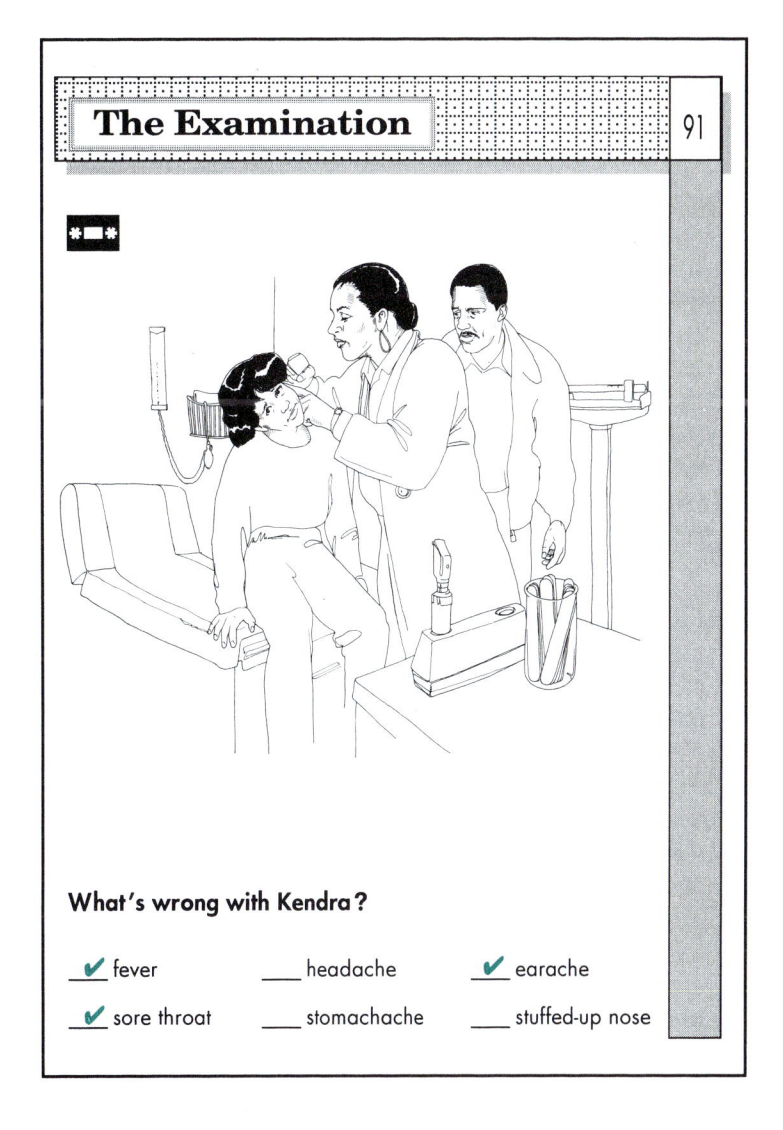

2. Ask learners if they have ever been to a doctor or clinic. Ask *Why did you go to the doctor/clinic? Who did you see? What did he/she do? What did you do?*

3. Play the audiotape and have learners listen to the conversation.

4. Ask *Does Kendra's ear hurt? Does her stomach hurt? Does her throat hurt? Does Dr. Johnson use a stethoscope? a flashlight? a thermometer? Does Kendra cry? giggle? say "Ahhh?" Is Dr. Johnson going to talk to the nurse? Fred Wilson?* Replay the audiotape to verify responses.

5. Together, read the question and words at the bottom of page 91. Then have learners check Kendra's problems. Replay the audiotape if necessary.

Expansion/Extension

See **TRF HANDOUT 9.2**, *Check-up*
TRF HANDOUT 9.3, *In the Doctor's Office*

- Introduce the names of other equipment in the examination room: *scale, blood pressure cuff, swabs, bandages.*

More *Expansion/Extension* on page 148

UNIT 9 • 141

Doctor's Advice

Purpose: To give practice in describing symptoms; to introduce taking medication

Teacher Preparation and Materials

1. Pictures of people with health problems used for page 91; new pictures: flu, backache
2. Index cards with sight words: *sore throat, headache, stomachache, earache, fever, cold, flu, backache*
3. Pictures of common types of medicines
4. Copies of TRF Handout 9.1, *A Sick Family (Expansion/Extension)*
5. Collect information on childhood diseases and health problems, or invite a guest speaker *(Expansion/Extension)*

Warm-up

1. Use pictures of health problems to review vocabulary. Have learners respond with simple sentences.
2. Tape the pictures of health problems on the board. Have volunteers read sight-word cards for the health problems and attach them under the appropriate pictures.
3. Say *My back hurts. What can I do (to get better)? Can I rest? Can I go to work? Can I drink tea?* Elicit a list of things to do or take for the various health problems.
4. Introduce new health problems. Show a picture of a man with the flu. Say *He has the flu. His head hurts. He has a sore throat. He has a fever. He's very tired, too. He feels terrible.* Show a picture of a woman with an earache. Say *She has an infection in her ear. Her ear hurts. There is a problem inside her ear. She feels terrible.*
5. Introduce common types of medicine by showing pictures. Model and have learners repeat *medicine, aspirin, antibiotic.* Ask *When do you take medicine? aspirin?*

Presentation

1. Have learners turn to page 92 and look at the pictures. Ask *What is the matter with Kendra? What is in the bottles? What is Kendra doing? What is she drinking? Where is she going in the last picture?*

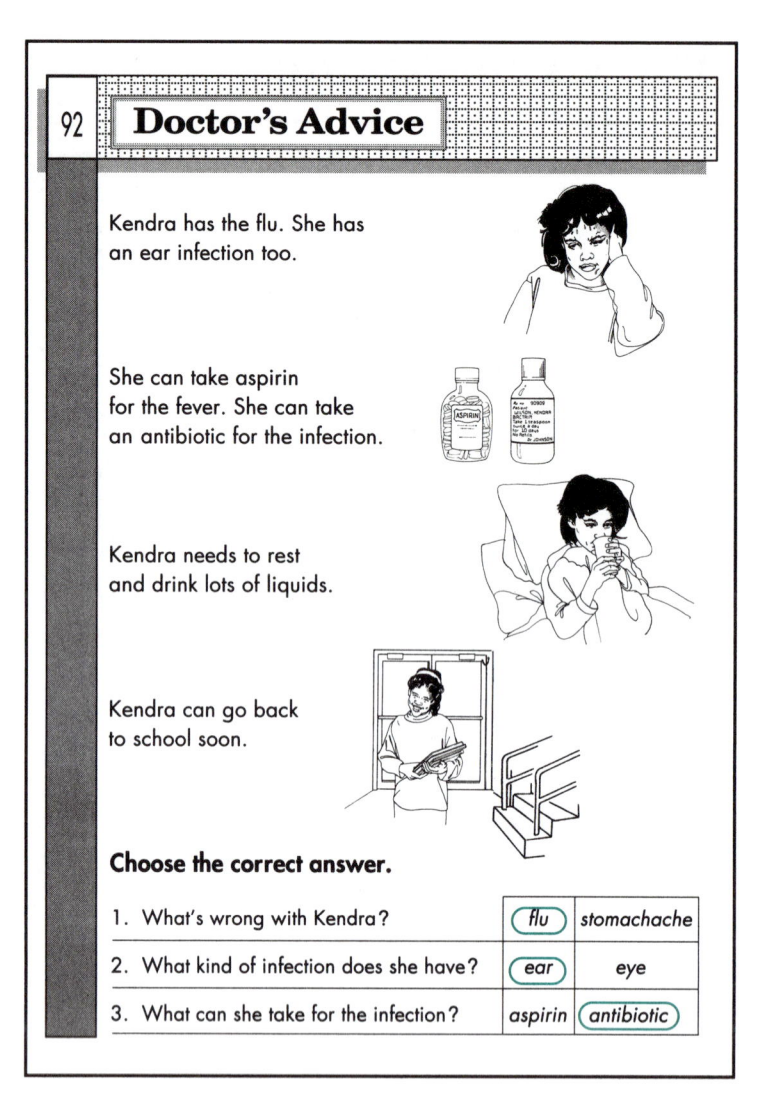

List the words and comments on the board. Be sure to include *flu, infection, aspirin, antibiotic,* and *liquids*. Explain what "Drink lots of liquids" means.

2. Have learners describe the pictures, using the words on the board.
3. Read the story together. Have learners find the new vocabulary words in the reading.
4. Ask *Does Kendra have the flu or a cold? Does she have a sore throat or an ear infection? Should Carol give her aspirin? Do antibiotics cure infections or headaches? Should Kendra play outside or rest? What should she drink? When can Kendra go back to school?*
5. Read the questions as a group. Then have learners underline or circle the answers to the questions.

Expansion/Extension
See **TRF HANDOUT 9.1,** *A Sick Family*

- Learners can share experiences of being sick or having a child who was sick. As a group, write an LEA story about the experiences.

More *Expansion/Extension* on page 149

Health Problems

Purpose: To give practice in describing symptoms, expressing need, and giving information

Teacher Preparation and Materials

1. Pictures of people with health problems used for page 92; new pictures: toothache, broken arm, broken leg
2. Sight words used for page 88
3. Magazines with pictures of health problems and/or first aid procedures *(Expansion/Extension)*
4. Copies of TRF Handout 9.7, *What Happened to You? (Expansion/Extension)*

Warm-up

1. Use picture cues to give practice in describing health problems. (FOR EXAMPLE: *My . . . hurts. I have a sore . . . . I have a/an . . . ache.*)
2. Introduce broken bones by showing pictures of people in casts. Model and have learners practice *I have a broken . . . .*

Presentation

1. Write the three expressions as headings for a chart on the board:
   My ... hurts. I have a/an ... ache. I have a broken ....
2. Hold up a sight-word card with the name of a body part. Ask *Which sentence can I use?* Repeat with other sight-word cards. Have learners list the words that fit in each of the expressions. *My . . . hurts.* (everything) *I have a/an . . . ache.* (stomach, ear, head, back, tooth) *I have a broken . . . .* (tooth, arm, elbow, hand, finger, leg, knee, foot, toe, back). (**Note:** Some parts can be used in more than one expression.) Also point out that certain health problems are expressed only one way. We don't say "I have an armache" or "I have a broken stomach."
3. Have learners turn to page 93 and look at the pictures. Ask *What's the matter with Kendra? What's the matter with the man?* Have learners describe the health problems.
4. Together, read the expressions in the bubbles at the top of the page.
5. Then have learners choose an expression for each of the pictures that follow.
6. In pairs, have learners practice asking for and giving information about health problems.

Expansion/Extension
See **TRF HANDOUT 9.7,** *What Happened to You?*

- Learners can look back on page 87 and find the item(s) needed for broken bones. Introduce vocabulary: *cast, crutches, sling, brace, bandage.*
- Introduce adverbs of frequency and severity, such as *all the time, sometimes, often, usually, a lot, a little.* Also introduce expressions to describe pain. FOR EXAMPLE: *It's a sharp/dull/constant pain. It hurts right here. It aches. It hurts when I walk.* Learners can practice describing a problem and its severity.
- Learners can assemble a first-aid booklet by making drawings or using pictures from magazines. Include advice on what to do for burns, cuts, nosebleeds, fainting, broken bones, unconsciousness, choking, and poisoning.

At the Drugstore

Purpose: To introduce reading medication labels; to introduce prepositional phrases of time and adverbs of frequency

Teacher Preparation and Materials

1. Samples of prescription and over-the-counter medicines: tablets, pills, creams, liquids, capsules, ointments
2. M&M's® or other pill-shaped food, teaspoons, water

Warm-up

1. Bring in medicines. Ask *What is in this bottle? Where can you get medicine? Why do people take them? Do you take medicine?* Model and have learners repeat new vocabulary: *liquid, pill, tablet, cream, capsule, ointment.* Have learners identify the medicines.
2. Separate the medicines into over-the-counter drugs and prescription drugs. Ask *What is different about these labels? How do you buy each of these?* and so on.
3. Place M&M's® (or other pill-shaped food), water, and teaspoons on a table. Give instructions to learners. FOR EXAMPLE: *Take two pills. Take one teaspoon.*
4. Introduce adverbs of frequency by making a chart on the board. FOR EXAMPLE:

Times Daily	Linda	Ramón
1 (once)	2 pills	1 teaspoon
2 (twice)	cream	1 tablet
3 (three times)	1 teaspoon	2 pills

Point to the chart and say *Linda and Ramón are sick. Linda takes two pills once a day. She puts on cream twice a day. And she takes one teaspoon (of medicine) three times a day.* Ask *What does she take once a day? What does she use twice a day? When (how often) does Linda take the pills?*

5. Repeat the procedure with Ramón. Model sentences with the adverbs of frequency and have learners repeat.
6. Write times on the board as you tell about Ramón. *Ramón has a bad cold. He takes two pills at 8:00 in the morning, 4:00 in the afternoon, and 12:00 at night.* Ask *How many times a day does he take the pills?* (three times) *How many hours apart does he take the pills?* (eight hours)
7. Repeat the procedure using other examples.

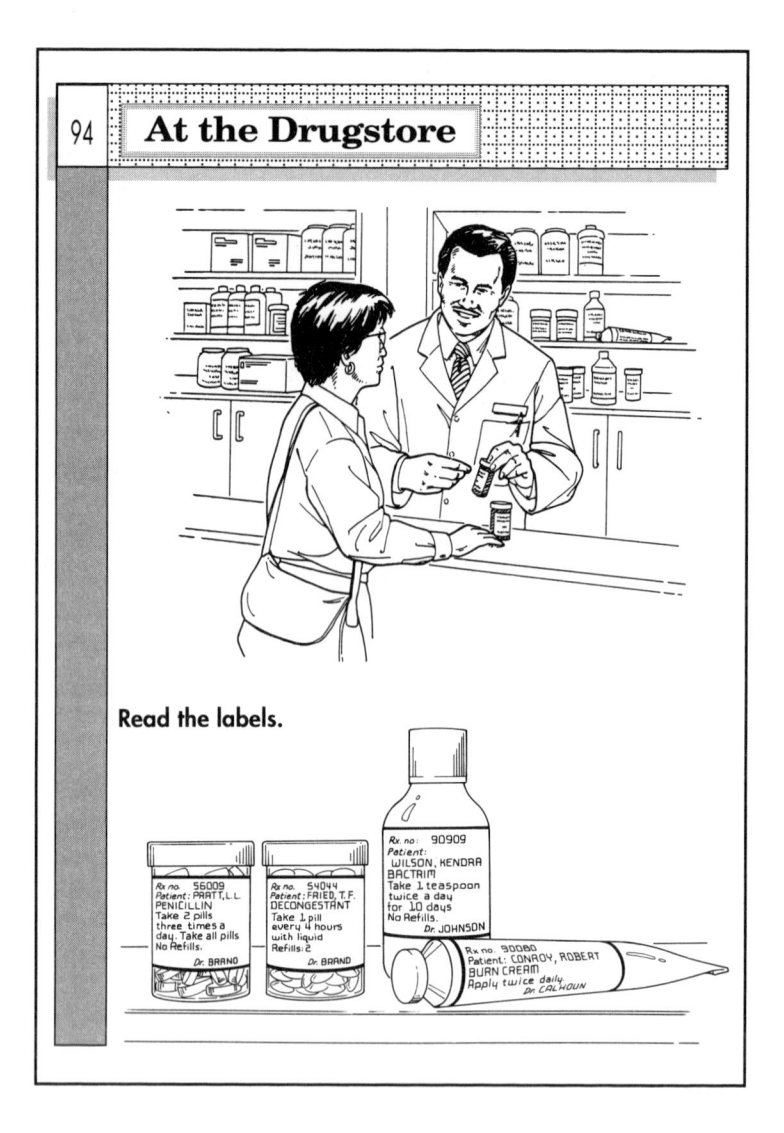

Presentation

1. Introduce prescription labels by writing one similar to those on page 94. Have learners find the information on the label. Ask *Who can take this medicine? How much does he/she take? How often does he/she take it? What is the prescription number?*
2. Have learners turn to page 94. Ask *What do you see? Where are these people?* List words and comments on the board.
3. Have learners look at the medicine labels and find the information. Medicine 1: *Who takes this medicine: Kendra or Dr. Johnson? Does she take one teaspoon or two teaspoons twice a day?* and so on.
4. Have learners mark parts of the medicine labels. Say *Circle how much medicine to take (or use). Underline the number of times a day (or how often).*

***Expansion/Extension* on page 149**

144 • UNIT 9

Reading Labels

Purpose: To give practice in reading medication labels and giving information; to give practice with adverbs of frequency and prepositional phrases of time

Teacher Preparation and Materials

1. Samples of prescription and over-the-counter medicines used for page 94, a teaspoon
2. Index cards with sight words: *patient, medicine, amount, times daily, special directions*
3. Copies of TRF Handout 9.4, *Prescriptions* (Expansion/Extension)
4. Copies of TRF Handout 9.5, *Poison!* (Expansion/Extension)
5. Copies of TRF Handout 9.6, *Medicine Cabinet* (Expansion/Extension)
6. Arrange a trip to a local drugstore (Expansion/Extension)

Warm-up

1. Show learners various types of medicines and a teaspoon and have learners give the names. (medicine, tablet, pill, etc.)
2. Write a sample prescription label on the board. Ask questions about it. *What's the patient's name? (Who takes this?) Where's the name of the medicine?* (Learners do not have to say the name, but should be able to find the type of medicine.) *How much does he/she take? How many times a day does he/she take it?* Depending on learners' skills, they can answer orally or point to the correct information.
3. Show sight-word cards: *patient, medicine, amount, times daily, special directions.* Have learners tape the cards next to the appropriate information on the prescription label.

Presentation

1. On the board, make a chart similar to the one on page 95. Together, read the column headings.
2. Have learners look at the prescription label used in the *Warm-up* and find the appropriate information. Ask a volunteer to copy the name of the person in the appropriate column. Have other volunteers come and fill in the rest of the chart.
3. Have learners turn to page 95 and look at the picture. Ask *Who do you see? What is Carol doing? What is Kendra doing? Why is Carol reading the label? Why is it important to follow the directions?*
4. On page 94, have learners find the medicine that is for Kendra. Ask *Where is the name of the medicine? How much does Kendra take? How often does she take the medicine?* Have learners fill in the information about her medicine on the chart on the board.
5. In pairs or small groups, have learners fill in the chart on page 95 with the information from the medicine labels on page 94.

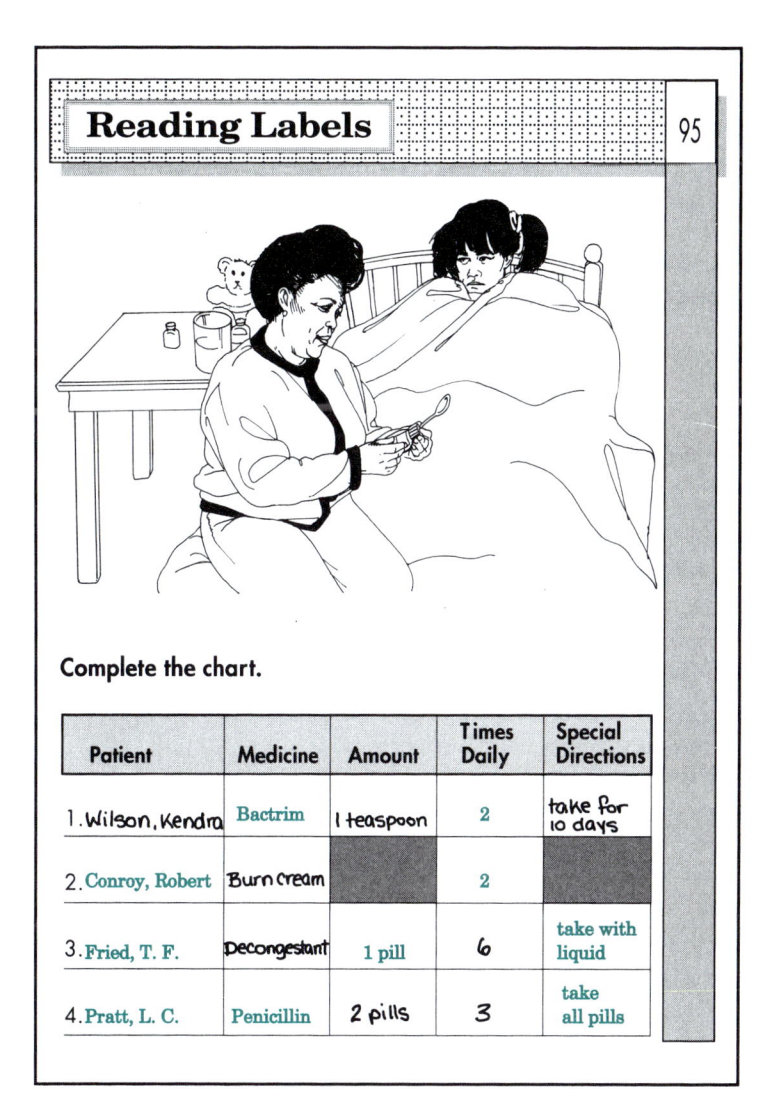

Expansion/Extension

See **TRF HANDOUT 9.4,** *Prescriptions*
  TRF HANDOUT 9.5, *Poison!*
  TRF HANDOUT 9.6, *Medicine Cabinet*

More *Expansion/Extension* on page 149

Reading Labels — 95

Complete the chart.

Patient	Medicine	Amount	Times Daily	Special Directions
1. Wilson, Kendra	Bactrim	1 teaspoon	2	take for 10 days
2. Conroy, Robert	Burn cream		2	
3. Fried, T. F.	Decongestant	1 pill	6	take with liquid
4. Pratt, L. C.	Penicillin	2 pills	3	take all pills

UNIT 9 • 145

Absence Notes

Purpose: To give practice in giving information; to introduce writing an absence note

Teacher Preparation and Materials
1. Pictures of people with health problems used for page 93
2. Thermometer *(Expansion/Extension)*
3. Magazines with pictures of healthful activities and habits, posterboard, scissors, and glue for all *(Expansion/Extension)*

Warm-up
1. Use picture cues to review identifying health problems with learners.
2. Introduce the past tense of the verb *have*. On the board, make a chart using some of the pictures of health problems:

	Now	Last Week
Kendra	[picture of person with a cut finger]	[picture of person with an earache]
Michael	[picture of person with the flu]	[picture of person with a headache]

Ask questions about the "Now" column. *What's the matter with Kendra?* (She has a cut.) *What's the matter with Michael?* (He has the flu.) Model and have learners repeat past-tense sentences about the "Last Week" column. *Kendra had an earache. Michael had a headache.*

3. Say sentences using the past and present of *have* and ask learners to respond with the appropriate column heading. FOR EXAMPLE: *Peter had a fever.* (Last Week) *Carol has a stomachache.* (Now) *Tom Lin has a broken foot.* (Now) *Anita had a cold.* (Last Week) Introduce *last month, last year,* etc.

Presentation
1. Have learners turn to page 96 and look at the picture. Ask *Who do you see? Where are they? What is Carol doing? What is Kendra doing? Is she still sick? How does she feel now? Why is Carol writing a note?*
2. Together, read the note. Ask questions about it. *Who is Ms. Brown? Why did Carol write a note to her?* and so on.
3. Ask *Did you ever write a note like this? Why do schools want absence notes? Why do some workplaces want a doctor's note when the worker is sick or hurt?*
4. Ask about the parts of the note: *What is written at the top of the page?/What is March 3, 1994?* (date) *Who is Ms. Brown?* (person getting letter) *What does Carol write about Kendra?* (reason for absence) *What does Carol write at the bottom of the note?* (signature)
5. Depending on learners' skills, have learners dictate an absence note for you to write on the board. Learners can copy it into their books. More advanced learners can write their own absence note. Learners can exchange books to correct each other's work. If learners do not have children in school, they can practice writing a note to an employer for an absence from work or to you for an absence from class.

Expansion/Extension
- Learners can practice calling in sick to school or work for themselves or for a family member. (My name is . . . . My son/daughter . . . cannot come to school. She is/has . . . . His/Her teacher is . . . . and so on.)

More *Expansion/Extension* on page 149

146 • UNIT 9

Look Back

Purpose: To give practice in identifying body parts, describing health problems, and reading and understanding directions for taking medication

Teacher Preparation and Materials

1. Full-length picture of a person (can be drawn on board)
2. Index cards with sight words used for page 88
3. Pictures of people with health problems used for page 93
4. Index cards with sight words used for page 92; new words: *toothache, broken arm, broken leg*
5. Index cards with phrases: *Take once/twice a day. Take three times a day. Take one teaspoon. Take two tablets. Take with food. Apply daily.* and so on
6. Posterboard and markers for all *(Expansion/Extension)*

Warm-up

1. Use picture cues to review identifying parts of the body and health problems.
2. Have learners match the pictures of health problems and parts of the body with the appropriate sight-word cards.
3. Give learners the sight-word cards with the direction phrases from medicine labels. As you say various phrases, have learners find the correct cards.
4. Make three simple drawings as column headings on the board: a medicine bottle, a sad face, a stick figure body. Write names of the column headings for each of the categories: *Directions, Health Problems, Body Parts*. Put all the sight-word cards in a pile and shuffle them. Demonstrate taking a card, reading it, and taping it under the proper column heading. Have learners take turns choosing a card and placing it in the correct column.

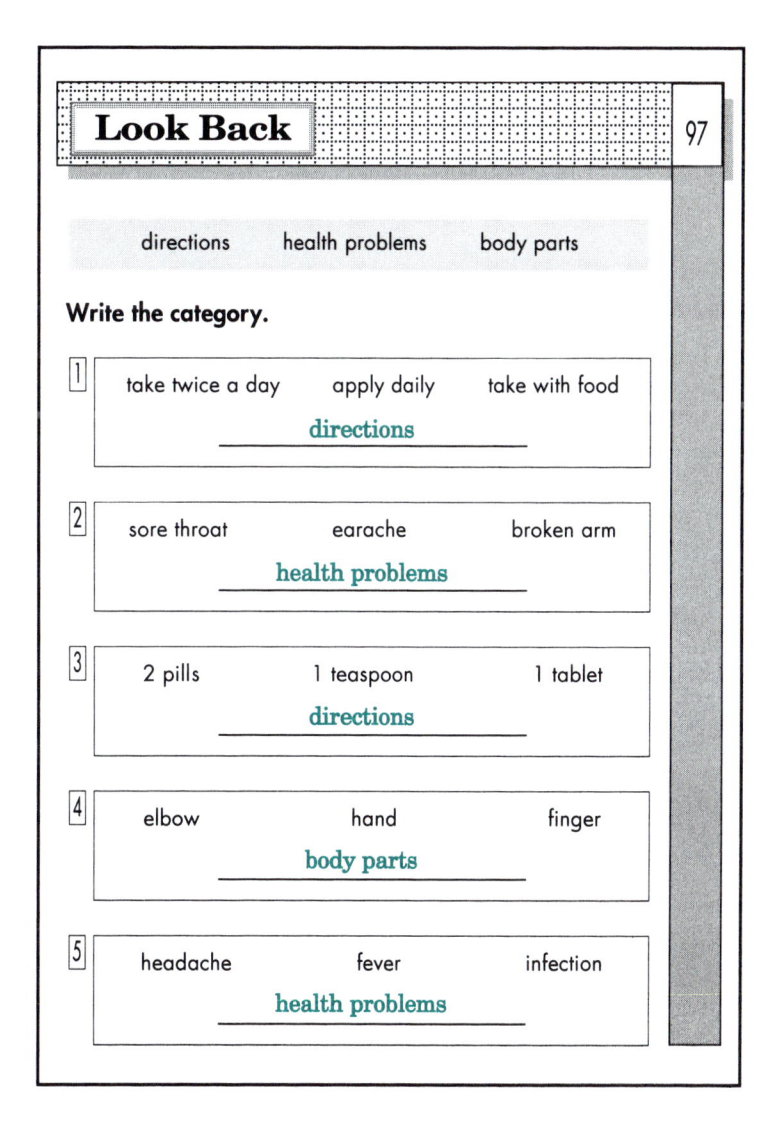

Look Back 97

directions   health problems   body parts

Write the category.

1. take twice a day   apply daily   take with food
   directions

2. sore throat   earache   broken arm
   health problems

3. 2 pills   1 teaspoon   1 tablet
   directions

4. elbow   hand   finger
   body parts

5. headache   fever   infection
   health problems

Presentation

1. Have learners turn to page 97. Together, read the categories in the box. Then read the three phrases in number 1. Ask *Are these parts of the body? Are they health problems? Are they directions?* Have learners write the correct category on the line.
2. Have learners complete the exercise on their own.

Expansion/Extension

- Discuss household hazards and how to prevent accidents. Some areas for discussion might be electrical outlets, fires, blocked doors, lead paint, and so on. Learners can make safety posters.

UNIT 9 • 147

UNIT 9: Getting Well
Expansion/Extension

What Hurts?
More *Expansion/Extension* for SB page 89

- Learners can look through magazines for pictures of people with health problems. In pairs, learners can use the pictures to describe the problems orally or they can label the pictures. (FOR EXAMPLE: What's wrong? His . . . hurts.)
- Refer to page 14 for emergency phone numbers. Add other emergency resources and their numbers to the list, such as those for a clinic, dentist, ambulance, emergency room, and Poison Information Center.
- Learners can categorize health problems according to the types of care needed, such as Emergency, Clinic/Appointment, and At Home. FOR EXAMPLE: Emergency: broken leg, large or severe burn/cut; Clinic/Appointment: ear hurts, throat hurts; At Home: nosebleed, head hurts.
- Learners can discuss what to do when a minor problem continues for an extended period of time. Discuss how keeping a record of when problems start can be useful in getting proper medical treatment.

Health Insurance Form
***Expansion/Extension* for SB page 90**

- Bring in samples of other clinic registration forms. Learners can compare the information required on the forms. Make copies of the samples and have learners practice filling them out for members of their families.
- Role-play filling out clinic registration forms. Often a receptionist or other clinic employee will check and verify information on the form with the insurance card. If learners have their own insurance cards, they can practice finding and giving the appropriate information. (FOR EXAMPLE: What's the company name? What's the policy number? Are you the employee?)
- Learners can share experiences of going to a doctor or clinic. Ask *Do you go to a doctor or a clinic? If you go to a clinic, do you see the same person all the time? What other people help you at a clinic?* (nurse, nurse practitioner, lab technician, and so on) *Do you fill out a form every time you go to the clinic?*
- Depending on learners' skills and interests, bring in information about various types of health insurance. Talk about types of plans. Introduce words such as *deductible, coverage, premium, copayment.*
- Learners can find out or bring in information on the costs of health care. You may want to include costs for checkups, emergency room visits, hospital stays, and X rays.

The Examination
More *Expansion/Extension* for SB page 91

- Create a TPR activity of a medical exam or parts of an exam.
  1. Say *You're sick. Go into the exam room. Open your mouth. Stick out your tongue. Say "Ahhh."*
  2. Say *You need an eye exam. Stand on the line. Cover your right eye. Read the chart. Cover your left eye. Read the first line.*
- Review the names of body parts by doing group exercises with commands. FOR EXAMPLE: *Put your hands on your waist. Bend your knees. Stand up straight.* or *Put your arms at your sides. Put your hands on your shoulders. Put your hands straight up. Stretch. Keep your arms straight. Put them down at your sides.*
- Learners can share experiences of medical exams and checkups. As a group, write an LEA story about medical exams.
- Discuss other medical professionals such as pediatricians, nurse practitioners, lab technicians, X-ray technicians. Ask *Who do they help? What do they do?*
- Learners can match pictures of medical equipment to the parts of the body or problems they are used on. FOR EXAMPLE: thermometer—mouth; blood pressure cuff—upper arm; eye chart—eye; stethoscope—chest (heart, lungs). Depending on learners' skills and interests, introduce the names of the various equipment.
- Introduce other health problems such as *virus, rash, cold, cut, scrape, nosebleed, burn, allergies, asthma, high blood pressure,* and *heart attack.*
- Give practice with expressions for sympathizing such as *I'm sorry to hear that. That's too bad. What a shame. I hope you feel better soon.* Learners can practice short conversations. FOR EXAMPLE:

  A. Hi, Tuan. How do you feel today?
  B. I don't feel well. I have a headache.
  A. I hope you feel better soon.

Doctor's Advice
More *Expansion/Extension* for SB page 92

- Discuss home remedies used in learners' native countries.
- Depending on learners' interests, discuss other common childhood diseases and health problems such as chicken pox, measles, German measles, lead poisoning, and lice. Bring in information about them or invite a guest speaker to discuss the topic.

At the Drugstore
***Expansion/Extension* for SB page 94**

- Introduce the terms *over-the-counter drugs* and *prescription drugs*. Learners can classify samples of medicines.
- Learners can share experiences of purchasing and using medications. Ask *Did you ever need medicine or a prescription? How did you know what medicine to get? Where did you buy the medicine? How much did it cost? Was it covered by insurance? How much did you have to take? How many days did you have to take it? Do you think the medicine helped you?* Write an LEA story about their experiences.
- Introduce other information found on medicine labels such as warnings, refills, names of medicines. *Why is this information important?* Find prepositional phrases such as *with meals, before meals, with liquid, for ten days, for one week.*
- Learners can role-play getting a prescription filled, picking up a prescription, asking for instructions on how to take the medicine, and asking for a refill.
- Learners can make a list of rules for proper use of prescription drugs. (FOR EXAMPLE: Keep out of reach of children. Don't use someone else's prescription. Don't drink alcohol when taking medicine. Follow directions. [Take with meals. Take with juice.] Talk to the doctor if unusual symptoms appear.) Discuss what unusual symptoms might be.

Reading Labels
More *Expansion/Extension* for SB page 95

- Present different problems involving medication. Learners can discuss what should be done in each case. FOR EXAMPLE:
  1. Carol forgot to give Kendra her medicine yesterday. Should she give Kendra four teaspoons today?
  2. Kendra takes the medicine for four days and feels better. Can/Should she stop taking the medicine?
  3. Carol sends the medicine to school for Kendra to take at lunchtime. (**Note:** A doctor's note is usually needed for children to be able to take medicine at school. The medicine also needs to be given to the school nurse or principal to make sure it is taken correctly.)
- Take a trip to a local drugstore. Find the place for ordering prescriptions. Find out if the drugstore accepts various types of insurance plans.
- Discuss generic and brand-name drugs. Ask *What is the difference in how they work? What is the difference in price? Why are they different prices? Which would you use?*

Absence Notes
More *Expansion/Extension* for SB page 96

- If learners have children in school, talk about appropriate health and medical issues. Ask *What immunizations are needed to enter school? Where can you get them? What happens when children get sick at school? What are common contagious diseases that children get? Can children take medicine at school? Is there a nurse at the school? What types of checkups can children get at school?*
- Learners can practice taking a person's temperature and reading a thermometer. Compare temperature readings in Fahrenheit and Celsius. Ask *What is a person's normal temperature? What do you do when someone has a fever? When should you call the doctor/clinic?*
- Talk about ways that people can stay healthy. Learners can make a collage of healthful activities and habits. Learners can find magazine pictures to cut out (or draw their own) and glue them on posterboard. They can label the collages.
- Introduce the negative and interrogative forms of the past tense of *have.* FOR EXAMPLE: *Did you have a cold last week? No, I didn't.*

1 2 3 4 5 6 7 8 9 10 11 12 Summary
Asking for Help

Objectives

Functions
- Describing problems
- Expressing need for service
- Requesting assistance

Life Tasks
- Calling 911
- Calling for repair work
- Writing a note to a landlord regarding a problem

Structures
- *Need* + passive infinitive
- Passive adjectives
- *Wh-* questions: *when, how*
- Past tense: regular verbs
- Past tense: irregular verbs
- Imperatives

Culture
- Community services in the United States and in native countries
- Understanding tenants' rights and responsibilities

Vocabulary

Key words:

911	kitchen
bed	lamp
bedroom	leaky
bookcase	lights
broken	living room
chair	lock
clean	paint
coffee table	peeling
curtains	refrigerator
desk	replace
dirty	rug
dishes	sink
door	smoke
doorknob	sofa
dresser	stairs
emergency	stove
faucet	table
fire	TV
fix	wall
floor	window

Related words:

ambulance	fire engine
building	fire fighters
burned	landlord
ceiling	pan
damaged	problems
destroyed	ruined
dinner	smoke detector
electric company	stained
fire department	utilities

150 • UNIT 10 • SUMMARY

A Kitchen Fire

Purpose: To introduce housing vocabulary

Teacher Preparation and Materials

1. Pictures of rooms in a house or apartment: kitchen, living room, bedroom
2. Pictures of housing features: walls, windows, doors, curtains, stove, smoke detector
3. Pictures of actions: sit, read, cook, call, watch (TV)
4. Smoke detector *(Expansion/Extension)*

Warm-up

1. Use picture cues to introduce the names of rooms and various housing features.
2. Review the present continuous tense. If necessary, model *What are you doing? I'm reading a book.* Give each learner a picture of an action. Learners can practice asking and answering questions according to their pictures. Also give practice with questions and answers in the third person. FOR EXAMPLE: *What is Ramón doing? He's watching TV.*

Presentation

1. Have learners turn to page 98 and look at the picture. Ask *Who do you see? What rooms do you see? What do you see in the rooms?* List the words and comments on the board. Be sure to include *kitchen, pan, living room, curtains, stove, fire, smoke,* and *smoke detector.*
2. Ask questions about the Wilson family. *Where do the Wilsons live? Who is in the family? Where do you think Carol is? Kendra? Michael?*
3. Together, read the question *What's happening?* If necessary, ask questions to guide the discussion. *Where is Fred? What's he doing? What's on the stove? What's burning?*
4. Have learners suggest things that Fred should do.

1 2 3 4 5 6 7 8 9 10 11 12
Asking for Help ■ ■ ■ ■ ■ ■ ■ ■

A Kitchen Fire
What's happening?   **Answers may vary.**

Expansion/Extension

- Write an LEA story about the picture using the words and phrases from the board.
- Bring in a smoke detector. Demonstrate how it works. Learners can think about where smoke detectors should be put in houses/apartments. Learners can suggest what people should do if the alarm goes off.
- If learners have had any experiences with fires, let them share their stories. Ask *Where was it? How did it start? What did you do?* and so on.

Calling for Help

Purpose: To introduce calling for help; to give practice with emergency vocabulary

Teacher Preparation and Materials
1. Pictures of emergency vehicles and people associated with them: fire engine/fire fighter, police car/police officer, ambulance/paramedic, doctor, nurse
2. Audiotape for Level 1
3. Copies of TRF Handout 10.1, *Dial 911 (Expansion/Extension)*
4. Copies of TRF Handout 10.2, *911 Conversation (Expansion/Extension)*
5. Arrange a trip to a local fire station or invite a guest speaker on fire-safety procedures. *(Expansion/Extension)*

Warm-up
1. Use picture cues to introduce or review names of emergency vehicles and the people associated with them: *fire engine/fire fighter, police car/police officer, ambulance/paramedic, doctor, nurse.* Ask *What is this? Who uses it? When can they help you?*
2. Have learners turn to page 14 and review the emergency phone numbers for their area. *What number do you call for a fire? What number do you call for an emergency? What are some emergencies?* If necessary, explain that in some parts of the United States, 911 is the number used to report all emergencies.
3. Review asking and answering questions about personal information. This can be done in a chain drill. (FOR EXAMPLE: *What's your address? What's your apartment number? What's your name? How do you spell it?*)

Presentation
1. Have learners turn to page 99 and look at the picture. Ask *Who do you see? What are they doing? Where are they?* List the words and comments on the board. Be sure to include *fire, 911, emergency.*
2. Have learners give ideas about whom Anita is calling and what she is saying.

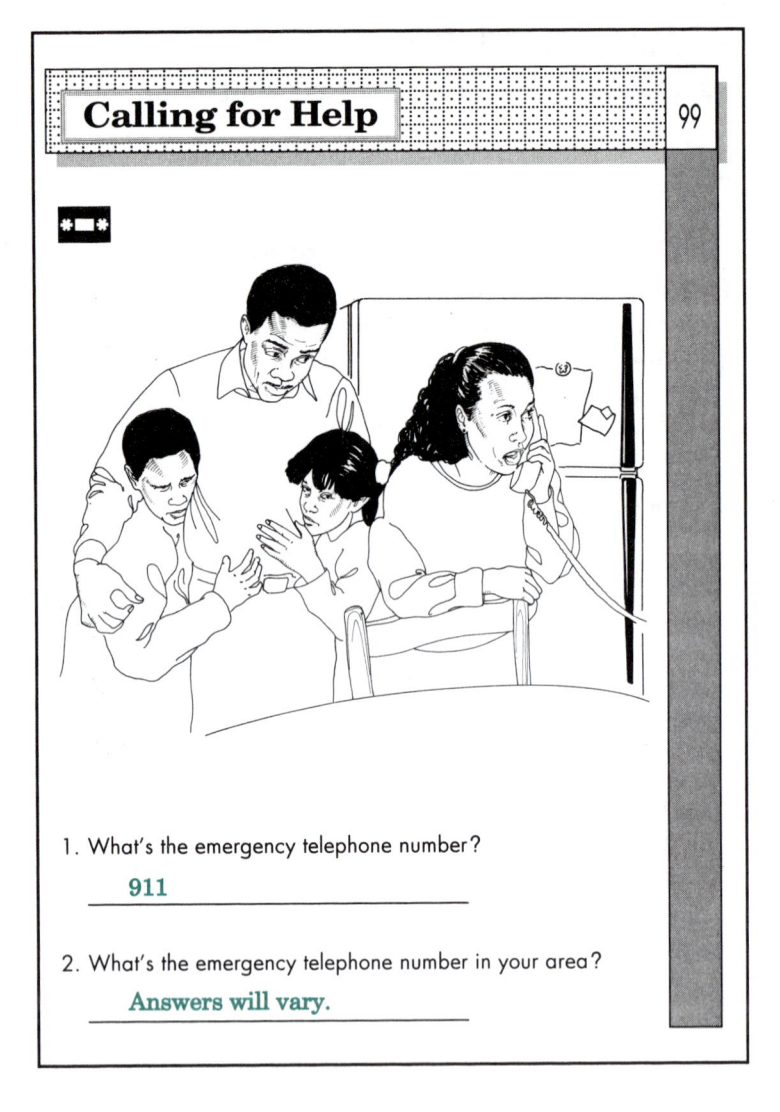

3. Have learners listen to the audiotape. Ask comprehension questions about the telephone call. *Who is Anita calling? What information does she give? What must everyone do?* Replay the audiotape to verify comprehension.
4. Discuss where the other tenants might be and how Anita can alert them. Ask *Who else lives at 127 Center Street? Where do you think they are? How should Anita tell them about the fire?*
5. Have learners answer the questions at the bottom of the page. If necessary, they can look back at page 14 for the emergency number used in their local area.

Expansion/Extension
See **TRF HANDOUT 10.1,** *Dial 911*
  TRF HANDOUT 10.2, *911 Conversation*

- Discuss the fact that the emergency number may be different in certain areas. Say *If you do not know the emergency number in your area, you can dial 0 for operator and report your emergency.*

More *Expansion/Extension* on page 162

Calling for Help

1. What's the emergency telephone number?
   911

2. What's the emergency telephone number in your area?
   Answers will vary.

152 • UNIT 10

More About the Fire

Purpose: To give practice in handling emergency situations; to give practice in using *Wh-* questions and past tense of regular verbs; to introduce past tense of some irregular verbs

Teacher Preparation and Materials

Newspaper articles or photos of fires (Expansion/Extension)

Warm-up

Have learners review the events and pictures on pages 98 and 99. Have learners summarize the events. Ask questions such as *Where did the fire start? Where was Fred? What did he do? What did Anita do?*

Presentation

1. Have learners turn to page 100 and look at the picture. Ask questions using the past tense. *Who came? Why did they come? What did they do? Where did the fire start? Who called for help?* and so on.
2. Together, read the story. Help learners with new vocabulary: *fire fighters, dinner, curtains.*
3. Ask questions about the reading. *Where was the fire? Where did it start? What did Fred burn? What caught on fire? What number did Anita call? Who came and put out the fire?* and so on.
4. Have learners find the regular and irregular verbs in the reading. List them on the board in separate columns. (*started, burned, called; was, caught, came, put*)
5. Have learners complete the exercise individually or in pairs. If necessary, read the statements together.

Expansion/Extension

- Learners can correct the false statements to make them true. (1. There was a fire in apartment *2A.* and so on.)
- Using the list of regular and irregular verbs on the board, learners can practice making statements and questions based on the story. (FOR EXAMPLE: Did the fire start in apartment 2B? No, it started in 2A.)

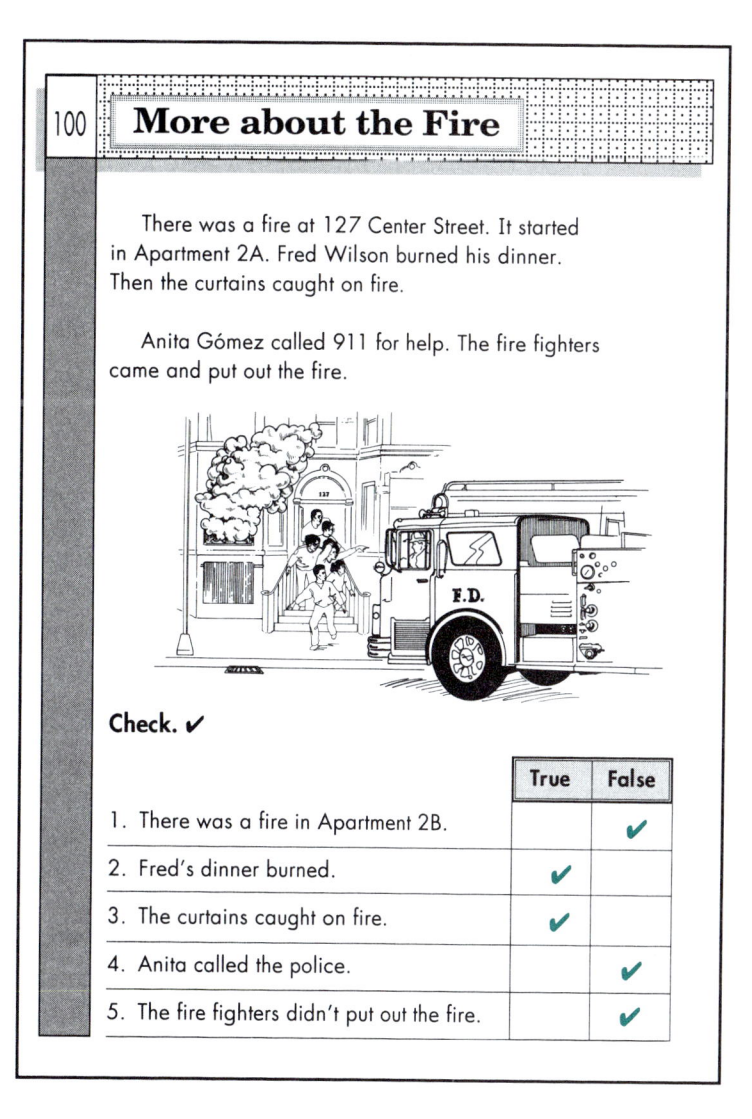

---

100 More about the Fire

There was a fire at 127 Center Street. It started in Apartment 2A. Fred Wilson burned his dinner. Then the curtains caught on fire.

Anita Gómez called 911 for help. The fire fighters came and put out the fire.

Check. ✔

	True	False
1. There was a fire in Apartment 2B.		✔
2. Fred's dinner burned.	✔	
3. The curtains caught on fire.	✔	
4. Anita called the police.		✔
5. The fire fighters didn't put out the fire.		✔

- Learners can find stories or pictures of fires in newspapers. Have them scan the articles or photo captions to find information such as the address, where the fire started, and so on.
- If learners have seen or been in a fire, write an LEA story about their experiences.
- Compare emergency help in the United States with help in learners' native countries. Ask *Who helped in emergencies? How did you get help?* and so on. Have learners prepare a chart showing similarities and differences.

Waiting for News

Purpose: To give practice with past tense of regular verbs and some irregular verbs

Teacher Preparation and Materials

1. Pictures of rooms used for page 98; new pictures: outdoor scenes with trees and grass
2. Audiotape for Level 1
3. Pictures of fire-fighting equipment: hydrant, hose, ax, ladder, etc. *(Expansion/Extension)*
4. First aid information for burns *(Expansion/Extension)*

Warm-up

1. On the board, make a chart with words and the pictures.

	Now	Before
Fred	[picture of a kitchen]	[picture of a living room]
Michael and Kendra	[picture of a bedroom]	[picture of outside scene]

Model present- and past-tense sentences with the verb *be*. *Now, Fred is in the kitchen. Before, he was in the living room. Now, Michael and Kendra are in the bedroom. Before, they were outside.* Have learners form sentences as you point to various parts of the chart.

2. Give practice with *Wh-* questions and answers based on the chart. Ask questions and have learners respond with the appropriate information and tense. FOR EXAMPLE: *Where is Fred now?* (He's in the kitchen.) *Where were Michael and Kendra?* (They were outside.)

Presentation

1. Have learners turn to page 101 and look at the picture. Ask *Who do you see? What are the fire fighters doing? What are the other people doing? What do you think they are talking about? How do you think they feel?*

2. Play the audiotape and have learners listen to the first conversation. Ask *Where are Lily and David? How did the fire start? Who was at home?* Replay the audiotape to verify comprehension.

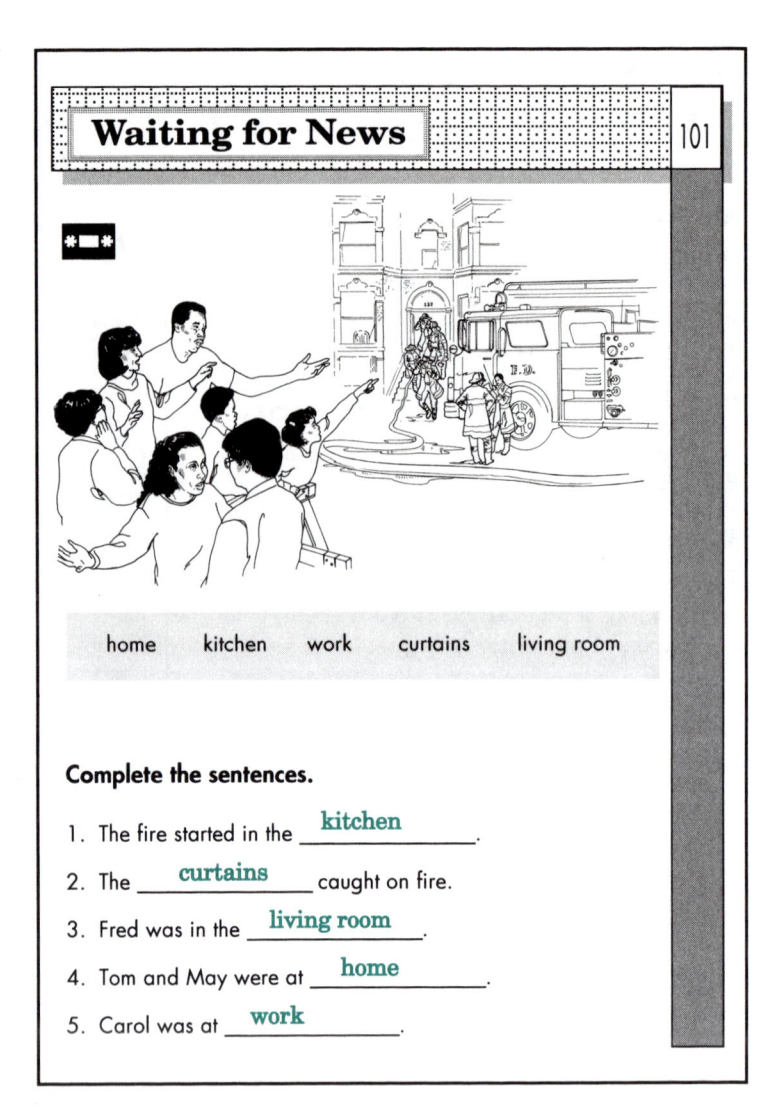

Waiting for News 101

Complete the sentences.

1. The fire started in the __kitchen__.
2. The __curtains__ caught on fire.
3. Fred was in the __living room__.
4. Tom and May were at __home__.
5. Carol was at __work__.

home   kitchen   work   curtains   living room

3. Play the audiotape and have learners listen to the second conversation. Ask *Where's Carol? Is anyone hurt? Where was Fred? What caught on fire? Who says the Wilsons can stay at her apartment?* Replay the audiotape to verify comprehension.

4. Together, read the words in the box.

5. If necessary, read the statements together. Then, have learners complete the sentences at the bottom of the page individually or in pairs. Replay the audiotape and have learners listen again to check their answers.

Expansion/Extension

- If learners are interested, use picture cues to introduce names of equipment used by fire fighters: *hydrant, hose, ax, ladder,* and so on.

- Discuss what happens to people who get hurt in fires. Ask *Who takes care of them? Where do they go?* Also, go over first aid for burns.

More *Expansion/Extension* on page 162

After the Fire

Purpose: To give practice with housing vocabulary; to introduce furniture vocabulary

Teacher Preparation and Materials

1. Pictures of rooms used for page 98
2. Pictures of furniture and appliances: sink, stove, refrigerator, table, chair, lamp, sofa, bed, dresser, rug, dishes, TV, coffee table, desk, bookcase
3. Magazines with pictures of furniture and rooms, or department store ads for household goods
4. Store catalogs or newspaper ads for household goods *(Expansion/Extension)*

Warm-up

1. Use picture cues to review or introduce the names of rooms in a house and the names of furniture and appliances.
2. Have learners look through magazines for pictures of various rooms. Have them identify the furniture and appliances found in the pictures. Alternatively, have learners look through store ads for various items. Say *Show me a table. Can you find a sofa?* and so on.

Presentation

1. Have learners turn to page 102 and look at the picture. Have learners find various rooms and furniture in the picture. Say *Show me the kitchen. Where's the coffee table? Point to the sink.* and so on.
2. Introduce descriptive words: *broken, burned, dirty, clean.* Have learners find the window. Ask *Is the window OK?* Model *It's broken/The window is broken.* Have learners find other items in the apartment that are broken, such as some of the chairs, the dishes, and a lamp. Repeat the procedure for *burned.* Have learners find the burned stove and curtains. Repeat the procedure for *clean* and *dirty.* Have learners identify items for each word.

Expansion/Extension

- As a group, write an LEA story about what happened after the fire. (FOR EXAMPLE: There was a fire in apartment 2A. Now the window is broken. The rug is dirty.)
- Learners can add names of other items found in the kitchen, living room, and bedroom to the picture on page 102.
- Learners can look through ads and circle the names of various pieces of furniture. Point out that some items have more than one name (sofa/couch, dresser/bureau, etc.).
- Give learners store catalogs or ads for household goods. In small groups, learners can find items to replace those that were damaged in the fire. Give learners a limit of $600 to spend. Learners can list items and cost of things needed. Then have the groups compare their lists.
- Introduce other rooms such as *dining room* and *bathroom.* Also introduce items commonly found in those rooms.
- Introduce other adjectives to describe the furniture on page 102, such as *damaged, destroyed, ruined, stained.*

UNIT 10 • **155**

Furniture

Purpose: To give practice with furniture and housing vocabulary

Teacher Preparation and Materials

1. Pictures of rooms used for page 98
2. Pictures of furniture and appliances used for page 102
3. Copies of TRF Handout 10.3, *Floor Plans* (Expansion/Extension)
4. Copies of TRF Handout 10.7, *Poetic Dog License* (Expansion/Extension)

Warm-up

1. Use picture cues to review the names of the rooms and furnishings.
2. Tape the pictures of the three rooms on the board. Place the pictures of the furnishings on a table. Model giving directions and taping the items under the correct room. FOR EXAMPLE: *Put the table in the living room. Can you move the rug to the bedroom? The stove should go in the kitchen.* Learners can give each other directions about where to place items.

Presentation

1. On the board, make a chart similar to the one on page 103. Have learners identify the rooms. Show a picture of a table. Ask *Where do I need a table?* Have learners name the room(s). Write *table* under the room(s). Give another example, such as *Where do I need a refrigerator?*
2. Have learners turn to page 103. If necessary, read together the names of the furniture and rooms.
3. Have learners work individually categorizing the furnishings. Learners may arrange the furniture in different ways. Some items may appear in two or three columns.
4. As a group, compare the results. (*Raoul, where did you put the rug? Lisa, did you put the rug in the living room? Where did you put it?* and so on.)

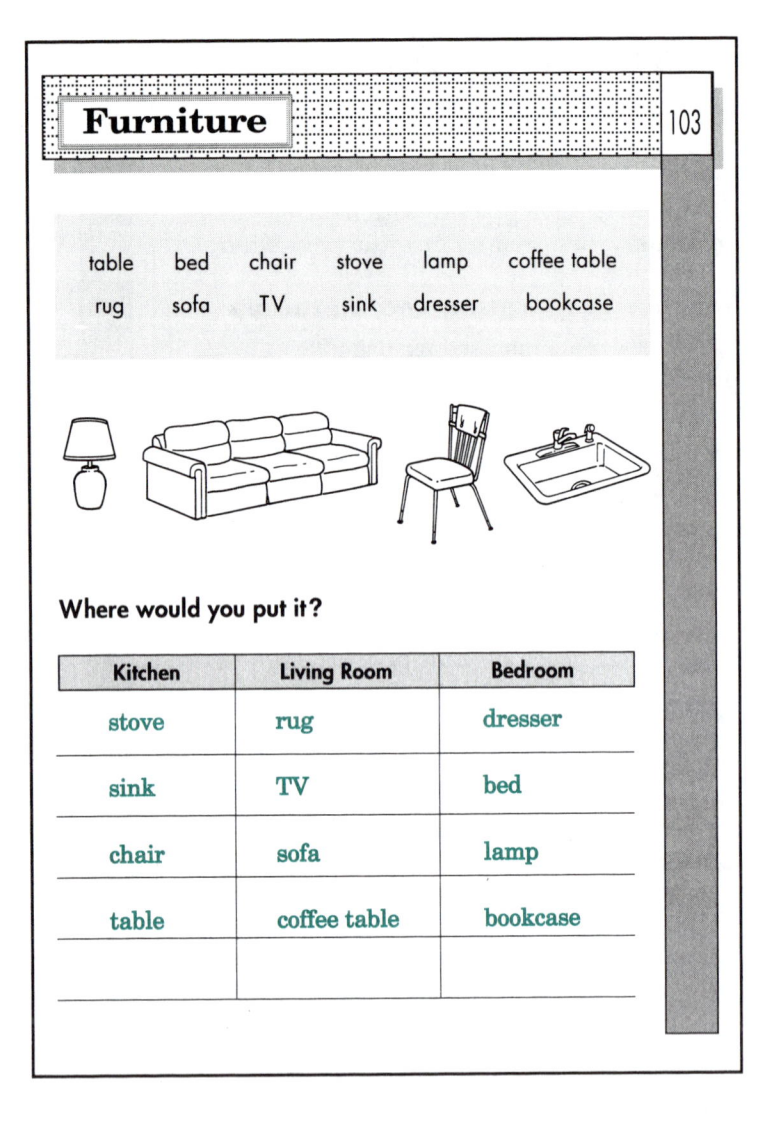

Furniture 103

table bed chair stove lamp coffee table
rug sofa TV sink dresser bookcase

Where would you put it?

Kitchen	Living Room	Bedroom
stove	rug	dresser
sink	TV	bed
chair	sofa	lamp
table	coffee table	bookcase

Expansion/Extension

See **TRF HANDOUT 10.3**, *Floor Plans*
TRF HANDOUT 10.7, *Poetic Dog License*

- Learners can write sentences to summarize their charts. (FOR EXAMPLE: *In the kitchen, I put a table, three chairs, a stove, and a refrigerator.*)
- Learners can add any number of items needed for each room and, if desired, include the colors or styles of the items. (FOR EXAMPLE: *I put a white electric stove in the kitchen.*)
- Talk about where to buy furniture: furniture stores, department stores, second-hand stores, yard sales, and so on. Compare prices and condition of furniture found at the various places.
- Learners can categorize furniture according to things that they need and things that they would like to have. Learners can also list other items they would like, such as radios, stereos, and washing machines.

Making Repairs

Purpose: To introduce describing problems; to give practice in asking for help; to introduce *need + to be + past participle*

Teacher Preparation and Materials

1. Pictures of furniture and appliances used for page 102
2. Pictures of repair tools: screwdriver, wrench, pliers; pictures of cleaning items: sponge, soap, scrub pad, mop; pictures of painting items: can of paint, brush, roller; ads for appliances
3. Audiotape for Level 1
4. Sample rental agreement or lease *(Expansion/Extension)*
5. Store catalogs or ads for appliances *(Expansion/Extension)*
6. Information from gas company *(Expansion/Extension)*

Warm-up

1. Use picture cues to review the names of furniture and appliances.
2. Have learners turn to page 102 and look at the picture. Review items that are broken and dirty. Ask *What's broken? (Is the window broken or OK?) What's dirty? (Is the wall dirty or clean?)*
3. Tape the pictures of the repair tools, cleaning items, painting items, and appliance ads on the board. Number the pictures *1, 2, 3,* and *4*. Say a sentence and have learners give the number of the picture that shows what is needed to correct the problem. FOR EXAMPLE: *The wall is dirty. What do I need?* (3) *The table is broken. What do I need?* (1) *The floor is dirty.* (2) *The stove is broken.* (4)
4. Model and have learners repeat sentences about repairs. *(1) It needs to be fixed. (2) It needs to be cleaned. (3) It needs to be painted. (4) It needs to be replaced.* Then, point out various problems in the apartment and have learners respond with the appropriate solutions.

Presentation

1. Have learners turn to page 104 and look at the picture. Ask *Who do you see? What are they doing? What is broken? What is dirty? What is burned? What do you think Anita is writing? Why is she writing things?*
2. Together, read the words in the box. Have learners identify these items in the picture above.
3. Play the audiotape and have learners listen to the phone conversation.
4. Ask *Are the lights working? What's ruined? What's broken? What things are dirty? What made the walls and rugs dirty? What things are burned? What is Anita going to do?* Replay the audiotape to verify comprehension.
5. Learners can work individually or in pairs completing Anita's work list and answering the question at the bottom of the page.

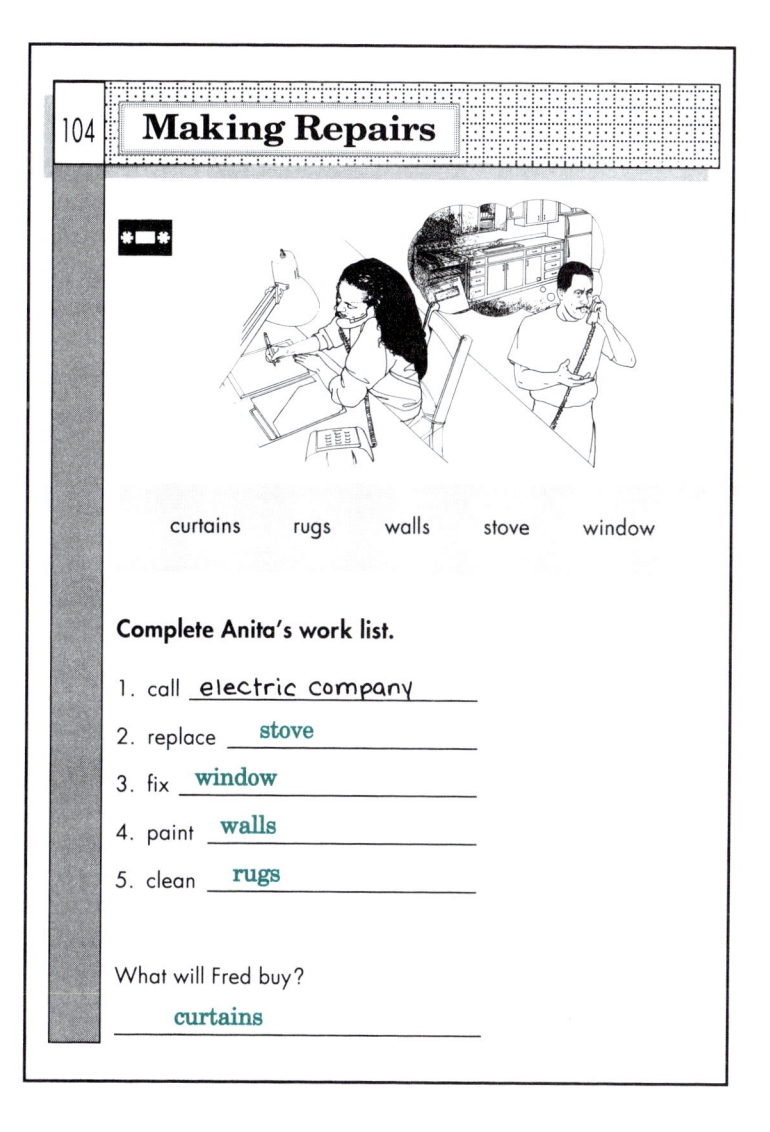

Expansion/Extension

- Introduce the names of various tools and equipment needed for household repairs and cleanups, such as *wrench, screwdriver, pliers, sponge, mop, paintbrush,* and *roller*.

More *Expansion/Extension* on page 162

---

104 Making Repairs

curtains   rugs   walls   stove   window

Complete Anita's work list.

1. call   electric company
2. replace   stove
3. fix   window
4. paint   walls
5. clean   rugs

What will Fred buy?
curtains

UNIT 10 • 157

Calling for Repair Work

Purpose: To introduce passive adjectives; to give practice in expressing need for service

Teacher Preparation and Materials

1. Pictures of furniture and appliances used for page 102
2. Audiotape for Level 1
3. Copies of TRF Handout 10.6, *Work to Do* *(Expansion/Extension)*
4. Toy telephones *(Expansion/Extension)*
5. Blank index cards *(Expansion/Extension)*
6. Local yellow pages *(Expansion/Extension)*

Warm-up

1. Use picture cues to review the names of furniture and appliances.
2. Have learners look at the picture on page 102. Review broken and dirty items.
3. On the board, write *The window is broken. I have a broken window.* Model the two sentences and have learners repeat.
4. Say sentences about broken appliances and furnishings and have learners give the alternative form. FOR EXAMPLE: *The stove is broken.* (I have a broken stove.) *The TV is broken.* (I have a broken TV.)
5. Repeat the procedure for the adjective *dirty*, using *rug, walls, floor, sofa*.
6. Introduce *utilities*. Give examples of utilities: *water, gas, heat, lights (electricity)*. Explain that these cannot be "broken." Model and have learners repeat sentences about problems with utilities. *The water doesn't work. (I have no water.) The lights don't work. (I have no lights.)* and so on.

Presentation

1. Have learners turn to page 105 and look at the pictures. Ask *Who do you see? Where is she calling? (Find the electric company. Show me the glass company.) Why is she calling the electric company? What is the problem? What will they do?*
2. Play the audiotape and have learners listen to each of the four conversations separately. Have learners identify the picture that goes with each phone call.
3. In pairs or small groups, have learners decide what the main problem is in each conversation. Have learners write the problem on the blank line.

Expansion/Extension
See **TRF HANDOUT 10.6,** *Work to Do*

- Learners can role-play calling companies using the toy telephones. In pairs, one learner can role-play the worker and the other learner can be the person reporting a problem. The worker should be prepared to give a day and time when he or she can fix the problem. The person with the problem should give his or her name and address, and describe the problem.
- Make a matching game using sentences about apartment problems. Write the two forms of sentences on separate index cards. FOR EXAMPLE: *I have a broken stove. The stove is broken.* Learners can match the sentences that describe the same problem. They can also play Concentration.

More *Expansion/Extension* on page 162

158 • UNIT 10

About You

Purpose: To introduce more housing vocabulary; to give practice in using passive adjectives and *need* + *to be* + past participle; to give practice in describing problems

Teacher Preparation and Materials

1. Pictures of furniture and appliances used for page 102
2. Pictures of housing features: faucet, pipe, stairs, doorknob, furniture with peeling paint
3. Picture of running water
4. Copies of TRF Handout 10.4, *Finding an Apartment (Expansion/Extension)*
5. Copies of TRF Handout 10.5, *It's Your Responsibility. (Expansion/Extension)*
6. Sample rental agreement or lease *(Expansion/Extension)*
7. Brochures and information on tenants' rights, or guest speaker from housing authority or tenants' association *(Expansion/Extension)*

Warm-up

1. Use picture cues to review names of appliances and housing features. Introduce new items: *stairs, faucet, pipe, doorknob, peeling paint.*
2. Tape the picture of running water on the board. Ask *What is this? What things in your home use water?* Have learners identify the appropriate items.
3. Introduce describing household problems. Model sentences and have learners repeat as you point to pictures. FOR EXAMPLE: *I have a leaky pipe. The faucet is leaky.*

Presentation

1. Have learners turn to page 106 and look at the pictures. Ask *What's the problem? What needs to be fixed?*
2. Ask *Do you have problems in your home? What problems do you have?* Make a list on the board.
3. Ask about solutions. *What can you do about this problem? Did you fix it? Did you tell someone? Did you call someone to fix it?*

Let learners share experiences. If necessary, review the story of how Fred told Anita about the problems and then Anita called for repairs.

4. If learners are renting, introduce and ask about *landlords* and *building superintendents*. *Do you ever see the landlord/superintendent? Does he/she live in the same building? Does he/she help with repairs?* If learners are not renting, ask how things get repaired. *Who helps you when something is broken? Can you fix things? Do you ask for help?*
5. Have learners individually make a list of things they need repaired.

Expansion/Extension
See TRF HANDOUT 10.4, *Finding an Apartment*
TRF HANDOUT 10.5, *It's Your Responsibility*.

- Learners can expand their list of household problems to include location of the problems. (FOR EXAMPLE: broken window in the kitchen, leaky faucet in the bathroom)

More *Expansion/Extension* on page 162

Writing a Note

Purpose: To give practice in describing problems, using housing vocabulary, expressing need for service, and using *need* + *to be* + past participle

Teacher Preparation and Materials
None

Warm-up

1. Have learners look back at the picture on page 102. Orally review the problems in the Wilsons' apartment. (FOR EXAMPLE: The walls are dirty. The window is broken.)

2. On the board, draw a simple three-story building. Ask *What floor do the Wilsons live on?* (the second floor) *Who lives on the first and third floors?* (Anita and the Lins) Ask learners if they think there are any problems in the other apartments in the building. *What problems do you think Anita has? What problems do you think the Lins have?*

Presentation

1. Have learners turn to page 107 and look at the picture. Ask *Who do you see? What is he doing? Whose apartment is 1A?*

2. Together, read the note on page 107.

3. Ask questions about the note. *Who is the note to? What is the problem with the kitchen walls? Why are they black? What's dirty? Do the lights work? What needs to be fixed in the apartment? Who wrote the note? What apartment does he live in?*

4. Ask learners whom they talk to if there is a problem in their apartment or house. *Do you have a landlord or building superintendent? What is his or her name?*

5. Have learners think of things they need fixed. They can refer to their lists on page 106.

6. Then, learners can write a letter to their landlord or superintendent. If learners do not have a landlord or superintendent, they can choose one particular problem and write a letter to an appropriate repair company. Depending on learners' skills, they can either write their own letters or dictate a letter for you to write on the board. Learners can then copy it into their books.

Expansion/Extension

- Learners can decide if the problems they wrote about are health or safety hazards. If there are unsafe situations, encourage learners to send the letters to their landlords.

- Discuss communication with landlords. Learners should date letters and keep copies of them. Learners can share experiences they have had with landlords.

160 • UNIT 10

Look Back

Purpose: To give practice with housing vocabulary; to give practice in expressing need for service

Teacher Preparation and Materials

1. Pictures of furniture and appliances used for page 102
2. Index cards with sight words: *paint, fix, clean, replace*

Warm-up

1. Use picture cues to review names of furniture and appliances.
2. Tape the sight-word cards on the board. Have learners read each word aloud.
3. Show a picture of a piece of furniture or an appliance. Model a sentence and question about a problem with the item. Have learners reply with a sentence using the word for what should be done. FOR EXAMPLE: *In my apartment, I have a broken window. What should be done?* (Fix it.) *There's a leaky faucet in my kitchen. What should be done?* (Fix it.) *The curtain is dirty.* (Clean it.)

Presentation

Have learners turn to page 108 and complete the exercise individually.

Expansion/Extension

- Learners can role-play a tenant talking to a landlord/superintendent about various apartment problems. The landlord/superintendent can make a work list from the information given.

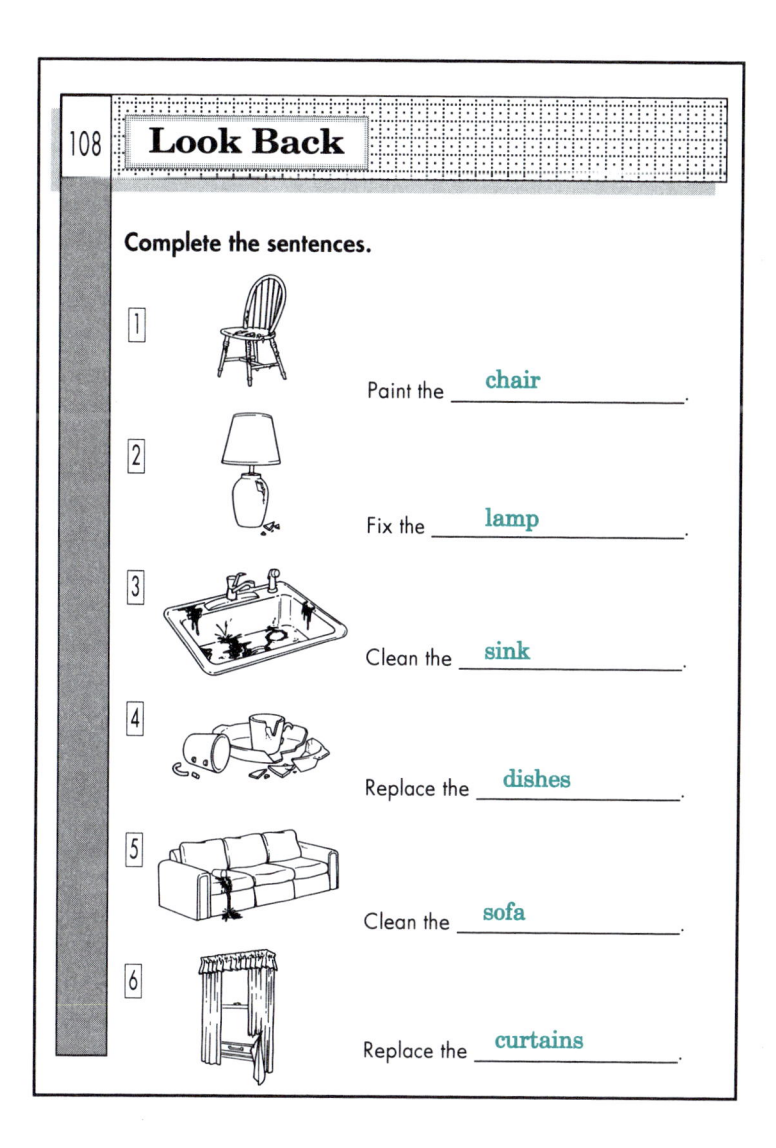

---

108 Look Back

Complete the sentences.

1. Paint the __chair__.
2. Fix the __lamp__.
3. Clean the __sink__.
4. Replace the __dishes__.
5. Clean the __sofa__.
6. Replace the __curtains__.

UNIT 10 • 161

UNIT 10: Asking for Help
Expansion/Extension

Calling for Help
More *Expansion/Extension* for SB page 99

- Arrange for learners to take a trip to a local fire station or have a guest speaker come to talk about fire-safety procedures.
- Locate any fire extinguishers or fire alarms in the building. Discuss when they should be used. Find any emergency exits from the building. Have a fire drill to practice going to the proper exit. Discuss safety procedures for getting out of a burning building. FOR EXAMPLE: Crawl to avoid breathing smoke. Touch doors before opening them. Don't hide under beds or in closets. If your clothes are burning, you should stop, drop, and roll.
- Learners can make a floor plan of their house or apartment building and then draw emergency escape routes. Learners can practice giving oral directions. (FOR EXAMPLE: Go out the door. Turn left. Go down the stairs. Go through the kitchen and out the back door.)

Waiting for News
More *Expansion/Extension* for SB page 101

- Talk about fire hazards and how to prevent fires. Make a list of rules and things to check in houses and apartments. (FOR EXAMPLE: Don't overload electrical outlets. Don't smoke in bed. Don't put paper near the stove. Be careful with electrical heaters.) Talk about equipment to have in the home in case of fire, such as a fire extinguisher.

Making Repairs
More *Expansion/Extension* for SB page 104

- Learners can talk about things they are able to take care of or fix in their houses and apartments. Ask *Can you fix sinks? Can you fix lights? Can you paint walls?* and so on.
- Discuss landlord responsibilities. Bring in a lease and find sections that relate to landlord responsibilities and tenant responsibilities.

- Compare *need + to be + past participle* (to be replaced) with *need + infinitive* (to replace). On the board, write the sentence *The stove needs to be replaced.* Ask learners who is responsible or who needs to do it. Write the sentence *Anita needs to replace the stove.* Have learners find the differences between the two sentences. Write other sentences for learners to change. FOR EXAMPLE: *The walls need to be painted. The rug needs to be cleaned. The curtains need to be replaced.*
- Bring in store catalogs or ads. Learners can find different types of appliances. (FOR EXAMPLE: stoves—gas, electric, microwave) Compare uses and features.
- Bring in information on natural gas. Gas companies often have special papers to make people aware of the odor of natural gas. Talk about what to do and not do if there is a gas leak in a building.
- Discuss the dangers of exposure to lead paint, especially for young children. Landlords are responsible for the removal or containment of lead paint in apartments.

Calling for Repair Work
More *Expansion/Extension* for SB page 105

- Learners can look through the local yellow pages to find names and phone numbers of local companies that do repairs and cleaning.
- Ask learners if they have ever needed help with broken appliances or utilities that did not work in their houses or apartments. If so, what did they do or who did they call? Allow learners to share experiences.

About You
More *Expansion/Extension* for SB page 106

- Bring in a sample rental agreement or lease. Review the responsibilities of the landlord and responsibilities of the tenants. Help learners find the rights of both the landlord and tenants written in the lease. Discuss possible action for both parties if rights are disregarded.
- Bring in information on tenants' rights or arrange for a guest speaker from the local housing authority or tenants' association. Learners can prepare questions beforehand.

1 2 3 4 5 6 7 8 9 10 **11** 12 Summary
The Spice of Life

Objectives

Functions
- Identifying and categorizing
- Understanding and giving oral directions
- Expressing likes and dislikes
- Comparing and contrasting
- Dealing with numbers
- Expressing needs

Life Tasks
- Reading food ads in the newspaper
- Reading signs in the supermarket
- Reading labels on food products
- Understanding U.S. weights and measures

Structures
- Imperatives
- Nouns: count/noncount
- Questions: *how much, how many, where*
- Present continuous tense
- Comparatives
- Superlatives

Culture
- Diet in the United States and in native countries
- Shopping and cooking in the United States
- Meals as social gatherings

Vocabulary

Key words:

apple	egg	peas
bag	expensive	pie
banana	fish	potato
beef	flour	pound
box	food	quart
bread	fruit	rice
broccoli	gallon	roll
butter	haddock	sausage
cake	lettuce	snow peas
carrot	loaf	strawberry
cheap	margarine	sugar
cheese	meat	taco
chicken (breasts)	milk	tomato
cookies	muffin	tortilla
cream	onion	turkey
donut	orange juice	vegetable
dozen	ounce	yogurt
each	package	

Related words:

aisle	homemade
bakery	macaroni
check-cashing card	meal
coupon	net weight
dairy	oatmeal
dessert	paper
dinner	plastic
enjoy	poultry
favorite	produce
fresh	seafood
frozen	total
fruit salad	unit price
halibut	

Planning a Meal

Purpose: To introduce food and meal vocabulary; to give practice with the present continuous tense

Teacher Preparation and Materials

1. Pictures of meals and various food items
2. Supermarket fliers, or newspapers with food ads *(Expansion/Extension)*
3. Magazines with pictures of food, posterboard, scissors, and glue for all *(Expansion/Extension)*

Warm-up

1. Use picture cues to introduce names of meals: *breakfast, lunch, dinner.*
2. Ask questions about food and meals. *What time do you eat dinner? Do you eat breakfast alone or with your family? Do you cook the food? Who cooks in your family? Do you go shopping for food? Where do you get your food?* and so on.

Presentation

1. Have learners turn to page 109 and look at the picture. Ask *Who do you see? Where is she? What is in the refrigerator? What is she thinking about?* List the words and comments on the board. Be sure to include *kitchen, food, dinner, shopping list, calendar.*
2. Together, read the question: *What's Anita doing?* If necessary, ask questions to guide the discussion. *What is Anita looking at? Why? What is she planning for Saturday? Who is coming on Saturday?* and so on.
3. Have learners suggest things that Anita needs to get or do to prepare for the dinner.

Expansion/Extension

- Together, write an LEA story about the picture. Learners can use the words and phrases from the board. They can suggest a menu for the dinner or give ideas of what she will buy at the store for the dinner. Learners can copy the story in their notebooks.

1 2 3 4 5 6 7 8 9 10 **11** 12
The Spice of Life ▪ ▪ ▪ ▪ ▪ ▪ ▪ ▪ ▪

Planning a Meal
What's Anita doing?   **Answers may vary.**

- Give learners supermarket fliers or newspapers with food ads. Learners can look through them for items that they like or use. At this point it is not necessary for learners to know the names of the items. They can share their findings with the group. (I like this. I don't like that. I use this for dinner. I don't use these. and so on.)
- Give learners pictures of food or food ads. Learners can identify food items that they associate with different meals.
- Learners can cut out magazine pictures of food for breakfast, lunch, or dinner. They can glue them on posterboard and then label the collages.

Making a Grocery List

Purpose: To introduce more food vocabulary; to introduce count/noncount nouns

Teacher Preparation and Materials

1. Pictures of food: apples, butter, chicken, cheese, tomatoes, flour
2. Audiotape for Level 1
3. Pictures of tacos and apple pie *(Expansion/Extension)*
4. Blank index cards *(Expansion/Extension)*

Warm-up

1. Use picture cues to introduce names of food items: *apples, butter, chicken, cheese, tomatoes, flour.*
2. Draw a large box on the board to represent a refrigerator. Tape the appropriate food items in the box. Model *In my refrigerator, I have apples. I have butter.* and so on.
3. Take out the butter and tomatoes and tape them on the side of the board. Model *Now, I have apples. I have chicken. But, I don't have any butter. I don't have any tomatoes.* Point to the various pictures and have learners give the correct sentences. Rearrange the items so some are in the box and some are outside. Learners can talk about things they have and do not have.
4. Erase the box. On the board, make a chart:

How many?	How much?

    Model *I don't have any apples. How many do you need? I need five apples.* Tape the picture of apples in the appropriate column. Model sentences and questions for the other pictures. Have learners tape the pictures in the correct columns.
    FOR EXAMPLE: *I don't have any flour. How much do you need? I need a bag of flour.*

Presentation

1. Have learners turn to page 110 and look at the picture. Ask *Who do you see? What is Anita doing? What is she thinking about? What do you think they are talking about?*
2. Play the audiotape and have learners listen to the conversation. Ask *Where is Anita going? Does Carol need anything? How many apples does she need? Does she need flour? Does she need butter? What does Anita need?* Replay the audiotape to verify comprehension.
3. Depending on learners' skills, read the sentences together. Have learners underline or circle the names of the various food items. Then, have learners complete the exercise individually or in pairs. Learners can listen to the audiotape again to check answers.

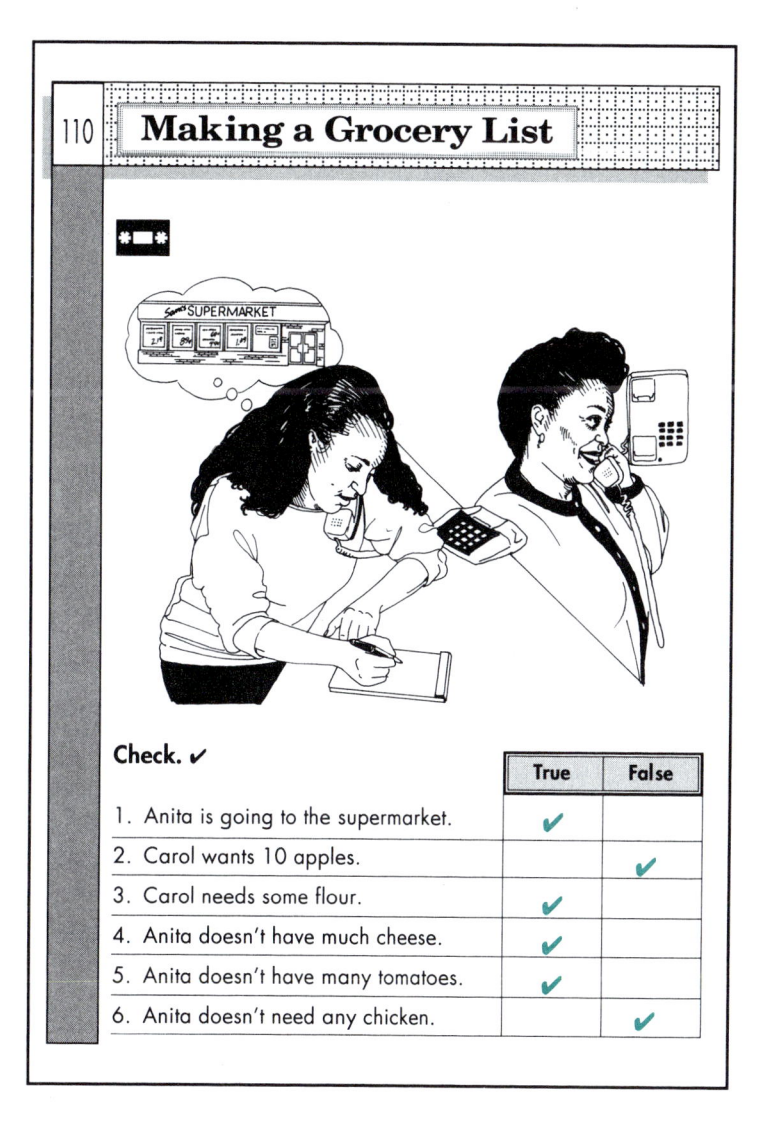

Expansion/Extension

- Learners can rewrite the sentences that are false to make them true. (2. Carol wants *six or seven* apples. and so on.)
- Talk about the food Carol and Anita are planning to make: tacos and apple pie. Bring in pictures of the items. Learners can talk about types of food they enjoy making.
- Learners can listen to the audiotape again and make a complete list of what Carol and Anita need.

More *Expansion/Extension* on page 175

---

110 — Making a Grocery List

Check. ✓

	True	False
1. Anita is going to the supermarket.	✓	
2. Carol wants 10 apples.		✓
3. Carol needs some flour.	✓	
4. Anita doesn't have much cheese.	✓	
5. Anita doesn't have many tomatoes.	✓	
6. Anita doesn't need any chicken.		✓

Supermarket Specials

Purpose: To introduce food categories, more food vocabulary, weights and measures; to introduce comparatives

Teacher Preparation and Materials

1. Pictures of food used for page 110; new pictures: fish, milk, orange juice, pie, bread, rolls, rice, macaroni, oatmeal, chicken parts
2. Quart, 1/2 gallon, gallon containers
3. Supermarket fliers or newspapers with food ads
4. Scale, or food packages of various weights, with weights marked on them.
5. Copies of TRF Handout 11.1, *Food Sets 1* (Expansion/Extension)
6. Copies of TRF Handout 11.6, *Special of the Week* (Expansion/Extension)
7. Store and manufacturers' coupons (Expansion/Extension)

Warm-up

1. Use picture cues to review and introduce names of food items.
2. Show various size containers and introduce the names: *quart, one-half gallon, gallon*. Ask *What comes in these containers?* (milk, juice, etc.) On the board, write the full and abbreviated forms: *quart = qt., one-half gallon = 1/2 gal., gallon = gal.*
3. Give learners supermarket fliers or food ads. Have them circle liquid measurements.
4. Weigh various items on the scale. (*It weighs one pound. It weighs six ounces.* and so on.) Alternatively, show food packages of various weights. Point out the number of pounds or ounces. On the board, write the full and abbreviated forms: *pound = lb., ounce = oz.* Have learners circle weight measurements in store ads.
5. Introduce other quantity terms and abbreviations: *loaf, dozen (doz.), package (pkg.).* Have learners look for them in store ads.
6. Review reading prices. Have learners find prices in store ads.
7. Model sentences about the prices.
   FOR EXAMPLE: *Tomatoes are expensive. Apples are less expensive.* Have learners compare other items and prices using the model sentences.

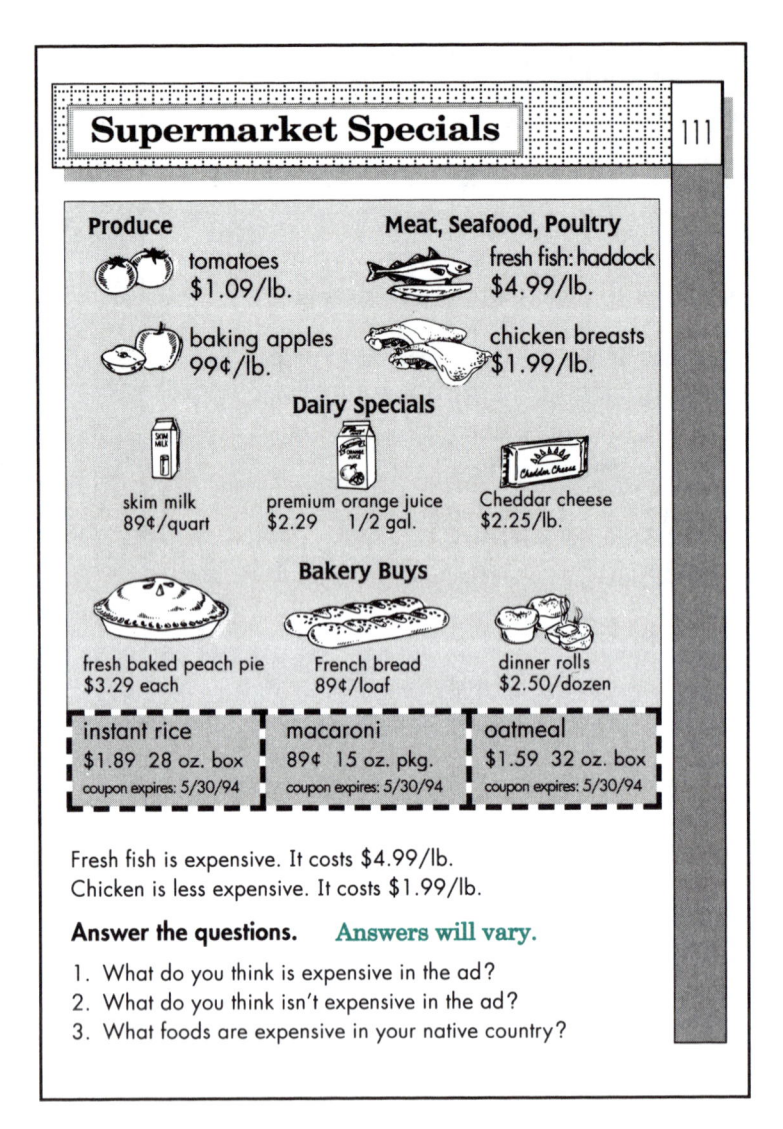

Presentation

1. Have learners turn to page 111 and identify the food items. Say *Show me the fish. Point to the cheese. Can you find the box of rice?* Depending on learners' skills, have them circle the names of the food items.
2. Have learners find quantity and weight measurements on the page. (lb., oz., quart, 1/2 gal., loaf, pkg., dozen)
3. Give practice with questions and answers about prices.
   FOR EXAMPLE: *How much are the tomatoes?* (They cost $1.09 a pound.) *How much is the bread?* (It costs 89¢ a loaf.)
4. Have learners compare prices on the flier. *Which is more expensive: the milk or the orange juice? Which is less expensive: the rolls or the bread?* and so on.
5. Together, read the sentences. Have learners make similar sentences. Then read and discuss the questions.

***Expansion/Extension* on page 175**

Supermarket Specials — 111

Produce
- tomatoes $1.09/lb.
- baking apples 99¢/lb.

Meat, Seafood, Poultry
- fresh fish: haddock $4.99/lb.
- chicken breasts $1.99/lb.

Dairy Specials
- skim milk 89¢/quart
- premium orange juice $2.29 1/2 gal.
- Cheddar cheese $2.25/lb.

Bakery Buys
- fresh baked peach pie $3.29 each
- French bread 89¢/loaf
- dinner rolls $2.50/dozen

- instant rice $1.89 28 oz. box — coupon expires: 5/30/94
- macaroni 89¢ 15 oz. pkg. — coupon expires: 5/30/94
- oatmeal $1.59 32 oz. box — coupon expires: 5/30/94

Fresh fish is expensive. It costs $4.99/lb.
Chicken is less expensive. It costs $1.99/lb.

Answer the questions. *Answers will vary.*

1. What do you think is expensive in the ad?
2. What do you think isn't expensive in the ad?
3. What foods are expensive in your native country?

Down the Aisle

Purpose: To introduce reading signs in the supermarket; to introduce asking for help in the supermarket; to introduce more food vocabulary

Teacher Preparation and Materials

1. Pictures of food used for page 111
2. Pictures of food categories: bakery; dairy; produce; meat, seafood, and poultry
3. Blank index cards *(Expansion/Extension)*
4. Arrange a trip to a local supermarket. *(Expansion/Extension)*

Warm-up

1. Use picture cues to review names of food items.
2. Tape the food category pictures on the board. Have learners identify various items in the pictures. Model the category names: *produce; dairy; bakery; meat, seafood, and poultry*
3. Write the categories under the pictures.
4. Choose a picture of a food item, such as apples. Have learners identify the proper category. (produce) Repeat with the other pictures of food items.
5. Draw vertical lines between the category names on the board.

Produce	Meat, Seafood, and Poultry	Dairy	Bakery

Introduce the word *aisle*. Point to the produce "aisle" and say *In this aisle, there are carrots, tomatoes, and lettuce.* Point to the dairy aisle and ask *What is in this aisle?* (milk, butter, etc.) Repeat for the other aisles.

Presentation

1. Have learners turn to page 112 and look at the top of the page. Ask questions about the aisles and signs. *What aisle number is the dairy section? What's in aisle 4?* and so on.
2. Give practice in asking for items. Learners can respond with the aisle number.
   FOR EXAMPLE: *I'm looking for milk. Where's the milk?* (It's in aisle 3.) *I need some chicken.* (It's in aisle 2.)

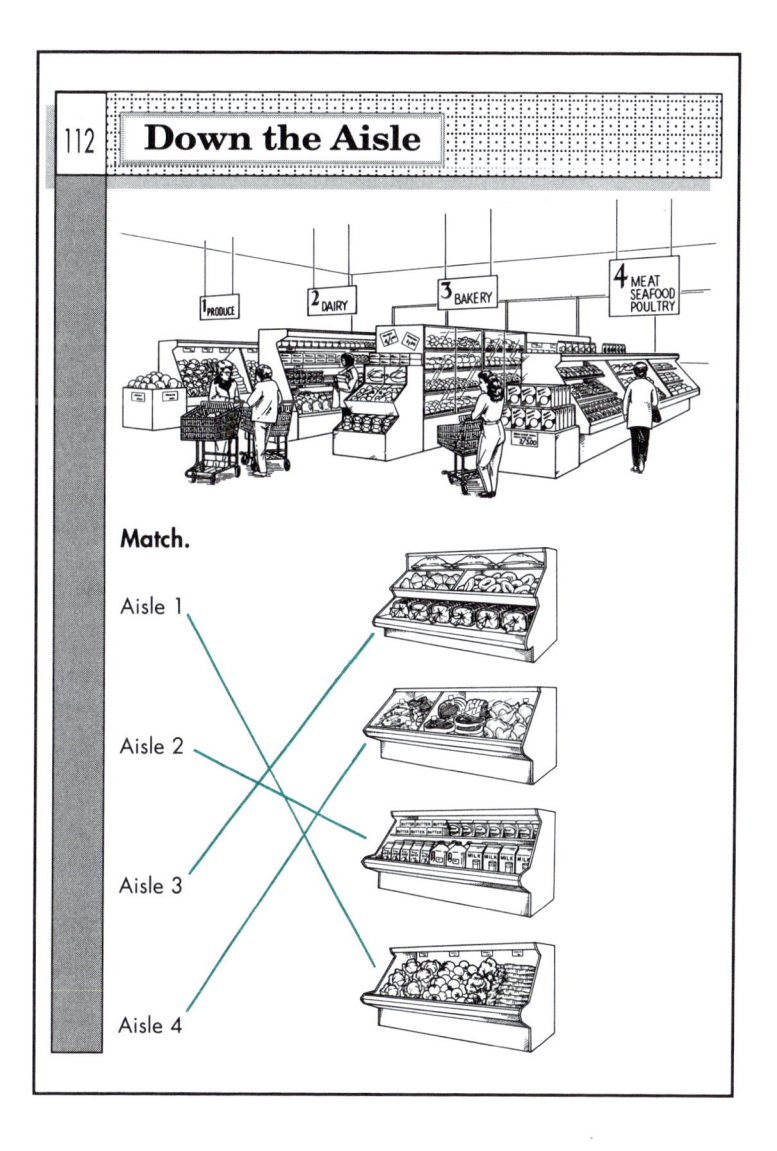

3. Have learners work individually or in pairs matching the aisles to the food groups.

Expansion/Extension

- Learners can suggest other examples for each of the food categories. Write the examples on the board. Learners can copy them in the correct aisle on page 112.
- Introduce names of new items pictured on page 112, such as *pies, muffins, fish, clams*.
- Arrange chairs into four aisles. Learners can make food category signs and aisle numbers on blank index cards. Learners can arrange the pictures of food in the correct aisles. Then, learners can role-play asking for the location of items in the store. (FOR EXAMPLE: Excuse me, I need some tomatoes. They're in [the] produce [section]. Where's that? [That's] in Aisle 1. Thank you.)
- Take a trip to a local supermarket. Learners can look for the category signs and aisle numbers. Give learners a list of items. Learners can write the aisle number where the different items can be found in that store.

More *Expansion/Extension* on page 175

In the Produce Department

Purpose: To introduce more food vocabulary; to give practice with weights and measures; to give practice in using count and noncount nouns

Teacher Preparation and Materials

1. Pictures of food used for page 111; new pictures: onions, carrots, potatoes, broccoli, bananas, strawberries, snow peas
2. Pictures of food categories used for page 112
3. Samples of containers: pint basket, five-pound bag of potatoes or onions
4. Supermarket fliers or food ads used for page 111
5. Seed catalogs *(Expansion/Extension)*

Warm-up

1. Use picture cues to review names of food. Have learners identify the food items that belong in the produce section. *Is this found in the produce section?*
2. Use picture cues to introduce the names of other produce: *snow peas, carrots, onions, potatoes, broccoli, bananas, strawberries.*
3. Tape the produce pictures on the board. Ask for items and have volunteers come and point to them. Use different units of quantity in the sentences. FOR EXAMPLE: *I need a five-pound bag of potatoes. I want a bunch of carrots and two pounds of snow peas.*
4. Arrange the produce pictures according to quantity words.

Bunch	5-lb. Bag	Pint
carrots broccoli bananas	onions potatoes	strawberries

   Show an example of each quantity term or make a simple drawing to illustrate. Model sentences and have learners repeat. *I need a bunch of carrots. I need a pint of strawberries.* and so on.

Presentation

1. Have learners turn to page 113, look at the picture, and identify the produce items.
2. Have learners circle or underline the quantity terms. Say *Find the word* bunch. *Circle* 5-lb. bag.

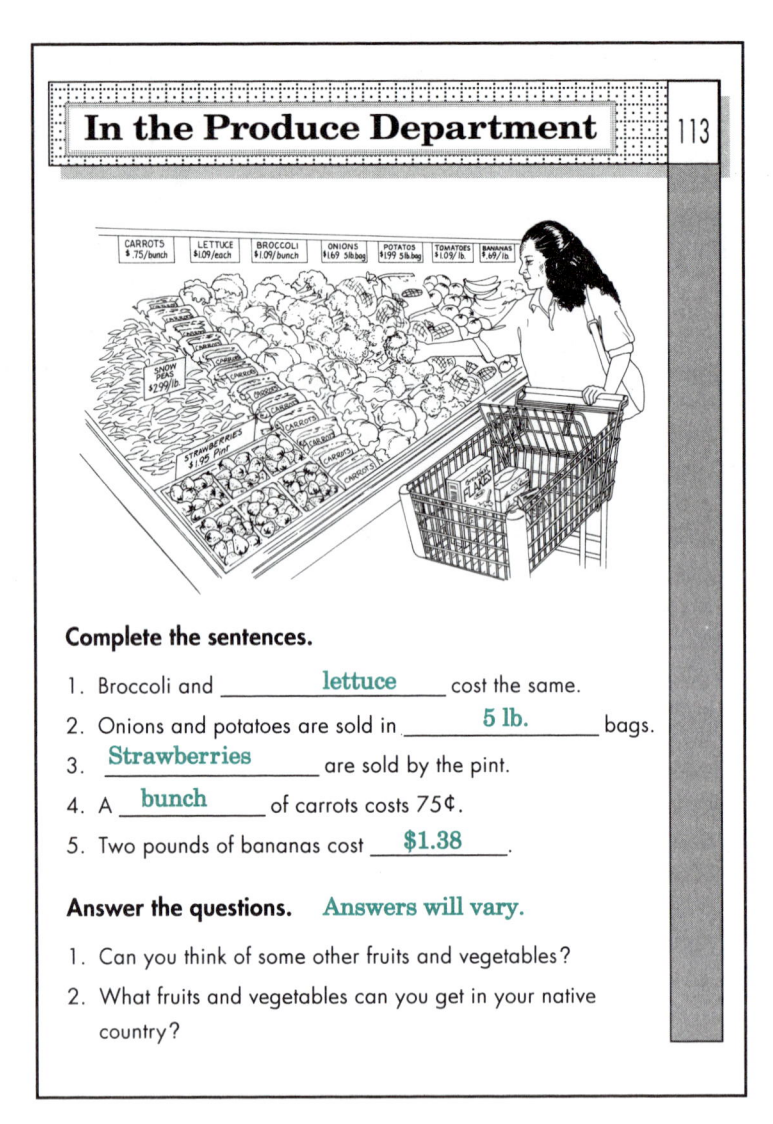

In the Produce Department — 113

Complete the sentences.

1. Broccoli and _____lettuce_____ cost the same.
2. Onions and potatoes are sold in __5 lb.__ bags.
3. __Strawberries__ are sold by the pint.
4. A __bunch__ of carrots costs 75¢.
5. Two pounds of bananas cost __$1.38__.

Answer the questions.   Answers will vary.

1. Can you think of some other fruits and vegetables?
2. What fruits and vegetables can you get in your native country?

---

3. Ask questions about the picture. *How much are apples? onions? What costs 69¢ per pound? What costs 75¢ a bunch? Which foods are sold by the bunch? Which are sold in five-pound bags? Which are sold by the pound? Which are sold in pints?*
4. Give some simple problems calculating costs. FOR EXAMPLE: *I need a head of lettuce and one pound of tomatoes. How much do they cost? How much are two pounds of apples?*
5. Depending on learners' skills, read the sentences together before having learners complete the exercise.
6. Together, read the questions at the bottom of the page and discuss the answers.

Expansion/Extension

- Introduce the categories *fruits* and *vegetables*. Learners can categorize produce items as fruits or vegetables. (**Note:** Do not get too technical. Tomatoes are classified as fruit but are usually placed in the vegetable section in stores.)

More *Expansion/Extension* on page 175

Meat, Seafood, and Poultry

Purpose: To give practice with comparatives; to introduce superlatives and reading labels on food products

Teacher Preparation and Materials

1. Supermarket fliers or food ads used for page 111
2. Scale (optional)
3. ▭ Audiotape for Level 1
4. Samples of meat price labels *(Expansion/Extension)*

Warm-up

1. Review reading prices. Have learners look through supermarket fliers or ads for prices of food items that are sold by the pound. On the board, record items and prices. FOR EXAMPLE:

   | apples | $1.09/lb. |
   | tomatoes | $1.29/lb. |

2. Point to two items on the board and model the comparative *cheaper than*. FOR EXAMPLE: *Apples are cheaper than tomatoes.* Have learners repeat and then compare other items. Repeat the procedure with *more expensive than*.

3. Point to three items and model superlatives. Say *Apples are the cheapest. Snow peas are the most expensive.* Have learners repeat and then compare items using superlatives.

4. Explain *net weight* and *unit price*. Use an item on the board as an example. Say *I need some apples. How much are they?* Act out choosing five or six apples, weighing them, and putting them in a bag. *I have two pounds of apples. How much does the bag of apples cost?*

5. On the board, use semantic webbing to review or introduce words for meat, seafood, and poultry items. FOR EXAMPLE: meat: beef, pork; seafood: halibut, haddock, cod, tuna, snapper, shrimp, crab; poultry: chicken, turkey, duck. Have learners look through supermarket fliers for items to use in the webbing.

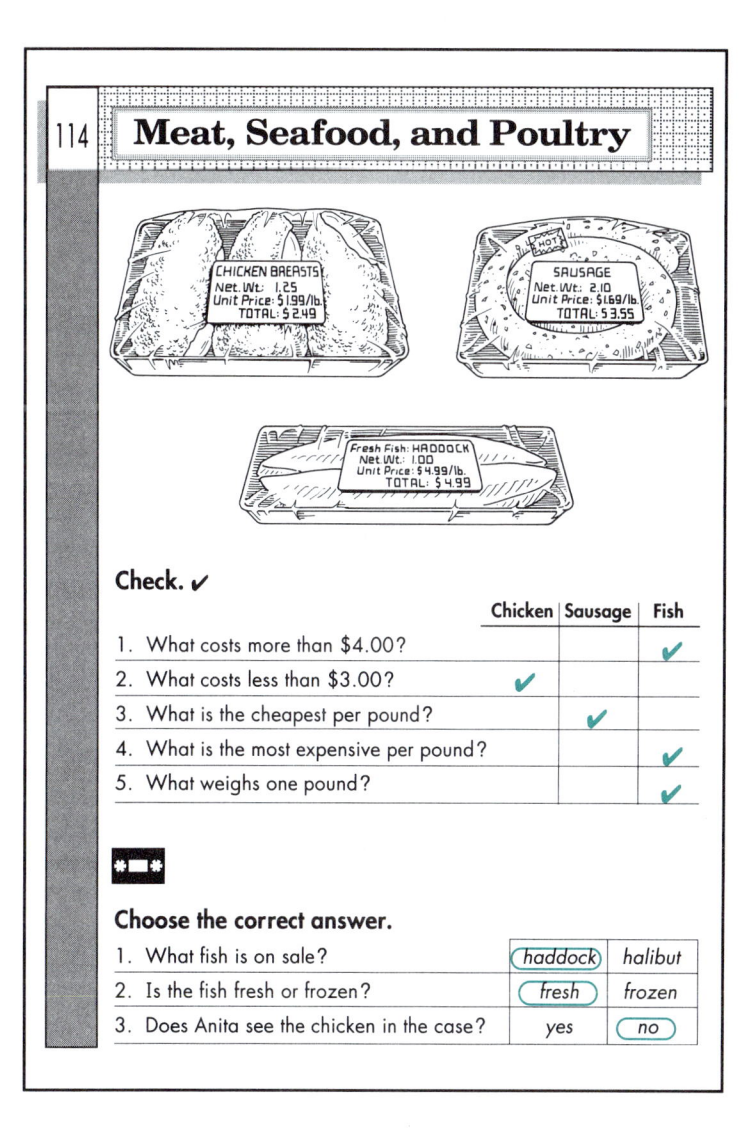

Presentation

1. Have learners turn to page 114. Ask *What type of food is shown here? How much does the chicken weigh? How much does the fish weigh? How much do the sausages cost per pound?* and so on.

2. Have learners underline the weight of each package, circle the unit price (or price per pound), and put a check mark next to the total price.

3. Ask *Which package weighs more: the chicken or the sausages? Which package weighs the most? Which is cheaper per pound: the fish or the chicken? Which is the cheapest per pound?*

4. In pairs, have learners complete the first exercise.

5. ▭ Play the audiotape. Ask *Where is Anita? What is she looking at? Is haddock fish or poultry? How much is it? Is it fresh or frozen? What else does she want? What is the grocer going to get?* ▭ Replay the audiotape to verify comprehension.

6. Have learners complete the second exercise. ▭ Have learners listen again to check answers.

Expansion/Extension on page 175

UNIT 11 • 169

Dairy and Bakery

Purpose: To introduce more food vocabulary; to give practice in using count/non-count nouns

Teacher Preparation and Materials

1. Pictures of food used for pages 110, 111, 113; new pictures: eggs, cookies, sugar, doughnuts, tortillas
2. Samples of containers with expiration dates *(Expansion/Extension)*
3. Supermarket fliers or newspapers with food ads used for page 111, additional store ads from competing supermarkets *(Expansion/Extension)*

Warm-up

1. Use picture cues to review food names.
2. Use pictures to introduce new foods: *eggs, cookies, sugar, tortillas, doughnuts.*
3. On the board, make a chart with two headings:

   | Dairy | Bakery |

   Have learners tape the food pictures under the correct categories.
4. Say items from a grocery list. Have learners identify the items that can be found in the bakery department. FOR EXAMPLE: *I need bread, carrots, apples, and doughnuts.* (bread, doughnuts) Learners can point to or repeat the items. Do several other examples.
5. Repeat the procedure with learners identifying items that can be found in the dairy department.

Presentation

1. Have learners turn to page 115 and look at the picture. Ask *What do you see? What food do you see in these departments? Show me the bread. Where is the milk?* and so on.
2. Have learners look at Anita's shopping list. Explain that these are things that Anita needs to buy at the store. Have learners read the list and find the pictures of the items. Ask *Does she need any meat or poultry? Does she need any produce?* and so on.
3. Together, read the items listed in the first exercise and the instructions. Have learners look at Anita's list and then choose the dairy items she needs.
4. Repeat the procedure for the second exercise.

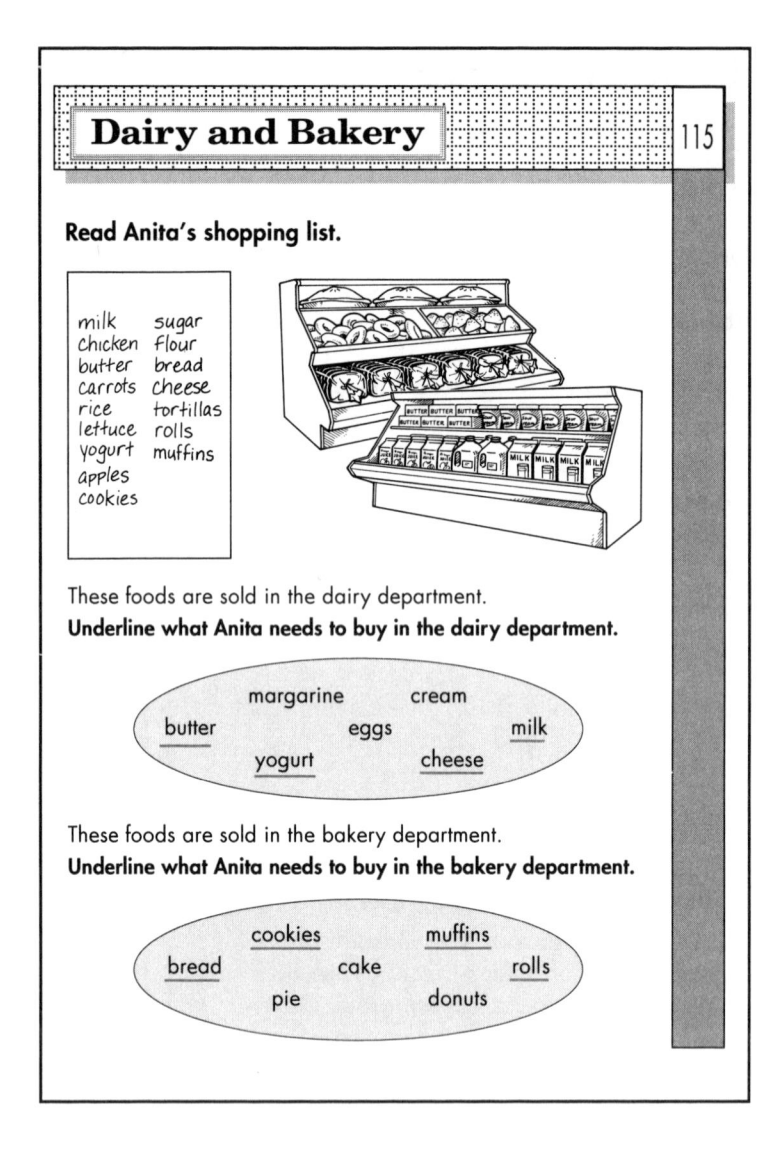

Expansion/Extension

- Learners can look back at page 112 and find the aisle number for each item on Anita's list. They can write the aisle number after each item on the list on page 115.
- Introduce names of other dairy and bakery items: *ice cream, cheeses* (various types), *milk,* and *bread.* Learners can identify items they use or that they have tried.
- Bring in milk and egg cartons or other containers that have expiration dates. Learners can find the expiration dates on the containers. Talk about why these products have dates.
- Discuss what to do if food is not good. Learners can share any experiences they have had. Introduce words to describe spoiled food, such as *moldy, sour, rancid, rotten.* Learners can role-play returning an item with the receipt to the store.

More *Expansion/Extension* on page 175

170 • UNIT 11

At the Checkout

Purpose: To give practice in using weights and measures; to introduce shopping in the United States

Teacher Preparation and Materials

1. Pictures of food used for page 115
2. Pictures of food containers: box, bag, package, gallon, quart
3. A check-cashing card
4. 📼 Audiotape for Level 1
5. Pictures or samples of containers: jars, bottles, cans *(Expansion/Extension)*
6. Store and manufacturers' coupons, or fliers with coupons *(Expansion/Extension)*
7. Copies of TRF Handout 11.4, *What's in Your Cart? (Expansion/Extension)*

Warm-up

1. Use picture cues to review food names.
2. Use pictures of containers to review quantities: *box, bag, package, gallon, quart.*
3. Have learners identify foods that are associated with the different containers. FOR EXAMPLE: *What food do you get by the gallon?* (juice, milk) *What do you buy in bags?* (flour, sugar, potatoes, apples) *What food do you get by the loaf?* (bread)
4. Tape the pictures on the board. Then, hold up a picture of some rice. Model *I need a bag of rice.* Hold up other pictures. Have learners identify the appropriate container for each food picture and then practice asking for quantities.
5. Act out a brief shopping trip by selecting pictures of food items. *I need a quart of milk, a loaf of bread, and a bunch of bananas.* Ask *What do I need to do before I go home? What do I give the checkout clerk?*
6. Discuss paying for groceries. Ask *Where do you pay? How do you pay?* (cash, check, food stamps) *What do you need to use a check?* Show a check-cashing card and explain its use. *What does the checkout clerk do with the food? What kind of bags does the store use?*

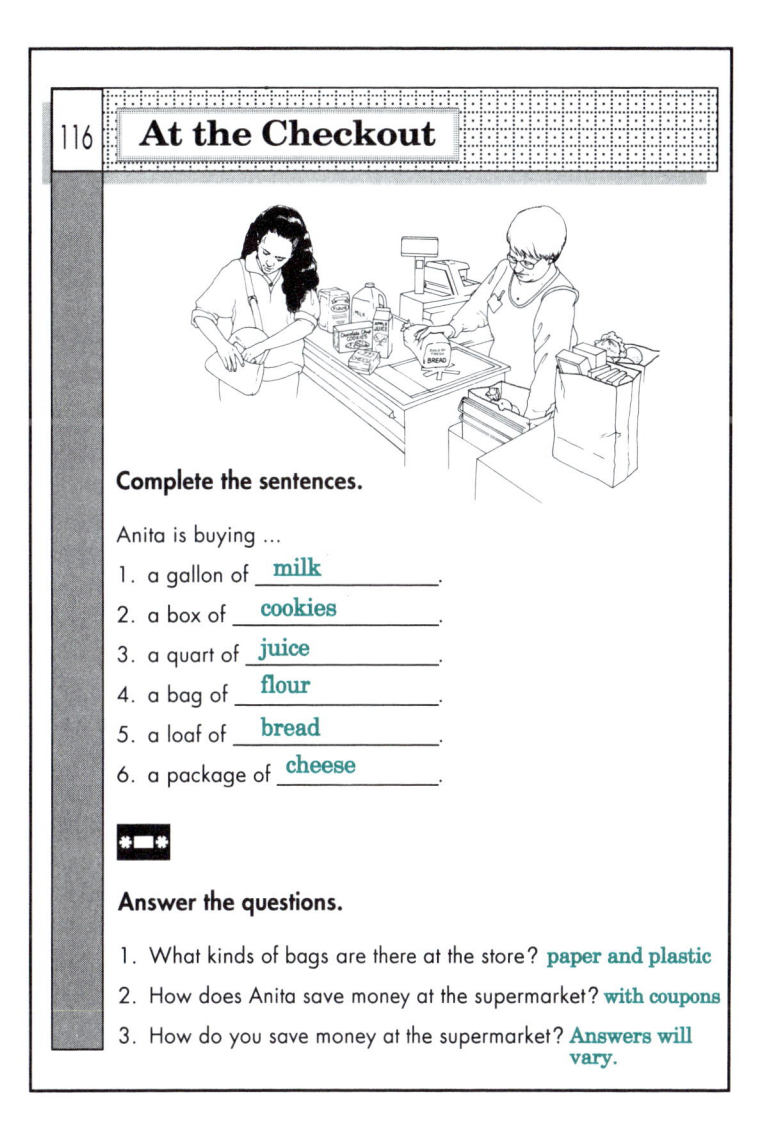

---

116 At the Checkout

Complete the sentences.

Anita is buying ...

1. a gallon of __milk__.
2. a box of __cookies__.
3. a quart of __juice__.
4. a bag of __flour__.
5. a loaf of __bread__.
6. a package of __cheese__.

📼

Answer the questions.

1. What kinds of bags are there at the store? **paper and plastic**
2. How does Anita save money at the supermarket? **with coupons**
3. How do you save money at the supermarket? **Answers will vary.**

Presentation

1. Have learners turn to page 116 and identify the items on the checkout counter.
2. Ask *Who do you see? What is the checkout clerk doing? What is the clerk looking at? What is Anita buying? What else do you think she bought?*
3. Read the first exercise together. Then, have learners complete the sentences.
4. Ask questions about checkout conversations. *What will the clerk say to Anita? How much do you think the food will cost? How do you think she will pay for the food?*
5. 📼 Play the audiotape and have learners listen.
6. As a group, read and discuss the second exercise. 📼 Replay the audiotape for learners to check their answers.
7. Ask additional questions about the conversation. *What kind of bag does Anita want? What kind of bags do you use at the store? Why? Does she have any coupons? Do you use coupons? Why or why not? How is Anita going to pay?*

Expansion/Extension on page 176

UNIT 11 • 171

Dinner with Friends

Purpose: To introduce cooking in the United States; to give practice in expressing likes/dislikes

Teacher Preparation and Materials

1. Pictures of food used for page 115; new pictures: apple pie, tacos, fruit salad
2. Audiotape for Level 1
3. Copies of TRF Handout 11.5, *Try It. You'll Like It. (Expansion/Extension)*
4. Recipe, ingredients, and equipment needed to make apple pie *(Expansion/Extension)*
5. Samples or pictures of herbs and spices *(Expansion/Extension)*
6. Utensils and items used for place settings, or pictures of place settings *(Expansion/Extension)*

Warm-up

1. Use picture cues to review names of food items.
2. Ask *What food do you like to eat? What do you eat for dinner? What do you use to make these things?*
3. Use pictures to introduce and talk about the food items on page 117: *tacos, apple pie,* and *fruit salad.* Ask *What do you (think you) need to make tacos? apple pie? fruit salad? Have you ever tried these? Did/Do you like them?*
4. Talk about dinner. Ask *What time do you eat dinner? Do you eat with your family? Do you eat with friends? What do you talk about at dinner?*

Presentation

1. Have learners turn to page 117 and look at the picture. Ask *Who do you see? What are they doing? What is on the table? What do you think they are eating? What do you think they are talking about?* Learners can look back at Unit 5 to identify Joe, the mail carrier.
2. Together, read the description of the dinner party. Have learners circle or underline new words: *dinner, tacos, favorite, homemade, apple pie, dessert, fruit salad,*

flowers. Learners may also want to circle or underline past tense verbs: *invited, made, brought, enjoyed.*

3. Ask questions about the reading. *Who invited Fred, Carol, and Joe for dinner? What did Anita make? Is it her favorite dish? What is for dessert? Who brought the apple pie? Did Carol buy it or make it? Who brought the fruit salad? What else did Joe bring?*
4. Play the audiotape and have learners listen to the conversation. Ask general questions about the small talk. *Are the people coming to Anita's house or going home? Are they talking about the food or work? Did they enjoy themselves?* Replay the audiotape to verify comprehension.
5. Together, read and discuss the questions at the bottom of the page.

Expansion/Extension
See **TRF HANDOUT 11.5,** *Try It. You'll Like It.*

Dinner with Friends

Anita invited some friends for dinner. She made chicken tacos. It's her favorite dish. Carol and Fred brought homemade apple pie for dessert. Joe brought fruit salad. He brought flowers for Anita too. Everyone enjoyed the dinner.

Answer the questions.   Answers will vary.

1. Do you enjoy having friends come to your home?
2. What do you make for your friends?

More *Expansion/Extension* on page 176

Favorite Foods

Purpose: To give practice in expressing likes/dislikes; to give practice in talking about food categories; to introduce meal planning

Teacher Preparation and Materials

1. Pictures of food used for page 117; new picture: peas
2. Pictures of food categories used for page 112
3. Copies of TRF Handout 11.2, *Food Sets 2* (Expansion/Extension)
4. Copies of TRF Handout 11.3, *My Partner and I* (Expansion/Extension)
5. Copies of TRF Handout 11.7, *Trail Mix* (Expansion/Extension)
6. Samples of restaurant or fast food menus (Expansion/Extension)
7. Magazines with pictures of food, posterboard, scissors, and glue for all (Expansion/Extension)
8. Information on nutrition; food containers with nutritional information (Expansion/Extension)

Warm-up

1. Use picture cues to review names of food items and food categories. Introduce *peas* if they have not already been taught.
2. Review desserts. Ask what Anita made for dessert on page 117. Ask learners for other types of desserts. List them on the board.
3. Give practice with questions and answers about favorite foods in a chain drill. FOR EXAMPLE: *What's your favorite fruit?* ([My favorite fruit is] pineapple.) *What's your favorite dessert? vegetable? meat?* Learners can refer to the list of desserts on the board when talking about desserts.

Presentation

1. On the board, make a chart similar to the one on the top of page 118. Ask questions about the categories. *What is your favorite fruit? Can you name some favorite vegetables? What types of meat do you like the most?* and so on.
2. Demonstrate interviewing a learner and filling in the chart with the responses.

3. If necessary, ask a volunteer to interview you or another learner and to fill in the chart.
4. Have learners interview four people and write the responses on the chart. Help with new food names if necessary. ■ In a one-to-one situation, have the learner interview friends or neighbors.
5. Learners can report their findings to the group. (FOR EXAMPLE: Mario's favorite foods are grapes, beans, fish, and ice cream.)
6. On the chart on the board, list all the favorite food items. Have the group summarize the results. (Oranges, peaches, and grapes are our favorite fruits. and so on.)
7. In pairs or individually, have learners plan a meal using items from the food categories listed in the book. Have learners share their meal plans with others in the class.

Expansion/Extension

See **TRF HANDOUT 11.2**, *Food Sets 2*
TRF HANDOUT 11.3, *My Partner and I*
TRF HANDOUT 11.7, *Trail Mix*

More *Expansion/Extension* on page 176

---

118 Favorite Foods

Interview.
What are your favorite foods?   Answers will vary.

Name	Fruit	Vegetable	Meat Seafood Poultry	Dessert
1. Anita	bananas	peas	chicken	apple pie
2.				
3.				
4.				
5.				

Make a meal with your favorite foods.   Answers will vary.

Vegetable	
Meat, Seafood, Poultry	
Dessert	
Fruit	

UNIT 11 • 173

Look Back

Purpose: To give practice with food categories and food vocabulary

Teacher Preparation and Materials

1. Pictures of food used for page 118
2. Pictures of food categories used for page 112
3. Index cards with sight words: *Bakery; Dairy; Produce; Meat, Seafood, and Poultry*

Warm-up

1. Use picture cues to review names of food items and food categories.
2. On the board, tape the sight-word cards: *Bakery; Dairy; Produce; Meat, Seafood, and Poultry*. Ask questions about various food items. *Where can I find milk?* ([In the] dairy [department].) *I'm looking for some bread.* ([It's in the] bakery [department].) and so on.

Presentation

1. Display four food pictures, such as chicken, turkey, carrots, and fish. If necessary, ask learners which food category is associated with each picture. Then, ask which food is in a different category from the other three. Remove the picture of the carrots and say *These are in the meat, seafood, and poultry section.*
2. Repeat the procedure with another set of pictures. FOR EXAMPLE: onions, eggs, milk, yogurt.
3. On the board, write the names of four food items: *bread, milk, muffins, doughnuts*. Repeat the procedure but demonstrate crossing out the item that does not belong. *(milk)* Then, write the name of the category under the food items. *(bakery)* If necessary, repeat with another set of four food items: *lettuce, broccoli, cheese, tomatoes*.
4. Have learners turn to page 119. Together, read the instructions.
5. Have learners complete the exercise individually. Learners may want to go through and cross out the items that do not belong and then go back and write the correct food categories for the remaining words. (**Note:** Numbers 1 and 2 can be categorized as either produce (both), or vegetables and fruits, respectively.)

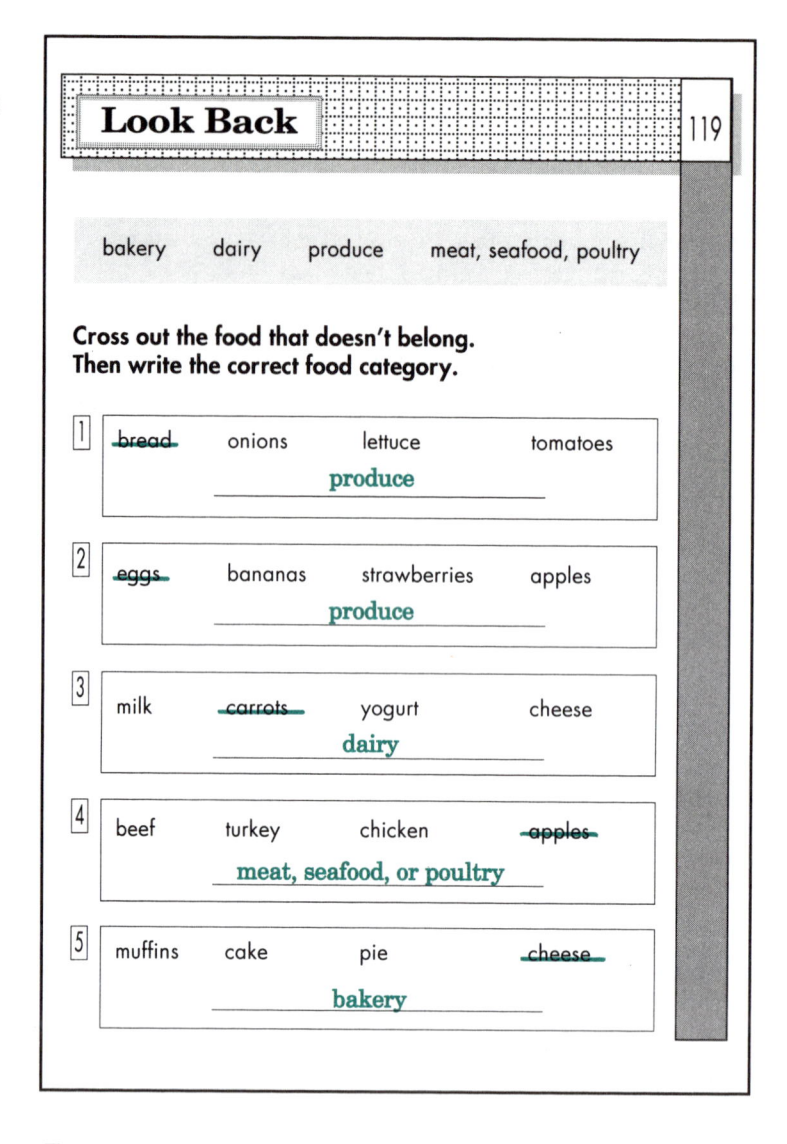

Look Back

bakery   dairy   produce   meat, seafood, poultry

**Cross out the food that doesn't belong.
Then write the correct food category.**

1. ~~bread~~   onions   lettuce   tomatoes
   produce

2. ~~eggs~~   bananas   strawberries   apples
   produce

3. milk   ~~carrots~~   yogurt   cheese
   dairy

4. beef   turkey   chicken   ~~apples~~
   meat, seafood, or poultry

5. muffins   cake   pie   ~~cheese~~
   bakery

Expansion/Extension

- Play Twenty Questions about food items. Have one learner think of or choose a picture of a food item. Other learners can ask *Yes/No* questions to determine the item. (FOR EXAMPLE: Is it a dairy food? Do you eat it for dessert? Is it cold? Is it green? Is it sweet?)
- On the board, make a chart with five columns. Tape the sight-word cards with the four food categories on the board. Write four different letters in the left-hand column. Learners can work in pairs filling in the names of food items that start with those letters for each of the categories. FOR EXAMPLE:

	Bakery	**Dairy**	**Produce**	**Meat, Seafood, and Poultry**
C	cake	cheese	carrots	chicken
A	apple pie		apple	
M	muffin	milk		mussels
B	bread	butter	banana	beef

UNIT 11: The Spice of Life
Expansion/Extension

Making a Grocery List
More *Expansion/Extension* for SB page 110

- Talk about food shopping and shopping lists. Ask *Do you make a list when you go shopping? Do you make your list in English or in your native language? How do you decide what to buy? Do you go shopping every day or once a week? How often do you shop? Do you always go to the same store?* and so on.

- On the board, write:

    I don't have any . . . . I don't have many . . . . I have enough . . . .
    I don't have much . . . .

- On index cards, write or draw various amounts of food items: *3 tomatoes, 0 tomatoes, 10 tomatoes; 2 pieces of cheese, 0 pieces of cheese, 20 pieces of cheese;* and so on. Demonstrate taking a card and making up a sentence for it. (FOR EXAMPLE: 2 apples—*I don't have many apples.* 0 apples—*I don't have any apples.* 12 apples—*I have enough apples.* 1/2 bag of flour—*I don't have much flour.* 2 bags of flour—*I have enough flour.* 0 bags of flour—*I don't have any flour.*) Learners can take turns selecting cards and making sentences about them.

Supermarket Specials
***Expansion/Extension* for SB page 111**
See TRF HANDOUT 11.1, *Food Sets 1*
   TRF HANDOUT 11.6, *Special of the Week*

- Bring in samples of store and manufacturers' coupons. Ask *What are these? How do you use them? When can you use them? Can they be used in any store? Are there special dates when they can be used? What does* expire *mean?* and so on.

- Discuss the four categories in the flier: Produce; Meat, Seafood, and Poultry; Dairy; and Bakery. Learners can suggest other items that belong in the categories.

Down the Aisle
More *Expansion/Extension* for SB page 112

- Talk about different types of places to buy food. Ask *Are there cooperative stores in the area? farmers' markets? ethnic food stores? wholesale food stores? convenience stores? What are the advantages and disadvantages of each?*

In the Produce Department
More *Expansion/Extension* for SB page 113

- Bring in seed catalogs with pictures of vegetables, fruits, and herbs. Learners can identify items they use or cannot find in local stores. Learners may want to purchase herb seeds to grow indoors.

- Learners can create their own math problems involving prices. (FOR EXAMPLE: Anita buys two bunches of carrots and two pounds of tomatoes. How much do they cost?)

- Learners can bring in local supermarket fliers and compare Anita's prices with local prices.

- Learners can talk about vegetables or fruits they have tried and those they have not tried yet. Learners can share recipes for cooking new vegetables.

- Learners can compare shopping in their native countries and shopping in the United States. Ask *Where do you shop? What are the stores like? How often do you shop? Are prices marked or do you bargain for the prices?* Learners can make a chart comparing the shopping systems or write an LEA story about shopping differences.

Meat, Seafood, and Poultry
***Expansion/Extension* for SB page 114**

- Bring in samples of meat labels. Have learners examine them and record the price per pound.

- Ask learners what else is unit-priced in stores. Learners can go to a grocery store and look for items that are unit-priced.

- Learners can look through store fliers and use comparatives and superlatives to talk about prices of various items.

Dairy and Bakery
More *Expansion/Extension* for SB page 115

- Plan a cooking project or party. Learners can prepare a shopping list of items and quantities based on what will be made. Learners can check ads and fliers from different local supermarkets to find the best prices.

At the Checkout
Expansion/Extension for SB page 116
See TRF HANDOUT 11.4, *What's in Your Cart?*

- Introduce other kinds of packaging, such as *cans, jars,* and *bottles.* Bring in samples of containers and have learners find the names of the items and the weight or quantity.

- Introduce common metric weights and measurements and their abbreviations: *liter (l), kilogram (kg), gram (g),* and so on. Many containers have both measurements on the labels. Learners can find and record examples from products in the store or in their homes. Learners can bring in their findings to share with the group. Ask learners how things are measured in their native countries. Ask *In your native country, do you buy rice by the pound or kilogram? Which measuring system do you prefer? Why?*

- Bring in samples of coupons or have learners look through fliers for coupons. Talk about different offerings and restrictions: *buy one get one free, $1 rebates, good with $10 minimum purchase, good when you buy two or more, good for 10 oz. jar only,* and so on. Compare store coupons and manufacturers' coupons. Some stores offer double the amount on manufacturers' coupons.

- Learners can classify the items on Anita's list (on page 115) and on the checkout counter (on page 116) as either count or noncount nouns. On the board, make a list for each category. Explain the differences between *count* and *noncount*. Count nouns have singular and plural forms. (FOR EXAMPLE: I want an apple. I want some apples.) Noncount nouns have only one form. (FOR EXAMPLE: I need sugar/some sugar.) Count nouns are items that you can easily count: apples, oranges, cookies, and so on. Noncount nouns include items that are more difficult or impossible to count: rice, cereal, flour, and so on. Many noncount items use an additional quantity word: a *box* of cereal, a *head* of lettuce, a *bag* of sugar, a *cup* of coffee, and so on.

Dinner with Friends
More *Expansion/Extension* for SB page 117

- Give practice with the past tense of regular and irregular verbs: *invite, enjoy, make, bring.* Learners can practice asking and answering questions about the story using the past tense verb forms. (FOR EXAMPLE: Who did Anita invite? She invited Carol, Fred, and Joe. What did she make? She made tacos.)

- Bring in a recipe for apple pie. Introduce common recipe measurements: *cup, teaspoon, tablespoon.* Learners can read the names of the different ingredients. If possible, bring in the ingredients and make the pie. Have a volunteer bake it at home and bring it to the next class for everyone to eat.

- Learners can share their own recipes with the group. In pairs or individually, learners can write a list of ingredients and instructions for making the dish. Make copies of the recipes and compile them in a class cookbook. Include the name of the food, the name of the writer, and the name of the writer's native country for each of the dishes.

- Plan a potluck meal. Learners can each bring in a favorite dish to share with the group.

- Discuss hospitality customs. Ask *Do you usually bring something for the host or hostess? What do you bring? Do you arrive on time or fashionably late? How long do you stay? Do you help clean up? Do you help serve? Do you bring the kids along?* and so on.

Favorite Foods
More *Expansion/Extension* for SB page 118

- Bring in samples of restaurant and fast food menus. Learners can find the names of various food items and food categories.

- Learners can make collages of their favorite foods. Learners can cut out pictures of food items from magazines and glue them to posterboard. Learners can label the posters.

- Talk about special diets. Ask *What does it mean if someone is a* vegetarian? *What does* low-salt diet *mean? Why do some people not eat some foods?* and so on.

- Bring in information on nutrition, vitamins, and minerals. Talk about how many servings of each food group are needed each day. Explain RDA (Recommended Daily Allowance). Learners can examine food packages for nutritional information.

1 2 3 4 5 6 7 8 9 10 11 12 Summary
Discovering Patterns

Objectives
- To help learners discover grammatical patterns
- To teach and give practice with those patterns
  The structures covered are:
  - prepositions of place
  - present tense: *have*
  - modals: *can/can't*
  - nouns: count and noncount
  - verbs: verb + *to be* + past participle.

About the Structures

• Prepositions of Place
This is one of the hardest structures to master in English. It should be taught early and practiced often, but it will be acquired late. Even advanced speakers will make mistakes with prepositions of place.

• Present Tense: *Have*
This page deals with *have* as a main verb signifying possession. Learners may ask about other uses of *have* in the present tense:
(a) as a main verb imperative
   (FOR EXAMPLE, *"Have a good day"* or *"Have a cup of coffee."*);
(b) as an auxiliary verb with *to* (FOR EXAMPLE, *"I have to go to work now."*).

• Modals: *Can/Can't*
You may want to tell learners that modals are "helping verbs." As used here, *can/can't* indicate ability/possibility in the present tense.

• Nouns: Count and Noncount
Like prepositions of place, this concept should be taught early, but mastery is not expected. Advanced learners still have trouble with noncount nouns, which take a lot of time, practice, and memorizing.

• Verbs: Verb + *to be* + Past Participle
This page presents the passive form of the present infinitive. The passive form always takes the simple form of the verb *be* followed by the past participle. None of these details need to be explained to the learners, but have them practice the pattern so they are comfortable with the formation of the past participle.

Prepositions of Place

Purpose: To give practice with prepositions of place

Teacher Preparation and Materials
1. Two boxes of different colors and sizes
2. Classroom objects: pens, pencils, bags, books

Warm-up
1. Give different commands involving locations of the boxes or classroom objects and have learners place the items correctly. FOR EXAMPLE: *Please put the green box on the yellow box. Put the box on the table. Put the pen in the box. Please put the small box near the large box.*
2. Ask questions about locations of people and things in the room. *Who is next to Pierre? Who is in front of you?* and so on.

Presentation
1. Have learners turn to page 120 and look at the "Prepositions" chart. Point out that each preposition is followed by a place. Learners can use the words in the chart to create sentences. Point out that *between* needs a plural or two places. Also, point out the two-word prepositions: *across from* and *next to*.
2. Have learners look at the picture on page 120. If necessary, ask learners to identify places in the picture and then to make up sentences using the prepositions. (FOR EXAMPLE: *Show me the post office. Where's the park? Where's the supermarket?*)
3. Learners complete the first exercise by matching the prepositions and the places in accordance with the picture.
4. In the second exercise, have learners fill in the correct preposition in each of the sentences.

Expansion/Extension
- Learners can mark the places mentioned in the first exercise on the picture. They can draw arrows to indicate the prepositions used with the places.

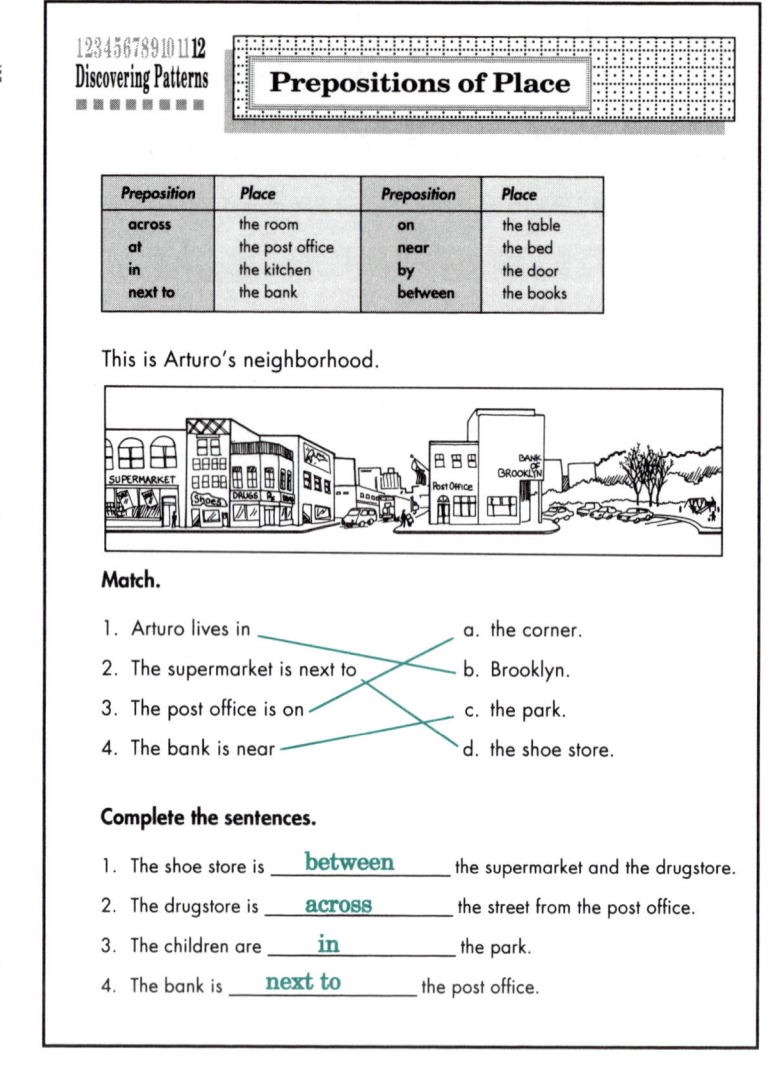

Discovering Patterns

Prepositions of Place

Preposition	Place	Preposition	Place
across	the room	on	the table
at	the post office	near	the bed
in	the kitchen	by	the door
next to	the bank	between	the books

This is Arturo's neighborhood.

Match.

1. Arturo lives in — b. Brooklyn.
2. The supermarket is next to — d. the shoe store.
3. The post office is on — a. the corner.
4. The bank is near — c. the park.

Complete the sentences.

1. The shoe store is __between__ the supermarket and the drugstore.
2. The drugstore is __across__ the street from the post office.
3. The children are __in__ the park.
4. The bank is __next to__ the post office.

- In the second exercise, learners can circle the place(s) that follow the prepositions.
- Learners can write questions for each of the sentences in the exercises. (FOR EXAMPLE: Who lives in Brooklyn? Where does Arturo live? Where is the post office?)
- Learners can write additional sentences about the picture using the prepositions of place. (FOR EXAMPLE: The . . . is next to the shoe store. The park is near the . . . .)
- Learners can write about their neighborhood or classroom, using prepositions.
- Learners can make up questions about locations of things in the room, building, or neighborhood. Learners exchange questions and answer each other's questions.
- Draw a simple street map of the local area. Learners can tell where various buildings and landmarks should be placed on the map. Together write an LEA story about the map.
- Learners can group prepositions that have the same or similar meanings. FOR EXAMPLE: *near, next to, by; in, at.*

Present Tense: *Have*

Purpose: To give practice with the present tense of the verb *have*

Teacher Preparation and Materials

1. Pictures of people with health problems: headache, stomachache, sore throat, broken leg, cold, fever, and so on
2. Classroom objects used for page 120

Warm-up

1. Use picture cues to review describing health problems. Model *I'm sick. I have a headache.* Have learners describe other problems. If learners do not use the model format, then ask *Is there another way to say that?* Alternatively, give each learner a picture of a health problem. Ask questions to elicit answers in the first and third person. *What's wrong with you? What's the matter with Inez?* and so on.

2. Ask questions about classroom objects. *Do you have a yellow pencil?* (Yes, I do./No, I don't.) *Does Hoa have a red book?* (Yes, he does./No, he doesn't.) *Who has a blue pen?* (Henri has one.) and so on.

Presentation

1. Have learners turn to page 121 and look at the "Present Tense: *Have*" chart. Ask questions as necessary. *Which words (pronouns) use* have? *Which words (pronouns) use* has? *Which ones use* don't have? *Which ones use* doesn't have? Point out that *have* is used with all the negatives. Point out that *do* and *does* with *have* follow the same pattern as the Yes/No questions with *Do* from page 61. Have learners give the full form of the contractions *don't* and *doesn't*.

2. Ask learners to look at the picture on page 121 and to identify the characters and their problems.

3. Have learners complete the exercise individually.

4. Then, have learners complete the second exercise with the negative forms.

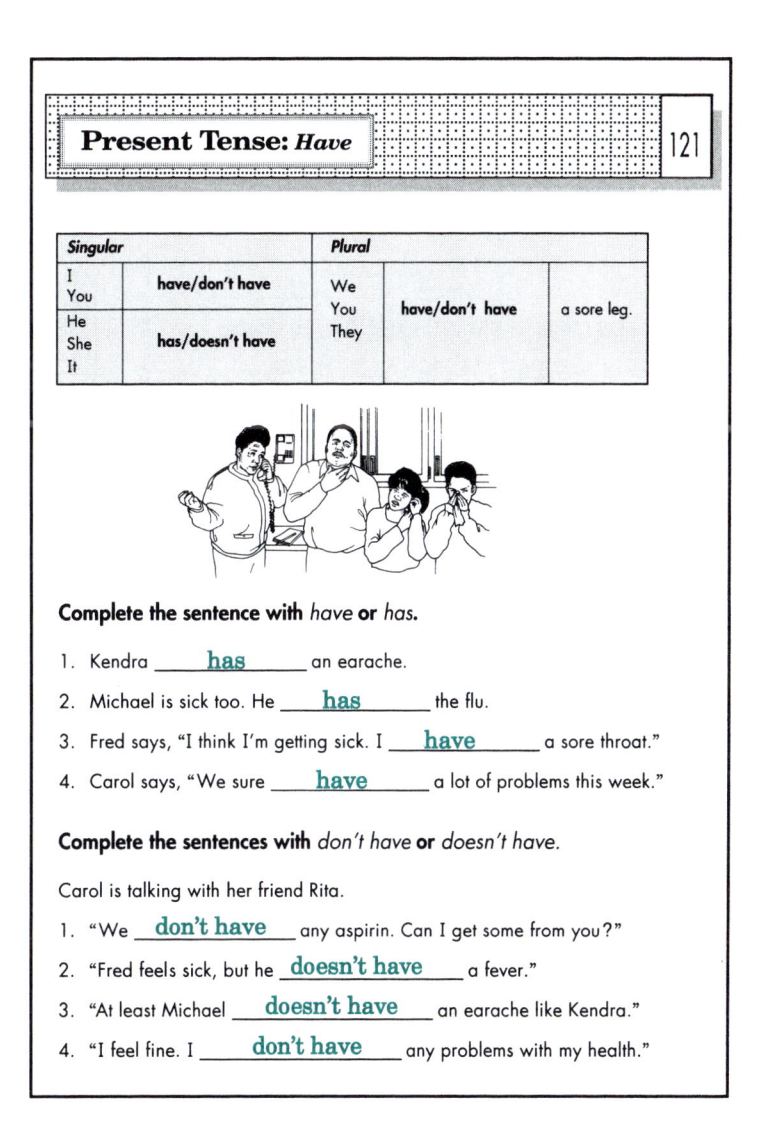

Present Tense: *Have* 121

Singular		Plural		
I You	have/don't have	We You They	have/don't have	a sore leg.
He She It	has/doesn't have			

Complete the sentence with *have* **or** *has*.

1. Kendra ___**has**___ an earache.
2. Michael is sick too. He ___**has**___ the flu.
3. Fred says, "I think I'm getting sick. I ___**have**___ a sore throat."
4. Carol says, "We sure ___**have**___ a lot of problems this week."

Complete the sentences with *don't have* **or** *doesn't have*.

Carol is talking with her friend Rita.

1. "We __**don't have**__ any aspirin. Can I get some from you?"
2. "Fred feels sick, but he __**doesn't have**__ a fever."
3. "At least Michael __**doesn't have**__ an earache like Kendra."
4. "I feel fine. I __**don't have**__ any problems with my health."

Expansion/Extension

- Learners can write Yes/No questions for the sentences in the first exercise. (FOR EXAMPLE: Does Kendra have a headache?)
- Learners can write about the Wilson family. It is a week later and now everyone is healthy. Make all the statements negative using the verb *have*. (FOR EXAMPLE: Now, Kendra doesn't have an earache. Michael isn't sick. He doesn't have the flu.)

UNIT 12 • 179

Modals: *Can/Can't*

Purpose: To give practice with the modals *can* and *can't* to express ability

Teacher Preparation and Materials
Pictures of various actions: cook, drive, paint, and so on

Warm-up
1. Use picture cues to encourage learners to talk about their skills and abilities. (FOR EXAMPLE: I can drive, but I can't cook. I can paint and cook.)
2. Ask questions about skills and abilities. *Can you drive?* (Yes, I can./No, I can't.) *Can you speak English?* (Yes, I can./No, I can't.) *Can Ana use a computer?* (Yes, she can./No, she can't.) and so on.

Presentation
1. Have learners turn to page 122 and look at the "Modals: *Can/Can't*" chart. If necessary, ask questions: *What form is used with he? I? they? Does can or can't change with the different pronouns? What kind of word comes after can or can't?* (A verb, or something you do.) *Does that verb change with the different pronouns? What is the full form of can't?* (cannot) and so on.
2. Together, read the examples of questions and answers. Point out the order of words in questions and sentences (the order of subject pronoun and modal are switched).
3. In the first exercise, have learners look at the picture and identify the items and prices. If necessary, read the sentences together. Then, have learners fill in the correct modal for each sentence.
4. In the second exercise, have learners make up a sentence for each picture, using the modals.

Expansion/Extension
- Learners can make up Yes/No questions or Wh- questions about the pictures in the second exercise.
- Learners can write questions and answers about themselves using the picture cues. (FOR EXAMPLE: Can you ride a bike? No, I can't. Can you reach that? Yes, I can.)
- Learners can write other sentences about their abilities and skills.
- Give practice with pronunciation of the final clusters of the modals. On the board, write:

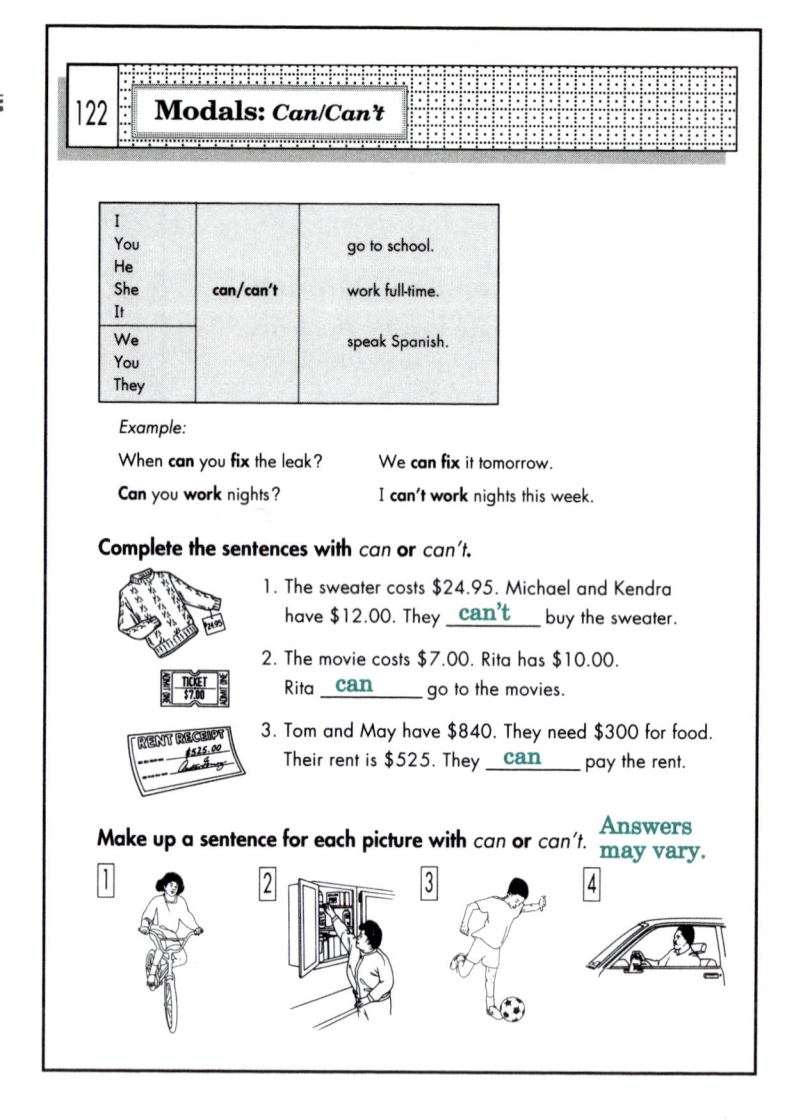

can	can't
1	2

Say a sentence and have learners give the number of the modal used. FOR EXAMPLE: *Arturo can't come to visit Anita.* (2) *Rita can work nights.* (1) Then, have learners practice saying sentences with the modals.

---

122 Modals: *Can/Can't*

I, You, He, She, It	can/can't	go to school.
We, You, They		work full-time.
		speak Spanish.

Example:

When **can** you **fix** the leak?   We **can fix** it tomorrow.
Can you **work** nights?   I **can't work** nights this week.

Complete the sentences with *can* **or** *can't*.

1. The sweater costs $24.95. Michael and Kendra have $12.00. They __can't__ buy the sweater.
2. The movie costs $7.00. Rita has $10.00. Rita __can__ go to the movies.
3. Tom and May have $840. They need $300 for food. Their rent is $525. They __can__ pay the rent.

Make up a sentence for each picture with *can* **or** *can't*. **Answers may vary.**

1 2 3 4

Nouns:
Count and Noncount

Purpose: To give practice with count and noncount nouns

Teacher Preparation and Materials
1. Pictures of foods and kitchen utensils
2. Recipe for chocolate chip cookies *(Expansion/Extension)*

Warm-up
1. Show pictures of foods and kitchen utensils. On the board, make a chart for singular and plural forms of the items. Learners can also look back at Anita's shopping list on page 115 for other food items. FOR EXAMPLE:

1	2 or more
a carrot	some carrots
sugar	some sugar
a spoon	some spoons

2. Have learners circle the items that do not change form for singular and plural.

Presentation
1. Have learners turn to page 123 and look at the "Nouns: Count and Noncount" chart. Ask questions about the chart. *Which word do you add an -s to (to make it plural): letter or mail? What are other examples of words that add -s (to make them plural)? Which word does not use* a *or* one *(in the singular form)? What are some other examples of words that do not use -s (in the plural) or use* a *or* one *(in the singular form)? Which words use* many? *Which words use* much?

2. Together, look at the picture and read the description. Have learners identify or point to the various food items and cooking utensils. Have learners decide which are count nouns and which are noncount nouns.

3. Together, look at the example in the exercise. If necessary, ask learners if *bowl* needs an *-s* in the plural form. Ask if it uses *much* or *many*.

4. Then, have learners complete the exercise individually.

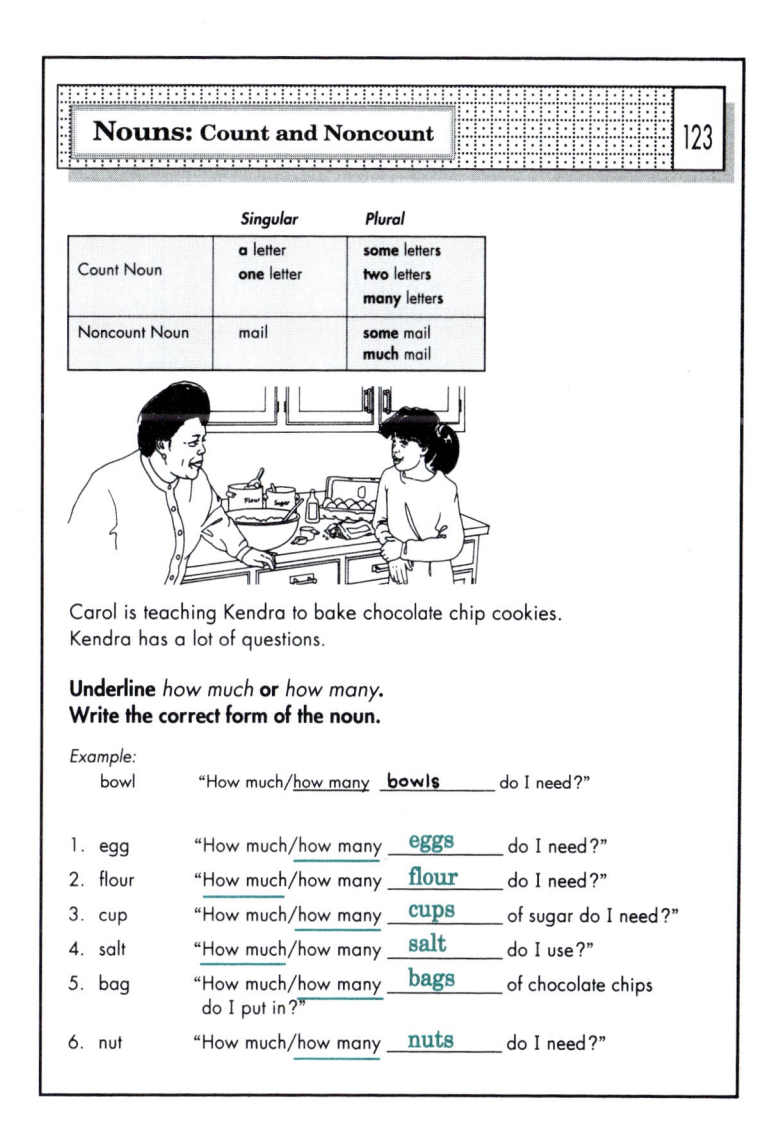

Nouns: Count and Noncount | 123

	Singular	Plural
Count Noun	a letter one letter	some letters two letters many letters
Noncount Noun	mail	some mail much mail

Carol is teaching Kendra to bake chocolate chip cookies. Kendra has a lot of questions.

Underline *how much* or *how many*.
Write the correct form of the noun.

Example:
bowl "How much/<u>how many</u> **bowls** do I need?"

1. egg   "How much/how many **eggs** do I need?"
2. flour "How much/how many **flour** do I need?"
3. cup   "How much/how many **cups** of sugar do I need?"
4. salt   "How much/how many **salt** do I use?"
5. bag   "How much/how many **bags** of chocolate chips do I put in?"
6. nut   "How much/how many **nuts** do I need?"

Expansion/Extension

- Learners can look at a recipe for chocolate chip cookies and then write Carol's answers to Kendra's questions in the exercise. (FOR EXAMPLE: You need one bowl. You need two eggs.) Point out that the quantity or container words can be made plural.

- Learners can practice making up other sentences using the nouns. (FOR EXAMPLE: Kendra has some eggs. She has some sugar. She has one bowl. She puts two eggs in the bowl. She mixes two eggs with some sugar.)

- Learners can write additional questions for *how much* and *how many,* using the correct plural forms of the items. (How many spoons does Kendra have? and so on.)

- Learners can bring in recipes. Help learners list the ingredients and utensils needed. Learners can ask and answer questions about amounts and steps in the procedure, using the correct count or noncount forms.

- Learners can write shopping lists for household products or school supplies. Learners should include amounts or quantities on the list. FOR EXAMPLE: 2 pencils, 1 package of paper, 1 roll of tape.

UNIT 12 • 181

Verbs: Verb + *to be* + Past Participle

Purpose: To give practice with *have, need, want* + *to be* + past participles

Teacher Preparation and Materials
Pictures of various actions used for page 122; new pictures: clean, call (on the phone), fix, move, cook, help, paint, replace

Warm-up
1. Have learners look around the room and think of some of the furniture and items that need cleaning, fixing, or replacing. Then use the picture cues to give practice with questions and answers. *What needs to be cleaned?* (The floor needs to be cleaned.) *What needs to be fixed?* and so on.
2. On the board, write some of the responses: (The lights need to be replaced. The window needs to be fixed.)

Presentation
1. Have learners turn to page 124 and look at the "Verb + *to be* + Past Participle" chart. Ask *What word comes after* to? (be) *What kind of word comes after* be? (a verb, an action word) *What ending is on the word (verb) that comes after* be? (-ed) Point out that only the first verb agrees with the subject pronoun.
2. Have learners look at the picture. Ask *Where is Fred? What is he thinking about? What needs to be painted? What has to be fixed?*
3. Together, read the instructions and the words in the box. Have learners complete the sentences using the structure.

Expansion/Extension
- Learners can write *Yes/No* or *Wh-* questions for the sentences. (Do the curtains need to be replaced? What has to be moved? and so on.)

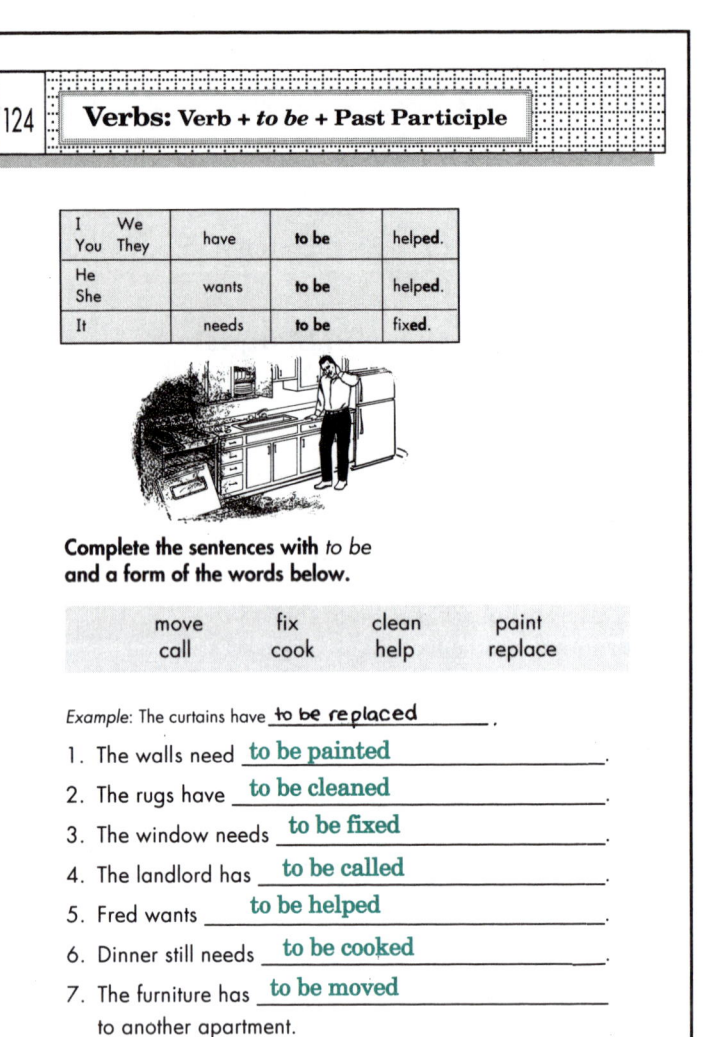

---

124 | **Verbs:** Verb + *to be* + Past Participle

I We You They	have	to be	help**ed**.
He She	wants	to be	help**ed**.
It	needs	to be	fix**ed**.

Complete the sentences with *to be* **and a form of the words below.**

| move | fix | clean | paint |
| call | cook | help | replace |

Example: The curtains have __to be replaced__.

1. The walls need __to be painted__.
2. The rugs have __to be cleaned__.
3. The window needs __to be fixed__.
4. The landlord has __to be called__.
5. Fred wants __to be helped__.
6. Dinner still needs __to be cooked__.
7. The furniture has __to be moved__ to another apartment.

- Learners can look at page 102 or another picture of the Wilsons' apartment and then rewrite the statements on page 124 as negative statements. (FOR EXAMPLE: The walls don't need to be painted. The landlord doesn't have to be called.)
- Using the structures, learners can write sentences suggesting improvements to the classroom or, as a group, write a letter to the school principal or building owner about repairs that are needed.

Tapescripts

UNIT 1
Neighborhoods

page 6 At Home
Narrator: Listen to the story.

This is 127 Center Street in Chicago.

Anita Gómez is from Mexico. She lives in Apartment 1A.

Fred and Carol Wilson are from the United States. Michael and Kendra are their children. They live in Apartment 2A.

The Lin family is from China. Tom and May Lin live in Apartment 3A. They have two children: David and Lily.

page 7 Languages
Narrator: Listen to the story.

Anita Gómez speaks Spanish and English.

Fred and Carol Wilson speak English. Michael and Kendra speak English too.

The Lin family speaks Chinese at home.
Tom Lin speaks English at work.
David and Lily speak English at school.
May Lin doesn't speak English.

UNIT 2
Families

page 22 Hello!
Narrator: Listen to the conversation between Janet and Fred.
Janet: I'm so happy to see you again, Fred!
Fred: Me too! We're glad you're visiting us!
Janet: Thanks. So am I!

◆ ◆ ◆ ◆

Narrator: Listen to Carol greet her friend Rita.
Carol: Hi! Good to see you. Come in.
Rita: Hi!

◆ ◆ ◆ ◆

Narrator: Listen to the conversation. Anita is talking to Harold Jones.
Harold: Nice to see you again, Anita. How are you?
Anita: Fine, thanks. And you, Mr. Jones?
Harold: Very well, thanks.

page 23 Nice to Meet You
Narrator: Listen to the conversation between Carol, Tom, and Alma.
Carol: Tom, this is my mother, Alma Jones. Mother, this is our neighbor, Tom Lin.
Tom: How do you do? I'm glad to meet you, Mrs. Jones.
Alma: I'm glad to meet you too, Mr. Lin.

◆ ◆ ◆ ◆

Narrator: Listen to the conversation. Fred and Richard are talking to David and Lily.
Fred: Richard, these are my neighbors, David and Lily Lin.
Richard: Nice to meet you, David.
David: Hi. How are you?
Richard: Fine, thanks.
Lily: Hi there!
Richard: Hi! I'm glad to meet you too, Lily.

page 24 Days of the Week
Narrator: Listen to the conversation between Anita and Janet.
Anita: Janet, let's get together for lunch.
Janet: What a good idea. I'm staying with Carol for two weeks.
Anita: How about next week sometime?
Janet: What about Tuesday?
Anita: Oh dear. I have an appointment that day.
Janet: OK. How's Wednesday?
Anita: Let's see. That's October 6th. That's fine. I can meet you here at 12:30.
Janet: Twelve-thirty on Wednesday, October 6th. That's great. I'm looking forward to it.

UNIT 3
Keeping in Touch

page 27 An International Call

Narrator: Listen to the conversation between Tom and the international operator.
Operator: This is the operator. How can I help you?
Tom Lin: I'd like to call Shanghai, China. I know the person's number. What do I do?
Operator: You can dial direct. First, dial 011 for a direct line. Then, dial 86 for the country code. Next, dial 21, the city code. Finally, dial the person's number.
Tom: Could you repeat that slowly, please?
Operator: First, dial 011 for a direct line. Then, dial 86 for the country code. Next, dial 21, the city code. Finally, dial the person's number.
Tom: That's 011, then 86, then 21, and then the person's number?
Operator: That's right.
Tom: Thank you. Good-bye.

page 28 Long-Distance Information

Narrator: Listen to the conversation between Anita and the long-distance operator.
Operator: New York City. Mrs. Miller.
Anita: I'd like the telephone number of Arturo Soto, *S-o-t-o*, on Hill Avenue in Brooklyn.
Operator: One moment, please.
Machine voice: Please make a note of the number. The number is 965-2029. Repeat, 965-2029.

page 33 Sending Money

Narrator: Listen to the conversation. Anita is in the post office.
Anita Gómez: Excuse me. I'd like to buy a money order. How much does it cost?
Clerk: A money order costs 75 cents.
Anita: I'd like to buy a money order for $25.
Clerk: That will be $25.75. Please fill out the money order right away.

page 35 Insuring a Package

Narrator: Listen to the conversation. David is in the post office.
David: I'd like to mail this package to China.
Clerk: Let me weigh it. That will cost you $20.50. Would you like to insure it, too?
David: Yes, that's a good idea.
Clerk: What's in the package?
David: Clothing.
Clerk: How much is it worth?
David: Around $100.
Clerk: The fee is $2.40 for $100 worth of insurance.
David: All right. I'd like to insure the package for $100.
Clerk: The postage is $20.50. The insurance is $2.40. That comes to $22.90. Please fill out this form.
David: Thank you.
Clerk: You're welcome.

UNIT 4
Getting from Here to There

page 39 Getting Information

Narrator: Listen to the conversation. Anita is calling the bus company.
Voice: Good morning. City Bus Service.
Anita: Hello. I live on Center Street. How can I get to City Hospital?
Voice: The number 3 bus goes right to the hospital. Buses leave every half hour from Sandburg Park.
Anita: The number 3 bus from Sandburg Park. So the next bus leaves at 10:30?
Voice: Right.
Anita: How much is the fare?
Voice: It's $1.50.
Anita: Thank you.
Voice: You're welcome.

page 44 Finding the Right Room

Narrator: Listen to the conversation. Anita is at the hospital.

Anita: Excuse me. Could you tell me what room Sonia Díaz is in?

Clerk: She's in room 305.

Anita: How do I get there?

Clerk: First, go across the lobby. Then take the elevator to the third floor. On the third floor, turn left and go down the hall. Room 305 is next to the nursery.

Anita: Across the lobby to the elevator. On the third floor, I turn left. And then?

Clerk: Go down the hall, and 305 is next to the nursery.

Anita: Down the hall and next to the nursery. Thanks.

UNIT 5
Feelings

page 54 Talking to Friends

Narrator: Listen to the conversation between Joe and Anita.

Joe: Hi, Anita. Please give this package to Tom Lin.

Anita: Sure, Joe.

Joe: What's wrong, Anita? You look sad.

Anita: I *am* sad. I miss my mother and father.

Joe: I'm sorry to hear that. I bet they miss you, too.

Anita: You're right. I'm going to write them a letter. Thanks, Joe. Bye.

Joe: Bye, Anita.

◆ ◆ ◆ ◆

Narrator: Listen to the conversation between Anita and Tom.

Anita: Hi, Tom. This package is for you.

Tom: Why didn't the mail carrier give it to May?

Anita: She didn't answer the door.

Tom: She doesn't know the mail carrier. She is afraid of strangers. She doesn't understand what they're saying.

Anita: Why doesn't she study English? I went to Lane School and studied English. It felt good to learn. It will make May feel good too.

Tom: That's a good idea. I'm going to talk to May.

page 56 Good News

Narrator: Listen to the conversation between Fred and Carol.

Fred: You wouldn't believe the day I've had!

Carol: You're so wet!

Fred: First I missed my bus. It took off just as I got to the bus stop.

Carol: How annoying.

Fred: Then it started raining cats and dogs.

Carol: You *really* got soaked, huh?

Fred: To make matters worse, I kept getting splashed by cars and trucks . . .

Carol: Well, listen, honey . . . Why don't you get out of those wet clothes? We have some good news to share with you.

Fred: Good news? What happened? Tell me now.

Carol: OK. Take a look at Michael's report card.

Fred: Wow! Look at all these A's and B's.

Carol: Isn't it great? I'm so proud of him.

Fred: Michael's becoming quite a student.

Carol: Well, hon, I hope this report card cheered you up a bit after the day you've had.

Fred: It sure did!

page 58 What's the Matter?

Narrator: Listen to the conversation between Carol and Kendra.

Carol: What's the matter, Kendra? You look upset.

Kendra: I'm angry! You like Michael better than me.

Carol: What makes you say that?

Kendra: You're not paying any attention to me. You're making a big deal out of Michael's dumb old report card.

Carol: Oh, Kendra. I'm sorry you feel that way. It's just that today is a special day for Michael. He got some good grades and we're proud of him.

Kendra: Well, I can't stand *him* and I can't stand *you*.

Carol: You don't really mean that. Remember when you sang in the school show last month? We all went out for ice cream to celebrate.

Kendra: Yeah, but . . .

Carol: That was a very special day for you. But you know, we're always proud of both of you, and sometimes it's nice to make a big deal out of times like this.

Kendra: Yeah, I guess so. I'm sorry I said those things.

Carol: That's O.K.

Kendra: I just wish *my* report card was as good as Michael's.

UNIT 6
What Did You Do Before?

page 65 Looking for Work

Narrator: Listen to the story.

Carol Wilson is looking for a job. She hasn't worked for 10 years. She has been busy raising her children. She used to be a cashier. She thinks she'd like to work in a bank. She'd like to be a manager one day. Her friend, Rita Pérez, is looking for a job too. Rita doesn't know what she wants to do yet.

page 70 Getting Advice

Narrator: Listen to the conversation between Rita and an employment counselor.

P. Willis: Hello, Ms. Pérez. My name is Paul Willis. May I help you?

Rita: I'd like to find a job.

P. Willis: What kind of work did you do before?

Rita: I worked in a factory.

P. Willis: Would you like to work in a factory again?

Rita: No. I didn't like it. It was noisy and dirty and hot.

P. Willis: I see you finished high school in El Salvador.

Rita: Yes, I did. I went to school here, too. I learned English at Lane School.

page 72 Making Choices

Narrator: Listen to the conversation between Rita and Paul Willis.

P. Willis: Let's look at what you can do.

Rita: I speak Spanish and English. I like to work with people.

P. Willis: Where would you like to work?

Rita: I'm not sure. I would like to work near my home, though.

P. Willis: Do you want to work full-time or part-time?

Rita: Full-time.

P. Willis: Can you work nights sometimes?

Rita: I'd like to work days, but I can work some nights.

P. Willis: There's a job open at Southside Health Clinic.

Rita: Tell me about it.

UNIT 8
The Cost of Things

page 80 In the Shoe Department

Narrator: Listen to the conversation. David and Lily are in the shoe department. David is talking to the salesclerk.

David: Can you help me? How much are these slippers?

Clerk: They cost $25.

David: That's too much. Do you have anything less expensive?

Clerk: Yes. Those slippers are on sale. They cost $11.

◆ ◆ ◆ ◆

Narrator: Listen to the conversation. Lily is talking to the salesclerk.

Lily: Do these slippers come in size 7?

Clerk: Yes, we have all sizes from 5 to 10.

Lily: Do they come in red?

Clerk: No. They come in pink, blue, and white.

Lily: Thank you. We'll think about it.

page 81 Using Cash

Narrator: Listen to the conversation. Lily is talking to the salesclerk.

Lily:	I'll take these pink slippers in size 7.
Clerk:	Here you are. The slippers cost $11 plus tax. The total is $11.96.
Lily:	Here's $12.
Clerk:	Your change is 4 cents.
Lily:	Thanks.
Clerk:	You're welcome.

page 83 Looking for a Present

Narrator:	Listen to the conversation between Tom and a salesclerk.
Clerk:	Can I help you, sir?
Tom:	No, thanks. I'm just looking.
Clerk:	Let me know if you need any help.
Tom:	I will.

◆ ◆ ◆ ◆

Narrator:	Listen to the conversation. Tom is in the jewelry department.
Clerk:	Can I help you, sir?
Tom:	I'm looking for the watches that are on sale.
Clerk:	They're right here. Usually they cost $50. This week they're only $25.
Tom:	They are very nice. Can I see one?
Clerk:	Yes. Let me show you.

page 84 Writing Checks

Narrator:	Listen to the conversation. Tom is talking to the salesclerk.
Tom:	I'll take this watch.
Clerk:	The watch is $25 plus tax. The total is $27.19. Is that cash, check, or charge?
Tom:	Check.
Clerk:	Please make the check out to "Danner Stores." I'll need some identification and your phone number.
Tom:	Here's my driver's license. My phone number is 884-4725.
Clerk:	Thank you.

UNIT 9
Getting Well

page 89 What Hurts?

Narrator:	Listen to each person calling the doctor.
	Number 1.
Caller 1:	My wife has a terrible cold. Her nose is red and runny and very stuffed up.
Narrator:	Number 2.
Caller 2:	Doctor, I fell down the stairs. I bumped my head. I can't walk. I think I broke my leg.
Narrator:	Number 3.
Caller 3:	I can't eat anything. I have a stomachache.
Narrator:	Number 4.
Caller 4:	My baby is sick. He's crying. He's holding his ears.
Narrator:	Number 5.
Caller 5:	I can hardly talk. I have a sore throat. I also have a terrible headache.
Narrator:	Number 6.
Caller 6:	My son is sick. His nose is running, and his stomach hurts. Can the doctor see him right away?

page 91 The Examination

Narrator:	Listen to the conversation between Kendra and Dr. Johnson.
Doctor:	Hi, Kendra. I'm Dr. Johnson. How do you feel today?
Kendra:	Hello, Dr. Johnson. I don't feel good.
Doctor:	I'm sorry to hear that. Tell me what hurts.
Kendra:	I have an earache. My throat hurts, too.
Doctor:	OK, Kendra. Let's take your temperature. Hmmm. You do have a bit of a fever.
	Now I'm going to look at your throat. Please stick out your tongue and say "Ahhh."
Kendra:	Ahhh.
Doctor:	Next, I'm going to look in your ears with this little flashlight. I'll be very careful not to hurt you.
Kendra:	That doesn't hurt.

TAPESCRIPTS • 187

Doctor: Good. Now I'm going to listen to your chest with this stethoscope.

Kendra: Oooh. That tickles!

Doctor: You're a good patient, Kendra. I'm going to talk to your father now.

UNIT 10
Asking for Help

page 99 Calling for Help

Narrator: Listen to the conversation. Anita is calling 911 Emergency.

911: 911 Emergency. What is your emergency?

Anita: There's a fire at 127 Center Street! Send someone right away!

911: That's 127 Center Street. Everyone must leave the building. Someone will be right there.

Anita: Please hurry! Everyone must leave the building! Let's go!

page 101 Waiting for News

Narrator: Listen to the conversation between Anita and Tom.

Anita: Are you all right?

Tom Lin: Yes, we're OK.

Anita: Is everyone here? Where are Lily and David?

Tom: Only May and I were home. The children are out. How did the fire start?

Anita: I think the fire started in Fred and Carol's kitchen.

◆ ◆ ◆ ◆

Narrator: Listen to the conversation between Rita and Fred.

Rita: Are you OK?

Fred: I think so. I was afraid someone would be hurt. Everyone is all right.

Rita: Where's Carol?

Fred: She's working late at the bank.

Rita: How did it happen?

Fred: It started in the kitchen. I was in the living room. The curtains blew over the stove and caught on fire. I hope our home isn't ruined.

Rita: I hope so too. You and your family can always stay with me.

Fred: Thanks, Rita. You're a good friend.

page 104 Making Repairs

Narrator: Listen to the conversation between Anita and Fred.

Fred: Hello?

Anita: Hi, Fred! This is Anita. What needs to be fixed in your apartment?

Fred: All our lights are out.

Anita: I know. Most of the lights in the building are out. I'm going to call the electric company right away. What else needs to be fixed?

Fred: The stove is completely ruined. It needs to be replaced.

Anita: Replace the stove . . .

Fred: A kitchen window is broken.

Anita: Fix the broken window . . .

Fred: The walls and rugs are dirty from smoke.

Anita: Paint the walls . . . Clean the rugs . . .

Fred: My curtains are burned too, but I'll buy some new ones myself.

Anita: OK. Now let me check this list again. Replace the stove. Fix the window. Paint the walls. Clean the rugs. And I'll call the electric company for you, too.

Fred: Well, thanks for your help. I'm sorry about the fire. I'm glad that no one was hurt.

Anita: Me too. Talk to you later.

Fred: OK, bye.

page 105 Calling for Repair Work

Narrator: Listen to the conversation. Anita is calling the electric company.

Voice: Illinois Electric Company. May I help you?

Anita: This is Anita Gómez at 127 Center Street.

Voice: Hello, Ms. Gómez. What's the problem?

Anita: We had a fire. Most of the lights are out. Can you send someone over right now?

Voice: Well, let's see. I can send someone over this afternoon.

Anita: All right. Tell them to go to Apt. 1A.

Voice: Could you repeat the address?
Anita: It's 127 Center . . .

◆ ◆ ◆ ◆

Narrator: Listen to the conversation. Anita is calling Danner Stores.
Voice: Danner Stores. May I help you?
Anita: Appliance department, please.
Voice: Appliance department. Good morning.
Anita: Good morning. I want to order a new stove. I want the Cookbest model in white.
Voice: We have that in stock.
Anita: How soon can you deliver it?
Voice: We're all booked for today. Thursday is our next delivery day.
Anita: That will have to do. Send it to . . .

◆ ◆ ◆ ◆

Narrator: Listen to the conversation. Anita is calling the glass company.
Ernesto: No-Shatter Glass Company. Hello.
Anita: Hi, Ernesto. It's Anita.
Ernesto: Hi, Anita. What's up?
Anita: We had a fire.
Ernesto: Yes, I heard. Is everyone OK?
Anita: Everyone is fine. There's lots to do, though.
Ernesto: I bet. What can I do for you?
Anita: One of the windows is broken. I need a pane of window glass one foot by two feet.
Ernesto: We have that in stock. I'll be here until 6 p.m.
Anita: Can you deliver it? I can't get over there.
Ernesto: Sure. I'll send the windowpane over right away.
Anita: Thanks. See you soon.
Ernesto: OK, Anita. Bye.

◆ ◆ ◆ ◆

Narrator: Listen to the conversation. Anita is calling the rug company.
Voice: Spotless Rug Service. Hello.
Anita: Hello. I need to have some rugs cleaned. When can you come?
Voice: First, tell me how many rugs.
Anita: Just two rugs.
Voice: OK, we can be there Friday morning.
Anita: Friday? That's good. My address is . . .

UNIT 11
The Spice of Life

page 110 Making a Grocery List

Narrator: Listen to the conversation between Anita and Carol.
Carol: Hello?
Anita: Hi, Carol. I'm going shopping for our dinner on Saturday night.
Carol: Oh, great. Did you know that there's a terrific sale at Sam's Supermarket this week?
Anita: I know. I was just looking at the ad. Do you need anything?
Carol: Oh, yeah. I need some apples. Can you get me six or seven baking apples? I'm going to make my special apple pie.
Anita: OK. Apples. Anything else?
Carol: Let's see . . . Oh, you know what? I need flour. Can't make a pie crust without flour! Could you get me a five-pound bag?
Anita: Sure. Do you need any butter or margarine?
Carol: No, I've got plenty. Thanks for asking. So, what are you making for the dinner?
Anita: I'm going to make tacos and I need some chicken. Chicken is on sale this week, so that works out great! And I just checked my refrigerator and I don't have much cheese—or many tomatoes, either. So I need to stock up!
Carol: Now is the time to do it if they're on sale!
Anita: You can say that again. Well, I'll see you when I get back. Apples and flour, right?
Carol: Right.

page 114 Meat, Seafood, and Poultry

Narrator: Listen to the conversation. Anita is in the supermarket.
Anita: What fish is on sale this week?
Grocer: Haddock's on sale at $4.99 per pound.
Anita: Is it fresh or frozen?
Grocer: As fresh as you can get!
Anita: Fine. I'll take one pound, please.
Grocer: OK. Anything else?

Anita: Could you tell me if you have any more chicken breasts? I don't see any in the case.
Grocer: We're selling a lot of them today. I'll get some more from out back.
Anita: Thanks a lot.

page 116 At the Checkout

Narrator: Listen to the conversation. Anita is paying for her groceries.
Checker: Paper or plastic?
Anita: Excuse me?
Checker: Do you want your groceries put in paper or plastic bags?
Anita: Oh, paper, please.
Checker: Any coupons today?
Anita: Yes, I have some.
Checker: Thanks. Oh, this one expired last month.
Anita: Oh, I'm sorry. I didn't notice the date.
Checker: That'll be $75.42.
Anita: OK. I'm going to pay by check today.
Checker: That's fine. I'll need your check-cashing card too.
Anita: Oh, yes, I almost forgot!
Checker: Thank you.

page 117 Dinner with Friends

Narrator: Listen to the conversation between Joe and Anita.
Joe: Thanks for inviting me, Anita. Your dinner was terrific. I had a great time.
Anita: I'm glad you could come.
Joe: I enjoyed talking with Carol and Fred. And Carol's homemade apple pie was delicious.
Anita: It sure was. That's my favorite dessert. Your fruit salad was really good, too. And thanks for bringing the lovely flowers.
Joe: My pleasure. Well, I'll see you during the week.
Anita: OK. Good night.

Index of Functions

	Unit(s)
asking for/giving information	3, 4, 7, 9
clarifying/verifying	3, 4, 9
comparing/contrasting	11
dealing with numbers (phone, time, money, sizes, weights)	1, 3, 4, 8, 11
describing/observing (physical surroundings, things, problems, symptoms)	1, 8, 9, 10
expressing abilities/skills/responsibilities	7
expressing emotions	5
expressing greetings	Preliminary Lessons, 2, 3
expressing likes/dislikes/preferences	5, 7, 8, 11
expressing needs	3, 7, 9, 10, 11
giving/following oral and written directions	4, 9, 11
giving/getting personal information	Preliminary Lessons, 1, 2, 9
identifying/categorizing (people, places, things)	1, 2, 9, 11
introducing oneself/others	Preliminary Lessons, 2
requesting assistance	3, 8, 10
sympathizing	5, 9

Index of Structures

	Unit(s)
adjectives: descriptive	8
adjectives: passive	10
adjectives: possessive	2
adjectives: with *be*	5
adverbs of frequency	9
adverbs of time	7
articles	1
comparatives	11
contractions	1
count/noncount nouns	11, 12
imperatives	4, 10, 11
intensifiers: *too, very*	8
modals: *can, can't*	8, 9, 12
negatives	1, 2
past tense	7, 10
politeness markers	3
possessives	2, 6
prepositions of direction	4
prepositions of place	1, 4, 12
prepositions of time	9
present tense	1, 2, 6, 12
present continuous tense	2, 3, 5, 6, 11
pronouns	Preliminary Lessons, 1, 6
questions: *wh-*	1, 2, 4, 5, 6, 7, 8, 10, 11
questions: *yes/no*	1, 5, 6
sequence words	4
superlatives	11
verb + *to*	3, 8, 10, 12
would + *like*	7